SHE BROUGHT THE
ART OF WOMEN

SHE BROUGHT THE ART OF WOMEN

A SONG OF SOLOMON, NABONIDUS, AND THE GODDESS

JANET TYSON

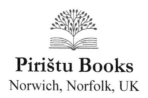

Pirištu Books
Norwich, Norfolk, UK

Images: Cover images licensed through AdobeStock.

ISBN   978-1-7393154-4-3

British Library Cataloguing in Production Data. A catalogue record for this book is available from the British Library.

The goddess ... lived in the form of a woman, who had the knowledge of words of power. Her heart turned away in disgust from the millions of men, and she chose for herself the millions of the gods....

Papyrus de Turin

*For all who strive to comprehend
what is hidden.*

CONTENTS

PART TWO: THE SONG OF SOLOMON

ABBREVIATIONS

General

Ag. Ap.	*Against Apion*, Josephus
Ant.	*Antiquities of the Jews*, Josephus
	Whiston, W. Trans. *Josephus: Complete Works*. Michigan: Kregel, 1960
Abarim	Abarim Publications
	https://www.abarim-publications.com
ETCSL	*The Electronic Text Corpus of Sumerian Literature*
	Black, J.A., et al. Oxford 1998- . http://www-etcsl.orient.ox.ac.uk/
HB	Hebrew Bible
Hist.	*Histories*
	Rawlinson, G. Trans. *Histories: Herodotus*. Hertfordshire: Wordsworth, 1996
NRSV	New Revised Standard Version
Strong's	*Exhaustive Concordance*
	https://biblehub.com/strongs/songs/

Nabonidus Inscriptions

H1	Harran Inscription 1
H2	Harran Inscription 2
	C. J. Gadd, "The Harran Inscriptions of Nabonidus" *Anatolian Studies* 8 (1958): 35–92.
Nab Chr	Nabonidus Chronicle
Nab 1	Imgur-Enlil Cylinder
Nab 10	Eulmash Cylinder
Nab 19	Eigikalama Cylinder
Nab 24	Ebabbar Cylinder
Nab 26	Ebabbar-Ekurra Cylinder
Nab 28	Elhulhul Cylinder from Sippar
Nab 34	Ennigaldi-Nanna Cylinder
Nab 47	Harran Stele
Nab 2001	Adad-guppi Stele

Continued...

R Chr   Royal Chronicle
Weiershäuser, Frauke and J. Novotny. *The Royal Inscriptions of Amēl-Marduk (561–560 BC), Neriglissar (559–556 BC), and Nabonidus (555–539 BC), Kings of Babylon.* The Royal Inscriptions of the Neo-Babylonian Empire, Vol. 2. University Park: Eisenbrauns, 2020

VA   Verse Account of Nabonidus
Livius.org. https://www.livius.org/sources/content/anet/verse-account-of-nabonidus

INTRODUCTION

This book will challenge everything you ever learned about the Song of Solomon. It will place this most enigmatic biblical text under the microscope and forensically analyse each and every verse, in an effort to demonstrate that it is neither an allegory, nor a bucolic love poem, nor a collection of ancient marriage songs. It is, in fact, a historical account, presented in the nature of a Mesopotamian praise poem or song, of three profoundly significant people who lived during the final years before the fall of Babylon to Cyrus the Great: Nabonidus, King of Babylon (556–539 BCE), Nitocris II, the elusive daughter of Ahmose III[1] and First Prophet of Amun-Re (Dynasty 26, Egypt), and the author of the Song. This particular song, however, has a profound twist, for it does not exalt the king it sings about, it admonishes him.

The Song is a dark, sombre composition; it does not tell of romantic love, or instruct on how to act as God's "chosen." It sings of secret, unrequited love; unwanted physical/sexual demands; death, deception, and blackmail; and the hubris of acquiring a "little knowledge." Feminist themes prevail, from the early demonstrations of female power and dominance within the central relationship, to the concentration on menstruation, contraception, and motherhood, to the depictions of fertility idols and the lechery of men of power, to the female authorship of the Song. Occult rites and practices are alluded to throughout the narrative, including priestly purity rituals, cultic initiation, and the seldom discussed, controversial blood-rite known in esoteric circles as the Elixir Rubeus, i.e., a heady blend of male and female efflux. This is the "crimson cord" that weaves its way from the very start of the Song, to its final exclamations. Probably the most unorthodox aspect of the analysis, it is, I shall demonstrate, a vital aspect of the Song that has gone unrecognised, or has been wilfully suppressed. Without it, the Song of Solomon cannot tell its full story. No holds are barred

---

[1] As of March 2012, this pharaoh is no longer Ahmose II. See Sébastien Biston-Moulin, "King Sénakht-en-Rê Ahmès of the XVIIth Dynasty," Égypte Nilotique et Méditerranéenne 5 (2012), 61–71, here 66.

in this investigation.

A century ago there was a promising new interpretation of the Song suggesting the narrative was a deliberate emulation of the sacred marriage of the Mesopotamian deities Ishtar and Tammuz, whose union was ritually re-enacted once a year, usually by the king and the high priestess of the temple.[2] The ceremony celebrated the renewal of Life in the spring with the return of Tammuz from his banishment to the underworld and the reconfirmation of the king's divine right to rule, bestowed upon him by Ishtar. The theory was beginning to take hold, with more and more apparent literary parallels between the Song and the many cuneiform texts being newly deciphered, but dissenters ruled the day and the idea was rather speedily swept under the carpet.

This book attempts to breathe new life into the old cultic view, adding to it on many levels, employing information its original proponents did not have access to. So many more inscriptions have been translated over the last century, and interdisciplinary research and writing has grown exponentially. In fact, the Song of Solomon is replete with allusions to mythology, i.e., predominantly that of Ishtar and Tammuz of Mesopotamia, but also that of the Egyptian Hathor, which has never been mooted before. Rather than simply finding appropriate precedents to show the potential for a Mesopotamian context (which I do provide), I aim to show how this mythology is used to depict Nitocris II as an Ishtar/Hathor avatar. Ishtar legends are used to convey the author's perception of the 'spoilt', sexually adept, dangerous princess, and is employed to make the overall narrative familiar and comprehensible to its original audiences, i.e., the migrants (Jews and non-Jews) who flee Babylonia in 538 BCE, and the Canaanites who receive them (back) into their territories, many of whom religiously identify with the cult of Ishtar (or her local cognates).

The fundamental nature of the Song is revealed using an array of approaches, including literary analysis (symbolism, allusion, puns, etc.); etymology of specific Hebrew words; gematria (giving letters of the Hebrew alphabet numerical value); occult rituals and magic; and cross-cultural historical information. Ancient Sumerian texts, for instance, offer precedents for the Ishtar/Tammuz themes, building an impressive body of evidence that points to a predominantly Babylonian context for the Song's composition.

---

[2] See T. James Meek, "Canticles and the Tammuz Cult," *American Journal of Semitic Languages and Literatures* 39.1 (1922): 1–14; and "Babylonian Parallels to the Song of Songs," Journal of Biblical Literature 43.3/4 (1924): 245–52; Samuel Noah Kramer, "The Biblical 'Song of Songs' and the Sumerian Love Songs" *Expedition Magazine* 5.1, Penn Museum (1962) Online version, http://www.penn.museum/ sites/expedition/?p=488; Marvin H. Pope, *Song of Songs*, The Anchor Bible (New York: Doubleday, 1977), 145–153.

There are also public, Neo-Babylonian inscriptions pertaining to Nabonidus that all but mirror what we find happening in the Song, making it almost impossible to deny some sort of common experience connecting the two. Then there is the mysterious Egyptian element in the Song that has remained elusive to this day; many scholars discuss it, many ignore it, but here it is made abundantly clear that Egyptian themes permeate the entire text because the leading woman of the Song *is* Egyptian.

That this woman in the Song could be Solomon's legendary bride, i.e., the "daughter of Pharaoh" (1 Kgs 3:1), is not a new theory, in fact it is a very old one. Theodore of Mopsuestia (350–428 CE, Antioch, Turkey) understood the Song to be a record of this marriage but his ideas were condemned by the Council of Constantinople in 553 CE. Milton, Wordsworth, and Blake, all wrote poetry about Solomon and his corruption by this particular wife, whom they clearly understood to be the woman of the Song. Perhaps the lack of proponents of this interpretation today is due to the stumbling block of identifying solid evidence for Solomon (the man) in the historical/archaeological record. Even Herodotus, the fifth-century BCE teller of flamboyant historical tales, knew nothing of him, his kingdom, or his grand temple. Once the conceptual leap is taken to replace "Solomon" with Nabonidus, however, things start to make much more sense and the Song reveals its true nature. Such a simple adjustment creates a wholly new paradigm for the Song, clarifying its mysteries.

Around the time of the first cultic theory it was also argued (by Raymond. P. Dougherty) that Herodotus's "Nitocris, Queen of Babylon" (in *Hist.* 1.185–7) was Nebuchadnezzar's daughter, whose mother was an unknown Egyptian princess; Nabonidus, it was thought, could not have married a full-blooded Egyptian princess before he was made king, as he was a commoner, so he must have married a half-blooded Egyptian.[3] As Belshazzar, Nabonidus's eldest son, was old enough to be left in charge of Babylon for several years, the marriage of his assumed parents was argued to have taken place many years before Nabonidus headed off to Arabia (in early 553 BCE). This theory left many unanswered questions and it remained an incomplete hypothesis, with no one since attempting to complete the picture. I suggest, however, that Nabonidus *is* already King when he marries Nitocris II, and that Belshazzar is his son from a previous marriage.

The Song's warlike imagery sets the scene for a battle of wills between the man and the woman, and between the Egyptian religion and the personal religion of the King of Babylon; the former is solar-based, the latter lunar-based. The religion of Nabonidus revolves around his desire to re-

---

[3] Raymond. P. Dougherty, *Nabonidus and Belshazzar: A Study of the Closing Events of the Neo-Babylonian Empire*, 1929 repr. (Eugene: Wipf & Stock, 2008), 42–63.

establish the ancient, female priesthood of the *entus* who were, many centuries earlier, devotees of the Mood God Sîn, at Ur. This ambition came to define his life but only really began once he had moved away from Babylon and settled in Tayma, Arabia. The most significant cuneiform inscription pertaining to Nabonidus is a reference to a lunar eclipse, supposedly dating the dedication of his daughter as the new *entu*; a second eclipse is proposed in this analysis, however, which challenges this dating and provides a *terminus post quem* for the composition of the Song.

The Song of Solomon has several secrets that can now be revealed, with but a little imagination and an open, curious mind. Conventional commentaries tend to rest their arguments on those of preceding generations, yet the Song's ultimate meaning has remained elusive and many questions still abound. It is a difficult thing to offer a new perspective in light of such monumental tradition but I hope potential dissenters will at least acknowledge that something very different happens to the Song when you change just one word—"Solomon."

It is recommended that you follow the text of the Song of Solomon as you travel through this new territory; the NRSV is used here, with constant references to the Hebrew text and its countless hidden gems. The Interlinear version on the Biblehub website is most helpful. The two main characters of the Song will be called Nabonidus and Nitocris, for clarity, but the Sumerian Inanna/Dumuzi and the Babylonian Ishtar/Tammuz are used interchangeably, depending on the context or quotation.

Research for this book was extensive and some topics had to be limited for brevity within the restraints of the analysis, but included at the end of the book are few Supplemental Notes that provide a little more insight. These include further information concerning Nabonidus's mother; the significance of Queen Tahpenes; and the amazing parallels to this 'new' paradigm that have actually been with us throughout the centuries, hidden in at least three other well-known legends. A further Supplemental Note on the potential relationship between Nitocris and Ankhnesneferibre is posted on Academia.edu.

Because the bibliography proved to be so long, an exhaustive Works Acknowledged list has been posted on Academia.edu.

PART ONE: CULTURAL CONTEXT

1. THE MOON GOD SÎN REQUIRES A HIGH PRIESTESS

The last King of Babylon, Nabonidus, is often described as the world's first archaeologist, as he had a unique fascination with the ancient structures he renovated and appears to have inspired the creation of a museum at Ur, where replicas of interesting objects that long-predated his own reign were found with museum-like tags attached.[1] Some scholars have written about his clever use of language, suggesting he was highly skilled in many fields of study.[2] These assessments, however, pale into insignificance when the character of the king is put to the test within the narrative of the Song of Solomon. He proves to be a man who likes to have his own way, who wants people to like him (in a laddish sort of way), who pursues his own agenda at the cost of his own reputation and even his kingdom, and who makes the mistake of thinking a little insight into the secrets of the universe is enough to make him invincible.

Perhaps one of the most famous of the Babylonian inscriptions pertaining to Nabonidus is the clay cylinder that tells of his mission to reinstate the long-defunct female order of priests at Ur, with his daughter Ennigaldi-Nanna as the high priestess, or *entu*. The *entu* priesthood, i.e., consecrated dream interpreters who practised their craft in a tiny sanctuary at the top of the ziggurat, had been sacred to Sîn, the lunar deity, many centuries earlier and Nabonidus's unswerving loyalty to Sîn is often cited as being one of the reasons he was deemed unpopular within Babylonia.[3] The

---

[1] Sir Leonard Woolley and P. Moorey, *Ur of the Chaldees* (Book Club Associates/Herbert Press: 1982, first published 1929), 251–5.

[2] Piotr Michalowski ("The Doors of the Past," *Eretz-Israel: Archaeological, Historical and Geographical Studies* [2003]: 136–52, here 138–9) argues that Nabonidus was not only literate but highly trained in the ways of the scribe, could understand and write both Akkadian and Sumerian, understood the astrological omens and formulae, and had a formidable grasp of ancient lore.

[3] In Mesopotamia, dreams were thought to be texts written by the gods on the heart of the dreamer, the heart being where the memory resided. Nabonidus refers to Ennigaldi (Nab 34, 1.24) as "daughter of my *heart*," not "of my loins/body" which was more common (and how he refers to Belshazzar on Nabonidus Cylinder 86, 2.51 [A. R. George, "Other Neo-Babylonian Royal Inscriptions" (2011): 171–86,

priests of Marduk (Babylon's city god), especially, resented his challenge to their long-standing primacy when he gradually began to elevate Sîn above Marduk.

The cylinder begins with a claim that a lunar eclipse portended Sîn's desire for a high priestess for his temple:

> "The Fruit" became eclipsed in the month Ulūlū, (on) the thirteenth day (of) the month of "the work of the goddesses" and set while he was eclipsed. "The god Sîn desired an *entu*-priestess," such was his sign and his decision.

> Nab 34 (1.8–10)

The first translation of this cylinder was by Albert T. Clay, in 1915.[4] His was a more poetic representation, which promoted Ishtar's significance to the scene, i.e., the "goddess of increase was aroused, and greatly awakened joy" (1.9); Ishtar, the goddess of procreation had permitted the conception/birth of a child (the "joy"). This early translation has since been downplayed, even ignored, but I suggest it provides a thematic link to the Song, and to a dream omen presented to Nabonidus, discussed later. The more recent, technically precise translation (above) loses some of the spirit of the original, perhaps.

Ulūlū is the month of August/September, presided over by Ishtar. It is generally accepted that the partial lunar eclipse of 26 September 554 BCE is the best candidate for Nabonidus's 13 Ulūlū omen, and the cylinder is presumed to have been made at about this time. I will show that this is only half of the story concerning the eclipse; the other half lies hidden within the Song of Solomon, and shifts the dating of the cylinder to about a decade later.

According to the (Persian) propagandistic Verse Account of Nabonidus (VA 5.4), when the king is presented with a collection of tablets that depict the astrological omens, he apparently refuses to employ them, preferring his own rendition of the signs, which breeds animosity amongst the diviners and priests. Scholars suggest he makes what seems to be a fundamental error by referring to this eclipsed moon as *inbu*, which translates from the Akkadian as "Fruit." This is one of the esoteric names attributed to Sîn as the new moon crescent, not the full moon, which must have appeared on that day, if there had been an eclipse.[5] A detailed

---

here 186, https://eprints.soas.ac.uk/12832/1/CUSAS-17-8.pdf]), i.e., "daughter of my *dream*; the daughter who is the word/will of the god (Sîn)."

[4] Albert T. Clay, *Miscellaneous Inscriptions in the Yale Babylonian Collection* (New Haven: Yale University Press), 1915, §45.

[5] Piotr Michalowski, "The Doors of the Past," *Eretz-Israel: Archaeological,*

discussion of the eclipse(s) is found in Part Two, Chapter 6.

Unfortunately, an eclipse of any sort is normally a portent of evil and danger; the darkening of the moon or the disappearance of the sun is directly linked to the fate of the extant ruler. As the moon loses its brightness, so the ruler will lose his authority, health, power, etc., if the correct rituals are not performed to assuage the danger. This is broadly referred to as "astral magic." One of the *worst* days for an ominous eclipse, traditionally, is the thirteenth of the month. It is far from a propitious sign, and is specifically recorded as one of the "wrong times" for portents, predicting "evil to (the king of) Akkad" (Babylon).[6]

We learn from VA 2.5–7 that Nabonidus sets out for Arabia at the beginning of his third year, i.e., a few months after the 554 BCE eclipse, ostensibly on a military expedition. The king records that when he let it be known that Sîn had shown him in a dream that the deity's temple needed to be rebuilt, the people of Babylon mocked and were hostile: "… they were speaking lies and untruths" (Nab 47, 1.19–22a). Famine and disease (1.21) created chaos and disharmony.[7] He claims the gods appointed guards for him, i.e., "for [his] safety and life" (1.30–1). He was, it seems, in fear of personal attack. A warning from the Sippar omen tablets reads: If "in Ulūlū an eclipse occurs [at the wrong] time: rebellion against the king, downfall of numerous people."[8]

Can this supposedly inauspicious eclipse, which creates an ominous atmosphere for the king, be what triggers *not* the joyful dedication of his daughter but his (contrived) *exit* from Babylon? The famine and fever could well be exaggerated in the reports to the king, suggesting the astral magic is not enough to protect Nabonidus, indeed Babylon, from danger. The normal procedure, after all, is to remove the king completely if there is any perceived

---

Historical and Geographical Studies (2003): 136–52, here, 145.

[6] The fourteenth day could also be a "wrong time," as was "the evening watch"; T. G. Pinches, "Review: L'Astrologie Chaldéenne. Le Livre intitulé enuma (Anu) îlu Bêl by Ch. Virolleaud," *Journal of the Royal Asiatic Society of Great Britain and Ireland, 1909*, 535–38. Also, in Ulla Koch, "Babylonian Views of Eclipses," Démons et merveilles d'Orient (2001): 71–84, here 71.

[7] The month of Kislimnu is mid-summer in Babylon, and one of the epithets given to Nergal is "the burner," which some have attributed to his role as the bringer of drought, i.e., scorching the earth, which reduces the quality of the crops. Then comes the flood season in the next month, Shabatu, bringing with it the beginnings of chaos, i.e., storm damage to crops, etc. This month is ruled by Adad (son of Sîn and brother of Ishtar); he is, along with Shamash, the God of Storms. In the VA there is reference to "the former favourite of the gods (i.e., Nabonidus) … now (being) seized by misfortunes" (1.5).

[8] F. N. H. Al-Rawi and A. R. George, "Tablets from the Sippar Library XIII Enuma Anuellil XX" *Iraq* 68 (2006) 23–57, here 53.

threat, and even to install a fake king in the interim, so the expedition to Arabia, initially, may not even be Nabonidus's idea, as is commonly thought. That his eldest son, Belshazzar, left in charge of the administration of Babylon for several years, continues with the orthodox, Marduk-favourable propaganda,[9] does tend toward a devised plan by the diviners/priests (and perhaps the prince) to get the dissident king out of their hair.

The ritual of the substitute king is carried out for solar *and* lunar eclipses, or for any other seriously worrying omen. As an eclipse is seen to have a direct relationship to royal sin or inadequacy, lamentation priests carry out specialised divinations that isolate the nature of the king's alleged sin and prescribe the proper subservient, or apologetic, action that the deities demand. The king is dressed in ragged clothing, a sign of his office removed, and is sent away to hide until the danger has passed. During this time, he is referred to as "the farmer" or "gardener," to illustrate his humble, or common, nature (thereby hiding him from the wrath of the gods). To make king and country safe once again through ritual purification, the substitute king is killed and all the royal robes and official accoutrements are burned and buried along with the sacrificed body-double. Although cuneiform evidence to prove this took place with Nabonidus is yet to be found, it may just be extant in the tale of Daniel's warning to a king that he must leave and live as beast until it is time for him to return (Dan 4:28–33). I suggest, in line with current scholarship, that Nebuchadnezzar in Daniel (Dan 1–6) is in fact Nabonidus;[10] this is substantiated as we progress through the analysis.

The diviners set expiry dates on the validity of omens, ranging from thirty to three hundred days. This means that between the eclipse of 13 Ulūlū and their deadline, Nabonidus's priests have to either declare that all is well for him to return to duty, or claim the gods are still very angry with him and he should, for the sake of the nation, remain at a distance (and there is evidence for Assyrian kings doing this).[11] The biblical Daniel seems to be

---

[9] Paul-Alain Beaulieu, *The Reign of Nabonidus King of Babylon 556–539 B.C.* (New Haven: Yale University, 1989), 63.

[10] E.g., see A. M. Davis Bledsoe, "The Identity of the 'Mad King' of Daniel 4 in Light of Ancient Near Eastern Sources," *Cristianesimo nella Storia* 33 (2012): 743–58; John Joseph Collins and Adela Yarbro Collins, *Daniel: A Commentary on the Book of Daniel* (United States: Fortress Press, 1993), 217. The argument on authorship of Daniel suggests Chapters 1 through 6 are far earlier than those of 7–12 and, according to Collins, have been deemed most likely applicable to the reign of Nabonidus since the discovery of the Prayer of Nabonidus (Dead Sea Scroll) in 1854.

[11] See "Lamentation and ritual," http://oracc.museum.upenn.edu/saao/knpp/essentials/lamentationritual.

the one chosen to confront the king, suggesting that he must atone for his sin against the gods and will be banished until he makes amends.

THE KING'S SIN

In Dan 2:1, the king's bad dreams are said to begin in his *second* year, i.e., just as Nabonidus's disturbing eclipse comes in his second year (554 BCE). The first dream, about the statue, is discussed later but in Daniel 4, he dreams that the gods plan to cut down a huge tree; its branches and all the creatures within it are scattered. He is warned that he will lose his mind for seven years ("times" in Dan 4:25). The tree, Nabonidus is told, is the king, whose power has become too great; the gods will diminish him but leave his roots in the soil so his kingdom can regenerate—*when* he subjugates himself to the heavens, i.e., to the gods.

This story has elements of the Sumerian tale of Inanna and the *huluppu* tree, in which the awesome and terrifying Anzu-bird rests in the branches of the goddess' tree and is violently evicted by Gilgamesh, who then cuts the tree down. A half-lion but with the feathers and talons of an eagle, just as is inflicted upon the 'mad' Nabonidus (Dan 4:33), the Anzu-bird is renowned for stealing Enlil's Tablet of Destinies, which holds the key to the fates of all living things. The king, I suggest, is seen to be emulating Anzu, i.e., in attempting to usurp the powers of the gods. Nabonidus is thereby accused of seeing himself as the controller of Fate, the manipulator of worship (the Storm Dragon, one of the guardians of the idol of Sîn ridiculed in VA 1.6–7, is a euphemism for Anzu), for he is systematically attempting to raise Sîn above the status of Marduk. The only way, so Daniel infers, for the king to be brought back from this calamitous eviction from his kingdom is to (symbolically) return the Tablet of Destinies to its rightful owner(s), the *shamayin*, literally, the sky, or "visible heavens." The forefather of the gods, Enlil, is gradually assimilated into Marduk, making the insult, or sin, all the more germane; Nabonidus is perceived as being arrogant, self-aggrandizing, and a threat to the Marduk-based establishment.[12]

---

[12] "[T]he omens in Enuma Anu Enlil not only created expectations and suspicions of possible political developments heralded by an eclipse, they also portrayed human opponents of the king as agents of the divine will. A lunar eclipse therefore supplied the religious justification for treason, as well as the social conditions conducive to such an endeavour." John Z. Wee, "Grieving with the Moon: Pantheon and Politics in The Lunar Eclipse," *Journal of Ancient Near Eastern Religions* 14.1: 29–67 (2014), 50. Wee goes on to explain how diviners could be in personal competition with each other, and that King Assurbanipal, who had a similar reputation for 'getting things wrong', might have exaggerated his own knowledge of such matters in order to counter overzealous "experts" who became, ultimately,

The exact same imagery, i.e., the tall tree, the animals scattered etc., and the same warning against rulers/nations becoming too powerful, appears in Ezekiel 31, first in relation to the Assyrians, then the Egyptians. Daniel and Ezekiel share a common theme, i.e., the same memory of what happened to Nabonidus.

Only Daniel is brave enough to push the king into action, i.e., into leaving Babylon. It is likely that the Jew in 4Q242 Prayer of Nabonidus (found amongst the Dead Sea Scrolls),[13] the exorcist who pardons the king his sin, is none other than Daniel, the head exorcist, or magus, of Babylon. Exorcists diagnose and remedy physical maladies in terms of a perceived offense to gods or demons; in Nabonidus's case, according to the Prayer, the physical representation of his sin is said to be an ulcer (Nabonidus is recorded as becoming "sick" whilst on military campaign just after the eclipse, i.e., Nab Chr 1.11–22; the Prayer intimates he is "afflicted" for "seven years" in Tayma, matching the seven-year eviction of Dan 4:25). This is why Daniel can both tell the king his sin (arrogance towards the King of Heaven, Enlil/Marduk) *and* prescribe the remedy (banishment and humiliation).

Around the time of Ennigaldi's eventual dedication as *entu*, Nabonidus claims he pays extra homage to "the god Lugal-Marda" (Nab 19, 2.16–26; 33–37), which proves fascinating, but only if the above link to the Anzu-bird is made—for Lugal-Marda is none other than the warrior god who *rescues* the Tablet of Destinies and returns it to Enlil! Nabonidus makes great show of restoring the ancient battle chariot of this deity, suggesting he is making doubly sure his penance is being noted in heaven.

ARABIA

The plan to establish his daughter as *entu* does not fully manifest until about three years *after* the eclipse of 554 BCE. Nabonidus travels through Arabia for a total of ten years (Nab 47, 1.22b–27a), the last seven of which we know he spends in Tayma, a bustling, cosmopolitan trading hub for both the Frankincense Trail, which brings spices from southern Arabia, and the King's Trail, as it diverts across the desert from Gaza; it is situated halfway between Babylon and Egypt. The king makes Tayma his second capital, building a replica of his Babylonian palace and preferring to stay there, even though his presence in Babylon is expected for such duties as the yearly Akitu festival and the sacred marriage rite. Leaving Belshazzar in charge of the city, Nabonidus is seldom seen in his kingdom.

The worship of Ishtar (locally called Atar) is strong in Tayma and the

---

a challenge to royal supreme authority (51).

[13] Find at https://www.livius.org/sources/content/dss/4q242-prayer-of-nabonidus/.

worship of the lunar-deity was ensconced even before Nabonidus's day; it is thought by many that the king goes there *because* of its holy-to-Sîn status, i.e., to immerse himself in the cult of Ter (the local name for Sîn), to emulate the distant ancestors whose golden age he longs to revive. In fact, the anti-Nabonidus VA names Ilteᵢ as the deity who sends a "vision" to the king, thereby confirming he is directly influenced by the Tayma cult.

The Song of Solomon is a record of what transpires in the palace of Nabonidus during these seven years in Tayma.

COALITION AND CONCILIATION

In 550/49 BCE, Cyrus the Great (c. 559–530 BCE) conquers Media and declares himself King of Persia. Soon thereafter, a coalition to stem his advance is created between Pharaoh Ahmose III, Croesus of Lydia, Polycrates of Samos, Sparta, and Nabonidus. Although there is no direct historical evidence to prove there is a conciliatory marriage between any two of these coalition members, it is the traditional thing to do in times of war; this proposed union I argue to be the foundation of Herodotus's strange and jumbled account of a marriage between an Egyptian princess and a foreign king. According to 1 Kgs 3:1, "Solomon made a marriage alliance with Pharaoh, king of Egypt"—this is where the Song begins its tale.

Herodotus tells us (*Hist.* 3:1–3) that at some point before the Persian invasion of Egypt in 525 BCE, Ahmose receives a request for one of his daughters from either King Cyrus or his son, Cambyses. Ahmose is concerned that if he sends his *own* daughter, she will not be given the status she deserves and will probably end up a concubine, so he sends Nitetis, the daughter of his nemesis, the previous (deceased) pharaoh, Apries. He provides three versions of the event (3.1–3): 1) Ahmose sends his best eye-doctor to Cyrus, forcing the man to leave his family. Disgruntled, the doctor convinces Cambyses to ask for Ahmose's daughter in marriage. Ahmose sends Apries's daughter instead and when this is discovered ("some time afterwards"), Cambyses attacks Egypt; 2) Apries's daughter marries Cyrus and Cambyses is their child, making him of Egyptian blood; 3) Cambyses seeks belated revenge for his mother's shame and hurt feelings when the Egyptian woman catches his father's eye. Each of these explanations for Persia's invasion of Egypt is somewhat implausible, and Herodotus allows for a period of about twenty years for the date of the marriage, i.e., from the childhood of Cambyses to the invasion in 525 BCE.

Nitetis is described as being "a tall and beautiful" woman; Ahmose decks "her out with gold and costly garments" and sends her to Persia "as if she had been his own child" (*Hist.* 3:1). It is often argued that Ahmose himself marries a daughter of Apries on his succession to the throne, suggesting this is a tactic to legitimise his reign, having taken the throne by force. Herodotus is clearly ignorant of such a marriage, assuming the daughter of a defeated pharaoh would be something to be ashamed of and therefore the cause of Cambyses's anger; in reality, it would seem, there is no such stigma.

Herodotus's accounts have been proven erroneous on several counts. He was a storyteller who wrote for audiences hungry for thrills and salacious gossip, so "history" is a bit of misnomer. If we agree, however, that somewhere in Herodotus's account there is a kernel of truth, we can say with of a degree certainty that *something* happened between Pharaoh Ahmose and a foreign king, involving the sending of a princess for marriage to said king, at a time of war. It would be easy, with Herodotus's limited hindsight, to assume this second party to be the imminent Persian king, sweeping into Egypt but I suggest it is not; it is Nabonidus.

Upon hearing the various versions of the tale (much of his material relied on second-hand anecdotes from passing traders, priests, etc.), Herodotus *presumes* a Persian link, even though he cannot figure out who the husband was in this political marriage, or even when it occurred. After the fall of Babylon, Cambyses is made "King of Babylon" for just a few months, before Cyrus, his father, removes him from office and takes the reins. When Cyrus dies in 530 BCE, Cambyses inherits the full title of "King of Babylon, King of the Lands," so if the rumour reaches Herodotus that Ahmose had sent a bride to the "King of Babylon," he would naturally assume it was either Cambyses or Cyrus, and have no reason to imagine it could have been the humiliated and defeated Nabonidus several years earlier. The invasion of Egypt seems to be a convenient context for the legend but the whole point about a conciliatory marriage is the *avoidance* of war; Herodotus presumes too much, and is left with conflicting accounts and no plausible rationale for the invasion. Once, again, put Nabonidus into the frame and the legend makes sense.

Would Ahmose give his daughter away so readily? Well, yes, given what is at stake. Herodotus does make a note of saying the Egyptian king only makes the alleged switch because he thinks his daughter will not receive the honour or status due to her. If this is in any way plausible, it means there is a potential for Nitocris being the price of peace in a conciliatory marriage, as long as the arrangement *is* agreeable. It may also suggest a lingering doubt as to the status of this Egyptian princess within the Babylonian king's court, and this will play directly into the Song's narrative.

If Herodotus misheard the tales, or embellished them, it may be that no such grand gesture, i.e., of sending Nitetis out with much pomp and ceremony, ever happened. With the Persians on the prowl, catching wind of this arrangement could tip the balance and risk everyone's safety (the alleged "anger" of Cambyses may stem from the discovery of the marriage itself, "some time later"). It could well have been quite a subtle, clandestine affair, but this does not make for a good tale for a writer like Herodotus. It needs spicing up. A switch is a classic audience pleaser.

Despite the previous confrontations with Nebuchadnezzar, it would seem that Ahmose and Nabonidus have more in common than might, at first, be evident. Both come to the throne in rebellious circumstances, neither being of royal blood; both are steadfast and somewhat isolated worshippers of lunar deities (Ahmose is a worshipper of Iah, an Egyptian moon god); they both attempt to revive antiquarian interests within their respective realms; both are relatively peaceful rulers. They are now allies, united against a mutual enemy.

DAUGHTER OF PHARAOH

The name Nitetis (*njtt-jj.tj*), meaning Neith is Come, is Egyptian but as the name of a royal it is not documented in any historical source; there is, however, another name that has a very similar meaning, i.e., Nitocris (*nj.t-iḳr.t*), or Neith is Excellent.[14]

Ahmose has a daughter called Nitocris, who appears in the historical record as Nitocris II (or B). Evidence for her includes a bronze statue of Amun-Re which refers to her as "First Prophet (i.e., High Priest; the male form is retained) of Amun-Re." There is also a clay seal, originally published by Percy E. Newberry (in 1943) which reads: "The First Prophet of Amun-Re, King of Two Lands, the Royal Daughter, Nitocris"; Newberry attributed it to Nitocris of Dynasty 6 but subsequently it has been argued that the early Nitocris never had the title of First Prophet (as the post was always held by men), so the seal must be attributable to Nitocris II.[15]

Even less well known is a clay seal impression with the cartouches, purportedly, of "King Ahmose and Queen Nitocris" but no one seems to be mentioning it in the literature.[16] Perhaps this is not a seal of the pharaoh and his *wife* but a (small and discrete) commemorative seal depicting the pharaoh with his beloved daughter. It is unusual for daughters to have their own cartouches but not unheard of. Princess Herit, known from a tiny fragment of a vase found by Harold Carter in the tomb of Amenhotep I at Thebes, shows her name in a cartouche opposite her father's. The seal inscription in

---

[14] Hermann Ranke, *Die Ägyptischen Personennamen, Bd. 1: Verzeichnis der Namen.* (Glückstadt: J.J. Augustin, 1935), 181.25, 27.

[15] H. De Meulenaere, "La Famille Du Roi Amasis," *Journal of Egyptian Archaeology* 54 (1968): 183–87, here 186.

[16] Los Angeles County Museum of Art. https://collections.lacma.org/node/245409. The damaged RH cartouche has caused identification issues, so this is probably why it is not used as evidence by academics.

question is translated as "Queen Nitocris" but perhaps it signifies an increased esteem granted to the status of the First Prophet of Amun-Re (previous First Prophets had used the cartouche, and the God's Wives names were usually in cartouches). It might also represent the occasion of a father giving away his daughter to *become* Queen. Ahmose is an unorthodox pharaoh who makes some radical changes in many areas; granting his daughter this token of respect might not seem *de rigueur* (to historians) but it has at least one precedent. There is further evidence (presented at the end of the analysis) that may substantiate such a theory.

Nitocris inherits the role of First Prophet of Amun-Re from her cultic, so-called "adoptive" mother, Ankhnesneferibre; she has been named, possibly, in honour of the most famous and most powerful God's Wife, Nitocris I, daughter of Pharaoh Psametik I; she is the heir apparent to her "mother's" cultic position. Ankhnesneferibre is also the Divine Adoratrice and God's Hand (variously attested on her sarcophagus, her Adoption Stele, and a statue from Karnak), so it seems likely Nitocris II is in line for these roles, too.[17] With so little evidence to work with, however, Egyptologists assume that with the invasion of the Persians in 525 BCE, the office of the God's Wife and the associated positions simply ceased, and Nitocris II "probably" never served in the higher roles. A potential connection between Nitocris and the obscure service of the God's Hand, however, can be gleaned from subtle clues in the Song of Solomon.

GOD'S HAND

The consensus of scholarly opinion is that the function of the woman who is God's Hand is to facilitate ritual masturbation in the context of emulating the moment of divine Creation, which is deemed to have been an act of ejaculation by the supreme deity. The original (human) God's Hand was called "the Wife of Min" (c. 2181–2040 BCE), a lunar deity who later became a god of human sexuality and fertility. He is depicted with an erect phallus, around the base of which he clasps his left hand, and he wears a red ribbon tied around his head that trails to the ground behind him. This is known as a *seshed* band and signifies sexual energy, rebirth, and renewal. A description of the God's Wife Shepenwepet II at Karnak suggests: "A skull cap, secured in place by a tied ribbon, covers her hair. Of unequal lengths, the loose ends of the ribbon fall behind the God's Wife's head, brushing past her left shoulder and reaching down to her left elbow."[18] The discovery of

---

[17] See Supplemental Note "Ankhnesneferibre and Nitocris II: A Question of Filiation" on Academia.edu.

[18] Mariam Ayad, "On the Identity and Role of the God's Wife of Amun in Rites of Royal and Divine Dominion," *Journal of the Society for the Study of Egyptian*

an offering table inscribed with: "God's Wife Pure of Hands in Karnak, God's Hand Shepenwepet," however, uniquely identifies her as God's Hand.[19] This ribbon/cord becomes a vital motif in the Song.

There is reference to the position of God's Hand in the Septuagint (LXX) version of 1 Kgs 11:19–20. In the Masoretic Text, the name of the queen is Tahpenes but in the Septuagint it is Thekemina, which Albright suggests means "The Female Attendant (or concubine) of Min."[20] Albright continues by claiming the *kemi-* aspect of the name, in Egyptian, has a potentially pejorative connotation, i.e., "prostitute," as it may stem from the (Egyptian) word for vulva, perhaps implying that the author of 1 Kings LXX wished to denigrate the Egyptian queen, which is a scribal technique that we will see elsewhere in the Hebrew Bible (HB) and even in the Song.

NITOCRIS'S RELIGION

Nitocris is first and foremost a priest, i.e., First Prophet of Amun-Re. She lives in the world of the God's Wife, the Divine Adoratrice, and the God's Hand serving, predominantly, in the temple at Karnak, Thebes. She worships Amun-Re, the great solar god of Creation, the king of the gods of whom it is said: "None of the gods knows His true form, His image is not unfolded in the papyrus rolls, nothing certain is testified about Him."[21] He is "One"; he is mysterious; the gods and goddesses (the *neteru*) become aspects of his identity, e.g., theophanies, or avatars. The religion of Amun-Re has been described as the "theology of the hidden."[22] As such, it is a sort of mystery-initiation cult, the head of which is Pharaoh, who is Amun-Re's representative on earth, as his divine "son" (hence the pharaoh is identified as Horus incarnate).

On the other hand, Nitocris comes from a family who also worships Neith, the goddess of Sais, the capital of the Saite Dynasty. Neith is a goddess of war, (pro-)creation, and wisdom. Though a mother goddess (i.e., the mother of Re), she remains a virgin. Neith is associated with the primeval

---

Antiquities 34 (2007): 1–13, here 2.

[19] H. M. Hays, "A New Offering Table for Shepenwepet," *Journal of the American Research Center in Egypt* 40 (2003): 47–60, https://hdl.handle.net/1887/16164.

[20] W. F. Albright, "New Light on Early Recensions of the Hebrew Bible," *Bulletin of the American Schools of Oriental Research*, 140 (1955): 27–33, here 32. See Supplemental Note "Tahpenes and Hadad: Nabonidus and his Alter Ego?".

[21] Wim van den Dungen, "Amun, the Great God: Hidden, One and Millions" (2016; version 5), citing Hymns to Amun, Papyrus Leiden I 350, chapter 200, lines 22–4. c.1213 BCE (end of the reign of Ramesses II), http://www.sofiatopia.org/maat/amun.htm.

[22] J. Assmann, J. *Egyptian Solar Religion in the New Kingdom* (New York: Kegan Paul, 1995), 153.

waters of Creation, and she is said to produce "perfumes and pharmacological mixtures such as the 'two kinds of stimulating drugs' mentioned in an inscription from Medamoud (Neith, doc. 224)."[23] She is mentioned again, in the context of pregnancy and the 'drugs' of initiation, in Part Two, Chapter 5.

For the purposes of understanding Nitocris's words and actions in the Song, however, I offer a few other ancient Egyptian religious concepts based upon parallels found within the narrative:

✶ The concept of *maat* is one of truth, righteousness, justice, and divine (cosmic) order. "From an early period, the king would describe himself as the 'Lord of Maat' who decreed with his mouth the *maat* he conceived in his heart."[24]

✶ When a person dies, his/her soul is weighed against the feather of the goddess Maat; if that person is judged to have an honourable soul, he/she is deemed *maat kheru*, which is usually translated as "True of Voice." The original meaning of this phrase comes from the story of Osiris, who was summoned to be judged by the gods after (unknown) false accusations by the scheming Set; Thoth intervened on Osiris's behalf, resulting in the god's judging Osiris "true of word or voice" or as is now commonly translated, "justified."[25]

✶ The lotus is a symbol of rebirth, the sun, and sexuality/fertility. It is said to be the product of Re's semen (see Book of the Dead, Chapter 81a) and is associated with Hathor.

✶ The most important moment of a pharaoh's coronation is his initiation as priest. This is signified by the Divine Embrace. The embrace is depicted (in the context of kingship) only in the Holy of Holies of the temple (e.g., at Karnak) and is considered the final sanctification of the king.[26] (This has a parallel in the Mesopotamian *hieros gamos* ritual.)

✶ Hathor's *menet* necklace represents the (magical) powers of the

---

[23] Edward P. Butler, "Neith," Henadology: Philosophy and Theology, https://henadology.wordpress.com/theology/netjeru/neith/.

[24] "Maat," 1, https://www.pgliterarytranslation.com/resources/Maat.pdf.

[25] For an in-depth analysis of the term see Rudolf Anthes, "The Original Meaning of Mꜥ Ḥrw," *Journal of Near Eastern Studies* 13.1 (1954): 21–51. Examples of this attribution for living persons have been found.

[26] Stephen D. Ricks, "The Sacred Embrace and the Sacred Handclasp in Ancient Mediterranean Religions," *Interpreter: A Journal of Latter-day Saint Faith and Scholarship* 37 (2020): 319–330, here 323.

goddess, which she relays to the pharaoh by offering the necklace to him. It represents life, fertility, and the esoteric union of male and female sexual energies.[27] Hathor is the original "Hand of God." Priestesses re-enact this relationship by shaking their *menet* necklaces at the king in the temple.

PERFECT CHOICE

In order to achieve his goal of establishing the *entu* priesthood at Ur, Nabonidus must have a daughter to put into the office, for this was the ancient tradition; even if he has daughters already, they are clearly not deemed suitable for the role, for he declares that Sîn rejects all other females dutifully suggested for the position (Nab 34, 1.14–21). This has a bearing on the assumed dating of Nab 34, as we shall see.

The choice of a mother for the first *entu* of Ur for centuries must be important to Nabonidus; that she is of the necessary quality is vital. Nitocris II is ideal. Not only is she young ("nubile," i.e., sexually mature) and beautiful, with the royal blood of the ancients in her veins, she is also the acting High Priest of Amun-Re. She brings with her a certain sacredness, prestige, spiritual knowledge, and ritualistic knowledge. She will add an air of authenticity and teach the young *entu* how to be a priestess. It is hoped she can bring gravitas and respect to the new order which, unfortunately, had been the butt of ridicule and sexual innuendo even in the Old Babylonian period (perhaps a portent of doom the king would have done well to acknowledge).

---

[27] Robert Schmidt and Barbara Voss, *Archaeologies of Sexuality* (London: Taylor & Francis, 2005), 256.

2. THE RIDDLE OF SOLOMON

A FAMILIAR KING

The character and behaviour of King Solomon (e.g., in 1 Kings and Ezra/Nehemiah) is, predominantly, a conflation of known characteristics and actions peculiar to Nabonidus. The postexilic authors create a bridging tale of this familiar king, to highlight the expectations of the new regime. They use "Solomon" as a benchmark, as an example of how *not* to rule Israel; they had witnessed first-hand the fallout of Nabonidus's reign, so this is their blueprint for the future. You can discern the repeated but varied renditions of the good-ruler-gone-bad theme (and the ensuing threat to the nation) throughout the HB; if you look carefully enough, most instances lead you back to the last Babylonian king and his poor example (e.g., the tale of Samson [see below], the fate of King Hiram of Tyre,[1] etc.). Below is a list of some of the most significant parallels between the life of Nabonidus and the Bible's depiction of Solomon (mostly in 1 Kings):

Nabonidus …

★ builds palaces and renovates temples, making them better than before; he is said to use the finest craftsmen and the best resources (Solomon: 1 Kgs 4–7)

★ is extremely close to his mother, who intercedes for him in becoming king; she is a powerful woman in her own right (Solomon: 1 Kgs 1–2)

★ rules over all territories west of the Euphrates, down to the border of Egypt; he is constantly receiving property and possessions from the people, and claims all kings bow down at his feet (Solomon: 1 Kgs

---

[1] Hiram builds palaces and temples to various gods; gives his daughter in marriage to a foreign king (Solomon); is praised for his wisdom and his access to hidden knowledge (Ezek 28:3–4); because he becomes arrogant and abuses his wisdom, his nation is destroyed; worships Astarte; accused of "profaning … sanctuaries" (Ezek 28:18); told he is wiser than Daniel and "no secret is hidden" from him (Ezek 28:3).

4:24; 10:24–5; 2 Chr 9:23–4)

★ goes against conventional worship practices in Babylon by elevating the Assyrian lunar deity Sîn above the Babylonian city god Marduk; in the Song, is inculcated into Nitocris's religion (Solomon: 1 Kgs 11:1–8)

★ is known for seeking out esoteric wisdom that surpasses the greatest of the Babylonian sages (Solomon: 1 Kgs 3:3–28; 10:4, 8, 24; Eccl 1:12–18)

★ fails to save his kingdom from falling to his enemies (Solomon: 1 Kgs 11:9–40)

★ is posthumously mocked for his "desire"; probably inherits the royal, multicultural harem; is said (by Herodotus) to have married a woman called Nitocris, i.e., an Egyptian name (Solomon: 1 Kgs 3; 11; Neh 13:26)

★ apparently enters a conciliatory marriage with Pharaoh Ahmose's daughter (Solomon: 1 Kgs 3:1)

★ builds a structure called the *majal* just beyond the communal residence (*giparu*) of the *entu*-priesthood at Ur (Solomon: builds the "Millo" 1 Kgs 9:24 [see below])

★ is a "peaceful" king, e.g., he makes a peace treaty with Egypt (and others); he does not fight the Persian invasion of Babylon (Solomon: 1 Kgs 3:1)

★ is told by Daniel that he will go mad for seven years and live far from his kingdom (Solomon: loses his senses for many years and roams as a beggar far away from home [in the rabbinic tale of Ashmedai, Gittin 68])

★ is said to force the people of Tayma into building a replica of his palace in Babylon (VA 2.9) (Solomon: 1 Kgs 5:13; *"The Arabs have a legend that Tayma was built by Solomon"*[2])

★ spends more time in Arabia than in Babylon (Solomon: Associated with Arabia only marginally less than with Jerusalem)

★ *leaves Babylon in his third regnal year, settles in Tayma from his fourth year (c. 550/49 BCE) for seven years, returning to Babylonia (potentially the temple at Ur, where the new entu is dedicated) in his*

---

[2] Raymond P. Dougherty, "Nabonidus in Arabia," *Journal of the American Oriental Society* 42 (1922): 305–16, here 306, note 6.

> **thirteenth regnal year (543 BCE), on 17 Tishritu, i.e., in the seventh month (Solomon: According to 1 Kgs 6:37–8, spends seven years, from his fourth to his eleventh regnal year building the temple; "his own house" he builds over thirteen years [1 Kgs 7:1], where "house" [bayith] can suggest palace, or family/dynasty; he dedicates the "temple" in the seventh month, Tishrei)**[3]

There is one glaring contradiction that should be mentioned. In 1 Kgs 11: 42–3 and 2 Chr 9:30, it is stated that Solomon reigned for "forty years" and was buried with his ancestors. We know that Nabonidus reigned only seventeen years, and was probably not buried with his kin (discussed again, later). The Book of Daniel seems to be more of a first-hand account of Nabonidus, as shall be demonstrated, and there, the hints at chronology match both historical evidence and clues within the Song. The ubiquitous biblical use of "forty" to delineate a leader's rule, the sojourn in the wilderness, and Moses's days up the mountain, etc., suggests a metaphorical, or symbolic usage of the number, i.e., it was never intended to be precise. In the context of the exodus, for instance, as in Josh 5:6–7, it was the time for a new generation to be raised; a generation fully indoctrinated into the new religion (and circumcised). Thus, "forty" represented a sloughing off of the life associated with captivity, a period of metamorphosis, cleansing. I suspect it was in reference to the life-span not of a man (considered to be seventy), but the life-span of the office or endeavour.

In terms of gematria (where Hebrew letters are assigned a numerical value), the number forty is represented by the thirteenth letter of the Hebrew alphabet, *mem*; this means "water," as in the waters of Creation and of the womb/childbirth. The gematria of "Life" itself is forty. Intriguingly, *mem* also pertains to the *secret teachings* of Torah; perhaps where "forty" is used, we should be looking for hidden meaning? It could allude to a trial, or endeavour in the "Wilderness of Sîn," i.e., a reference to the time spent in exile in the perceived spiritual wilderness of Babylon (where the reference to Sîn may be an allusion to the reign of Nabonidus). Regardless, I do not see any problem with this one generalization, given the extent of the substantiating details elsewhere provided. (See comment regarding Daniel in "Eternal Nothingness" in the discussion of Song 1:2–3.)

Solomon changes in depiction in the later biblical texts; earlier accounts are broadly forgiving but by the time of Ezra/Nehemiah there is little left to be praised. The king of the Song is not a hero or a romantic lover; he is the Nabonidus of ill-repute, the self-centred, distracted, somewhat

---

[3] See "Dedication?" in Part Two, Chapter 7 and also the Supplemental Note "Ziv, Bul, and Ethenim."

uncouth soldier with delusions of grandeur that eventually bring him to his knees.

The bitter memory of Nabonidus's controversial reign and its consequences (at least in terms of the political and religious institutions, if not the general public) can be discerned in several biblical texts; those who leave Babylon do not leave the Babylonian experience behind them.

GEZER, GAZA

The issue of the dowry-gift of Gezer from Solomon's father-in-law (1 Kgs 9:16) has always seemed rather underwhelming, i.e., the wedding present from an illustrious pharaoh to a great king is this small, isolated piece of land in northern Palestine which, according to the all-encompassing description in 1 Kgs 4:21, seems to be in Solomon's territory anyway.

Gezer lies on the busy trade route between Egypt and Syria; it was a significant site once, and it has been suggested that the "control of Gezer was a mark of supremacy in the affairs of the land"; this was in its heyday, centuries before Solomon's alleged dates (i.e., tenth century BCE), by which time it had been lowered to a state of "cringing subservience" and was a "relatively insignificant border city."[4] Furthermore, there is no archaeological evidence in the vicinity to support the claim that any Israelites lived there at all.[5] So, the wedding gift clearly does not fit the chronology, the history, or the archaeology.

The apparent addendum (in parentheses, suggesting it could have been added at a later date) of 1 Kgs 9:16–17 tells of the pharaoh capturing and burning Gezer and this *is* reflected in badly charred areas of the site but the general consensus seems to be that this dates from the attack on Gezer by Thutmose III, who lived almost 500 years earlier. So, how could the same pharaoh who destroyed the city give it to Solomon on his wedding day? Perhaps this is a case of Chinese Whispers, where the original circumstances have been confused over time. Given the emphasis on Solomon's marriage to an Egyptian princess, and the rabbis' concentration on how this brought ruin to the nation, I can see how the "wedding" motif might become associated with the story of a significant place. If Solomon is based on Nabonidus, however, there is a more satisfying explanation.

An ancient tradition holds that there is an "old watercourse called *Ḳanâet Bint el-Ḳafir*, i.e., 'the Conduit of the Infidel's Daughter,' running west of the mound in the direction of Ramleh" (i.e., north-western Israel,

---

[4] James F. Ross, "Gezer in the Tell El-Amarna Letters," *Biblical Archaeologist* 30.2 (1967): 62–70, here 70.
[5] R. A. Macalister, *The Excavation of Gezer, Vol. 1* (London: John Murray, 1911), 21.

enroute to Gaza if following trade routes from the northeast, e.g., Babylonia); this is presumed by most to refer to "Pharaoh's daughter."[6] Ahmose is called many things by many people but nowhere have I come across the notion he, personally, was deemed an "infidel"; it does not fit what we know of him. Of course, it could just be a generalised admonition against all Egyptians, who were not popular with the Jewish people of the time but with the stipulations of "*the* infidel" and this one daughter, it seems unlikely. Nabonidus, on the other hand, *would* be considered an "infidel" for turning against the orthodox Marduk-led religion of Babylon.

If Nabonidus is implied by the term "infidel," this "daughter" would be Ennigaldi-Nanna. Nothing has ever been found to shed light on what happens to young Ennigaldi after Cyrus takes Babylon. She may be allowed to leave with Nabonidus for Carmania, where he is supposedly sent by Cyrus (*Ag. Ap.* 1.153) but as this research progresses it will prove highly unlikely, so I contend that she leaves with the first wave of emigrants, to escape the wrath of the remaining Marduk priesthood. Gezer may be a stopping-off point, where Ennigaldi is known to have remained for a while. This is not an endearing, positive memory, as the term "infidel" attests; it is a derogatory reminder and it has its parallel in Gaza and in the story of Samson which, I argue, is an earlier (or contemporaneous but alternative) attempt to illustrate the delinquent Nabonidus in edifying terms.

SAMSON AND THE MENSTRUANT

The place-name mentioned in Judg 16:4, where Samson meets Delilah is "the valley of Sorek." The term used for "valley" is *nachal*, which suggests a torrent, or a valley through which water flows, i.e., for most interpreters, a *wadi*, hence Jewish translations refer to this as the Wadi Sorek. Sorek is often understood as relating to "a choice vine" or vineyards (which, as we will see in the Song, is a female-sexual euphemism), for the term relates to a ruddy-red colour. Together with the concept of a "valley" through which fluid runs, it seems quite probable that a woman's menses is implied.[7]

The name Delilah stems from the verb *dalal*, to hang or transport; the noun *dalla* denotes a hanging bundle of hair or threads, i.e., representing sexual energy. Coupled with the idea of a woman's vulva (the "valley"), flowing with "water" (i.e., blood/menstruation), the dangling ribbon, i.e., Min's *seshed* band, is employed here to portray Delilah in the most sexual and taboo terms. This is a castigation of Samson; he is being shown to be a

---

[6] Macalister, 20–1.

[7] See "A Critical Appraisal of Theories of Menstrual Symbolism," in *Blood Magic: The Anthropology of Menstruation*, eds. Thomas Buckley and Alma Gottleib (Berkeley: University of California Press, 1988): 3–50.

degenerate, by virtue of his sexual union with her while she is menstruating. It is a strong parallel to the legend of Solomon and Ashmedai, discussed below, and it emphasises the "type" of woman this leader associated with, for all three of his liaisons are with women that are deemed (within the context of the biblical text) prostitutes, i.e., he brings his ex-wife a "kid" when he knows she has found another man (Judg 15:1)—a kid is the going rate for a prostitute; he meets a working prostitute (16:1); and Delilah is reckoned a prostitute, for she is paid for her services (16:18).

The name Gaza stems from the verb *azaz*, to be strong, so it is a fitting name for the site of Samson, the strong man's, deeds. According to 1 Kgs 4:24, Gaza lies on the western boundary of Solomon's kingdom, providing the only access to Egypt from the Arabian Desert (*Hist.* 3.5: Gaza is here called Cadytis). Pharaoh Apries, sometime between 581 and 572 BCE, sets his sights on Phoenicia and successfully conquers Sidon; the surrounding territories, *including Gaza*, submit to Egyptian rule. In 568 BCE, however, Palestine falls to the Babylonians and records indicate that the king of Gaza becomes a vassal to Nebuchadnezzar. So, we see Gaza transferred from Egyptian to Babylonian rule, i.e., from pharaoh to Babylonian king, just twelve years prior to Nabonidus's reign. This may be enough to spawn a legend, perhaps several generations later (when the addendum of 1 Kgs 9:16 is added?), of the transfer of "Gezer" at the time of Solomon's marriage to his Egyptian princess.

The name Gezer stems from *gazar*, to cut, divide, or slice off—and this is precisely what is done in the story of Samson, i.e., in the shaving or slicing off of his hair. Might a conflation of Gaza and Gezer have occurred during the formative years of the legend of Solomon?

The story of Samson does parallel that of Solomon/Nabonidus on several levels, including:

* Samson means Sun Man (*shemesh*); the Mesopotamian solar deity is Shamash. Nabonidus, of course, is the Moon Man (there is a later discussion on why Nabonidus is not mentioned in the HB).

* He is chosen by God in the womb (as a Nazarite). Nabonidus is supposedly chosen to be king in his mother's womb. See 2 Sam 12:24 for Solomon.

* He goes with several women, i.e., foreigners. Ditto for Solomon/Nabonidus.

* An uncontrollable rage comes over him–a form of madness; he is revived after drinking miraculous water. Nabonidus has nightmares, paranoia, and probably hallucinations; he is known in the VA (4) for being "mad"; he has a moment of rage in the Song *caused* by an elixir.

19

* Samson gathers foxes. Nabonidus "gathers the little foxes" in the Song.

* He hides in "clefts of the rocks." Nabonidus (in the Song) describes Nitocris as hiding in "clefts of rocks."

* He carries the gate of Gaza to a hill opposite Hebron, which means "place of alliance," approximately halfway between Gaza (the entry into Egypt) and Israel. Tayma is halfway between Egypt and Babylon; it is possibly the site of the alliance in 549 BCE.

* Samson judges Israel for twenty years (round figure). Nabonidus is king for seventeen years.

* In Gaza, he sleeps with prostitutes. Prostitute innuendo is common in the Song, and this is linked to Babylonian prostitution mentioned by Herodotus, and to Ishtar, goddess of prostitutes, both connected with Nabonidus.

* With Delilah, he has sexual relations with a menstruant. Nabonidus in the Song is obsessed with women in menses; in the legend of Ashmedai, the "demon king" orders that menstruants be brought to him.

* Samson sets a riddle (lion/honey). Solomon is said to share riddles with the Queen of Sheba and Hiram of Tyre. Nabonidus demonstrates a penchant for occult matters and devising his own cultic symbolism that baffles everyone.

SOLOMON'S IDOLS

According to 1 Kings 3, Solomon was already deeply affected by his associations with women by the time he had settled into his reign as monarch; 1 Kgs 11:4 states he was "old" when his "wives turned away his heart after other gods." Nabonidus is in his sixties when he becomes king.

Both Exod 34:16 and Neh 13:26 make it clear that intermarriage is a direct route to idolatry and emasculation; by marrying foreign women, Israelite men are forced to 'prostitute themselves' to other gods. The prohibition is later reiterated in *direct* relation to Solomon in 1 Kgs 11:1–2. Rather than just including Egyptians in the list of prohibited marriages, the precedent of Nabonidus, who had married "the daughter of Pharaoh," is directly implied.

The account of Solomon's chastisement by God and the punishment of the loss of the kingdom after his death (1 Kgs 11:5–8; exactly what happens to Nabonidus, recall), is inextricably linked to the king's leniency toward the heretical worshipping practices of his wives. The one marriage that seems to have caused the most consternation amongst the court of Israel, however, and the one most vividly remembered by subsequent generations, is that to the Egyptian princess.

> When Solomon married the daughter of Pharaoh, she introduced to him a thousand different kinds of musical instruments, and taught him the chants to the various idols.
>
> Shabbath, 56.2

Of course, Nitocris, versed in the rituals and chants/prayers of her Egyptian deities, is expected to use her knowledge and experience to teach the new priestly order at Ur, especially the young Ennigaldi. The gods have different names, the language is different, but the similarities between the cults of the God's Wives and the *entus* are enough to make the transition potentially effective.[8] Perhaps Nabonidus does not find quite as much insightful material in the archaeological record as he boasts (e.g., he claims to have discovered everything he needed, just at the right moment, on a stele dated to Nebuchadnezzar I's reign); it may be that Nitocris has more of an influence than is acknowledged.

JOSEPHUS'S SECRET

Josephus claims: "I have discovered from our own books, that after Pharaoh, the father-in-law of Solomon, no other king of Egypt did any longer use that name" (*Ant.* 8.6.2), yet he does not provide the name of that pharaoh. There were many pharaohs using the title after the period assigned to Solomon, so is he mistaken, or are we?

As most of what little we know of Psametik III, Ahmose's son, comes from a few references by Herodotus and from much more modern excavations, it may be that the fleeting reign (less than a year) of this rather inconsequential pharaoh left no immediate or lasting impression. Ahmose *was*, for all intents and purposes, the last true Pharaoh of Egypt; all the subsequent pharaohs ruled as foreigners, usurping the title to assuage rebellion. Perhaps Josephus, a Solomon-apologist, did not wish to expose the whole truth because it would put his entire argument about Solomon in jeopardy.

THE LINK TO NECHO

The search for Solomon's Egyptian father-in-law has largely overlooked the

---

[8] For a comprehensive comparison, see Lloyd D. Graham, "King's Daughter, God's Wife: The Princess as High Priestess in Mesopotamia (Ur, ca.2300–1100 BCE) and Egypt (Thebes, ca. 1550-525 BCE)," https://www.academia. edu/34248896.

specification of Pharaoh Necho II (609–594 BCE) in the Palestinian Talmud. Gribetz has suggested that this "requires further investigation, as here the rabbis are either deliberately anachronistic in their recounting of Solomon's life, or they are simply wrong in their chronology."[9] The issue is written off by most scholars as a mere aberration on the part of the rabbis, which is unhelpful and rather patronizing. Could they truly be so wrong, or is there a reason why the rabbis chose to make this claim: "R. Levi said: … Solomon married into [the family/dynasty of] Pharaoh Necho the king of Egypt" (Avodah Zarah 1:2, 39c)?

The accounts of Necho II in both the HB and the rabbinic literature are less than flattering, equating his name with danger, cunning, self-aggrandisement, being a useless ally, and a threat to the nation of Israel. The entire Necho dynasty becomes anathema and, by association, so does the fabled wife of Solomon.

Recall that Dougherty posits that Queen Nitocris of Babylon is possibly the granddaughter of Necho II, being the mixed-blood offspring of a nameless Egyptian princess and Nebuchadnezzar. I argue, however, that Nitocris II, the *great*-granddaughter of Necho II, marries Nabonidus *after* he becomes King. She is pure Egyptian, of the Necho dynasty. The rabbis were not wrong.

MERED AND BITHIAH

The wedding of Solomon and this Egyptian princess is said to have taken place on the very day the new temple was consecrated; in the Palestinian Talmud (Avodah Zarah 1:2, 39c) this woman is given a name, i.e., Bathya. There is no historical record of an Egyptian princess called Bathya but there is a woman called Bithiah in the HB; she is, remarkably, a "daughter of Pharaoh" who marries a descendent of Judah called Mered (1 Chr 4:17–18). The name Bithiah means Daughter of the Moon.

> *Once [Solomon] built [the temple] and married Bisiya bas Paroh....*
> Vayikra Rabbah 12:5

Mered's name means rebellion (from the noun *meri*) but the verb *mara* means argumentative or disobedient, *particularly* with respect to God. An alternative understanding of the name is Ruler. The early rabbis saw a connection to Moses and attempted to rationalise Mered by suggesting he was actually Caleb; this is why a tradition later arose that Moses's adoptive mother was called Bithiah, when the Book of Exodus does not name her.

---

[9] Sarit Kattan Gribetz, "A Matter of Time: Writing Jewish Memory into Roman History," *Association for Jewish Studies Review* 40.1 (2016): 57–86, here note 30.

Caleb, however, means Dog and thus has the connotation of faithfulness, devotion, and bravery. How does this tally? There must be a better fit. Who else can be seen to be a "rebellious ruler"? I suggest Mered is another name (among many) for Solomon, i.e., Mered is an alternative rendition of Nabonidus.

The postexilic generation, in varying degrees, perceive Solomon as wicked, as rebelling against God's stipulations regarding foreign women and idolatry. This is a far more significant rebellion to warrant the name of Mered than Caleb's stand against the reluctance of the spies in Numbers 13, which is the usual explanation. This is on a par with Nabonidus's rebellious actions in metaphorically stealing the Tablet of Destinies (i.e., usurping the right to supremacy for Sîn), especially in light of the "infidel" epithet (above).

Take a look at Mered's children with Bithiah (his "Judean wife" is discussed later). Their firstborn is recorded as being Miriam, a *daughter* (unusual to be mentioned at all). Miriam can *also* be translated as rebellion (like father like daughter) but there are two alternatives, i.e., from the Egyptian, "beloved" (which would link, etymologically, to Jedidiah, see below) and from the Hebrew, "myrrh."

In 1 Kgs 4:11, 13, two daughters of Solomon are mentioned, i.e., Taphath and Basemath. Taphath is derived from the verb *nataph*, which suggests dripping; the same word is employed in Song 4:11; 5:5, 13, in reference to the dripping of honey and "liquid myrrh." Basemath, from the feminine of *bosem*, means fragrance, i.e., a spicy, sweet odour. Both daughters reflect the fundamental character/nature of their mother, Nitocris of the Song, in that they personify the art of women, they are identified with the "liquid myrrh" and spices of the Elixir Rubeus (see Part One, Chapter 3). These are both possible addenda (in parentheses), so perhaps it was after the Song had revealed the intimate/private life of Nabonidus/Solomon and his notorious wife that someone thought it necessary to include these other daughters, but why?

It is possible that these two women are invented, to add verisimilitude in an ever-increasingly negative perception of Solomon (by insinuating that his daughters are "harlots," like their mother). It is also possible that there were other, older daughters of Nabonidus; Beaulieu suggests there are two princesses connected with the Ebabbar temple in Sippar.[10] As Nabonidus's immediate family, and as 'temple women', they too would be if not rejected, certainly cast in an ill light by the early Jews (expanded upon further in due course). These daughters of Solomon are described as being married to

---

[10] Paul-Alain Beaulieu, *The Reign of Nabonidus King of Babylon 556–539 B.C.* (New Haven: Yale University, 1989), 136–7.

Israelite men, making them prime targets for those in the Ezra/Nehemiah anti-mixed-marriage camp (Ezra 9; Neh 13).

The name Miriam can also stem from *tamrur,* meaning bitterness, but this can be a pun on the identical noun *tamrur*, meaning a marker or sign post, from the root verb *tamar*, to be stiff or erect—an identifying attribute of Ishtar, i.e., as the symbolic palm (the noun *tamar* translates as "palm"). Both biblical Tamars prove significant to the interpretation of several of the Song's verses.

HAND OF A GOD

Solomon's divine name is Jedidiah (2 Sam 12:25), traditionally translated as Beloved of Yah, from the verb *yadad,* to love, in an intimate, physical, i.e., sexual way (see Prov 5:19; Ezek 23:3; and cf. Gen 30:14). The suffix, *-iah* or *-yah,* is usually explained as "the name of the Lord." The noun *yad* (i.e., Jed) denotes *the hand* (there is another verb *yadad*, linked to the casting of lots, which, of course, is done with the hand). The hand is a euphemism for the penis in Mesopotamian texts.

Although a name supposedly given from God via a prophet, Solomon's sacred name is never used again. Why would that be, given that every other instance of God implementing a name-change (e.g., Abram, Sarai, Jacob) results in that name being adopted from that moment on? I suggest that it is because 2 Sam 12:25 is either a later addendum, or an intentional (contemporaneous) link to the Song of Solomon, which can only be rationalised in Part Two, Chapter 9, once this new version of the Song is explained. If this is the case, the name Jedidiah is not divine but very subtly derogatory.

"Jedidiah" thus breaks down into three elements: *Jed*: Hand (sexual), *did*/*dod*: Beloved (cultic, explained later), and *–iah*, the Egyptian lunar deity. The name *could* mean: Beloved hand of the moon god. This could be a deliberate signpost to the Egyptian women who serve as God's Hand. In that capacity, it would be intended as an *insulting* sexually-charged inference that the king (Nabonidus), himself, is "the hand" to Ahmose III (as a personification of Iah/Yah), a slur on the Babylonian king's strength as a man and ruler, e.g., that he is capitulating and/or emasculated even. This potential emasculation or ridicule of the king finds a parallel in the Song and it has been suggested by some current scholars that the depiction of Solomon therein is a parody of kingship. I would argue that this is the result of him being the representation of Nabonidus, the Babylonian king publicly mocked and derided after his death.

WOMAN IN THE WORKS

The Palestinian Talmud states that on Solomon and Bathya's wedding day, the people of Jerusalem are so busy flattering the newlyweds, they forget to pay homage to God in his new house. God responds by planning the future destruction of the temple. At the moment the royal couple consummate their marriage, an Archangel descends with a reed in his hand. He plants the reed in the sea and around it grows, in time, a thickly forested island; upon the island grow the seeds of the Roman Empire, which will eventually carry out God's revengeful plan (Avodah Zarah, 1:2, 39c). Solomon, by marrying the Egyptian princess, sows the seeds of his own destruction and that of his kingdom.

Meanwhile, the new queen seduces her husband day and night, teaching him the songs of her pagan religion and the names of all the gods (Shabbat 56b). She uses her wiles by sewing gems into their bed's canopy; when the king wakes, she convinces him that the gems glittering above him are stars, so he goes back to sleep, neglecting his duties (Midr. Lev. Rabbah 12.5). That is, Solomon is detrimentally influenced, i.e., deceived, by his Egyptian bride. Nabonidus, of course, is notorious for not fulfilling his royal duties in Babylon, especially at the Akitu festival; we learn from the Song that it is the beguiling Nitocris and her alleged deceptions that keep the king otherwise engaged.

The guards in the legend need Solomon to give them the keys to open up the temple but he keeps them under his pillow; they dare not attempt to wake him, so they go to his mother, Bathsheba, for advice. Her response is to march over to Solomon's palace, where she rebukes him for remaining in bed, claiming that she had never asked for a son who would reign *well*, but at least he might have been pious (Lev. Rabbah 12:5; Sanhedrin 70b). Such a scene finds a parallel in a myth of Enki and his mother: "Are you really lying there asleep, and ... not awake? ... My son, wake up from your bed!" (*ETCSL t.1.1.2*, §12–23). Recall, it is supposedly largely due to Bathsheba's intercession that Solomon attains the throne in the first place, and it is Adad-guppi, Nabonidus's mother, who gets the credit for interceding with the kings of Babylon (and Sîn) on behalf of her son, Nabonidus (Nab 2001, 1.44b–2.4).

THE MILLO

In 2 Chr 8:11, Solomon brings his Egyptian wife to her own house some distance away from the city of David because she is not to reside anywhere the "ark of the Lord" has been, as the land itself becomes holy, yet back in 1 Kgs 3:1, it is said he takes her to live in the city until his own house and the temple are complete. 1 Kgs 6:37–8 tells us this all takes thirteen years.

So there is a conundrum: Does the foreign ('pagan') wife live on allegedly sanctified ground for well over a decade before Solomon has a brainwave that perhaps this is not kosher, or are we being told something else? I suggest this has more to do with the memory of Nabonidus and his plan for the *entu* priesthood; the author of 2 Chronicles realises the inherent problem with 1 Kgs 3 and tries to make amends for his Jewish audience who, by now, have their own stringent rules concerning ritual cleanliness and the proximity of women, especially menstruating women, to the temple. The key to the riddle is the strange edifice Solomon builds in 1 Kgs 9:24, i.e., the Millo.

The term Millo comes from the verb *male/mala*, which means to be full/to fill and suggests completion, or fulfilment. In the original translation of Nab 34 by Clay is the transliterated word *majal*: "... the wall of the *majal* (resting place) of the ancient votaries, as it was of old, I constructed around it anew."[11] The same word (*majal*) appears in an Assyrian letter to Esarhaddon, where it is translated as "nocturnal [dreams]."[12] The ancient *entu* priestesses greatly revered their predecessors, creating a veritable cult of the dead, referring to them as the "resting ones."[13] Near the *giparu*, the *entus'* residential complex, was a walled cemetery; the wall was constantly renovated by the *entus* themselves, then, after hundreds of years, by Nabonidus.

So, I posit that the word Millo in the HB, meaning completion, and the Akkadian word *majal*, used in a context of graves of those who have completed their lives/duties (i.e., the "resting ones"), seems a link that deserves further investigation. For instance:

✶ Nabonidus repairs the *giparu* (Nab 34, 1.39–40), wherein is found the cella, or sanctuary; *then* he builds the royal/priestess' residence at some distance from the sacred site ("Near the boundary of Egipar I built anew the house of En-nigaldi-Nanna," 2.6); *then* he renovates the *majal* ("As [it had been] in the [distant] past, I surrounded the burial ground of the ancient *entu*-priestesses anew with a wall" [2.12–14]).

Thus: Cella (sacred site), then residence, then cemetery.

✶ Solomon moves the Egyptian queen away from the Yahweh-sacred

---

[11] Albert T. Clay, *Miscellaneous Inscriptions in the Yale Babylonian Collection* (New Haven: Yale University Press, 1915), 2.15.

[12] Simo Parpola, *Letters from Assyrian Scholars to the Kings Esarhaddon and Ashurbanipal* (University Park: Eisenbrauns, 2007), 211.

[13] Penelope N. Weadock, "The Giparu at Ur," *Iraq*, 37.2 (1975): 101–128, here 103–4, and note 31.

city of David, to her own residence (1 Kgs 9:24) — "then" the king builds the Millo.

Thus: Tabernacle (sacred site), then residence, then cemetery.

The order of Nabonidus's building projects is retained in this account of Solomon. Clearly, this has something to do with purity concerns, e.g., either in terms of the creation of a cemetery at Jerusalem, or (by choosing to clarify 2 Chr 8:11) in terms of negating any suggestion of contamination of temple grounds by (menstruating) women. That Solomon moves his wife away from the city does imply she lives there first, and this demonstrates the king's lack of insight into priestly purity concerns; uncannily, this does become a significant theme in the Song (Part Two, Chapter 5).

THE SOLOMON SPELL

King Solomon is renowned for four things, i.e., the temple; his foreign women and their idols; paradoxically perhaps (once this analysis is complete), wisdom; and magic. If Solomon is based on Nabonidus, as I suggest, it makes sense that this biblical king has an aspect of Nabonidus's personality that reflects *his* fascination with occult practices, e.g., Nabonidus was ridiculed (after his death) for trying to interpret omens and gain superior, occult wisdom. Although this facet of Solomon's character does not find *much* representation in the HB, it *is* there, and it finds firmer footing in the rabbinic literature.

Perhaps the early sages/scribes found the prevalence of the occult in Babylonia just too fascinating to resist. We see a double-standard at work here, for in the public texts, e.g., the law allegedly found in the ruins of the old temple in Jerusalem (2 Kgs 22:8), we get this vehement diatribe against such practices:

> No one shall be found among you who makes a son or daughter pass through fire, or who practices divination, or is a soothsayer, or an auger, or a sorcerer, or one who casts spells, or who consults ghosts or spirits, or who seeks oracles from the dead. ... [D]o not give heed to soothsayers and diviners ....
>
> Deut 18:9–14

On the other hand, in the rabbinic writings meant only for the sages and men of learning, it is declared that "none were allowed to sit in the Sanhedrin unless they had a knowledge of magic" (Sanhedrin, 17.1). Was sorcery still so commonplace that in order to be ready for any legal contingency, the Sanhedrin, many generations later, could justify flouting the law? Or perhaps it was a case of the old Babylonian magic casting its spell on the Jewish leaders, who simply did not wish to give it up, so they incorporated it into the legends of Solomon and thus could debate upon the matter at their leisure, with impunity. Before the esoteric nature of the Persian Zoroastrianism inspired the Kabbalah, the rabbis cut their teeth on the inherited magic of the Chaldeans.

It would seem that the character of Solomon was a gift that kept on giving, for legends concerning every aspect of his life, from the technological details of his (mechanised) throne, to the riddles the queen of Sheba asked him, sprouted from originally rather vague suggestions. By the time we get to Josephus (in the first century CE), Solomon's occult reputation is truly established: "God also enabled him to learn that skill which expels demons .... He composed such incantations also by which distempers are alleviated. And he left behind him the manner of using exorcisms ..." (*Ant.* 8.2.5). This alleged ability to interact with demons ties in with the legend of Ashmedai, which has significance to the Song.

Aware that the law dictates that no iron tool is to be used in making the altar for Yahweh (Exod 20:25), Solomon fears he will not be able to build the new temple with unhewn stones. The sages tell him he needs the *shamir* (variably translated as insect/worm, or a sharp stone), whose presence alone can split rocks. Only the king of the demons, Ashmedai, knows where to find the *shamir*, and the legend follows Solomon's strategy in exploiting Ashmedai to obtain it (Gittin 68a–b), including first capturing a male and a female demon. In Eccl 2:8, the king says: "I got singers, both men and women, and delights of the flesh, and many concubines"; the Babylonian Talmud (Gittin 68a) interprets these last two as "male and female demons."

Ashmedai, significantly, lives atop a mountain and on a daily basis he ascends into heaven, "to take part in the discussions in the celestial house of study"; in the evening, he descends to earth to participate ("invisibly") at "the debates in the earthly houses of learning."[14] The Mesopotamian sun god, Shamash, lives behind the mountains; he rises every day and then descends (becomes "invisible"); his iconography includes him holding in his hand an object, often referred to as a saw, which he uses to split the mountains, so that he can rise again in the morning. A Jewish house of study is called a *beth midrash* and is centred on teaching and discussing Torah, which is predominantly a collection of laws. Shamash is not just the Sun God; he is also the god of Law and Justice; Hammurabi (1792–1750 BCE) claimed his famous Law Code was given to him by Shamash. The *shamir* is thus an example of appropriated mythology and perhaps magical lore, to

---

[14] K. Kohler and L. Ginzberg, "Asmodeus, or Ashmedai [Ashmadai]," *Jewish Encyclopedia*, https://www.jewishencyclopedia.com/articles/2019-asmodeus.

create a story pertinent to the new Jewish religion.

A further aspect of the story that is significant here is that Ashmedai tricks the king out of his signet ring[15] (the one item that both identifies Solomon as King and is used to control demons) and sends him hundreds of miles away, to wander the countryside as a beggar for years. Of course, Nabonidus inscribes on a (public) stele that he "wandered around the country" (Arabia) for ten years (Nab 47, 22b–27a). Solomon, in the Ashmedai legend, is being reprimanded for his deviance from the law and for his pride and arrogance. Recall Daniel's words to Nabonidus in Daniel 4, i.e., the king's power has become too great and he will be brought low (for his sin against the gods) by being sent far away, living as an animal.

While Solomon is supposedly absent, however, the wise men and the court begin to question the king's behaviour. In the story this is Ashmedai, impersonating the king. He roams at night, and he demands that women who are menstruating, and even the queen mother, Bathsheba, lay with him (both of which are forbidden in Jewish law). In Nabonidus's case, we have surmised that there is a potential opportunity for a substitute king, which ultimately leads to him leaving Babylon and going several hundred miles away, during which time he is deemed to go "mad." As will be demonstrated, this "madness" is directly linked to women who are menstruating.

It was but a few words in Ecclesiastes that convinced the early rabbis that there *must* have been a time when Solomon was *not* on the throne: "I, Koheleth [the Teacher], son of David, *when king* over Israel" (Eccl 1:12). The reign of Solomon is placed in the past tense, though described in the first person. It was, they argued, because of his arrogance, his willingness to invoke demons, his foolishness in handing over his sacred ring, etc., that he was forced to undergo the humiliating sojourn—it was his *penance*, just like Nabonidus.

Both kings regain their senses and return to their thrones, temporarily.

---

[15] The ring-in-the-fish tale appears several guises throughout the world and throughout history. Perhaps the earliest we know of is the tale of Polycrates, in *His*.3.39–43, where the context is *also* a treaty with Ahmose III of Egypt and dream divination by the king's daughter. I suggest this has roots in the pharaoh's experience of Nabonidus, not Polycrates. It should also be reassessed in terms of Jezebel in 1 Kgs 21:8, and her relationship to Nitocris in the Song (e.g., in the context of usurping the king's power).

3. Blood, the Goddess, and Dangerous Women

Bloody Women

The postexilic Jews incorporate a profound degree of resentment into the very fabric of their existence, evidenced by the antipathy in their texts, and this runs all the way from the returnees' generation to the Book of Revelations in the New Testament. Old wounds still fester, it seems:

> I saw a woman sitting on a scarlet beast that was full of blasphemous names …. The woman was arrayed in purple and scarlet, and adorned with gold and jewels and pearls, holding in her hand a golden cup full of abominations and impurities of her fornication; and on her forehead was a written name, a mystery: "Babylon the great, mother of whores and of earth's abominations." And I saw that the woman was drunk with the blood of the saints ….
>
> Rev 17:3–5

Notwithstanding the interpretation given in the subsequent verses, we can see how vivid the memory of the cultic influences of Babylon remains many generations later. At its heart is the image of a "harlot," dressed in the manner of a priestess in the act of some ritual. The personification of Babylon seems familiar, for this fearsome, blood-thirsty, "mother of whores" is the fiery Ishtar.

Each of the "whore's" attributes can be found in just one myth, for instance, i.e., "Inanna and Ebih."[1] There we see parallels to the scarlet beast; seven heads; finery and jewels; the name as symbol; and, most significantly, the golden cup. The golden cup is held by the *entu* during the sacred marriage ritual,[2] but it is also linked to feminine blood rites, as in the tale of Siduri, who prepares a sacred "wine" (blood) in a golden bowl, for the gods (see Part Two, Chapter 5). Blood figures heavily in the mythology of Ishtar

---

[1] Betty De Shong Meador, *Inanna: Lady of Largest Heart: Poems of the Sumerian High Priestess Enheduanna* (Austin: University of Texas Press, 2000), 91–102.

[2] E. Douglas Van Buren, "The Sacred Marriage in Early Times in Mesopotamia," *Orientalia*, NOVA Series, 13 (1944): 1–72, here 68.

(*ETCSL t.1.3.3*, 129; *t.1.3.2*, §1–6; t.*4.07.2*, §42–59; *t.4.07.3*, §39–48, etc.). Her colour is red (sexual/blood allusion), and this is the colour of her high priestess' vestments (the "whore" wears scarlet).

The "cup full of abominations and impurities of her fornication" refers to something few scholars feel comfortable discussing, i.e., the ingestion of bodily fluids within the context of sacred rites. These include menstrual blood and semen as potent elixirs of Life. This is an ancient, ancient practice but due to its many centuries of taboo status, it has received little or no attention by mainstream scholars, other than in anthropological field-studies.

ELIXIR RUBEUS

So called in esoteric circles today, the Elixir Rubeus, made from the revered menstrual emanation attributed to the Mother Goddess and the semen of her consort (e.g., the king), is said to be ingested by priests, kings, and pharaohs for cultic purposes, i.e., for rebirth rituals, and for facilitating spiritual and cognitive prowess. In Mesopotamian lore, it is the womb-blood of Ninhursaga (who is alluded to within the Song), wife of Enlil, Mother of the Gods; historically, however, it is the menstrual blood of specific temple women. These non-childbearing females are sacred, they are the hierodules (i.e., "beloved ones"), the red-robed Scarlet Women later vilified as prostitutes and "whores."[3]

> ...the childless though nubile female is prized more highly than the mother herself, because the magical energy of the latter has been to a certain extent dissipated and therefore impaired by the production of physical offspring.[4]

In their discussion of the phenomenon of ingesting menstrual blood, Seren and Azra Bertrand list its depiction in myth and the historical record. It was probably the mysterious *soma* in the tantric (Vedic) tradition, "euphemistically referred to as the juice from the stalk of a plant (tree of life) that was the god of the gods—the Mother God" (the "tree of life" here is equated to the womb); in Persia, it was called *amrita* and it gave the gods their immortality; it is called "the flower, and the life-giving river in many Indian traditions, still to this day"; it was "the fountain of life in Gnostic Christian tradition; it was "the Holy Grail of Celtic Grail and Arthurian legends, and was also known as claret wine in the European legends that

---

[3] See James Arthur, *Mushrooms and Mankind: The Impact of Mushrooms on Human Consciousness and Religion* (United States: Book Tree, 2000), 38; Laurence Gardner, *Genesis of the Grail Kings* (London: Bantom Books, 2000), 173–187.

[4] Kenneth Grant, *The Magical Revival* (1972), PDF version, 130, https://cdn. preterhuman.net/texts/religion.occult.new_age/Magick/Magical%20 Revival.pdf.

conferred enlightenment to the king who drank it."[5] The authors state:

> These are the elixirs of immortality that alchemists of old were connoisseurs of. The proteins and peptides found in menstrual blood and yoni fluids include many ... that are neurologically active or alter sensory perception ... the womb elixirs are entheogens, sacred gateways to [the divine].[6]

The Egyptian Gnostic sect known as the Phibionites (c. third century CE) were called Borborites by the Greeks who deemed their practices reprehensible; the term Borborites stems from *borboros*, or "filthy beggars."[7] They practised ritual ingestion of both menstrual blood and semen (the "fluids of begetting"), which they revered as *psyche*, i.e., the divine Life-force that permeated all living things; this was laced with strong spices, often assumed to make the mixture palatable but which could, themselves, be hallucinogens. The Phibionite fellowship's liturgical characteristics included:[8] Eating and drinking together, with the climax of the meal being the communal drinking of the elixir; "performing the *agape*" (a formalised phrase denoting ritual sex, often referred to in terms of being the "holy of holies"); prayer/dedication (an offering); and a closing statement, usually beginning "this is ...."

The "performing the *agape*" ritual was deemed a symbolic act, not intended for procreation but to experience a blissful union with the divine. The Phibionites purportedly aborted any unwanted pregnancies and ritually ate the foetuses.[9] Everything mentioned above exists within the Song, i.e., the sharing of blood and semen; the spices; the sexual union that does not result in children; the offering; and the final "this is ..." closing statement. Even the notion of eating the foetus finds a potential rationale. I argue, therefore, that these Egyptian Gnostics took their liturgy from their understanding of the Song of Solomon and its Egyptian high priest(ess), Nitocris. There is no better explanation for the profound similarities.

It is, without doubt, a radical thought that such a practice as the Elixir Rubeus (for want of any original name) could be hidden within the poetry of the Song but there are so many allusions to it that I now find the Song

---

[5] Seren Bertrand and Azra Bertrand, *Womb Awakening: Initiatory Wisdom from the Creatrix of All Life* (United States: Inner Traditions/Bear, 2017), PDF version, 385.
[6] Bertrand, 404.
[7] Kurt Rudolph, "Borborians," in *Religion Past and Present* (2011) doi: http://dx.doi.org /10.1163/1877-5888_rpp_SIM_02245.
[8] Stephen Benko, "The Libertine Gnostic Sect of the Phibionites According to Epiphanius," *Vigiliae Christianae* 21.2 (1967): 103–19, here 117.
[9] Benko, 110.

incomprehensible without it. That there is no Egyptian text, or inscription, or image that I can categorically assert as a precedent does not make the claim null and void: "It has not been characteristic for most cultures to reveal their most sacred ritual materials"; in over ten thousand verses of the *Rig-Veda* of ancient India, not one instance of an unequivocal identification for the drink/plant *soma* has been found.[10] It may be that the Song is the only surviving witness to such a ritual, especially within the sphere of a potential God's Hand; it is partly because the Song has not been taken seriously as *history*, that such a notion has not been discussed before.

In order to prevent the transference of iniquity (impurity) to their new order, the early Jews intend to make certain the role of women therein will be strictly controlled and legislated, i.e., the antithesis of what seems to be the Babylonian way. They use the sanctity of ritual and cultic space as their reason for inflicting draconian rules upon those who have the "way of women" upon them (Gen 31:35).

When you look at the way the early rabbis deal with the wholly natural aspect of womanhood, i.e., menstruation, you can begin to see how intent they are on eradicating any risk of corruption from women in menses. The extensive and detailed Niddah tractate defines how and when a woman enters the *niddah* state—the state of being ritually impure due to an issue of blood—and how she is dealt with under the law. Some sages (men) make it their speciality to codify and enforce the complex laws on female purity, a position that requires medical experience and which, at times, results in preventing a woman from engaging in a normal sexual (i.e., "married") life, and this includes enforcing separation. In some instances, there is no relenting and no leeway; female Samaritans, for instance, are considered menstruants from birth and are thus *always* impure (Niddah 4.1–3).

Koren argues that the priestly sources "used the term *niddah* as a symbol of evil—a metaphor to describe total separation from the sacred." She cites, for instance, Lam 1:17 ("Jerusalem is like a menstruous woman"), and 1:8 (Jerusalem is "like a *niddah*" because of her sins); Ezek 7:19–20 (concerning idolaters: "You will cast [your idols] out like a menstruous woman"); Ezra 9:11 (Israel is a "land of *niddah*," polluted "by the menstruous deeds ["pollutions" in the NRSV] of the people"). Koren concludes: "… these biblical priestly sources reflect a perennial distaste for the menstruant."[11] This sentiment, especially from Ezra, has an unexpected link to the Song, discussed in due course.

In the Babylonian Talmud, a debate ensues between a rabbi and a

---

[10] William A. Emboden, "The Sacred Narcotic Lily of the Nile: Nymphaea Caerulea," *Economic Botany* 32.4 (1978): 395–407, here 401.

[11] Sharon Faye Koren, *Forsaken: The Menstruant in Medieval Jewish Mysticism* (Hanover: Brandeis University Press, 2011), 34.

person called a *"min"* concerning the rights and wrongs of menstruant-related laws; the understanding of who or what this *"min"* is, is still under debate, and the overall current idea is that it relates to some sort of "heretic."[12] Is this a muted reference, however, to the Egyptian god Min and his red ribbon relating to sexual energy and the power of feminine blood? Min would thus be serving as devil's advocate (i.e., by suggesting the rules are too stringent).

The blood of women, while still worshipped by many, rapidly becomes something shameful and impure to the Jewish mind. The subject crops up, well-disguised, in the tale of Samson and his woman from the valley of Sorek, in the legend of Solomon and Ashmedai, *and* in the Song— the cultic reverence for Ishtar, the woman in red who dominates the sexual scene in Babylon, is abhorred by the exiled Jewish elite and this revulsion never wanes.

The Babylonian Talmud broadly considers sexual desire itself a demonic force, referring to it as the *yeser*, an evil entity that rules the souls of men. The rabbis preach that the *yeser* must (and can only) be extinguished through marriage but they warn that *all* women are sources of temptation and that *all* men can fall victim to the *yeser's* devastating power.[13] This, generally speaking, is the postexilic mind-set pertaining to women, their blood, and their supposed sexual wiles.

In Mesopotamia, conversely, a young girl's first menstruation, or menarche, is considered a rite of passage and is celebrated. The sacred rites surrounding this event can be compared to those of the inauguration of a high priestess, where the girl is treated as if she were holy, not impure; she is sat on a throne, attendants look after her every need, her feet are bathed and anointed, and she is given red garments. The older women surround her and initiate her into the mysteries of the female blood cycle and the prospect of procreation, which includes, of course, indoctrination into the cult of Ishtar.

MISOGYNY OR FEAR?

Women in the HB are generally transitory by nature, unimportant in their own right and usually mentioned in relation to a man, or as examples of

---

[12] Tirzah Meacham, "An Abbreviated History of the Development of the Jewish Menstrual Laws," in *Women and Water: Menstruation in Jewish Life and Law*, ed. Rahel R. Wasserfall (Hanover: Brandeis University Press, 1999), 19 and note 62.

[13] Yishai Kiel, "Dynamics of Sexual Desire: Babylonian Rabbinic Culture at the Crossroads of Christian and Zoroastrian Ethics," *Journal for the Study of Judaism in the Persian, Hellenistic, and Roman Period,* 47.3 (2016): 364–410, especially 368–77.

weakness, wickedness, or dangerous mystery. Yes, there are a few apparent heroines, like Miriam and Huldah, but delve a little deeper and you soon realise that even they, who are so often held up as examples of women overcoming adversity or achieving high status, fall victim to the dominance and insulting humour of the male writers.

We are given four main types of women by the male authors, i.e., the seductive prostitute/"harlot"; those who earn acceptance by performing a dangerous task or by taking on (symbolically) the role of a man (e.g., Deborah and Jael in Judg 4–5); the "witch"; and the "good" virgin/wife/mother.

The first (biblical) woman, of course, is Eve, the bewitching temptress who, making her independence known, listens to the serpent and seizes the fruit of the tree, i.e., carnal knowledge. Adam and Eve discover each other, sexually, in the garden, in Nature, and are punished for it. For Ishtar, the garden is where she meets Tammuz at the start of her emotional and psychological journey as a female; it is where they unite, sexually.

The difference between Mesopotamian and Jewish perspectives on the story of the first seductress could not be more polar. In the Epic of Gilgamesh, a prostitute from the temple of Ishtar is the instigator of Enkidu's cultural development; she leads the naive and pastoral man out of his ignorance and plants him squarely on the road to enlightenment, i.e., he becomes "wise, like the gods." She teaches him "the art of women." She is a force for good. In the HB, of course, we see the opposite depicted: Eve is a force for evil, the cause of man's downfall and unending struggle for forgiveness.

It is claimed in 2 Kgs 22:8–20 that "the book of the law" was discovered in the ruins of the temple (by the high priest, of course) and was immediately brought to King Josiah. What is astounding is that they then go to a woman for advice. Huldah is said to live in Jerusalem in the Mishnah ("Second Quarter" in the NRSV: 2 Kgs 22:14), which is a school, a place of Torah; she is potentially a teacher, a wise-woman. This seems quite a positive depiction, until you look a bit deeper.

Huldah is said to have descended from the prostitute Rahab, due to her identification as "the wife of Shallum son of Tikvah," and in light of Rahab's actions in Josh 2:18, i.e., "... you tie this length [*tikvat*] of crimson cord" (Sifrei Num. 78).[14] The sexual/blood connotations of the "crimson cord" are clear to us from the *seshed* band of Min. We also learn that Rahab lives "in the wall itself," with her window facing outwards: this is

---

[14] See Tamar Kadari, "Huldah, the Prophet: Midrash and Aggadah," *Jewish Women: A Comprehensive Historical Encyclopedia* (2009), Jewish Women's Archive, https://jwa.org/encyclopedia/article/huldah-prophet-midrash-and-aggadah.

traditionally the home of the prostitute, of Kilili, who leans out of the window, and of the prostitute-goddess Inanna-Nanaya (e.g., *ETCSL t.4.07.8*, §A/20A–9; *t.4.08.09*, §25–30). Rahab's "crimson cord," then, is the equivalent of the Passover blood, protecting her and her family from the onslaught to come, i.e., it is either a "red light" sign of the prostitute (she puts the cord up after the men leave, suggesting she is available; she would most probably be spared for the soldiers), or it is a signal that she is menstruating, in which case the purity laws of the incoming Israelites may save her.

Although Huldah is deemed a powerful enough person to seek advice from about this most important document, the men, though seemingly acting on her words, seem to resent her authority and subjugate her honour by *nicknaming* her "Huldah," which is the feminine of *choled*, i.e., interpreted widely as "weasel" (a burrowing animal) but which can also mean to breed abundantly, to populate. In Lev 11:29, *choled* is used in conjunction with *sherets*, i.e., things that swarm, in a list of animals the Jews must not eat; the weasel tops the list. Why would a seemingly illustrious female be given such a nickname if it was not to demean her status? Not only is she compared to something that crawls upon the ground (Ezek 8:10, where "creeping things" are considered an abomination), her role as a vessel of procreation is debased, perhaps as another allusion to the "temple prostitute" perception of these erudite, authoritative, sacerdotal women, whom the early Jews saw as "swarming" and thus dangerous. What is worse, these animals are considered "unclean" (Lev 11:31) and "detestable" (11:41), even when dead! Could the reality be that she actually says something the priests do not wish to hear, and the scathing diatribe attributed to her is their own composition? Her reputation amongst the early settlers means her word is significant, has authority, so the priests use her popularity to convey their own agenda, while degrading her in the subtext.

Note how a similar thing happens to Miriam in Numbers 12; questioning Moses's marriage to a Cushite, *both* Aaron and Miriam are summoned to the tent of meeting by God but only Miriam is punished. She is declared a "rebel" via her name, and is chastised with leprosy and thus expulsion for seven days. We know that in the Mesopotamian belief system of Nabonidus's day, illnesses are associated with sin in some way, and the diviners (exorcists) are the only ones who can discover what sin has been committed and how to rectify this spiritual imbalance. For the Babylonian king, an ulcer is deemed the outward symptom (i.e., in 4Q242 Prayer of Nabonidus) of a spiritual shortfall. Thus, Miriam's "leprosy" is not the medical condition we know of today, i.e., it is a ritualised form of punishment known in Judaism as *tzaraat*.[15] The translation of Num 12:11 (i.e., in the NRSV, "do not punish us") is "do not lay sin upon us."

In Exod 15:20–1, Miriam acts like a Mesopotamian priestess, an understanding that has become quite widespread today. She is allowed access to the sacred tabernacle; she shakes the tumbril and leads other women in a victory dance. In Exod 28:36, Aaron, receiving his vestments as the first high priest, is given a solid gold "rosette" to wear on his forehead— solid gold rosettes were one of the ritualistic emblems of Ishtar. Thus, Aaron symbolically usurps the role of divine intercessor and wears the rosette almost as a trophy. We then discover that the process of communing with the divine through dream visions, i.e., oneiromancy, as practised by the "prophets" but also the *entu* in the ziggurat, has been superseded: "I ... make myself known to them in visions / I speak to them in dreams / Not so with my servant Moses" (Num 12:6–7). Miriam (like Huldah), if once a "prophet" by virtue of her priestly visions or insights, is therefore made redundant. She dies an uninspiring death in Num 20:1 and is buried in Kadesh, a place that has homophonic allusions to sacred/temple prostitution (i.e., *qadesh* means a male temple prostitute—the feminine is *qedeshah*; Gen 38:21–2). Kadesh is thus a play on words that ultimately takes Miriam back to 'her own kind'; it removes her, and all she represents, from the new and aspiring male priesthood. By Deuteronomy 24, Miriam becomes an example to be remembered, i.e., if you do not do as the (new) priests tell you, the same thing will happen to you!

This is not simply a slapped wrist for a woman who dares to rise above her station; this is the androcentric, Jewish (postexilic) priesthood ousting the gynocentric, Mesopotamian goddess-priesthood. Huldah and Miriam are just two of the many commanding and influential women in the new court of Israel who must be brought down to a level the men can handle, or forcibly convert, in order for the patriarchy to maintain a sense of control and power.

In discussing the overthrow of Miriam and the anointing ritual she would have received before re-entering the community, Rabbi Hammer postulates that while "the blood of the biblical ritual came from an animal sacrifice, one wonders if [Miriam's anointing] might hark back to menstrual blood; the blood of a woman's life force."[16]

The Hebrew tradition of complex word-play, however, does manage to retain an element of the truth, or the original nature of these women, even if through metaphorically gritted teeth.

---

[15] Rabbi Jill Hammer, "Priestesses, Bibliomancy, and the Anointing of Miriam," 2013, https://rabbijillhammer.com/2013/11/25/priestesses-bibliomancy-and-the-anointing-of-miriam.

[16] Hammer, https://rabbijillhammer.com/2013/11/25/priestesses-bibliomancy-and-the-anointing-of-miriam.

Female sexuality is mysterious, subtle, often deemed subversive and therefore dangerous. The HB is replete with warnings against women, at least those three categories of women that seem to far outnumber the "good" virgins/wives/mothers. There is an almost universal belief that women, especially those who are different (e.g., foreign), can sap the strength of kings and force the nation into a spiral of destruction and foreign usurpation.

> *Do not give your strength to women,*
> *your ways to those who destroy kings.*
> Prov 31:1–3

With the strange affairs of the rebellious, occultist Nabonidus and his Egyptian princess bride, who (at least from the perspective of the Marduk priests) kept him from his responsibilities in Babylon, the new Jewish institution has its prime directive when it comes to women: Suppress and demean, get rid, or convert.

ISHTAR: BELONGING TO NO MAN

In Babylon, meanwhile, we have the epitome of sexual freedom and expression, the worship of procreation in all its contexts, and the most enduring, multi-faceted, commanding female deity, Ishtar (the Sumerian Inanna).

Ishtar is androgynous, represented by the planet Venus, which has both a male and female aspect (the male star of the morning, and the female star of the evening); this seems to explain why the goddess has diametrically opposed passive and aggressive traits. Festivals pertaining to her as such involve cross-dressed participants, and it is thought that during the act of sexual intercourse she magically melds the genders. As the shining "star" (Venus), Ishtar is the Light Bearer, i.e., Lucifer. Early Christian fathers denounced the temples "dedicated to the foul devil who goes by the name of Venus—a school of wickedness for all the votaries of unchasteness."[17] She has quite a reputation and many of her attributes are applied to the woman of the Song.

Ishtar's most representative colour is red, signifying her sexuality. The phases of the moon reflect the menstruation of the goddess, with the day of the full moon (normally the fifteenth) being the "evil day" of her period (the moon itself was seen to menstruate, suggesting it took on a feminine nature, and in later years the once-monthly observance was expanded to

---

[17] Barbara Walker, *The Woman's Encyclopedia of Myths and Secrets* (San Francisco: HarperCollins, 1983) 1045. Quoting John Holland Smith, *Constantine the Great* (New York: 1971), 287.

cover the four quarters of the moon). The fifteenth day thus becomes Ishtar's sacred day, and the number fifteen itself can be used as her occult name. This develops into the Babylonian sabbath day, during which the people are not to work, eat cooked food, or go on a journey. The king cannot ride in his chariot or deliver judgements, and the priests cannot grant oracles. A female deity's menstrual cycle, ironically, is thus at the root of the Jewish (and Christian) sabbath.

The earliest iconography for Inanna consists of a bunch of reeds (i.e., representing fertility) tied together to form a pole/post with a rounded head at the top; at the back there is attached what most interpreters refer to as a "streamer," or headband. This is reminiscent of Min's red *seshed* band, which hangs down his back. One of the sacred elements of Ishtar's apparel, as evidenced by the cultic statues, is a head-dress with "a tasselled band hanging down her back."[18]

The young Ishtar does get married, to Tammuz, her "beloved," but she does not adhere to anyone's concept of an ideal wife, for she is impetuous, possessive, and usually ends up killing or otherwise damaging those she attempts to love. Though in some myths she has children,[19] she is still regarded as the archetypal, uncontrollable virgin. In preparation for the ritual of the sacred marriage in the month of Ulūlū, she bathes in the river, which not only makes her ritually pure for the rite to come but also, magically, reaffirms her virginity. This concept of virginity is not akin to chasteness; it has more to do with sexual independence (male or female) and is a sign of personal fortitude, i.e., without being sexually bound to another. Ishtar and all her "temple harlots" are thus to be seen as 'belonging to no man', i.e., "virginal," despite enjoying multiple forms of sex! Young "maidens" are virginal only through lack of experience; the hymen can break long before sexual intercourse. It is considered a frame of mind. When Ishtar bathes, she reaffirms her independence. When Ishtar lusts, she does so unreservedly, when she loves, she consumes, when she is riled, she kills. Tammuz pays the price for his union with the goddess and is sacrificed to the underworld.

The Song of Solomon exploits the widely known, understood, and enjoyed Ishtar narratives to depict aspects of its central character, Nitocris. This leaves absolutely no doubt that the fate of the queen's counterpart, Nabonidus, is to succumb to the overwhelming power of her sexuality, her dominance. It follows, therefore, that this will ultimately lead to the king's

---

[18] Salvatore Gaspa, *Textiles in the Neo-Assyrian Empire: A Study of Terminology* (Berlin: De Gruyter, 2018), § 5.5.1.1.

[19] Diane Wolkstein and Samuel Noah Kramer, *Inanna, Queen of Heaven: Her Stories and Hymns from Sumer* (New York: Harper and Row, 1983), 70; 161, note 31.

fall; it is as unavoidable as Tammuz's fate.

The author of the Song masterfully intertwines the still-revered cult of the warrior-prostitute with the recent and familiar historical aspects of Nabonidus's reign. The parallels with Ishtar are predominant but not exclusive, for the telling of this story of Nabonidus and Nitocris requires a very important element not conducive to the Ishtar mythology: Pregnancy. For this aspect, the Egyptian Hathor is employed. In many ways she is identical to Ishtar, e.g., she is also the goddess of sexuality and childbearing; she, too, is Venus; she has a dual nature, both passive and aggressive, etc. Hathoric allusions are subtle at first, hinting at Nitocris's Egyptian heritage, but her significance as a mother goddess is unreservedly exploited in Song 7. Thereafter, she fades from the story, her relevance spent, to be replaced with the familiar but more mature Ishtar at the end of the narrative.

THE AUTHOR AS WOMAN

This study did not begin with a desire to prove female authorship. In fact, it was a late development, due to the cumulative effect of many clues, the apparent intimacy of the knowledge behind the poetry, the overall tone, and the nature of the subtext.

In 2000, the *Feminist Companion to the Song of Songs* was printed as the inaugural focus of a series of essays discussing the feminine perspective within the Bible as a whole.[20] Apparently, many female scholars refused to contribute for fear of backlash, censure, or sanctions to their academic pursuits. Although subjects dealing with goddess worship, for instance, have found representation in academia today, it remains evident that openly stating the case for a female author of the Song of Solomon is still considered daring, or brave. This could also be said of the focus on menstruation and rituals pertaining to menses; there is *still* stigma attached, it seems, or a level of distaste, and I am convinced there is more evidence for this subject in the ancient texts than has been acknowledged, let alone published. Several verses demonstrate an intimacy with female behaviour and emotions that a man might well imagine but a woman can empathise with and thus express on a more complex and deeper level, e.g., themes pertaining to menstrual problems and pregnancy.

One potential stumbling block to pinning down the feminine vein that runs through the Song is the apparently intentional confusion over gender representation within the language. For instance, in the HB the woman's feet are made masculine (Song 5:3), as are the "daughters of Jerusalem" (2:7;

---

[20] Athalya Brenner, ed., *A Feminist Companion to the Bible the Song of Songs: No. 6* Feminist Companion to the Bible: Second Series (Sheffield: Sheffield Academic Press, 2000).

3:5, etc.). Would a woman who could write so well do this, and if so, why? It has been suggested that "the scribes deliberately changed the gender of pronominal suffixes" in order to indicate that "something is not as it seems," thereby imbuing the text with subliminal meaning that only further investigation can expose.[21] So, if applying masculine suffixes in an obviously feminine context is a signal to the reader that something has been hidden within the text, surely this, on its own, is worth investigating.

Mayer Slonim suggests that this is a widespread biblical phenomenon and examples are categorised as intentionally elevating women, or demeaning them.[22] For instance, in 2 Sam 6:22, King David dances almost naked and Michal, the daughter of Saul who complains, is not granted "the honour" of a masculine suffix but the maidens, who are not shocked by his behaviour, are. This must be a case of elevating the maidens, as the next verse simply states that Michal had no children, i.e., a sure sign she is being denigrated for speaking her mind. Rahab, in Josh 2:17, 20, is also given this token of masculine approval because of her assistance, as do the maids who dance with Miriam (Exod 15:21) but, as we know, Miriam herself is demeaned.

Therefore, we are forced to ask the question: Does the author of the Song make these quirky gender changes or does someone else, later? It has been suggested that the Song was so well known "as to make alteration impossible," and that it had a wide accepting audience very early on.[23] I have found the narrative far too complex and coherent to withstand alteration from a redactor who was not fully in-tune with the original symbolism and subliminal themes. I therefore opt for the former; the author mixes up the gender on purpose, to exploit an already prevalent scribal technique for her own purposes.

Consider the two examples from the Song, i.e., the woman's feet, and the "daughters." The feet, we shall see, are profoundly significant in 5:3, as symbols of ritual purity, and the "daughters," discussed in due course, have a parallel in Ishtar's sacerdotal retinue. Both have cultic relevance in the Song. Slonim suggests that objects "becoming holy through their connection with sanctuaries and religious rituals … regularly assumed the masculine gender."[24] Thus, a female author cannot be ruled out on the basis of

---

[21] Mayer G. Slonim, "The Deliberate Substitution of the Masculine for the Feminine Pronominal Suffixes in the Hebrew Bible," *Jewish Quarterly Review* 32.2 (1941): 139–58, here 155–8.

[22] Slonim, 139–41.

[23] Jonneke Bekkenkamp and Fokkelien Van Dijk "The Canon of the Old Testament and Women's Cultural Traditions," in Brenner, *Feminist Companion*, 67–85, here 80.

[24] Slonim, 154.

masculine terminology, for she may just be using this known technique to focus the reader's attention on hidden meanings.

I submit that the Song sings with a woman's voice, with words penned by a female scribe who is in control, unharnessed, excelling in a sphere soon to be restricted by, and to, men. There are several clues that provide a potential identification for this author, and one amazing, hiding-in-plain-sight code within the Song that *could* be termed her "signature." She lived in close proximity to the couple, in Tayma, and served with Nitocris at Ur. She is a trained scribe, an insider privy to personal information, and a person well-versed in cultic ritual and magic. It explains so much.

PART TWO: THE SONG OF SOLOMON

1. DARK STRANGER

SONG OF WAR (1:1)

Songs are intrinsic to worship in Mesopotamia and constitute one of the *me* Ishtar receives from Enki: "He gave me the resounding musical instrument. He gave me the art of song."[1]

Like the Egyptians' emphasis on the significance of Name (i.e., that it carries the memory and essence of the individual), and also on the magical power of the *inscribed* name on monuments, sarcophagi, etc., so the Sumerian songs preserve the identity and essence of the person or deity by invoking attributes, actions, and Name: "Until the distant future may this song bless the name of me, the king .... Let them tell in song a perfect recital of all my praiseworthy deeds" (*ETCSL t.2.4.2.02*, §18–20).

Sometimes, however, it can work the other way round. In the tale of Ishtar's rape by Shu-kale-tuda, the goddess hunts her perpetrator down in an impassioned act of revenge; she finds him, kills him, and says: "Your name ... shall not be forgotten. Your name shall exist in songs and make the songs sweet. A young singer shall perform them most pleasingly in the king's palace. A shepherd shall sing them sweetly ..." (*ETCSL, t.1.3.3*, §290–310). It is not that Ishtar kills Shu-kale-tuda and then feels remorse and grants him immortality in a lovely song; it is the reverse. He is destined to be remembered for his actions, his heinous crime against her. He is ultimately banished to the desert (the place of dust and death); the song that is sung of the rapist is sung "sweetly" so that it *will* be sung forever. It is a song that keeps his name in ignominy and his soul in torment. That is his comeuppance. I suggest this is precisely what the Song of Solomon does, i.e., it records the deeds of Nabonidus not to exalt him but to keep him turning in his grave.

Immediately, the tone of the Song is set; this is not going to be a bucolic love song—it is going to be a battle cry! Ishtar's song *is* a battle cry:

---

[1] Diane Wolkstein and Samuel Noah Kramer, *Inanna, Queen of Heaven: Her Stories and Hymns from Sumer* (New York: Harper and Row, 1983), 17. The book's title is a quotation from the translation on pg. 26. The *me* are the various aspects that constitute civilization, e.g., technology, arts, science, institutions, etc.

"In her joyful heart she performs the song of death on the plain. She performs the song of her heart. She washes their weapons with blood and gore ..." (*ETCSL t.4.07.3*, §39–48). War is a major theme in the Song, expressed on a number of levels, and has been a matter of contention for many but in this new paradigm it is a necessity; Inanna/Ishtar is Nitocris's avatar in the Song and as the narrative unfolds, we see her depicted in the context of spiritual and sexual battle, but the author of the Song is also on a mission of war, i.e., a very personal battle with deep emotions and the need for vengeance.

The Song itself opens with what some call its "title" (even suggesting it is an addendum by a later hand) but others, including me, consider it the poem's first line. This is a declaration that the ensuing narrative is a story *about* and/or *for* a man called Solomon; it is not a claim of authorship. "Solomon" is used seven times as a running motif from beginning, through the middle, to the end (Song 1:1, 5; 3:7, 9, 11; 8:11, 12). It will become evident that including this line as part of the structure of the Song is important, as it helps define an internal chronology, e.g., suggesting the Song encapsulates the seven years ("times") of the king's banishment as stated in Daniel 4:25 (indicating that Daniel is dated after the Tayma years, i.e., post-543 BCE). It also instigates a very significant pattern that will potentially provide us with the identity of the author (see Chapter 9).

To the Babylonians, seven is the number of "powers" Ishtar wears as a protective girdle around her genitals (*ETCSL t.1.3.3*, §112–28), which is violated when she is raped. It is also the number of the planets (five actual planets plus the sun and moon), and the number of the corresponding levels of the great ziggurat in Babylon. In the case of the legendary Solomon, it is the number of steps leading to his throne plus the platform upon which he sits (1 Kgs 10:18–21). Relating "seven" to the king in the Song can thus be seen as a symbolic echo of the ziggurat and an example of a parallel between Solomon's and Nabonidus's hubris but also (by subtly alluding to the rape of Inanna), as a very clear foreshadowing of a scene later in the Song, where Nitocris is similarly faced with unwanted sexual advances.

"Solomon" stems from the verb *shalem*, to make complete, whole. Though often translated as "peace," this is a consequential meaning not a direct one, as the name carries the understanding of an act of restitution, of conciliation, or making amends. This necessitates a context of conflict. Abarim provides a fascinating discussion on the name, including an explanation of the biblical concept of "peace-making," which has relevance here.[2] The core of the idea is that one must "know one's enemy" before one can bring about conciliation (restitution); as the old adage says, "Keep your

---

[2] Abarim Publications, "Peace and How to Make It," https://www.abarim-publications.com/Dictionary /si/si-l-mfin.html.

friends close, your enemies closer." One must gauge one's opposition, comprehend the "whole."

As I claim "Solomon" is a pseudonym for Nabonidus, the restitution aspect is a link to his original banishment from Babylon, i.e., his sin of hubris, for assuming to take control of the fate of the nation, metaphorically stealing the Tablet of Destinies. Restitution is defined as the act of restoring something to its rightful owner, hence the previously mentioned connection to Nabonidus honouring Lugal-Marda, the one who returns the Tablet. As the Song's story unfolds, this somewhat oblique understanding of the name seems uncannily apt, for Nitocris must learn how to deal with the king, and how to suppress him as her adversary. This becomes clearer gradually, especially as the theme of war becomes more apparent, and with the discussion of the Shulammite in Song 6:13–7:9.

"Solomon," therefore, is a fictitious name. It may be that the author of the Song invented it, or that those biblical texts containing his name are contemporaneous and the pseudonym was adopted unanimously (more on this below). The Book of Daniel is a special case, and is discussed again later.

The opening dialogue, then, captures the audience's attention. It tells them this is going to be exciting, intriguing, as any war story would be. Just as the battleground is set, however, there is a stark contrast, a shift in tone that is almost startling, as if a strange non-sequitur (and this is probably why some see the first line as a disassociated title) but it is not. We are given the battle cry, and now comes the weapon of choice.

SEX, BLOOD, AND LOVE (1:2–3)

"Let him kiss me with the kisses of his mouth" is an odd sentence taken at face value. What else would one kiss with, other than the mouth? Kissing in Mesopotamian literature, however, is considered tantamount to sexual union, e.g., "at this one kissing he poured into her womb the seed of Ninazu" (*ETCSL t.1.2.1*, §91–116); "He had intercourse with her there, he kissed her there" (*ETCSL t.1.2.1*, §117–142). In the Hebrew text of the Song, various terms for the mouth are employed, in order to accommodate the shift in context, such as in Song 4:3, which will be explained at that juncture. Here in 1:2, the noun *peh* is used to describe the king's mouth; this term has the connotation of an open mouth, used for speaking or *tasting*, and it is used in Gen 4:11, for example, in the context of drinking blood. Nitocris is, therefore, effectively saying: "Let him have sex with me (taste me), with his mouth," i.e., cunnilingus. This a significant concept in the analysis; it sets the tone and context for much of what ensues.

The only other place in the HB where the noun *neshiqah* (a kiss) is employed is in Prov 27:6, where it is claimed, "profuse are the kisses of an enemy." I subscribe to the theory that the HB was written *in toto* during and after the Babylonian exile; the authors of those texts would have experienced the same Babylonian milieu and would have shared literary skills, terminology, attitudes, etc. (they might even have known each other). Rather than dismiss this proverbial allusion, as it clashes with most interpretations, we must retain it; at the very least it is a portent of concern.

The noun "love" in this verse is, in Hebrew, *dod*. Meek argues that in Isa 5:1, *dod* "reflects the god name Dod or Dodo; and … others long ago recognised in Dod the Palestinian counterpart of Tammuz."[3] The earliest audiences, therefore, would be aware of this pun and realise that the woman of the Song is going to be depicted in terms of Ishtar and her complicated, sexual, rollercoaster life, but that is only one aspect of this pivotal term, *dod*.

The noun *dod* is used five times (1:2, 4; 4:10 [twice]; and 7:12); each of the first four denotes "your love" (two spoken to the king, two to the queen), with the final instance rendered "my love" (spoken by the queen). This subtle distinction is meaningful, as it tips the balance in the queen's favour at the very end of the Song. The term is applied, I suggest, to the *type* of love that Nitocris brings with her, the type of love she wishes the king will find; it is the anticipated union with the Divine. This is why she calls Nabonidus her "beloved" (*dodi*), i.e., signifying she sees him as her spiritual student in pursuit of *dod* (the king never calls Nitocris "beloved"). There will be more to say on this later.

For "wine" is the noun *yayin*, used throughout the HB to denote the drink. In the Song, however, it takes on a very specific meaning, i.e., blood, which is how the early rabbis use it: "R. Yehuda says: "Every vine [woman] has wine [menstrual and virginal blood]" (Mishnah Niddah 9:11). Thus, *dod* is considered a far better prize, goal, etc., than the 'acquisition' of Nitocris's blood. It (*dod*) is supreme wisdom, it is the "hidden" knowledge, the "secret things" Nabonidus will later wish to comprehend (discussed in Part Two, Chapter 5); it is divine 'love', or more aptly, cosmic harmony/balance, etc. The king does not understand this at first, for his initial interest is in procuring a child. The link between Nitocris's blood and *dod* (i.e., the Elixir Rubeus, as we call it today) is yet to be made clear in the Song's narrative; only when the entire tale is understood can the reader return to the beginning and appreciate all these early warnings and declarations.

In Song 1:4, Nitocris convinces the king that everyone will "remember" (using the verb *zakar*) his wisdom far more than they will remember her wine/blood, which is utterly true, for the alleged "wisdom of Solomon" is legendary, and Nabonidus's claim to secret knowledge is

---

[3] T. James Meek, "Canticles and the Tammuz Cult," *American Journal of Semitic Languages and Literature* 39.1 (1922):1–14, here 5–6.

immortalised in stone, but who save a few relentless researchers speak a word about his wife's menstruation? It should also be remembered that the Elixir Rubeus is a sacred, secret, and protected rite that under normal circumstances would *not* be spoken of at all beyond the inner sanctum of the temple.

The word *dod* is not used anywhere else in the Song to mean love; it is too special a concept and its unique significance is only appreciated within the context of Nitocris's religion and the royal couple's personal relationship. In all instances of the king referring to Nitocris (e.g., Song 4:1; 5:2), the rather less than stirring *rea* is used, i.e., a companion, friend (used also by Nitocris, referring to the image of the king in Song 7; from the noun *raah*, an associate; see Judg 11:37). There is certainly no emotional commitment in this designation, though the English translators of the Song like to render it "darling." Also, elsewhere in the Song, the word for "love," e.g., the love of the girls for the king, etc., is depicted using the noun *ahabah*, from the verb *aheb* (predominantly sexual love). The "virgins" or "maidens" translation comes from the Hebrew noun *almah,* which simply means a girl, as in a female of marriageable age, nubile, or sexually mature; it has nothing to do with actual, physical virginity but means she has begun menses, i.e., another vital clue to understanding much of the Song and the king's relationship with women. These young women also "love" the king (*aheb*); this is almost a throw-away line but will prove highly significant.

Thus, we see from the start a distinction between the various applications of *dod, rea,* and *ahabah,* even though the English translations suggest they all pertain, generally to "love." We must also remember that *dod* is an integral part of Solomon's divine name, Jedidiah, as mentioned earlier, subtly reaffirming the connection between the Solomon of 2 Sam 12:25 and the male character in the Song of Solomon.

For our introduction to the Song's darker (redder) themes however, we simply need to be aware that blood—female blood—will prove as vital to the Song as it is to Life. Thus, the weapon of choice is neither sex nor love; it is actually female blood, menstrual blood—and this is held out by references to menstruation as "the weapon" in a Babylonian guide to physiognomy.[4]

ETERNAL NOTHINGNESS
The mention of "anointing oils" or ointments/unguents is significant, as fragrant Egyptian anointing oils are applied not only to the dead but also to the statues of the deities. Fragrance, e.g., from incense or oils, is deemed to

---

[4] Marten Stol, *Women in the Ancient Near East,* trans., Helen and Mervyn Richardson, (Berlin: De Gruyter, 2016), 438 and note 12.

be the breath of the gods and the statues of the deities are anointed on a daily basis in a ritual called Seneteri, in order to invoke the essence of the deity and thereby make the statues themselves divine.[5] In Song 5 we witness Nitocris seemingly constructing a cultic statue of Nabonidus, who attains demi-god status in the Song, i.e., he becomes divine. There is, however, a twist, an intentional play on words that allows for a surprising alternative interpretation.

The "perfume poured out" phrase has proven to be a curiosity, for commentators have long debated what *turaq* oil could be. Pope suggests, on the basis of Esth 2:3, 9, 12 and Prov 20:30, that the word is actually *tamruq* and this "applied to the purification of girls with a year's application of various perfume oils after first menses before they were presented to the king"; he also notes, that the Syriac version "rendered *turaq* as 'myrrh'."[6] In the Song, later, we learn that "liquid myrrh" is another euphemism for menstrual blood, so both these potential explanations from Pope inadvertently pertain to menses.

Interestingly, however, the word *turaq* stems from the verb *ruq*, to cast out, make empty/hollow (and thus only by association, "pour forth" from a vessel, i.e., making *it* 'empty', etc.). With this understanding, a profound insult is apparent, aimed at the king: "Your name is empty, hollow, cast out." The author demonstrates the biblical policy of not naming the "infidel," Nabonidus, which is why the pseudonym "Solomon" is invented. It is, perhaps, a pact, a universal postexilic agreement to remove Nabonidus from his self-imposed 'divinity' by cutting him off from the protection of Name. Daniel, for instance, refers to the perturbed king (who has nightmares, has visions, and is punished for his hubris) as "Nebuchadnezzar" but in Dan 5:1 the king is suddenly called "Belshazzar," which has been a matter of debate for generations. Today, we know that Belshazzar, Nabonidus's son, did not rule as king. Daniel would have known this. The context of this name-shift is when the capture of Jerusalem by Nebuchadnezzar is mentioned; Nabonidus is given another pseudonym (familiar to Daniel's audience) that allows for the historical veracity of the invasion/exile experience, whilst not allowing Nabonidus any mention for posterity. Anyone from this generation would comprehend such a simple 'adjustment'.

Suggesting the king's name is empty, worthless, is the very worst thing an Egyptian can say, for an empty name has no honour, a name cast aside means a soul cast aside for eternity. Recall the tale of Ishtar's rape by

---

[5] Shane Clayton, "The Seven Sacred Oils of Ancient Egypt" (2020), https://www.wandering -stars.net/the-seven-sacred-oils.

[6] Marvin H. Pope, *Song of Songs: A New Translation with Introduction and Commentary* (New York: Doubleday, 1977), 300.

Shu-kale-tuda, and the "sweet" song she creates to make his name and wrongful deeds live on in ignominy (*ETCSL, t.1.3.3*, §290–310), being sung by everyone from field to palace, forever. This, to the Mesopotamian, is parallel to the Egyptian "nameless"—both are eternal torment.

So, the first few words of the Song set the entire stage for what is to come, i.e., a tale of a king; an anticipated battle; a strongly sexual narrative; a concept of "love" that may differ from the norm; the future deification of the king; a potential harem setting; the idea of menstruation at the heart of Nitocris's depiction; the Egyptian influence; the sexually orientated "love" of a certain group within the harem; and an oblique cut at the king's dishonoured name (a very skilful scribe, indeed).

PRINCESS BRIDE (1:4)

Nabonidus has made a pact with Ahmose, with Nitocris's hand in marriage sealing the deal. At some point, she must leave Egypt and be with the Babylonian king; I have suggested she first lives at the new palace in Tayma. In these lines we can sense the movement, the transition, i.e., Nabonidus "draws" the princess away with him. There is no way of knowing how Nitocris feels about the deal but a subtle clue may be found in a play on the term *mashak*, to draw, or—to drag/seize. The fact that they are said to "run" (*ruts*) may well be an indication that the transference *is* done surreptitiously (as proposed earlier), hence speedily. However, it is the princess who seems to suggest haste; this is the first of several instances revealing the queen's dominance in the relationship, i.e., she is attempting to be in control from the start.

Back in 1 Chr 4:17, in the listing of Mered and Bithiah's children, Mered is said to "marry" Bithiah but the word used there is *laqach*, which means to take, and this also has connotations of seizing, taking away, capturing, etc. This word is used in 1 Kgs 3:1, to record the marriage of Solomon and his Egyptian wife. The more common Hebrew word for betrothal is *erusin*, and for the consummation it is *nissuin*; the aggressive choice of terminology for the marriage of Mered and Bithiah suggests it is more political, more war-related than romantic, e.g., part of a treaty.

The use of "we" suggests the young princess is initially desirous of being accepted among the court ladies, including herself as one of those who love the king. With the interjection of "they," however, we soon get a clue that things are not going to be that simple; Nitocris is one set apart from the "daughters of Jerusalem." (Ishtar, Queen of Heaven, uses the royal pronoun when she is speaking about herself [e.g., *ETCSL t.4.08.09*, §31–5]).

Nitocris is taken into the king's inner rooms, defined by the noun *cheder*, which has dubious connotations. It can suggest secrecy (e.g., 2 Kgs

9:2) and hiding (e.g., 1 Kgs 20:30; Judg 16:9, 12), and is used to describe the place where David's son Amnon rapes his sister Tamar (2 Sam 13:10). As the name Tamar proves significant in this analysis, and not for any positive reason, it is worth noting this early potential portent.

In the Epic of Gilgamesh, the hero is loved by the "singing girls," and is praised as the "most glorious of the heroes." In the tale of Ishtar and Tammuz, the goddess says of the king: "He brought me into his garden / ... He brought me into his house,"[7] where "garden" and "house" are known metaphors for the body (i.e., in a sexual context). We can safely surmise, therefore, that Nabonidus is keen to embark on his venture to sire the new *entu*.

BLACKNESS (1:5)

One of the most ancient names for Egypt is *kemt* (or *khame*), meaning dark, or black. Called the Black Country because of its dark, fertile, Nile-enriched soil, the term came to represent the magic that emanated from this land, i.e., "black magic" (and al*chem*y). Osiris, King of the Afterlife, is called the Black One, his black skin representing the regeneration and fertility of the black soil of the Nile floodplain. This alone could be enough to identify the Song's "black" queen as Egyptian.

The word Kedar (or Qedar) is also translated as black or dark. The nomadic Kedarites (who live in tents) are an Arabian kingdom and a force to be reckoned with by all accounts. They are mentioned in the HB (e.g., Ezek 25:4, 10; Isa 21:16–17) and in Josephus (*Ant.* 10.9.7) but of interest to us is the fact that they have a direct relationship with Nabonidus and Tayma. In Nab Chr 1.11–22, the king is said to advance on the Kedarite citadel of Amurru, before heading for Tayma; the moment he leaves Tayma, however, the Kedarites rise again to great strength, becoming a daunting foe of Judah. The "tents of Kedar" would thus be part of the Jews' recent (negative) experience, making the reference a little too sinister for a supposedly bucolic love song. This negative perception is echoed in Ps 120:5–6 and Jer 49:28–29.

One of Ishtar's epithets, Ishhara, is "traditionally construed as a derivation from the root *shhr*, 'to be black'"; she is called this during the sacred marriage rite.[8] As Venus, the goddess becomes invisible during the hours between dawn and dusk; in "the silent glare of noon she turns to

---

[7] Diane Wolkstein and Samuel Noah Kramer, *Inanna, Queen of Heaven: Her Stories and Hymns from Sumer* (New York: Harper and Row, 1983), 40; 48.

[8] B. Becking, "Ishhara," in *Dictionary of Deities and Demons in the Bible Online*, Karel van der Toorn, Bob Becking, Pieter W. van der Horst, eds., http://dx.doi.org/10.1163/2589-7802_DDDO_DDDO_Ishhara.

black"; hers is the power of "darkening the light"; her "frown blackens the light of noon."[9] In recounting her sexual union with Tammuz, Ishtar says with great pride: "He laid his hands on my holy vulva, / He smoothed my black boat with cream"; the "black boat," her vulva, i.e., her skin, is gloriously black.[10]

Nitocris's alleged darkness is, on one level, symbolic, i.e., representative of an assumed/alleged underlying iniquity (Sir 25:17; 2 Esd 7:125), which is alluded to throughout the Song. On a more mundane level, she *can* be considered black/dark, for she hails from the genetic lineage of the Libyan Necho dynasty. The ancient Libyans were a predominantly black people; their descendants, the Tuareg, or the Berbers, intermingled over the millennia, becoming somewhat lighter-skinned, though very dark lineages still exist.

Herodotus describes the Libyans in some detail, and two points in particular stand out. Firstly, he states that one of the many tribes of Libyans, the Atarantians, are known to curse the sun, when it is "high in the heaven … because (they say) he burns and wastes both their country and themselves" (*Hist.* 4.184). Secondly, he claims all "the wandering Libyans … sacrifice to the Sun and the Moon, but not to any other god" (4.188). This passage in the Aramaic Targum to Song of Songs 1:6, reads: "Do not despise me because I am darker than you, because I have … bowed down to the sun and the moon."[11] The specific determination of the rabbis that Solomon's Egyptian bride was from the family of Necho, i.e., of Libyan heritage, is (partially) substantiated by Herodotus's anecdotes.

CURTAINS

There are four potentially significant curtains: 1) in Exod 26, the second curtain to be made to protect the Ark is made of black goat skin/hair, just like the tents of Kedar, 2) in Mesopotamian temples, the sacred area that houses the statues of the deities has a curtain to separate them and to give them privacy whilst being ritually fed, 3) a *purdah* (curtain) separates the harem from the court, 4) the Divine Curtain (*perogod*) in Judaism, is said to separate God from his angels; it bears the divine name and the destinies of all souls (this has a direct correlation with Ishtar, who wears a robe upon which bears the destinies of all in heaven and on earth; the term *perogod* can also be rendered "coat," or "cloak"). This may have a link to Nabonidus's alleged stealing of the Tablet of Destinies. Then there is the curtain/canopy

---

[9] Betty De Shong Meador, *Inanna: Lady of Largest Heart: Poems of the Sumerian High Priestess Enheduanna* (Austin: University of Texas Press, 2000), 121; 129; 130.

[10] Wolkstein and Kramer, 44.

[11] See https://www.sefaria.org/Aramaic_Targum_to_Song_of_Songs.1.6?lang=bi.

of Solomon's wedding bed, in the rabbinic legend of Bathya sewing gems upon it to trick Solomon into thinking it is still night; this must have been black/dark, to serve as the night sky. It is the only one specifically linked to Solomon.

DAUGHTERS

The "daughters of Jerusalem" are persistently around the new queen, suggesting a harem situation. A royal harem has three levels of women: 1) the elite ladies and lesser wives, 2) unmarried princesses (referred to as 'daughters') and "the married ones who live with their own family," and 3) the concubines.[12] In Song 6:8 the noun *almah* is translated as maidens; in 6:8 and 6:9 the translation also reads "maidens" but the word changes from *almah* in v.8 to *bath*, or daughter, in v.9. The maidens of 1:3 and the "daughters of Jerusalem" are thus one and the same, i.e., it is they who love (*aheb*) the king. They represent the young, nubile women who do not have the experience and expertise of Nitocris. She is constantly reminding them not to be so keen, so eager.

In Ishtar's temple Eanna are the "daughters of Uruk" and the "daughters of Anu"; the latter are the unmarried daughters of the deity Anu who appear in the Akitu procession in Uruk.[13] They are, effectively, Ishtar's deified temple attendants, who are thought to be participants in the *hieros gamos* (sacred marriage rite).

SONS AND VINEYARDS (1:6)

Why should Nitocris's 'brothers' be angry with her? Is being a keeper of the vineyards a punishment? The Hebrew word for "angry" here is the verb *charar*, to be hot/to burn, which can also be used figuratively, i.e., to show or incite passion. Perhaps the "passion" ignited in these men needs a little more investigation.

In Prov 31:16–18 (the same proverb that warns the king not to give his strength to women, lest they destroy him), the good, capable, pious wife, the woman who "does him good and not harm," is the one who "plants a vineyard" (singular) of her own choosing, with her own hands, and she is diligent and efficient. This would suggest, then, that the Jewish writer of this proverb should deem the woman of the Song *honourable* for being a "keeper of the vineyards," so why does the Song introduce her in an almost apologetic way, forcing her to defend her apparent appearance, which she admits is a direct result of performing this admirable task?

---

[12] "Harem," https://iranicaonline.org/articles/harem-i.

[13] Julia Krul, *The Revival of the Anu Cult and the Nocturnal Fire Ceremony at Late Babylonian Uruk* (Leiden: Brill, 2018), 157 and note 94.

As it is highly unlikely that a single young woman would be put in charge of several physical vineyards, we can assume this is meant metaphorically. The motif of vineyards/gardens in both Mesopotamian *and* Jewish literature, is one of sexual fertility. If the rabbis compare one woman to a vine (Mishnah Niddah 9:11), then a vineyard must be a group of women. The word "vineyard" in the Song is interesting, for in the Hebrew it is *kerem,* which has no known derivation or etymology; it can mean vine, the "increase of the vineyard" i.e., fruit/wine, or vineyard. Thus, *kerem,* as "vineyard," serves as a euphemism for a group of fertile women (vines). Vineyards can produce fruit (for eating), or they can produce wine; these are mutually exclusive, as the fruit must be destroyed in the wine-making process. The "vineyard"/"wine"/"fruit" motif pervades the Song and is key to its interpretation. For the purpose of understanding Nitocris's immediate situation regarding being the caretaker of other vineyards, whilst not "keeping" her own, I submit that she is referring to her role as a cultic supervisor for a group of young women. She keeps them pristine, pure, safe, i.e., she protects them, but she is no longer that untouched vineyard, herself.

Nitocris, I suggest, held the position of God's Hand before she left Egypt (more on this later), a highly sexualised, symbolic role; she must therefore be highly knowledgeable and skilled, sexually (though she might still be a virgin, technically). Nitocris enters a new world, anticipating this will not be fully understood, so she treads cautiously. The Mesopotamians did once have a sexually-orientated priesthood, i.e., the ancient *entu* priesthood at Ur that Nabonidus is so keen to resurrect but, as previously mentioned, this had long since been a source of mockery and derision.

The fact that the author uses "my mother's sons," rather than "my brothers," or even "my father's sons," suggests the author is preferencing the maternal relationship. Nitocris's cultic mother is Ankhnesneferibre, i.e., an "adoptive" mother, in her role as God's Wife. The God's Wife's "sons" is a poetic parallel to Nitocris's cultic relationship as "daughter," i.e., they are the male priests of Karnak (Thebes).

The "vineyards" of Song 1:6, therefore, i.e., the group of young, fertile women under Nitocris's supervision, are potentially those young "wombs" that are designated for the Elixir Rubeus.[14] The Elixir is the privilege of

---

[14] The role of Adoratrice has also been called Mistress/Superior/Overseer of the Harem of Amun, which may confirm this notion, in that Nitocris could have attained the level of Adoratrice and been put in charge of the other women; she would thus be more likely to have ascended to the role of God's Hand, also. See Laurent Coulon, "The Quarter of the Divine Adoratrices at Karnak (Naga Malgata) during the Twenty-sixth Dynasty: Some Hitherto Unpublished Epigraphic Material," in *Thebes in the First Millennium BC*, E. Pischikova, J. Budka and K. Griffin, eds. (Cambridge: Cambridge Scholars, 2014), 56.

priests and royalty, and it may be that the idea of the former's "anger" comes from the sudden loss of their purest source. This suggestion finds corroboration in Song 7.

UTU GAZES, INANNA EATS

Ishtar (Inanna) is known for being the only female celestial deity (as Venus) within a family of males, i.e., all the other planets, the sun, and the moon constitute her "brothers."

The Hebrew word used for "the sun" here is *shemesh* and the Akkadian word for the solar deity is Shamash; in the Sumerian period, this is Utu. Utu is Inanna's twin brother, often described as "gazing" upon his people. Many scholars mention, reservedly, that the relationship between Inanna and Utu might border on incestual, especially as Utu seems so intimately involved in getting his sister sexually prepared for her husband, Dumuzi. In an ancient text, for instance, the young and apparently inexperienced Inanna says: "My brother ... let me ride with you to the mountains! ... I am unfamiliar with womanly matters ... with sexual intercourse (*ETCSL t.4.32.f*, §35–8). She wishes to learn the art of women and she wants her brother, Utu, to teach her.

The goddess goes on to suggest that they "eat" whatever there is in the "hills" and in the "mountains of cedars," and this, too, is possibly a reference to a sexual education for Inanna, for "cedar," the tree of Utu (and Tammuz), is a euphemism for the phallus, and "hills" for pudenda and/or breasts. The act of "eating" is itself an allusion to carnal pleasure. Once done, Inanna feels she is ready to be taken home to prepare for her wedding. She is, it seems, now wise to the art of women.

Thus, on both the historical and mythological levels of interpretation, Nitocris enters the new court as one already versed in the sexual arts.

VEIL (1:7)

"Where do you pasture your flock?" Nitocris asks the king. Mesopotamian rulers refer to themselves as being the shepherd of the people (e.g., Nab 1 2.12–16; *ETCSL t.4.08.30*, §45–79), in emulation of the first shepherd-king, Tammuz. The suggestive "Tell me where you make it *lie down* at noon" is an echo of Gen 29:7, where Jacob arrives at the well in "broad daylight," e.g., noon, only to learn from Rachel that the flocks are not to be gathered to the well at such a time but must remain at pasture until the well is uncovered in the coolness of the evening. It is a scene that emphasises the physical attraction and desire of two people who will eventually be married, only first, there is the little matter of deception, i.e., the substitution of Leah for Rachel, a scenario that involves a veil. What Jacob sees Jacob wants but it is not what Jacob gets! This could be a subtle confirmation of the basic premise of

Herodotus's tale that the foreign king who married Ahmose's daughter did not get the woman he thought he was getting (which becomes clearer as we progress).

Let me learn the way to the holy sheepfold, my Dumuzi's sheepfold!
ETCSL t.4.08.18, §C8–16

One aspect of this verse that should really make us aware of Nitocris's intensity is her command to the king, i.e., she *orders* him to "tell" (just as Ishtar would). No matter how this is dressed up to sound like the love-sick wishes of a young maiden, when taken in conjunction with the subsequent statement, there can be no doubt who is the stronger character here. With an indignant, almost arrogant air, Nitocris asks: "Why should I be like one who is veiled beside the flocks of your companions?" "Why should *I?*" On whichever word you place the emphasis, the result is the same; she sees herself as different, if not superior to those women who veil, or cover, themselves. Recall Ahmose's concern, as told by Herodotus, that such a fate might befall his daughter.

The term "veil" is complex, for the research to date is disparate; there are arguments for and against certain women who can or cannot wear a veil, both in Mesopotamia and in the Jewish tradition. Most commenters, however, refer to the stern Assyrian Law Code (five hundred years after the Code of Hammurabi) on this matter. The Code (A40–41) stipulates that married women and daughters must wear the veil outdoors, while women such as secular prostitutes should be severely punished if they are found wearing one; sacred prostitutes, however, are permitted to wear a veil for cultic purposes, as are concubines if they accompany a mistress. The rulings on veiling are based on a central tenet: Women belong to men. The veil serves as a sign to the outside world that the female is owned by, married to, or under the protection of a man. For the cultic prostitutes, this translates into the hierodule being under the protection of the deity.

It is the companions (*chaber*) who wear the veils. This same term is used again in 8:13 but there, because the people are in gardens (hinting at a cultic scenario), it is understood to mean worshippers. Thus, companions and worshippers are synonymous in the Song. In the Mesopotamian context of the new royal court at Tayma, it would probably be the companions/worshippers of Tammuz that are alluded to here, who don their veils of mourning and who follow (beside) the flocks (Nabonidus, of course, is the avatar of Tammuz). Nitocris is saying, in effect: "Why should I be like one of these women who follow you about and love you from afar?" She has been promised queenship!

There is also a more sexual interpretation of the veil: In The Great

Prayer to Ishtar, the goddess is said to open "the veils of all young women / elevated or cast down,"[15] hinting at a delineation between the strata of society that do or do not normally wear veils, but this particular phrase refers to the hymen: Ishtar is *every* girl's symbolic female companion at the moment this "veil" is torn, i.e., when she loses her (physical) virginity.

It has been conjectured that the form of the Mesopotamian temple mirrored the reproductive anatomy of the female body, with the "veil" constituting the vagina up to the hymen.[16]

SNIDE LADIES (1:8)

Rather than show the king's new bride the respect she warrants, the "daughters of Jerusalem" are sarcastic and mocking, telling Nitocris, more or less, to know her place. They see her as an upstart, an infiltrator, perhaps a threat. Though traditional perspectives seem to see this as jovial banter, or friendly advice to a young bride, it is not. It is a case of mutual disdain and necessary tolerance (e.g., 8:1: "… and no one would despise me").

If she is truly the "fairest among women," she would not have to "follow the *tracks* of the flock" in order to find the king's place of repose. She cannot even follow the flock itself, she must trail along in its wake, following only the footprints in the dust. Such a sign of desperation debases her, as if she is no better than a common camp-follower.

Echoing Rachel in Gen 29:7, Nitocris is portrayed as a shepherdess, but why would she have just kids to pasture? This is an allusion to Tamar and her encounter with Judah, when she dons the veil of a "temple prostitute" (Gen 38:21) in order to get pregnant. A kid is the (biblical) price for the prostitute's services (Gen 38:17; Judg 15:1). The insinuation, therefore, is that Nitocris has charged many men, as she has "kids," in the plural. Not only that, she is told to pasture them beside the "shepherds' tents," again, in the plural, suggesting that she will be able to find much business there. Of course, this has come only a short while after Nitocris has declared herself sexually knowledgeable. The women see in her the prostitute Ishtar, who charges one lamb for a good time against the city wall (*ETCSL t.4.07.8*, §A20A–9). A degree of disrespect, even contempt (not mere ambivalence), finds a persistent voice in the Song.

---

[15] E. Reiner, and H. G. Güterbock, "The Great Prayer to Ištar and Its Two Versions from Boğazköy," *Journal of Cuneiform Studies* 21 (1967): 255–66, here 261 (NB33).

[16] John M. Allegro, "The Sacred Mushroom and the Cross: A Study of the Nature and Origins of Christianity within the Fertility Cults of the Ancient Near East," 19, https://cochabambahotel.noblogs.org/files/2017/09/John-Marco-Allegro-The-Sacred- Mushroom-and-the-Cross.pdf.

BRIDLED WOMAN (1:9–11)

There is a very famous precedent for the mare amidst the chariots of the pharaoh, and this would have been known to scholars at the time, or even visitors to Egypt, for the record of the event is preserved for posterity on the walls of the Temple of Karnak and was already a popular story. Pharaoh Tuthmosis III in c.1452 BCE, defeated a coalition of Canaanite vassal states at Megiddo, led by the king of Kadesh. During the Battle of Kadesh, a mare was set loose by the Kadeshites amongst the Egyptian army, whose chariots were drawn by stallions; this was an obviously disruptive tactic. An elite soldier called Amenemhab took it upon himself to kill the mare and present the pharaoh with her tail; his tomb bears the inscriptions of his biography and his pride in performing this deed and winning "gold decorations" from the king of Egypt.[17]

The term for "chariots" here is *rekeb*, whereas later, in Song 6:12, the term *merkabah* is used. The former is slightly less specific, as it can suggest not only the vehicle but also the draught animals, or the riders in the vehicle or on the horses. The latter term is more precisely the equipment, rather than the beast(s) or rider(s). The author has made this subtle distinction because the subject of the king's simile in 1:9 is Nitocris (in 6:12, the chariot is undoubtedly intended as the mode of transport).

There has already been reason to discuss a potential lexical link to *qedeshah*, or temple prostitute. Nitocris is the female who will wreak havoc in the camp, the sexually potent, possibly promiscuous "rider" of the stallions (remember the "prostitute" allusion in the Greek Thekemina, for Tahpenes, the Egyptian queen of 1 Kgs 11:19). Thus, Nabonidus, naively, *intends* this to be a compliment, affirming Nitocris's royal heritage, asserting, perhaps, her role as cultic priestess but in doing so, the king actually emphasises the darker, more dangerous aspect of the female character. He does so with all the over-enthusiasm and blindness of a sexually attracted fool; this is a constant attribute, and one that will be his ruin.

In fact, one could also suggest that the king sees this new female as a prized possession, much *like* a grand horse; he examines her to be certain she will "bear" well; the teeth are the first thing a horseman would look at, and often the most telling of a horse's age and health. Her cheeks are adorned with ornaments, just as a horse's would be if dressed in a fancy bridle. "Strings of jewels" lie on her neck, like the reins against the horse's neck. To the king, she is a conquest, a woman to be bridled, though decked out in

---

[17] Alan Richard Schulman and Alan R. Schulman, "The Egyptian Chariotry: A Re-examination," *Journal of the American Research Center in Egypt* 2 (1963): 75–98, here 85, note 61.

fine array to suit her station.

> *...in the house you will indeed have hold of my halter, O Enki....*
> *ETCSL t.1.1.1*, §147–51

Nabonidus, though, is not seeing or thinking clearly, this is the whole point! Nitocris has no intention of being *under* control—she intends *to* control. To the early Jewish readers of the Song, she is the rider of men (the shepherds), the prostitute, the camp-follower. She is the Egyptian infiltrator, who comes to the Israelite court with all her wicked ways to enslave the nation (Nah 3:4) by conquering the king (Solomon).

PORTENTS OF DOOM (1:12–17)

The spikenard plant (nard) is native to Nepal, Bhutan, and the lower valleys of Tibet. In the Roman world, spikenard was seen as a symbol of the Elysian Fields, of eternity, the hereafter: "Sprinkle my ashes with pure wine and fragrant oil of spikenard."[18] Mark 14:3–9 and John 12:3 are the only other places in the Bible where this plant is mentioned (i.e., Jesus's crucifixion/burial). Spikenard is thus inextricably linked with death.

So, too, is myrrh. Isis, the goddess of death and mourning employs its powers to locate the missing body-parts of Osiris; she uses it as a magical ink to write her spells as she puts her husband's body back together. Myrrh is one of the most important elements of mummification, in preparation for the afterlife: "Death is before me today, like the fragrance of myrrh ...."[19] Myrrh is a product imported primarily from southern Arabia: Pliny the Younger wrote of it as "a bundle of tears," for the liquid sap dripped from the trees like tears, and this was often sold as a gum (the dried resin) wrapped up in bundles, which fits the imagery of Nitocris wearing a bundle of it around her neck.

Henna grows into a sturdy, very spiky plant; its flowers, which bloom in May/June, are sweet-smelling but mentioned in tandem with "vineyards" we see a potential reference to its use as a *protective* hedge, to exclude animals from the tender crops (see Isa 5:5). They bear large thorns and have deep roots, which makes them suitable as a deterrent and beneficial for preventing erosion. The presumption that the king is compared to the blooms/blossoms is not, technically, substantiated by the Hebrew text. It

---

[18] J. M. C. Toynbee, *Death and Burial in the Roman World* (London: Thames & Hudson, 1971), 63.

[19] From an Egyptian poem, ca.1900 BCE. "A close reading of 'Death Is Before Me Today'" *Litarus* (2018), https://litarus.net/2018/07/29/a-close-reading-of-death-is-before-me-today/.

reads "a *cluster* of henna," i.e., more than one shrub. Nabonidus is thus likened to the defensive henna that surrounds the vineyards, alluding to his protective capacity; the overall insinuation is that Nitocris is, initially, shielded by the king. The "vineyards" that require this hedge of protective henna are not grape-vineyards but the king's women (metaphorically). The concept of a protective barrier is utilised again later in the Song, forming an inclusio with this early scene.

The phrase "gave forth its fragrance," employs the word *nathan*, to give. This verb is used also in Song 7:12 and 8:11 (the former in the context of childbirth, the latter, menstruation/sex); in Arabic, it is understood to mean 'giving off an *evil* odour',[20] so nard, apparently, has a foul scent. The Targum actually plays on this understanding and incorporates it into the description of the calf-worshippers at Sinai, i.e., the "idolaters."[21] Such a potential allusion to the woman's idolatry is in keeping with the tone of the Song and echoes the earlier symbolic employment of "black/dark" in 1:5–6.

The noun for "fragrance" is *reyach*. This can have a literal meaning, as in the scent/odour of something but it can also have a more occult meaning, as a technical phrase for the "odour of soothing," i.e., the smell of sacrifices that goes up to the gods (Gen 8:21; Exod 29:18), considered calming, 'tranquilizing', appeasing. These various ominous elements, combined, provide the first hint that Nitocris is scheming, for there is contradiction here, polarity, and hidden meaning. Immediately after she is referred to as a "mare," with all its associated symbolism, she begins her manipulation of the king; she is already contemplating her battle plan. The allusion is to the eventual fate of Nabonidus, which is constantly referred to in the narrative in terms of capture and sacrifice.

Continuing with these portents of doom, so pleasingly disguised as passionate banter, the name En-gedi stems from the verb *gadad*, meaning to cut or invade; in nine out of eleven instances, this verb pertains to cultic self-laceration (e.g., Deut 14:1; 1 Kgs 18:28; Jer 16:6). This practice is an aspect of the Ishtar cult: "Lacerate your eyes for me, lacerate your nose for me .... In private, lacerate your buttocks for me" (*ETCSL t.1.4.1*, §37–40). Not only does this bring En-gedi into the sphere of the goddess, it sets up Nabonidus as the protector of those who worship her, and this is in perfect harmony with the HB's depiction of Solomon erecting high places for his wives' cults.

The name En-gedi is traditionally translated as Fountain/Spring of the Kid. An oasis, a fertile area west of the Dead Sea, En-gedi may be seen to be evoking the image of a garden, in order that the subsequent imagery of

---

[20] Keil and Delitzsch OT Commentary on Song 1:12, https://biblehub.com/commentaries/songs/1-12.htm.

[21] See translation at https://www.sas.upenn.edu/~jtreat/song/targum/.

the fruit trees and the obvious sexual tension in the Song will bring to mind the Garden of Eden and the awakening of sexual desire (but the kid motif brings its own undesirable connotation). To extend the allusion to its inevitable conclusion, however, we must anticipate a fall.

DOVE

The word used for dove here, in 5:2, 12, and in 6:9, is *yownah*, which emphasises a certain characteristic, e.g., the allusion is to the warmth of the bird's mating ritual but the term is linked to *yayin*, which implies intoxication. Thus, Nitocris's eyes are, from the very beginning, a source of intoxication to the king; his reason is jeopardised the moment she looks him in the eye. This sense of increasing unease for the king, caught in Nitocris's unnerving gaze, becomes more evident as the Song progresses.

The dove is Ishtar's emblematic bird; it is known as the "bird of destiny," as the goddess is the one who determines the fate of kings. The dove-like eyes are a significant image in the Song, used to convey this sense of fate and control, i.e., the gradual mesmerisation of the king.

IDOLATROUS BED

In the Sumerian tale of Inanna and Dumuzi, the concept of the couch, or bed, is central. The original setting of the lovers' first sexual encounter, the initial *hieros gamos*, is a bower, a little hut of reeds set in a leafy, woodland-like grove; hence, "our couch is green." The reed-hut is recreated for the sacred marriage rite and lavishly decorated with symbolic fresh vegetation, to emulate the place where the couple unite. The cedar tree is an emblem of Tammuz (Dumuzi). The cedar and pine also create the natural canopy for the bower, echoing the arched appearance of the couch (i.e., *eres*, which has a possible meaning of arch, suggesting a canopied bed, which then reminds us of the rabbis' tale of Bathya and the bed-canopy). This prepares us for Song 2, where the first of three *hieros gamos* allusions occurs.

Compare Isa 57:3–9, which tells of a conscious decision to turn away from Yahweh, to pay homage to pagan gods. There is reference to the marriage bed amongst the greenery, lust amongst the trees, sacrifices at high places, and even the use of oils and perfume. Isaiah 57 is a warning to change one's idolatrous ways, or accept the consequences. There are many parallels between the Song and Isaiah but this is a very early portent of doom, deeply set within a framework of an apparently positive and romantic liaison between the king and his new bride; it anticipates Nabonidus's soon-to-be-overwhelming desire to learn about Nitocris's religion.

2. NO EMBRACE

DOUBLE TROUBLE (2:1)

Song 2:1 is unique. It is one, solitary, loaded sentence, presented with no context and no further expansion by the speaker of that line. Every other instance of Nitocris speaking is within a set context, and she carries on to explain further what she means. In Song 1:5, she declares: "I am black and beautiful" and continues to discuss her darkness; in 2:5, "I am faint with love" sits neatly within the narrative. I suggest that what 2:1 represents is the first instance of the *author's* voice being heard. The sentence is spoken in such a way that it pertains to both women: Nitocris and the author. A fuller explanation must await the appropriate juncture but it serves our purpose here to understand 2:1 as a declaration of status, saying, in effect: "This is also me; I am important to this story."

Looking at these two lines more closely, it becomes clear that the two cultural influences, Mesopotamian and Egyptian, come into play.

SHARON

The name Sharon stems from one of two words, i.e., the verb *yashar*, to be level, or the noun *shiryan*, meaning body armour, from the root *sharar/shrh* (1 Sam 17:5; 1 Kgs 22:34), to be stiff or firm. The former is often accepted and interpreted as a plain or steppe in a mountainous region, hence the (not so precise) "valleys" in the NRSV's translation of this verse. The allusion to body armour suggests an all-embracing wall of protection, i.e., a theme repeated later in the Song, in the context of pregnancy.

One of the possible root words for Sharon is the verb *shara*, meaning to fill and release; the related noun *mishra* denotes grape juice, i.e., wine. The name could then potentially be a play on words to suggest blood filling the uterus and spilling out; in Talmud Niddah 21a, the Jewish laws pertaining to menstruants, the "wine of Sharon" *is* menstrual blood, under examination by the rabbis, to judge as pure or impure.

Sharon is noted for its fertility, as in Isa 65:10, where it is said that "Sharon shall become a pasture for flocks ... and the Valley of Achor a place for herds to lie down." The nouns *rebets* (to imply a resting place or shelter) and *naveh* (i.e., habitation, shelter) are used in this description. The Sumerian sign to indicate a shelter, a place of rest, for such beasts (sheep and/or cattle) is known as the Tur₃-sign, or the "cattle-pen." The cattle-pen is sacred to Ishtar, the goddess of cattle and sheep. This sign, in turn, is the foundation of the sign for a womb, known as Šag₄-Tur₃, i.e., "the interior 'birthing pen' of the female body."[1] Thus, the name Sharon and the "valley" in the Song are not only mirrored in Isa 65:10 but are symbolically linked, via an ancient common denominator, i.e., the symbols of pregnancy/birth.

There are two leading women in the Song, one seemingly overshadowed by the other, until you manage to hear her voice—then you cannot ignore her. Correspondingly, there are two distinct wombs in the Song; wombs provide two crucial things, i.e., blood and pregnancy. This echoes the "vine/vineyard" metaphor of Song 1:6, i.e., in that a vineyard (woman) can produce either fruit (a child) or wine (menstruation); one precludes the other at any given time.

ROSE

The "rose" of Sharon is *chabatstseleth*, a conflation of two words. One is the verb *chabab*, used in the Song only in this verse; it means to love/cherish, and this is used elsewhere in the HB only in Deut 33:3, to depict God's love for his people. The other is *basal*, meaning flower bud. Tammuz is symbolised by the date bud that grows each spring; Tammuz, of course, is the cultic representation of the king. We might read into this phrase, therefore: "I am ... the one who loves/cherishes ... the king." The fact that a unique term for love is embedded in the term for the "rose" offers its own riddle, for there are, as discussed in the previous chapter, several designations for "love" in the translation of the Song. That *chabab* should be an almost concealed reference in this wholly unique verse, suggests it has significant meaning, and this is further discussed in Part Two, Chapter 9.

The only other instance of *chabatstseleth* is in Isa 35:1, where it is said God will turn the desert into a rich swampland, and the "crocus" will blossom abundantly. Crocuses do not grow in swamplands; lotuses do. *Chabatstseleth* is also akin to the Akkadian *habasillatu*, which refers to a "flower-stalk, marsh plant, reed." This is fitting for Ishtar, Queen of Heaven, the goddess of the reeds, the lotus of the marshes. Furthermore, the root *shrh* has one derivative. i.e., the feminine noun *shirya*, which denotes some kind of weapon, most likely a ballistic one (Job 41:26). Ishtar is mistress of the bow and arrow (a ballistic weapon).

Isa 35:2 mentions the "majesty of Sharon"; there is a distinctly royal

---

[1] Gavin White, *Queen of the Night: The Role of the Stars in the Creation of the Child* (London: Solaria Publications, 2014), 38–9.

context for the name, i.e., the masculine noun *sar* means chief or ruler, while the feminine *sara* denotes a princess or noblewoman.

LILY

The lily of Song 2:1, when interpreted as a plant, is the (water/marsh) lotus, not a terrestrial plant. J. McDonald provides a fascinating analysis of the lotus plant in Near Eastern and Egyptian iconography; he suggests the depictions of the sacred tree, as found in the palace of Assurnasirpal II, for instance, though commonly described as a palm tree, actually have a form "inconsistent with palm morphology."[2] Rather, they have all the attributes of the lotus plant, with its long, upright, stiff stem, a large bud, tendril-like extensions, and large blue flowers; depictions of this supposed "tree" have remnants of blue pigment. Palm leaves are quite different and bear tiny, cream-coloured blossoms. McDonald goes on to argue that Ishtar shares "close iconographic relations with the sacred lotus."[3] Moreover, Tammuz is recognised as the "guardian of the blue-leaved (blue-petalled?) tree of life ...."[4] Perhaps the most compelling evidence, however, comes from the Ishtar Gate in Babylon, where the "sacred tree" is depicted as a lotus stalk, with a repeated pattern of alternating buds and flowers[5] (reminiscent of the Inanna symbol, i.e., the tied-together reeds, with the curved 'head' and the trailing cord/ribbon, which is uplifted on the Gate, to form a decorative flourish). The Song also uses the bud-and-blossom motif (Song 6:11 and 7:12). In 1 Kgs 7:19, 22, 26, the pillars of Solomon's temple are decorated with "lily-work," probably akin to the lotus decorations on the Ishtar Gate (which Nabonidus would have emulated at Tayma, perhaps, along with the replica of his palace in Babylon).

The lotus has a single, flamboyant flower. One of the primary symbols used for Ishtar is the single flower, often stylised into the rosettes adorning her statues, and the Ishtar Gate. The tall, beautiful, strong, independent (singular), voluptuous, perfumed lotus is the perfect match for Nitocris.

EGYPTIAN INFLUENCE

These several attributes also pertain to Hathor. She is the Shining (rising)

---

[2] J. Andrew McDonald, "Botanical Determination of the Middle Eastern Tree of Life," *Economic Botany* 56.2 (2002): 113–29, here 117.

[3] McDonald, "Botanical Determination," 127.

[4] J. Andrew McDonald, "Influences of Egyptian Lotus Symbolism and Ritualistic Practices on Sacral Tree Worship in the Fertile Crescent from 1500 BCE to 200 CE," *Religions* (2018) 9 (9): 256 §7, https://doi.org/10.3390/rel9090256.

[5] McDonald, "Influences," §5. The image of the lotus stalk on the Gate is reminiscent of the Inanna symbol, i.e., the tied-together reeds, with the curved 'head' and the trailing cord/ribbon (which is uplifted to form a decorative motif).

One, the dual-natured goddess of love and war, the Lotus.

Suggested transliterations of the Hebrew for "lily" include *shushan, shoshan,* and *shoshannah.* Morrow suggests that the noun *seshen* is the ancient Egyptian word for lotus; and that *sha* means to blossom,[6] so it is widely accepted that the Song's name for the flower in question *is* actually an Egyptian loan-word. The lotus is a symbol of Creation, rebirth, and regeneration, i.e., it represents the heavenly womb. The opening and closing of the lotus each day results in it being associated with the solar deity; in the Book of the Dead we read a hauntingly familiar phrase: "I am the pure lotus that cometh forth from the field [of Re]"; the lotus is said to "belong to the head of Hathor." This complex declaration in Song 2:1 might be understood as: "I am the lotus of Re, the Divine womb, I am Hathor." As suggested earlier, Nitocris assumes the identity of Hathor within the Song, subtly at first but rising to a significant and powerful climax in Song 7 and her womb is in divine service to Amun-Re. However, this is but one aspect of the riddle.

TWO WOMBS

The "rose of Sharon" and the "lily of the valleys" epithets pertain to the *two* women of the Song. Superficially, the words seem to herald from Nitocris, the Egyptian lotus, the representative of the solar deity (Amun-Re); hers is the womb that brings the sacred blood of eternal Life. Delve a little deeper, and it becomes evident that there is another womb, representing the fertile "cattle pen." The womb that bears *physical* Life is that of the author of the Song; she is staking her claim early in the narrative. While Nitocris is depicted via allusions to the mothering Hathor, this soon proves to be a sardonic representation, i.e., it is the author who is the true Hathor avatar in this story.

In explaining the meaning of "the rose of Sharon," Abarim says: "… the verb *salal* means to grow dark and derivation *sel* means shadow. The word that indicates this flower seems to mean, literally, Overshadowed by God's Love."[7] This is uncanny, for it is precisely what we will see depicted in the Song, i.e., the author feels overshadowed by Nitocris, the Egyptian priestess who brings with her the promise of divine love greater than anything the king can imagine; while *she* loves the king, Nitocris gets all his attention. Much more needs to be said about this, of course—but not yet.

BRAMBLES (2:2)

Throughout the Song, it will become apparent that the king is not cognisant

---

[6] Susan Brind Morrow, *The Dawning Moon of the Mind: Unlocking the Pyramid Texts* (New York: Farrar, Straus and Giroux, 2015), 195.

[7] "Sharon," https://www.abarim-publications.com/Meaning/Sharon.html.

of what is going on in Nitocris's domain and this is evidenced here, i.e., his response to this profound statement is weak and lacklustre; he has no apparent comprehension of what has just been announced. His response is the first of three (unfortunate) public declarations (i.e., Song 2:12, 4:12, and 6:9).

The king's mundane retort is that Nitocris is not *just* a lily, she is a singular lily amongst brambles, where the brambles are the other women of the court, the "daughters of Jerusalem." She is the one bedazzling, exotic flower in his collection. This is another confirmation that she is an outsider, superior, and probably resented, i.e., the thorns of the brambles reflect the prickly nature/behaviour of the other women at court; something else the king fails to recognise.

EAT OF THE FRUIT (2:3)

Commentators tend to focus on identifying the species of fruit Nitocris eats, rather than looking at the symbolism of the entire passage. The tree in this verse stands alone in a wood, thicket, or forest. It is broad, bears fruit, and casts beneficial shade, i.e., it is a *mature* specimen. It stands amongst the metaphorical forest of similar, younger, less impressive trees, i.e., "sons" (using the noun *ben*) but it is superior to them. This is Dumuzi, Inanna's "first-class fruitful apple tree" (*ETCSL t.4.08.05*, §1–4), so it is also King Nabonidus. As a seasoned soldier, a strong, powerful, mature man, and possibly quite awe-inspiring to a young woman, at first, his shade/shadow, as the fecund and dominant apple tree, echoes his keenness to protect the young princess upon her arrival, as is evident in the next verse.

The idea of "fruit" pertaining to offspring clearly does not fit the context here but it does fall within the sphere of procreation, i.e., sex. Ronald A. Veenker provides the comparison of two interchangeable Akkadian words, *kuzbu* and *inbu* for fruit as a sexual reference, i.e., "sexual charm."[8] Therefore, "fruit" can also pertain to the sexuality (or sexual organs) of both genders.

The apple tree is a common motif in Sumerian literature, most especially as a sexual euphemism in the poetry about (or to) Inanna: "Inanna speaks: My blossom-bearer in the apple-orchard / My bearer of fruit in the apple orchard."[9] "She leaned back against the apple tree. / When she leaned against the apple tree, her vulva was wondrous to behold."[10] There is also

---

[8] Ronald A. Veenker, "Forbidden Fruit: Ancient Near Eastern Sexual Metaphors," *Hebrew Union College Annual* 70/71 (1999): 57–73, here 59, note 10.
[9] Diane Wolkstein and Samuel Noah Kramer, *Inanna, Queen of Heaven: Her Stories and Hymns from Sumer* (New York: Harper and Row, 1983), 49.
[10] Wolkstein and Kramer, 12.

the undeniable allusion to a woman positioned lower than the man, so that she can partake of his fruit: "By an apple tree I knelt as is proper. ... O Dumuzi! Your fullness is my delight!"[11]

The noun used to denote "shadow" is *tsel*, and this often suggests welcome *shade*, as in *defence* from the sun. In other biblical usage, *tsel* is used frequently to refer to the safety and shelter of a benevolent being (Gen 19:8; Judg 9:15; Job 7:2; Ps 17:8, 36:7, 91:1, etc.). This is exactly how the Sumerian literature employs the concept: "Ur-Ninurta, may the Land refresh itself in your shade" (*ETCSL t.2.5.6.1*, §30–9); "Let their refugees refresh themselves in my shade" (*ETCSL t.2.4.2.04*, §168–74). The word *tsel*, however, stems from *tsalal*, meaning to be or grow dark, so this serves as a warning to the reader, for it is another hint of Nabonidus's fate, i.e., he is to grow dark like Nitocris is dark—to the postexilic Jewish audience, an allusion to immorality.

The combined imagery, therefore, speaks to sexual union but there is certainly a leaning toward oral sex. It becomes evident very quickly that Nitocris is toying with the king, letting him experience her only as far as she is willing; the oral preference is hers, for she is keen to keep the king content, whilst maintaining her physical sanctity. If she was a serving (or even a trainee) God's Hand back in her homeland, this might very well have been the type of sexual experience she would be familiar with, within a cultic setting.

It must be remembered that the ancient Egyptians, and certainly the Mesopotamians, had few inhibitions where sex was concerned and, perhaps even more so for the latter, sex was a constant and conspicuous theme in much of the literature. They had Ishtar to thank for that, i.e., the highly-sexed patron of prostitutes, whose feminine arts young women aspired to, and whose unlimited appetite and knowledge every man longed for! Bear this in mind, as the Song proves to be far more sexual and explicit than has ever been thought (or admitted).

HIEROS GAMOS 1: BETROTHAL (2:4–7)

The first sacred marriage allusion signifies the first stage in the marriage of Nabonidus and Nitocris, i.e., their betrothal. De-Whyte argues that this serves as a "probationary period," during which conception is expected to occur, i.e., a test of fertility before the finalities of a full marriage: "It can be argued that the marriage was not legitimated until the presence of the first child, thus the consummation of the union was not complete until it produced offspring ...."[12]

---

[11] Wolkstein and Kramer, 40–1.

[12] Janice P. De-Whyte, "Wom(b)an: A Cultural-Narrative Reading of the Hebrew

Where the NRSV has "his intention toward me was love," the Hebrew reads: "… his banner over me was love," where love is *ahabah*, from the verb *aheb* (i.e., not *dod*), the mundane aspect of love, e.g., sexual, familial, etc., rather than divine or altruistic (though there are a few exceptions). The sexual attraction between Isaac and Rebekah (Gen 24:67) and Jacob and Rachel (Gen 29:18), and of Samson for Delilah (Judg 16:4) and Amnon for Tayma (2 Sam 13:1), all use this verb *aheb*. In effect, the king has brought Nitocris to take what he sees as rightfully his; his "intention" is sex (i.e., procreation; *ahabah* is used in 2:5, where "I am faint with love" means she is tired from, or perhaps of, the sex, e.g., she has the proverbial "headache").

Nabonidus seems to make a public statement regarding his protection of Nitocris. The banner (*degel*) is a standard, a military/tribal symbol of identity. The noun *degel* stems from *dagal*, meaning to raise a flag, to make conspicuous, to flaunt; thus, the banner is metaphorically raised above her, identifying her as the king's property, his prize. He is showing off his trophy-wife (Egyptian women, let alone princesses, were highly sought after as wives by ancient Near Eastern kings). The banner imagery is used again later in the Song (6:4, 10) in a different context and with a different result.

Notice the wordplay, with respect to the "banqueting house"; in Hebrew, the phrase here is *beyt ha-yayin*, often translated by scholars as the "house of wine" but *yayin* literally means to effervesce, to intoxicate, making it more "the house of intoxication." It has also been stated that *yayin* (wine), in the Song, designates menstrual blood. It makes sense, therefore, for procreation to take place in the "house of (sexual) intoxication," e.g., in the bedroom, and in association with menstruation. This connection is further explained later but hints at the significance of Nitocris's monthly cycle, i.e., it foreshadows the intoxicating Elixir Rubeus.

Nitocris has tasted the king's fruit; she has picked the apple from the tree and has apparently found it sweet and satisfying (though perhaps a degree of flattery should be considered, here). The term for this fruit is *periy*, from *parah*, to bear fruit, to be fruitful, increase, etc. It is the same word that is used in Gen 3:3 to describe the fruit of the tree Adam and Eve were warned against (and thereby represents sexuality itself), and it is the same word that is used to denote a child in the womb (e.g., Gen 30:2; Isa 13:18). This reiterates the fruit-sexuality-genitals connection.

The first of three independent allusions to the *hieros gamos*, the sacred marriage rite, is thus presented and within these few lines we see the following aspects of the rite alluded to:[13] Sexual intimacy ("his fruit was

---

Bible Barrenness Narratives" (PhD diss., McMaster Divinity College, Ontario, 2014). 28–9.

[13] Philip Jones, "Embracing Inanna: Legitimation and Mediation in the Ancient Mesopotamian Sacred Marriage Hymn *Iddin-Dagan A*," *Journal of the American*

sweet to my taste"); post-coital banquet or festival (banqueting house / raisins and apples); a ritual embrace (2:6).

The ritual embrace, after the sacred couple emerge from their private bed-chamber, is the most significant aspect of the sacred marriage, representing the union between the divine and the mundane.

UNFULFILLED

Nitocris, having experienced the king sexually, is taken to the banqueting hall (a specific site for the ritual worship of idols in Mesopotamia, e.g., *ETCSL t.5.3.2*, §26–36; *t.4.80.1*, §303–10; *t.4.13.13*, §15–20; *4.13.05*, §49–55). She demands to be fed raisin cakes (*ashishah*; see Hos 3:1) and apples (the symbol of sexuality). Nitocris is speaking with the voice of Ishtar, embodying the proud Queen of Heaven at the time of her marriage to Tammuz.

A Sumerian poem recounts the ending of the sacred marriage rite: "The king embraces his beloved bride, / Dumuzi embraces Inanna."[14] The formal embrace comes after their sexual union and solemnises their marriage. That Nitocris phrases her comment in 2:6 as "O, that ..." does suggest this final symbolic act, that would confirm Nitocris as the one and only Queen, is not forthcoming. The lack-of-the-embrace theme is here at the start of the royal couple's relationship and it is there at the end of it, in Song 8, creating a thematic inclusio (one of many).

The adjuration of 2:7 is not a plea but a charge by oath, i.e., an oath made not by God, which would be the case for all Israelites (Gen 21:23; Deut 6:13) but by animals of Ishtar's world. This is in keeping with the ritual of swearing an oath in Mesopotamia, where symbolic items are incorporated to represent the deity; the gazelle is one of Ishtar's animals. Both male ("gazelle"/buck) and female (hind/"doe") beasts of the field are invoked in this adjuration: Ishtar is the goddess of sexuality, so it is fitting for the oath here to be taken in such a way as to evoke her (the hind/doe) ritual union with Tammuz (the "gazelle"/buck).

What must be understood, however, is that this animal we translate as gazelle, when referred to in the Sumerian literature, is usually being hunted, trapped, and killed: "The people living around the city hung up nets ... chased gazelles and killed the gazelles as one kills humans ..." (*ETCSL t.1.7.1*, §16–25).

HUNTRESS (2:8–9A)

The king is heard at a distance, represented by the word *qol* in Hebrew,

---

Oriental Society 123.2 (2003): 291–302, here 297–299.
[14] Wolkstein and Kramer, 108.

which can mean sound or voice, i.e., words. This, too, is an important theme in the Song.

Although there is a sexual connation to the gazelle (i.e., the word *tsbiy* stems from *tsabah*, to swell up/to grow turgid), the male gazelle appears in only three places in the HB, besides the Song. In 2 Sam 2:18 and Isa 13:14, the context is one of punishing those who anger God, whose fate is certain death. In Prov 6:2–5, however, the concept is linked *directly* to the idea being snared by one's own words in a pledge, or 'binding', to a "stranger" (6:1–5). Nabonidus will soon come under the influence of his Egyptian princess and her arts; he will be drawn into her intense and powerful sphere, binding himself to her; he will become the gazelle, the hunted one, *not* the hunter.

The gazelle is also directly associated with Tammuz in the context of being hunted; he is sought out and chased by demons and he calls out to his brother-in-law, the solar god Shamash: "Change my hands into the hands of a gazelle. / Change my feet into the feet of a gazelle. / Let me escape from my demons."[15] Despite a temporary escape, the fate of Tammuz is ultimately the fate of the hunted gazelle, and his demons get the better of him. For the early audiences of the Song, this is an ill omen for the king.

SNARE APPARENT (2:9B–C)

Why would Nabonidus act in such a subservient manner, peering at his bride from a distance, when he could simply order her to be presented?

In the narrative of Proverbs 7 we see the king supposedly remembering his own youthful experience of the power of feminine sexuality: "For at the window of my house I looked through my lattice, and I saw among the simple ones, I observed among the youths, a young man without sense ...." (Prov 7:6–7), i.e., himself. The Song's use of the same imagery cannot be sheer coincidence; we are meant to make the connection. Grossberg states: "In Proverbs 7 the woman is called ... *zarah* ('foreign woman') with the strong connotation of 'social outsider' or 'deviant'."[16] This provides a thematic link back to the underlying theme of the Song, i.e., beware the foreign female.

There is a play on words here, for the verb *zarah* means to arise, rise, come up, shine. A derivation of this verb is the masculine noun *zerah*, meaning a dawning or shining. The loose, foreign woman is Ishtar, goddess of the dawn, the shining light of morning, Venus. The king in Proverbs 7 warns the "child" not to let his heart be swayed by women who frequent the streets and the squares and will "eagerly" seize a man in a lustful way. This

---

[15] Wolkstein and Kramer, 81.

[16] Daniel Grossberg, "Two Kinds of Sexual Relationships in the Hebrew Bible," *Hebrew Studies* 35 (1994): 7–25, 20.

is Ishtar to a tee: "The pearls of a prostitute are placed around your neck, and you are likely to snatch a man from the tavern (*ETCSL t.4.07.4*, §109–15).

The woman's seduction remains bitter-sweet in the memory of this king. The result of his youthful lack of judgement, however, is made clear in the references to "an ox to the slaughter," a "stag" in a "trap" (Prov 7:22), and the woman's house being "the way to Sheol" (7:27). He could not resist, paid the consequences, and is now offering his wisdom to others. This is the fictional (wishful) aftermath of the Song of Solomon.

The Hebrew for "lattice" here in the Song is *cherek*, from *charak*, which means to braid (i.e., to entangle or snare), or catch (game) in a net. In 2 Kgs 1:2, Ahaziah, the notorious son of Ahab, falls through the lattice of an upper chamber, is badly injured, and dies; the term for lattice there is *sebakah*, which also denotes a sort of netting, e.g., in the context of trapping animals (Job 18:8). This would suggest that Ahaziah's "fall" is no accident, i.e., he apparently pays the price for turning to Baal-zebub, rather than to Yahweh. The synchronicity with 2 Kings seems to be intentional, for why does the Song's author not use the less provocative, more architectural term, *eshnab* (as in Judg 5:28 and Prov 7:6)? If this usage is pointing us to 2 Kings, it may be because a) Nabonidus is heading for such a snare and b) his fall will also be due, ostensibly, to his devotion to other gods.

Nabonidus, we are beginning to realise, is already being depicted as one who is entangled in Nitocris's net of sexuality and intensity, ignorant, at least initially, of his predicament.

SPRING FEVER (2:10–13)

Spring means it is the time of Tammuz's return from the underworld; it is the time of growth and mating. The "voice of the turtledove" heard throughout the land is Ishtar's voice; the dove represents the Great Star goddess. In Akkadian, the turtledove is known as "eye-star" and in Assyrian, even more bluntly, "star-bird."[17]

"The time of singing has come" implies, however, *not* the singing of birds (i.e., *zamir* means song and is used to imply only human singing, e.g., Isa 25:5; 2 Sam 23:1, etc.) but the festivities of the Akitu festival, when the public celebrate with much singing and dancing, while the king undergoes his solemn ritual in the temple. The Akitu-house, where the New Year festival culminates, is known as the "house of joyful singing."

The mention of the fig tree and its fruit is a sexual/fertility symbol

---

[17] William Houghton, "The Birds of the Assyrian Monuments and Records," *Transactions of the Society of Biblical Archaeology* 8 (London: 1885): 42–142, here 85,https://archive.org/stream/transactionssoc00nashgoog/transactionssoc00nashgo og_ djvu.txt.

used throughout the ancient Near East and elsewhere. It signifies the union of male and female, for the fruit itself can resemble the vulva and/or womb, and the sap, when the fruit is cut from the tree, is a white milk, like semen. The multitude of seeds within, like the pomegranate, attest to fertility.

In the phrase, "they give forth fragrance," we see the second of five uses of *reyach* to describe scent, or the "odour of soothing" (also, 4:11; 7:8, 13). As discussed earlier (Song 1:12), this is not a propitious omen in the Song.

There is a significant allusion here to the tale of "Enki and Ninhursaga." Enki finds the beautiful Ninhursaga in the garden paradise known as Dilmun. She is resting there, *through the winter*, tired from her efforts to help create the world. In the spring, when she awakens, Enki falls in love (lust) with her; he invites her to come away with him, they enjoy sexual union, and Ninhursaga gets pregnant. She has a daughter. Because Ishtar is not known for her role as a mother, the author of the Song subtly introduces Ninhursaga to pave the way for the imminent and paramount pregnancy theme. Early audiences would comprehend the parallels in the stories but would also be aware of the negative aspects of the myth; Enki goes a little "mad" and has sex with his own daughters, forcing Ninhursaga to resort to drastic measures to make thing well. The myth is a tale of a very strong female and a foolish male, in a web of deceit, sex, pregnancy, and grave danger. It is a fitting choice for an allusion, as we shall see.

VOICE AND HIDING (2:14)

The dove hiding in the clefts of the rocks and the "*covert* of the cliff" contrast sharply against the praise of Nitocris's "sweet" voice and "lovely" face, and this should be taken as a turning point, a warning. Things are going to change soon. The mood will darken, the atmosphere will become somewhat fraught. Why should she hide? Why be covert?

The clefts of the rocks are a recognised place of secrecy, of ill repute, e.g., "… you that slaughter your children in the valleys, under the clefts of the rocks …" (Isa 57:5). It is the place of refuge for those who are deemed wicked, evil, or unwelcome, e.g., because Saul banished all witches and wizards, those who remained in the land had to hide themselves in the caves and forests beyond the cities, up in the hills (1 Sam 28:3–25). In Judg 15:8, Samson, hiding after a confrontation with the Philistines, conceals himself "in the cleft of the rock at Etam," and in Jer 48:28, the wicked Moab is told to leave and hide, "like the dove that nests on the sides of the mouth of a gorge." Hiding is not Nitocris's idea. It is not what she does. This association is purely from the author's hand, intentionally painting this woman with the same brush as the sorceress and the enemy.

The very next phrases from the king, i.e., "let me see your face," and "let me hear your voice" prove more significant as the story progresses. In the HB, it is not really the face that the king wishes to see, it is the woman's overall appearance, i.e., *mareh*, a noun that is also used to denote a divine vision (e.g., Ezek 8:4), or something awe-inspiring (e.g., Judg 13:6). This is the subtlest of clues to what lies ahead for Nabonidus; it reveals the author's consistent tactic of placing the truth upon the unsuspecting king's lips. This, in turn, reveals his weakness. He wishes to see Nitocris's physical body, of course, because she is so beautiful and he wants to have sex with her, to procreate. The author knows, however, that Nitocris is far more than her sexual parts and a pretty face; the king claims to want to "see" her, but for now, he has no clue what that really means.

Similarly, Nabonidus asks to hear Nitocris's voice, i.e., her words; he seeks to access her wisdom. As will become clearer in Song 5, the king's wish to learn the "chants to the various idols" (Shabbath, 56.2) of his Egyptian wife manifests in a surprising way, and the notion of hearing/listening becomes central to his quest. Here, it is only just hinted at. He is showing enthusiasm to learn, which, of course, makes the rabbis' castigation of Solomon easier to understand, but it also suggests the king is instigating his own downfall, which is yet another underlying motif of the Song.

TIME TO BEGET (2:15)

Perhaps one of the most debated verses in the Song, the catching of foxes seems such an odd interjection at first glance. It is in the realm of mythology that the most potential explanation can be found.

In the Sumerian tale of Ninhursaga and Enki, mentioned earlier, the god unwittingly succumbs to his lust for the young women who are his daughters. The final daughter, Uttu, he rapes; she cries out in despair and Ninhursaga comes to her aid, removing the semen from the young woman and throwing it to the ground, from whence plants grow. Enki consumes these, in ignorance (again), and he, himself, becomes pregnant. As a male, he is unable to give birth and he is near death when, of all things, a fox comes by, promising he will get help. The fox is Ninhursaga's messenger. He prepares himself before approaching the deities he will seek help from: "The fox first anointed his body, first shook out his fur (?), first put kohl on his eyes" (*ETCSL t.1.1.1*, §228–34). Ninhursaga comes to Enki's side, places him inside her own vulva and gives birth to the new deities. She calls them "little ones."

The fox plays a crucial role in that he becomes the conduit between the sexual act and the resulting birth of the deities. He prepares himself as an avatar of Ishtar, goddess of procreation, i.e., he fluffs up and preens his *red* coat, just as the goddess wears her red mantle. He puts kohl on his eyes, and anoints himself with oils, just as the goddess does, e.g., "She blends (?) kohl. She lets down her hair which was combed up ... She anoints herself with sweet oil ... She paints her eyes with kohl. She covers her body with a queenly robe (*ETCSL t.4.08.31*, §B1–16).

The fox is inextricably linked to the act of procreation, at least in this mythological context. It is also strongly associated with Ishtar's Egyptian counterpart for whom it became an iconic symbol, i.e., Hathor's foxes were *identified* with sexuality. Darnell, in discussing Hathor and her attentive foxes, suggests that in the myth of the Solar Eye "the foxes may themselves ... suggest the birth" of the child (Horus).[18]

Unsurprisingly, in the biblical accounts of foxes, they are found scavenging on ruins like vultures and are thematically linked to destruction (Neh 4:3; Lam 5:18; Ezek 13:4). The Hebrew word for fox, *shual*, means a burrower (which, in itself, suits the hiding aspect of the previous "clefts of the rocks" phrase); *shual* stems from *shoal*, meaning to hollow out, or "the hollow of the hand." This links us back to two topics already discussed, i.e., the tale of Samson and the priestess Huldah. In Huldah's case, we saw how this nickname, given to the prophetess by the rabbis, was a play on words that ultimately denigrated her by ridiculing her feminine role as a vessel of procreation, and making her akin to a weasel, or other such creature that crept on or burrowed into the ground. Here in Song 2:15, the fox suggests a similar earth-living beast, i.e., a burrower. The fox, as the weasel, thus has a symbolic link to cultic females. Samson, in Judg 14:9, scoops out honey from the carcass of a lion, using the "hollow of the hand/palm" (*kaph*).

In Judg 15:4–5, Samson, in the midst of his wedding celebrations, offers the Philistines a riddle based on his scooping of the honey; when they fail to discern its meaning, they coerce the new bride into obtaining the secret information from her husband, which she does. Samson responds: "... if you had not ploughed with my heifer, you would not have found out my riddle" (Judg 14:18). Ploughing is a common Mesopotamian euphemism for sex. These are scathing words that put the wife in a very dark light, indeed. In revenge for this humiliation, Samson destroys the fields and *vineyards* of the Philistines by setting fire to torches tied to the tails of three hundred foxes. The story depicts foxes tied end to end because this is the manner in which dogs lock together during copulation. Samson (or rather the author of the story) is being *sarcastic*, insulting, alluding to the woman's lack of wifely virtue, for to him she is a foreigner, a loose woman (see also the discussion of Song 8:11). The Song's allusion to the hollow of the hand and its immediate reiteration of the word "foxes," in the context of marriage, sex,

---

[18] John Coleman Darnell, "Hathor Returns to Medamûd," *Studien zur Altägyptischen Kultur* 22 (1995): 47–94, here 88.

and vineyards points the reader in one, clear direction, i.e., to Judges 14–15.

From the historical perspective, this seems to be the point at which the author of the Song makes reference to Nabonidus's desire for a daughter. The entire verse is full of allusions to pregnancy and childbirth, and even to Ishtar/Hathor, the goddesses of procreation and childbirth, being present in the (symbolic) guise of the fox.

The term for ruin is *chabal*, or to bind, or pledge but also, to writhe, twist, hence travail, e.g., of a woman in labour; this same word is used in 8:5 of the Song in *just* such a context, making pregnancy/childbirth the central motif in both instances. The "little foxes that ruin the vineyards" are, I posit, children. As vineyards are representative of female sexuality, it is a simple progression to imagine pregnancy "ruining" both virginity and most sexual liberties. The little rascals (as foxes *and* children are often perceived) put an end to the frolicking in the grass! (The Assyrian equivalent of *chabal*, or ruin, is *na-balu*, and this has the significant connotation of a rope, or snare.)

If the author is attempting to depict (for the record) the desire of Nabonidus for a daughter to serve as Sîn's high priestess, the call to catch the little foxes must be a positive exclamation here. The effect is: "Let us 'bind' the 'little ones' to us … let us have children … for the time is ripe" (and recall that this is still the betrothal period, when the new bride is expected to conceive). This is spoken by the impatient king.

Knowing how important omens are to Nabonidus, and especially the timing of significant events based on those omens, it is possible he has been influenced by an oracle or omen in this instance, which is why he seems to be urging Nitocris on. There is potential historical substantiation for this in a cuneiform text called "Dream Portending Favour for Nabonidus and Belshazzar."[19] In this very short tablet text, a dream is recounted (by a priest/diviner) that is dated to 15 Tebet, i.e., December/January (the tenth month of the Babylonian year), 549 BCE, i.e., the king's seventh regnal year, the year of the treaty and the 'acquisition' of Nitocris. During the dream, the diviner sees the triad of Nabonidus's favourite gods; the moon (Sîn), the sun (Shamash), and the Great Star (Venus/Ishtar).[20] Two days later, he witnesses just the Great Star, i.e., *just* the goddess. Ishtar is the goddess of

---

[19] Albert T. Clay, *Miscellaneous Inscriptions in the Yale Babylonian Collection* (New Haven: Yale University Press, 1915) §39.

[20] There are several "Great Stars" listed in the *Great Star Lists*, including Venus, Jupiter, Saturn, and Mars but Venus fits this context throughout, especially as Ishtar's accepted iconography is the eight-pointed star, and "'Ish-shtar' means 'The Star' (Asia Haleem, "The Venus Cycle and Venus Worship in the Ancient Near East" [2013], 1–21, here 19, http://www.layish.co.uk/venusworship.pdf). See H. F. Lutz, "An Omen Text Referring to the Action of a Dreamer," University of Pennsylvania, https://www.journals.uchicago.edu/doi/ pdf/10.1086/369879.

childbearing, so this little cuneiform tablet seems to suggest to Nabonidus that the gods are giving their consent and Ishtar will grant him his daughter. Recall Clay's rendition of the inscription on Ennigaldi's dedication cylinder that promoted Ishtar's role in granting her conception. It is quite possible this little gem of a cuneiform tablet was a (sycophantic) gesture of support for the king's new marriage.

The historical tale of Nabonidus and Nitocris anticipating the conception of their special daughter is hinted at by the allusion to Enki and Ninhursaga. The subtle references to Samson and the echoes of Huldah demonstrate the postexilic animosity toward women not of the aspiring Jewish religion; they are temptation personified, they are under the influence of Ishtar, and they all seem to be setting a trap for men. The *yeser* is alive and well, they fear.

RABBIS' TALE (2:16–17)

The translation of "pastures his flock" in the NRSV is a little misleading, for "flock" is assumed, not extant in the Hebrew text; it should read "He feeds among the lilies." The allusion to feeding/eating in a sexual context is a reminder of the Sumerian story of the young Inanna and her brother Utu, who "eat" what "grows" upon the mountain; Inanna descends, having learnt the art of women. The lily, as well as being the esoteric symbol for the womb, represents the plurality of female associated genitalia, i.e., the pudendum (pubis, vulva, labia, vagina, clitoris). Feeding "among the lilies" is, therefore, another reference to cunnilingus.

The scene in 2:17 is set during the early hours of the morning, possibly before dawn, and the couple are probably in bed. Nitocris, becoming agitated because the king is so focused on procreation, attempts to distract him, for she does not wish to conceive; it would mean the end of her role as the guardian of the divine Elixir Rubeus.

The verb *puach* generally means breathing, or blowing, i.e., sighing, suggesting the evening, when the day cools down and the shadows begin to mingle with the ensuing darkness (they "flee"). Other translations of *puach* suggest the uttering of words, the kindling of a fire, or, most interestingly, bringing something into a snare. In this scene the "snare" of Nitocris's overwhelming intensity is first set. She tells the king to turn, i.e., to turn back to her, for he is about to get up from the bed; she stops him. For some reason it appears the king wishes to leave Nitocris in bed and go about his business.

The rabbis' legend of Bathya and the bejewelled bed canopy thus has a parallel in Song 2:17; the art of this foreign woman, her apparent guile, keeps Solomon from his duties and lures him into the "dark" world of her idolatry. In the Song, Nitocris constantly toys with the king, using her feminine charms, and her voice, to draw him into her world, in a bid to keep her "vineyard" to herself. Whatever her motivation, she is certainly manipulative.

> *With her smooth talk she compels him ... and [he] goes like*
> *an ox to the slaughter, or bounds like a stag*
> *toward the trap until an arrow pierces his entrails.*
> Prov 7:21–3

SACRIFICE AND SAMARIA

Nitocris distracts the king by suggesting he comes back to 'play' but the focus is on her breasts, i.e., the "cleft mountains," rendered from the HB's "mountains of Bether." She hopes to keep him satisfied without risking impregnation. The word *bether*, however, means piece, from *bather*, to cut in two, generally associated with sacrificial animals being cut up and divided. It is from this point in the Song we begin to see the king adversely affected by Nitocris's intensity. His identification with the gazelle in 2:8–9 evoked the imagery of Dumuzi being hounded by his demons and begging Utu to change him into a gazelle so he could escape (*ETCSL t.1.4.3*, §165–73). Now the king is drawn toward the "mountain of cutting and dividing"; the sacrificial allusion cannot be unintentional.

The use of *bether* is thus an allusion to the king's ultimate fate but there is another level to this, which takes into consideration the postexilic emigrants from Babylonia and the anti-Samaritan prejudice of the later HB authors. Mount Gerizim is the site of worship for the much-maligned Samaritans. The name Gerizim (from *garaz*) means to cut up, off, etc. (aligning it with the "mountain of cutting and dividing," above); therefore, it can suggest rocky, craggy, *cleaved*. The twin mountains of Gerizim and Ebal could be the "cleft mountains" of the Song, and could thus be interpreted as breasts (hence the king acts as a lusty stag upon them). By identifying Nitocris with such a place, she is seen to be the epitome of what is wrong for, and encouraging what is destructive to Israel, urging her king to stray into the path that will lead him (and his people) into danger.

The *Jewish Encyclopedia* suggests that Samaritan wine (the drink) was forbidden because it was used in the worship of an image of a dove on Mount Gerizim. The dove is Ishtar's symbolic bird.

3. MOTHER AND MARRIAGE

HONEYMOON OVER? (3:1–2)

When Ishtar and Tammuz consummate their marriage, they do so extensively. The goddess turns out to be insatiable; on their wedding night, Ishtar makes love with her husband fifty times! With both parties spent, Tammuz decides it is time to get back to his job as shepherd-king and, like a 'morning-after' cooling off, he returns to the palace, leaving his new wife in the marriage bed. In fact, he pleads with her: "Set me free!"[1]

The language we saw in the previous verses of the Song hinted at a trap, or snare, and a context of sacrifice. Nabonidus attempts to leave the marriage bed but Nitocris coaxes (tricks?) him into remaining. Echoing Tammuz, however, he eventually has enough and gets away on his own.

Hunted by the *galla* demons, who want to take him down to the underworld, Tammuz is turned into a gazelle and escapes; he hides but his whereabouts is revealed by a "friend" who betrays him for riches and gifts. This is the beginning of the end for the shepherd-king and perhaps a portent of Nabonidus's fate, for he too is sought, 'betrayed', found, and seized.

The streets and squares are where the prostitutes of Babylon work: Ishtar is "the mistress, the lady of the great powers who allows sexual intercourse in the open squares ..." (*ETCSL t.1.1.3*, §358–67); "I the maiden, in the streets and alleys ..." (*ETCSL t.4.08.08*, §A24–6). This does not bode well for Nitocris's reputation.

REMOTE VIEWING

King Sargon of Akkad, it is said, "lay down not to sleep, but lay down to dream" (*ETCSL t.2.1.4*, §12–24). In the Sumerian text "Lugalbanda in the mountain cave," the king follows suit, i.e., he "... [lies] down not to sleep, he [lies] down to dream" (*ETCSL t.1.8.2.1*, §326–350). The two states are distinguishable and the process is ceremonial: Lugalbanda imbibes an alcoholic drink, prepares a "couch" of special herbs, and dons a sacred garment in preparation for his "dream."

---

[1] Diane Wolkstein and Samuel Noah Kramer, *Inanna, Queen of Heaven: Her Stories and Hymns from Sumer* (New York: Harper and Row, 1983), 48.

Nitocris is not properly sleeping, nor is she dreaming in the familiar sense; she is attempting to "see" someone from afar, as in remote viewing, and this may be indicative of her Egyptian identity, for ...

> ...[i]n their descriptions of dreams, the Egyptians do not speak of the dreamer as physically journeying to another place, nor do they express the notion of the soul leaving the body during sleep, as do a number of other cultures ... the sleeper remains in his own familiar surroundings, but in a state where he can perceive things not normally within eyesight.[2]

Remote viewing is a process still used today in certain investigative contexts and can be learned; it might have been part of Nitocris's priestly training, or it might relate to her potential role as God's Hand and to the Elixir Rubeus (see Part Two, Chapter 5). It should be noted that this exercise of remote viewing is conducted over several nights, as the word for "night" here is in the plural—the king has *stayed* away!

Could there have been an episode that went down in local history, where the young, impetuous Nitocris overstepped the bounds of decorum and did, indeed, go abroad into the streets in search of Nabonidus, who could have been about his own business? Did she make a fool of herself?

> *She is loud and wayward; her feet do not stay at home;*
> *now in the street, now in the squares, and at every*
> *corner she lies in wait. ... "I have come out to meet you,*
> *to seek you eagerly, and I have found you!"*
> Prov 7:11–12, 15

SENTINELS 1 (3:2–4B)

There is a striking parallel in the tale of the marriage of Enlil and Ninlil, where Ninlil "chases" the king through the city: Enlil orders the gatekeepers not to tell her where he has gone (*ETCSL t.1.2.1*, §65–91) but she manages to pursue him. This may serve as a direct inspiration for the narrative of the Song, where the presence of the sentinels is somewhat ominous. This is Nitocris's first interaction with them and it seems fairly straight forward, for she simply asks if they have seen the king. They seem to offer no reply but allow her free passage and, almost immediately, she finds her itinerant lover. In this instance, the king, just like Tammuz, is apparently betrayed by the night-watchmen, who either point the way or tell the young queen which way he went.

---

[2] Kasia Szpakowska, *Behind Closed Eyes: Dreams and Nightmares in Ancient Egypt* (Swansea: Classical Press of Wales, 2003), 28.

The verb for "love" here ("whom my soul loves") is *aheb*, the sexual version of love in the Song.

> *I am running, but I cannot cat[ch up with him] ...*
> *I am weary for looking out for him.*
> *I keep thinking he will go through my neighbourhood,*
> *The day has gone by, where is [my darling]?*
> From a Sumerian Love Poem[3]

SEIZED (3:4C–5)

For the traditional interpreter, the image of the woman holding onto the man she admires is nothing more than an expression of her undying love, her desire to keep him close. The word for "held" in the Hebrew, however, is *achaz*, meaning to seize, grasp, or take possession (by force), providing consistency with the theme of the king becoming a sacrifice, a trapped animal. The verb *achaz* is used in Gen 22:13, where Abraham is about to sacrifice Isaac, only to find, at the last moment, a sacrificial ram caught up in a thicket, "trapped." In Judg 1:6 a man is chased, cornered, and mutilated. In 1 Kgs 1:51, a man in fear of his life seeks sanctuary by clinging onto the sacrificial altar. In Eccl 9:12 the simile of animals trapped in a snare is used to warn of an impending disaster. Not a promising omen, perhaps.

> *I hold you in restraint, as Inanna held Dumuzi ....*[4]

> *I have seized you and I will not set you free!*
> From a Sumerian sex spell[5]

Nitocris refuses to "let him go" until she gets him to her "mother's house." She is invoking the source of her spiritual/magical learning, passed on from parent to child. As a sign of desperation and of alternative strategy, she returns home in order to gain moral support or, as seems to be the case in the next chapter of the Song, to learn new magical techniques to 'deal with' her situation. The use of *hara* in the phrase "of her that *conceived* me," though relating to Nitocris's *conception* and thereby suggesting she is not merely the cultic but also the biological daughter of Ankhnesneferibre,[6] is a foreshadowing of her own pregnancy, which is depicted soon.

---

[3] Benjamin R. Foster, *From Distant Days: Myths, Tales, and Poetry of Ancient Mesopotamia* (Bethesda: CDL Press, 1995), 353.

[4] Foster, *Distant Days,* 334.

[5] Foster, *Distant Days,* 339.

[6] See Supplemental Note "Ankhnesneferibre and Nitocris II: A Question of Filiation" on Academia.edu.

81

That a fully grown man, and a king at that, should be dragged through the streets by a woman is an intriguing image and could, perhaps, only have taken place had he been weakened somehow. Once more within her sights, Nitocris steals the king away, proving she is the one in control. We begin to sense the "swarming" nature of women, the potential gathering together (e.g., of mother and daughter) against the men, that the early rabbis fear and ridicule.

Nitocris refuses to let go until she gets the king to her mother's "chamber"; this is linked not only to the concept of seizing but also to that of deity worship, i.e., the inner chamber is a sanctified space. The phrase "the mother who bore me" is common to many of the Sumerian myths, from the Epic of Gilgamesh (*ETCSL t.1.8.1.2*, §D16–23) to "Dumuzi's Dream" (*ETCSL t.1.4.3*, §5–14) but one instance stands out: "The goddess ... was pacing to and fro in the chamber of her mother who bore her, in prayer and supplication, while they stood in attendance on her respectfully ..." (*ETCSL t.1.4.4*, §31–6). The chamber is that of Ningal, Ishtar's mother, consort to Sîn. Ishtar is "in prayer and supplication"—she is in a sacred space, i.e., a temple, or shrine to Ningal.

As Nitocris is an Egyptian high priest, her "mother's" i.e., Ankhnesneferibre's, chamber is the temple at Karnak. Nitocris has taken Nabonidus into the heart of Egypt, into the bosom of her spiritual home, where she has moral support. This is where Nabonidus will discover the riches of Egypt first-hand, and where he will be introduced to his wife's religion in its native context. It is a monumental moment for Nitocris, for this will be the end of the betrothal stage of the marriage and the prelude to the full (consummated) wedding which will take place in Tayma.

In the Jewish tradition, a woman normally remains in her father's house during the betrothal period, where she can be kept chaste which, of course, Nitocris does not, as she is not Jewish. In Mesopotamia, however, a betrothed woman is called "bride" until she conceives, then she is deemed to have earned the title of "wife."[7] There is a distinct shift in the vocabulary and imagery by Song 4 that points to Nitocris being elevated from "bride" to "wife."

Still, though, Nitocris warns against "awakening" sexual love (using *ahabah*) too soon. The self-control required for transcending base sexual urges is a fundamental aspect of her religious training.

---

[7] Janice P. De-Whyte, "Wom(b)an: A Cultural-Narrative Reading of the Hebrew Bible Barrenness Narratives" (PhD diss., McMaster Divinity College, Ontario, 2014), 28–9.

WEDDING CARAVAN (3:6)

The trade route between Egypt and Palestine was dominated by the Via Maris, which passed through Gaza, along the coastline; it was a well-trodden and familiar journey for most merchants. There is another route of note, however, i.e., the Frankincense Route, which traversed the wilderness through the Arabian Desert, its most cosmopolitan and central hub was Tayma. The description of the frankincense, myrrh, and spices strongly suggests the king and his entourage have up come from Egypt via the Arabian Desert.

The "fragrant powders of the merchant" are clearly spices being brought along the Route to the hub of trade in Tayma; it has been conjectured that one of the reasons Nabonidus chooses this location to build his second capital is that he desires to control the trade of spices and gold through the region. The term "spices," however, has a different connotation in the Song, so the phrasing is adapted here.

The word for "wilderness" is *midbar*, which translates as "mouth" but is also used to denote a broad tract of land, i.e., either a pasture, or a desert. From the Arabic, there is a connection in *midbar* to becoming "black or brown, of a colour between black and red."[8] Another play on words to indicate a cultic context? Nitocris is black and is linked to crimson later (Ishtar is black and her symbolic colour is red). Egypt is "black" and the home of dark magic.

More profound, however, are the columns of smoke. The Hebrew word is *timarah*, meaning palm-like, from *tomer*, and ultimately from *tamar*, palm tree. It is in the plural, suggesting at least two such palm-shaped columns. The palm is the symbol for Tammuz; it is also a symbol for Ishtar where the lotus is not intended, and we see this again later in the Song. The columns reminiscent of palms thus allude to the divine couple at the time of the *hieros gamos*, the second of which is alluded to in the upcoming verses.

Although one may suggest a subtle allusion here to the legendary sojourn from Egypt to the land of Canaan, the smoke (*ashan*) is not akin to the "fire and cloud" of Exod 14:24. It is more the sacred smoke of an offering to the gods, be it one's soul, e.g., "His smoke went up to the sky" (*ETCSL t.1.8.1.4*, §A286–303); an offering on an altar (*ETCSL t.1.8.2.1*, §A371–93); or the offering of an entire temple (*ETCSL t.2.1.7*, §353–64). With multiple figurative meanings for *ashan* (smoke), including a simile of a dust cloud, God's anger, and as relating to "the destruction of Israel,"[9] combined with the "odour of soothing," the notion of sacrifice within the Song is reiterated. There is no way anyone standing at a distance could appreciate the scent

---

[8] "Midbar," https://biblehub.com/hebrew/4057.htm.
[9] As noted on https://biblehub.com/hebrew/6227.htm (*ashan*).

itself; it is an overall impression of the event, providing a sense of religious gravitas to the arrival of the couple returning from Egypt, and serving as an ominous portent.

In Genesis, "traveling to Egypt" is referred to as "going down," while leaving is called "going/coming up"; this is "not a mere geographical notation," Levenson states, e.g., Joseph's "descent into Egypt is a kind of death; his ascent to rulership, a kind of resurrection. Whereas the pit is a metaphor of Sheol in the case of Joseph's first descent, in the case of his second, the metaphor is Egypt ...."[10] Thus, it could be said that Nitocris has taken Nabonidus into the jaws of death, into the dark underworld of Egypt; time will tell how this affects the king. Perhaps it is the catalyst that instigates his fall.

There are, then, *two* fragrances—one highlighting the symbolic ascent from the darkness of Egypt, i.e., myrrh, with its associations to the underworld and death (discussed further later), and one representing the physical journey along the incense-route, i.e., frankincense.

It should also be noted that Hathor is known as the "Horizon-Dweller who appears in the horizon," making this a significant early allusion to Nitocris's Hathor-avatar. The "coming up from the wilderness" in this context is profoundly reiterated and expanded upon in Song 7, where the Hathoric connection culminates.

PIVOTAL MOMENT

Out of over a hundred instances of "pillar/column" in the HB, only the Song, here (alternative words are used in Song 3:10 and 5:15) and Joel 2:30 use the noun *tomer*, and both use it in the plural. In Joel, the context is the imminent Day of Judgement, one of the portents of which is columns of smoke; on that day, God promises "Egypt shall become a desolation" and all the oppressors of Israel will be avenged upon. Strange parallel, you may think, but not if the author of the Song is alluding to the disgrace of the king's erroneous ways and his ultimate punishment. Remember the rabbis' legend of the marriage of Solomon and Bathya; the future fall of Jerusalem is instigated on the day of their wedding. Seeing this cloud on the horizon, with the couple arriving back in Tayma for their official wedding (see below), is a warning.

FEAR (3:7–8)

The term for "litter" is *mittah*, i.e., a couch or bed but it can also mean a bier

---

[10] J. D. Levenson, *The Death and Resurrection of the Beloved Son: The Transformation of Child Sacrifice in Judaism and Christianity* (New Haven: Yale University Press, 1993), 152.

(as in 2 Sam 3:31), which is used to carry the corpse at a funeral. There is a play on words here (a different term is employed in 3:9), intended to remind the reader of Tammuz and Ishtar's marriage bed but also of their mutual descents into darkness (a form of death).

The "mighty men" are protecting the king because of "troubles" at *night*. In Sumerian literature, this is the time for demons, e.g., "The evil demons and the evil demonesses who beset mankind ... who enter by night ... who will not leave a man alone, stand before the man. He is robbed of sleep ..." (*ETCSL t.4.22.1*, §46–51). The night is also Ishtar's time of intense warlike power, shining brightly as Venus: "After the first watch of the night has passed ... you seize your battle-mace like a warrior ... you appear brilliantly ... you emit awe-inspiring splendour ... (*ETCSL t.4.07.4*, §22–36). The Sumerian concept of fear is directly related to the overwhelming and terrifying appearance of the deities (recall the comment made earlier about Nabonidus wanting to "see" Nitocris but not realizing what he was wishing for). In the Song, Nitocris is, effectively, a goddess. Her power is strongest at night (e.g., 2:17; 3:1; especially 5:2, i.e., to underscore her metaphorical darkness). It would seem as though the visit to Egypt has proven quite a dramatic experience for the king. It may be that Nitocris and her mother manage to influence him in some way, or that the reality of Nitocris's status and significance at Karnak is an intimidating revelation to him.

Nabonidus has many dreams that disturb him, as we saw earlier, but perhaps the most vivid comparison is the passage that tells of a military guard that protects him when he leaves Babylon for Arabia, for he fears danger to his person (Nab 47, §1.27b–31a). This is a public inscription, so would be common knowledge (to those who could read). I submit that *something* occurs during this trip to Egypt that makes Nabonidus even more paranoid than ever.

The Song's word for "troubles" is *pachad*, which actually denotes *fear and dread*, i.e., terror, not merely difficult circumstances, e.g., civil disruption, etc. This is serious for the king. Like Tammuz, Nabonidus is apparently afraid of his own demon, whose power is heightened during the night. He has "sixty" mighty men who encircle him, like some magical barrier he has inscribed around himself; it would be fitting in a time of impending war with the Persians for the royal couple to travel very well-protected on their return from Egypt, but the plural seems to have been left behind here—this protection pertains only to Nabonidus.

SIXTY

Sixty happens to be the number of queens mentioned in Song 6:8. That means there is, potentially, one soldier for each queen (not the concubines, who have less authority, scope, and access to the king).

Sixty is the numerical value (gematria) of the fifteenth letter of the Hebrew alphabet, *samech*. This letter is shaped like a closed circle and symbolises not only infinite light/power (e.g., of a deity) but also, a wedding band and thus, marriage. It is linked to the fifteenth day of the month Av, when Jewish girls traditionally dance in a circle, and boys choose their wife-to-be from among them. The number sixty is therefore inextricably linked to the number fifteen, and to the union of male and female.

The Chabad.org website states: "We are told that the fifteenth of any month is the zenith of the Jewish calendar since the Jewish people are compared to the moon, and on the fifteenth the moon is full."[11] This is a direct inheritance from the worship of Ishtar in Babylon, where the fifteenth day, the day of the full moon, is the goddess' holy day (just as fifteen is her symbolic number and occult name), eventually extended to the four quarters of the moon: 4 x 15 = 60. The gematria of the proper noun "Brilliance" or "Beauty," when relating to Venus, also has the numerical value of sixty. This would certainly point to Nitocris (the avatar of Ishtar) as the main threat.

So, Nabonidus is surrounded by sixty guards because he fears he is losing control; it is possible he fears others of his queens may follow suit and gain the upper hand with him.[12] He is overwhelmed by Nitocris's intensity; he is awed by her brilliance and beauty and is falling under her spell. The very next chapter of the Song reveals just how besotted and mesmerised he is when she is about.

The Talmud suggests that Solomon kept a guard around him for the very purpose of averting the demon-king Ashmedai's return (Gittin 68b) but I suggested earlier that the legend of Ashmedai was manufactured to help explain Nabonidus's strange 'bewitchment', his strange behaviour. If it is, indeed, Nitocris's influence that makes the king act so irresponsibly and foolishly as to be rendered unrecognizable by his own court, then it makes sense for the king to deploy guards during a moment of clarity.

A sudden change in tone is evident from this point onward. It is from this introduction of the soldiers bearing arms that the theme of war is made apparent in the narrative itself, not just in the allusions to Ishtar. There is a multi-faceted spiritual battle going on now that will permeate the rest of the Song.

---

[11]"Samech," Chabad.org, https://www.chabad.org/library/article_cdo/aid/1370 87/jewish/Samech .htm.

[12] During his visit to Egypt, Nabonidus might have learned of the famous court case concerning the murder of Rameses III, known as the "Harem Conspiracy." One of the pharaoh's wives was accused of using sorcery to kill Rameses, in order to seize the throne for her son. She had several accomplices within the harem.

HIEROS GAMOS 2: THE GROOM'S SEAT (3:9–10)

The ceremony of the sacred marriage begins with the consort of the deity being taken *by chariot* (or "litter") to where the wedding is to be solemnised (i.e., here, coming up from Egypt to Tayma); this is known as the "going up" of the procession. As the groom approaches, everyone comes out to greet him and female attendants minister to the couple. The pomp and ceremony, the lavish accoutrements, the entourage, the incense and finery portrayed in the Song echo the procession of the divine marriage.

Silver and gold represent sun and moon, masculine and feminine; combined, they represent the *hieros gamos* itself. In this particular ceremony, of course, the solar and lunar deities are vital components, being the respective divinities of Nitocris and Nabonidus.

In a text that tells the story of the sacred marriage between "Banitu and Her Consort" we read: "… they brought out the … chariot of silver, they harnessed the … chariot of go[ld]. They brought (it) out and laid over it red wool, blue purple wool and *red purple* wool."[13] The cushion cover, throw, blanket, etc., of this symbolic reddish colour is thus central to the vehicle used in the *hieros gamos*.

In the HB, the palanquin's interior is decorated for the king "*by*" the loving "daughters of Jerusalem"—the maidens, the companions who follow Tammuz in distant homage. This proves interesting, for it suggests they have decorated the most intimate part of the vehicle (which comes into contact with the king), the seat, with purple fabric; the concept of "purple" appears several times throughout this analysis in the context of sexuality and menstrual blood.

The palanquin is not on wheels, like a horse-drawn chariot, but is based on a wedding sedan-chair used for hundreds of years in Babylon: "I have had a sedan chair made for Ninlil …" (*ETCSL t.2.5.4.01*, §B1–24). It suggests that the king is not physically driving a chariot (as for war); he is being escorted, regally.

This type of mobile seat is also to be found depicted in ancient Egyptian tombs of the elite, both royal and non-royal. Evidence for the status-symbol of the palanquin being used in the funerary art of wealthy citizens is minimal and dates predominantly from the Old Kingdom; only a few later examples of kings being carried are preserved. These litters had ornate woodwork that often had a curtain or canopy on top, which was held up by "column-like piles,"; they were conveyed by a number of men who carried sticks or batons, who were recruited from two groups, i.e., the lower-

---

[13] Martti Nissinen, "Akkadian Love Poetry and the Song of Songs: A Case of Cultural Interaction," 13, https://helda.helsinki.fi//bitstream/handle/10138/231968/Druckfahne_Nissinen_fertig_.pdf?sequence=1.

class, semi-military cadets, sailors, etc., and/or noble youths associated with the palace. The number of carriers reflected the status of the person being carried, but extant records do not surpass twenty-four carriers for a canopied litter, taking turns.[14] For the king to have sixty such (armed) men, seems profoundly over the top.

It is not difficult to imagine Ahmose providing such a special vehicle for the marriage of his daughter to the king of Babylon. Both the pharaoh and the king are retrospective in their tastes and plans; reviving the once illustrious palanquin might well have been one of Ahmose's personal projects, much admired and coveted, perhaps, by Nabonidus.

SUBTLE INSULTS

The "wood of Lebanon" refers to two seemingly distinct but in fact related ideas. One, is the enforced labour for which Solomon is notorious: "He sent them to the Lebanon, ten thousand a month in shifts" (1 Kgs 5:13–14). The other, more significant reference, is to the building in Jerusalem, known as "The House of the Forest of Lebanon" (1 Kgs 7:2) because of the huge number of tall cedar trunks used in its construction. The upper story of this building, apparently, was used as the state treasury (10:17), only this wealth was actually the king's own, personal property; he held five hundred shields of beaten gold as a reserve in this storage house but while Jerusalem's resources were exploited to create the king's own palace and his own ideal temple, this private gold went untouched. Contrast this with 2 Kings 11–12, where similar elements (e.g., guarding of the king, "riches," idolatry, funding building projects, etc.) are combined in the *antithesis* of the king whose "palanquin" is approaching on the horizon; it serves as a scathing allusion.

We should also compare the Song's depiction of Solomon building *his own* palanquin (i.e., perhaps he drew up the design), to his building his own throne in 1 Kgs 10:18–20, and to his taking personal credit for building the temple (8:13, 43). He is coming across as proud, arrogant even.

The term for "pillars/posts" used here in Song 3:10, i.e., *ammud* (from *amad*), has multiple meanings including to appoint, to confirm, to establish, to raise up, etc. It is the term used for the great thundercloud of Exod 13:31; it is thus ominous. It is also used many times in the HB to describe pillars of grand stature, i.e., aspects of buildings, *not* chariots. In 1 Kgs 7:6, Solomon first builds his Hall of Pillars, then his own Hall of the Throne; he then builds "a house like this hall for Pharaoh's daughter, whom he had taken in marriage" (7:8). The "hall" referred to there is not necessarily the Hall of

---

[14] Vera Vasiljević, "How Many Porters?" *Egypt and the Levant* 25 (2015): 509–35, here 513, http://www.jstor.org/stable/43795220.

Pillars, but the Hall of the Throne. Solomon, according to 1 Kgs 7, makes the Egyptian princess Queen. He "confirms" her status, he "raises her up." By Song 4, Nitocris appears to have earned her position as "wife"; she is raised above the role of bride and above the slighted "daughters." More importantly, she is raised to the greatest heights, i.e., to that of a *deified* Queen.

The emphasis here in Song 3, however, is firmly on the king and his magnificent entry as Tammuz. There are two reasons for this, i.e., the author has her own motive for focusing on the king and the palanquin (discussed in Chapter 9), and this entire scenario serves as one of two date-specific calendrical markers within the narrative, to tell all future audiences when this event occurred.

MOTHER R.I.P. (3:11)

According to 1 Kgs 1:32–40, Solomon is made king by Zadok, Nathan, and Benaiah; in 1 Chr 29:21–3, the people anoint Solomon king. His mother, Bathsheba, though manipulative and intervening on his behalf, does not crown him.

The Babylonian king, in the role of bridegroom in the sacred marriage rite, must supplicate himself to the goddess and pray for a favourable oracular reply (in order to legitimise his rule for the coming year); if he receives a positive response, he is "seated on a throne and a crown [is] placed on his head and the sceptre of righteousness in his hand."[15] This scene, therefore, is the moment of Nabonidus's deification as the divine consort, not his coronation as king. Thus the "day of his wedding," during which he is "crowned" is actually an allusion to the *hieros gamos*, where his kingship is reconfirmed. This rite occurs in the first month of the Babylonian calendar, Nisanu, or March/April. The fact that such a ceremony seems to take place (at least three times) in Tayma may substantiate and explain the Chronicle's account of so many Akitu festivals (where the *hieros gamos* is performed) the king failed to attend in Babylon (e.g., Nab Chr 2.5–8; 10–12; 19–21a; 23–25).

This *hieros gamos* is also a symbolic representation of the second, consummation stage of the marriage between Nabonidus and Nitocris (as the first represented their betrothal); the solemnity of the sacred marriage rite sets the scene for the earthly marriage ceremony. As the assertion has been made that Nitocris begins as a bride, and only later is raised to the status of wife, and that this follows the Mesopotamian practice of assuring fertility before completing the marriage, we must assume that Nitocris is now

---

[15] E. Douglas Van Buren, "The Sacred Marriage in Early Times in Mesopotamia," *Orientalia*, NOVA Series, 13 (1944): 1–72, here 36–7.

pregnant. This is confirmed in Song 4.

ADAD-GUPPI

Nabonidus's mother, Adad-guppi (an Aramaic name) is immortalised in the lengthy epitaph on a stele that is written as though it were autobiographical (Nab 2001). She dies in the ninth year of Nabonidus's rule, i.e., in April, 547 BCE, at the ripe old age of one hundred and four, having apparently travelled 1500 miles from Harran to "Dur-Karashu, on the banks of the Euphrates upstream from Sippar" (Nab Chr 2.13). Scholars have debated why a woman of such advanced years would be travelling at all, let alone so far from home. I suggest she is either coming from or returning to her home in Harran, having been sent for to attend the royal wedding of her "darling" son. She rests at the militarily-protected stopover, Dur-Karashu, where she succumbs to the stresses of the journey. She becomes immortalised in the Song as having been at the wedding, handing Nabonidus his special marriage "crown."

This apparent reference to Adad-guppi in the Song is intended as a direct historical pointer, suggesting that the author is fully aware of the date of the Queen Mother's death. Adad-guppi's stele also contains a prayer for (the now aging) Nabonidus to be granted "offspring" (H1 2.38–9), presumably from the new marriage (for he already has adult children); this does suggest her death coincides with her son's marriage to Nitocris, give or take a few weeks.[16]

It could be conjectured that this surreptitious visit, made common knowledge on the death of Adad-guppi, lies at the root of the salacious claim that "Solomon" demanded that his own mother be brought to him, along with menstruants, i.e., in the rabbinic legend of Ashmedai.

ZION

The sudden inclusion of another group of "daughters," i.e., those of Zion, demands explanation. On the one hand, we see the repetition of a basic theme in the books of the Prophets, where both the daughters of Zion and of Jerusalem appear together in an invitation to rejoice because the king (human or divine) is soon to be in their midst (e.g., Zech 9:9; Zeph 3:14–19; Micah 4:8; Isa 12:6; 40:9). These express a hopeful, optimistic return to the legendary Davidic golden age, and offer a thematic parallel to the arrival of the king in the Song.

On the other hand, there is a negative, accusatory expression of the "daughters of Zion" that echoes the early Jewish perception of Babylonian priestesses. The most vicious diatribe comes in Isa 3:16–26, where the

---

[16] See Supplemental Note, "Adad-guppi and the 'Genius of Favour'."

detailed description paints a veritable portrait of the Near Eastern high priestess and her entourage. They are "haughty"; they glance "wantonly with their eyes"; they wear crescent-shaped adornments, and headbands; and they wear veils. Zion in this instance cannot reflect the hill where Yahweh dwells, for the "daughters of Zion" are demeaned and castigated.

In Ishtar's temple Eanna, there are the "daughters of Uruk" and the "daughters of Anu," the latter being unmarried women, affiliated with demons, witches, and magical medicine, who appear in the Akitu festival procession.[17] I posit, therefore, that the inclusion of two groups called "daughters of ..." in Song 3:10–11 is an allusion to cultic devotees, i.e., the women in Nabonidus's Tayma (the "daughters of Jerusalem" who honour Tammuz) and those of Babylon (the "daughters of Zion" who represent Ishtar's followers). This means Zion equates (symbolically) to Babylon, which is unconventional but the following discussion may help prove the point (an in-depth analysis is beyond the scope of this book, but I feel it is an intriguing lead and one that further confirms a very Babylonian-influenced context for the Song).

The name Zion literally means a parched place. In Isa 14:13, is the place-name Zaphon, or *tsaphon*; this is translated most often as "north," from the noun *sapon*. In Jeremiah (6:1, 22; 15:12; 46:20, 24) and Zechariah (2:10; 6:6, 8), the term *denotes* Babylonia (i.e., as the latest onslaught from the north). It can also stem from the verb *sapan*, to hide, or store, therefore a storage place.

In the context of a proclamation against Babylon by the prophet Isaiah, Zaphon is given a warning that it has become far too haughty and proud, believing itself to be on a par with the gods, and able to ascend the "mount of assembly," i.e., the "heights of Zaphon." In Isa 4:5 we read of Mount Zion and its "places of assembly."

The Israelites are instructed by God to rest at Baal-zaphon, on the shore of the Red Sea (Exod 14:2); this is where the Egyptian army will be destroyed. The site is known as a centre of worship for the Canaanite storm god Baal-zaphon (the equivalent of the Mesopotamian Adad). The waters of the Sea are said to be driven back by a "strong east wind" all night (Exod 14:21); the land beneath would thus have its water cut-off, i.e., it would be "parched." The site of Baal-zaphon is also a mountain or hill, just as the physical site of Zion is described.

Is it possible that the concept of a new promised land, a theological Zion that finds its house/home on a hill near Jerusalem, is in some way inspired by a memory of this concept of Zaphon as the lofty meeting place

---

[17] Julia Krul, *The Revival of the Anu Cult and the Nocturnal Fire Ceremony at Late Babylonian Uruk* (Leiden: Brill, 2018), 157 and note 94.

of the gods? The raised "storage house" of Zaphon (which must be a dry place) is reflected in the "dry" hill of Zion.

According to Isa 14:1, Israel will settle in their own land and "aliens" will join them there; this sounds very much like the mixed exodus (Jews and non-Jews) from Babylon to Jerusalem under Cyrus. Isa 14:12, declares: "How you are fallen from heaven, O Day Star, son of Dawn!" This uses (for Day Star) the term *helel*, or "shining one" (otherwise known as Lucifer); we have already seen that (the androgynous) Ishtar has this epithet. The subjugation of the feminine (i.e., the star falls) to the aspiring patriarchy, as seen in the accounts of Miriam and Huldah, is unmitigated here.

The "prophecy" in Isa 14:12 mentions Babylon's decline, which happens during Nabonidus's reign; it seemingly portends a humiliating fall from grace for the king that can only really pertain to Nabonidus (in hindsight). The king will be cast out, not to be buried with his kin, like other kings before him (Isa 14:19) and this is true, as there is an understanding that Nabonidus is exiled after the Persian invasion. Isaiah 14 reads like a paraphrase of the VA, the tabloid version of Babylonian history!

With Zaphon the heavenly, mountainous abode of the divine "assembly," the vitriolic abhorrence of everything Babylon-related might well have sparked the concept of Zion, i.e., as the antithesis of Zaphon, yet mirroring its familiar and adaptable ideology.

Isa 5:1–7 has similar vocabulary and imagery to the Song, e.g., "sing to my beloved," "my beloved had a vineyard," the protective "hedge" around the vineyard, etc.—a familiar source for both or one influencing the other?

4. A WOMB LOCKED

This is a rather more complicated chapter of the Song, with many details that need explaining; it tells a vitally important story, however, upon which a full appreciation of the Song is dependent. Nitocris is described in exotic and sometimes baffling terms but each layer of imagery and allusion builds upon the same theme, i.e., she is pregnant.

GOAT HAIR (4:1)

In Sumerian/Akkadian literature, saying something is beautiful is akin to saying it is blessed, or even divine. The majority of instances pertain to the beauty of deities, though some refer to kings and temples (which are, by default, sacred). The king, therefore, speaks of Nitocris as though she were his own, private goddess, and this becomes ever more apparent as the Song continues. He starts with her eyes, those pools of intoxication behind her veil, emulating the doves that ominously "hide" in the "clefts of the rocks." Is this coyness or deception? Ishtar's symbolic bird is the dove; the Song, alluding to the darting and flapping of doves, echoes this, said of Inanna: "Be it known that you have flashing eyes!" (*ETCSL t.4.07.2*, §122–138).

Nitocris's hair is said to be like a flock of black goats descending a mountain. Most interpreters suggest this is to highlight her long black hair falling over her back and/or shoulders. Ishtar's hair is described as: "Maiden, glossy mane, lovely beauty ... mane of the ibex ..." (*ETCSL t.4.08*.18, §A1–8). The Hebrew term for "hair" here, however, is *sear,* which is often used to represent a *male* goat with dense, *coarse* hair; this stems from *sa'ar*, to sweep, or whirl away (as tossed about in a storm). The allusion, therefore, could be understood as pertaining to Nitocris's *pubic* hair, which may seem odd, but subliminal symbolism is one of the author's greatest skills, so I ask that you bear with me.

The name of the mountainous land, Gilead, means Perpetual Fountain. Depending on the source, the etymology of the name is derived from either the verb *galal* (Abarim), suggesting whirling, reiterating *sear/sa'ar* and thus accentuating the curly nature of the pubic hair; or the verb *gala*, to expose, or quarrel (*Strong's*). The former, discussed at some length on the Abarim

93

website, offers further intriguing and relevant details, e.g., the related noun *gal* means heap or pile, and *gulla* means bowl, basin, or spring; both concepts feature in the description of the woman's reproductive physiology in Song 7, *in* the context of pregnancy. The etymology of Gilead is, in part, based on an assumed root, *'dd* (Abarim); only one derivative of this root remains in the HB, i.e., the feminine noun *ed*, which appears in Isa 64:6 as "our righteous deeds are like a *filthy cloth*." The word *ed* means menstruation, from the idea of being *ritually* unclean. Other Hebrew words related to the etymology of Gilead includes the verb *yaad*, to appoint, designate, e.g., to set a regular time for something (suggesting repetition). The Perpetual Fountain can therefore suggest a womb/pudendum (heap/mound) that repeatedly bleeds. Thus, Gilead becomes a symbol of menstruation (which is why the women in the television adaptation of Margaret Atwood's *The Handmaid's Tale*, who live in a place called Gilead, wear red cloaks; they are the menstruating, fertile ones).

Furthermore, the image of Gilead in Song 4:1 is one of a mountain (i.e., *har*; the symbolism of the mountain as womb is discussed later), forming an inclusio with the imagery of 4:6, where the king's focus rests, i.e., Nitocris's mound that perpetually bleeds, i.e., her pubic area. Curly black hair upon such a mound may evoke images of many black goats upon a mountain.

VEIL

Nitocris had said from the start that she did not want to be seen merely as yet another camp follower, i.e., "one who is *veiled* beside the flocks of [the king's] companions" (1:7); the word employed there is *atah*, to wrap/envelop oneself. In 4:1 the word for "veil" changes to *tsammah*; it is no longer the garment of the women mourning for Tammuz, it is, in the more mundane narrative of the Song, the sign that Nitocris is now a wife (rather than bride). We know that the marriage has taken place (in Song 3), through the allusions to the *hieros gamos* but now we see the new queen dressed to suit her station.

The word *tsammah* (veil) is used only once elsewhere in the HB, i.e., Isa 47:2. The post-Babylon generation is recounting the anger of God against his people and the giving up of Israel into the hands of their oppressors. The context is one of a foreign woman (i.e., the personification of Chaldea) who is proud and arrogant, who sees herself as majestic and powerful, who makes self-assured claims regarding her position, and who has practised sorcery from her youth. In an act of revenge, she is humiliated, forced to the ground, and exposed, and her veil and robe are stripped from her. This is *precisely* Nitocris's perceived nature *and* what will happen to her in Song 5. The intended emphasis, therefore, serves as foreshadowing.

> *...remove your veil, strip off your robe ... your shame shall be seen.*
> *...in spite of your many sorceries and the great power of your enchantments.*
>
> Isa 47:2, 9

SPEECH AND BEREAVEMENT (4:2)

The word for "teeth" is *shen*, from *shanan*, meaning prick, sharp, point; it can also mean to teach diligently, *to inculcate*, which makes it an intended pun relating to Nitocris's idolatrous ways and tutelage. The emphasis on her speech, her teaching, is directly linked to her role as priestess. In *heka*, the magic of ancient Egypt, perhaps the most potent of the skills, or attributes, of the magician (i.e., priest) is the articulation of spells, i.e., words. A pharaoh (who is also a priest) for instance, is described as "Effective/magical of spells, good of utterance, who pacifies the gods with his words."[1] There is also an echo of Inanna, whose command is absolute. Speaking to Utu, she says: "... my twin, I want to tell you something—pay attention to my speech" (*ETCSL t.1.3.5*, §B7–9).

The reference to the teeth also presents a foreshadowing of what is to come, i.e., Nitocris's imminent miscarriage. The metaphor is given the context of sheep-shearing, which seems rather odd for teeth, until you know what happens in the next few chapters of the Song. The author is putting the truth of what is *yet* to happen on the king's lips; in his ignorance, and his zeal in procuring a child, he sees only this young, nubile, seemingly healthy woman as the epitome of womanhood, ripe for impregnating. His words are prophetic and ironic, and not for the last time, for they hint at bereavement, and of *two* offspring.

The context of the sheep-shearing is discussed again in the analysis of 6:6.

THE CRIMSON THREAD (4:3A)

While it is not known whether Near Eastern women used any form of colouring on their (mouth) lips, the Egyptians did. Hebrew women (in polite society) certainly would not have done; in fact, they did not wear any red at all, due to its sexual (i.e., Ishtar) associations, as exemplified in Jer 4:30. The Aramaic Targum of the Song equates the Song's "crimson thread" with sin.

The noun *saphah* is used to denote the lips of the mouth but it can also mean speech or language, and this is fitting, given how Nitocris's words are so potent in the Song. Her teeth, mouth, and lips, together evoke the concept of provocative speech. Her speech is seductive, entrancing, bewitching; a "mellifluous mouth ... makes speech persuasive" (*ETCSL t.3.3.09*, §1–9).

---

[1] Robert Kreich Ritner, *The Mechanics of Ancient Egyptian Magical Practice*, ed. Thomas A. Holland, SAOC 54 (Chicago: University of Chicago, 1993), 40–9.

In the Hebrew tradition,

> …the heavenly Bath-kol … was called the 'daughter of the voice', and the voice which was called from the blackness was said to originate during a female's puberty. The womb was resultantly associated with the voice (the *qoul* or *call*), and Star Fire [the Elixir Rubeus] was said to be the oracular 'word of the womb', with the womb itself being the utterer or *uterus*."[2]

Thus, Nitocris, the Elixir blood-womb, is inherently a seer, which plays back into the two scenes in the Song where she is conducting remote viewing (3:1; 5:2).

Inanna uses the word "lips" to denote her labia: "May the lips, my labia, be lips of honey."[3] The mouth and the genitals are often used together in Sumerian poetry: "Like her mouth her genitals are sweet … (*ETCSL t.2.4.4.1*, §19–27), and this has a bearing on the analysis of Song 4:13, where the Mesopotamian concept of physiology comes into play. Similarly, in ancient Egyptian hieroglyphs there is a curved arrow-shaped symbol that "represents liquid issuing from lips"; this symbol is a constituent in the glyph for menstruation.[4]

Nitocris's lips, i.e., the lips of her mouth, are a hue of red, for she is an Egyptian, to whom the practice of staining the lips is familiar, but there is a double entendre intended, suggesting she is now at the peak of her innate (dangerous) sexual energy; she is menstruating. Ribbons/cords/threads—from the Egyptian god Min, to Inanna's fencepost symbol, to Rahab's rope signal—relate, symbolically, to sexual energy, blood energy. To the Jewish audience, she should be off limits to the king but once again, just like Samson and Ashmedai, the blood of the woman at the height of her femininity proves irresistible.

It was commonly believed that conception was most likely just after a woman's period because the uterus remains open for a time. It was also

---

[2] Laurence Gardner, *Genesis of the Grail Kings* (London: Bantom Books, 2000), 180.

[3] Benjamin R. Foster, *From Distant Days: Myths, Tales, and Poetry of Ancient Mesopotamia* (Bethesda: CDL Press, 1995), 350.

[4] Paula Veiga, "To Prevent, Treat and Cure Love in Ancient Egypt. Aspects of Sexual Medicine and Practice in Ancient Egypt," *Proceedings of the II International Congress for Young Egyptologists*, Lisboa, November 2009 (Centro de História, Faculdade de Letras da Universidade de Lisboa, 2010): 453–465, here 459 and note 41. See also Ulrike Steinert, "Concepts of the Female Body in Mesopotamian Gynecological Texts," in *The Comparable Body: Analogy and Metaphor in Ancient Mesopotamian, Egyptian, and Greco-Roman Medicine*, by John Z. Wee (Leiden: Brill, 2017), 275–357, here 291.

held that the woman's menstrual blood mixed with the man's semen to create a child, so there is no conflict in suggesting these verses speak of pregnancy *and* menstruation. Nitocris's menstruation is highlighted in order to indicate she is a normal, healthy woman at the time of conception; this has a bearing on the repeated verses in Song 6:5–7.

SLUR

Nitocris's mouth is mentioned in the next phrase, using the noun *midbar*, which was used in Song 3:6 to suggest a wilderness. It also represents a red/brown colour, i.e., the colour of menstrual blood. If there is a dual meaning to "crimson cord" and "lips," "mouth" may also have more than one meaning, i.e., the lips are the labia, the mouth is the vagina (i.e., the "mouth of the womb"). We see this connection even more directly in Song 7. Nabonidus, then, is praising Nitocris's sexual perfection, i.e., her (realised) potential for reproduction.

I further suggest, however, that the noun *midbar* is used here as a pun to form another of the author's vengeful slurs, this time alluding to the original "wilderness" use in 3:6. Much like the opening declaration between the lines of Song 1:3, where the king's name is cursed with beautiful words (his name is "empty"), the author is here saying to Nitocris, in effect: "Your vagina/womb is a wilderness." This is a profound insult and anticipates the action in the subsequent verses of Song 4.

CHEEKS, TEMPLES (4:3B)

There are two ways of looking at this verse; either you accept the NRSV translation as cheeks, or you go with the HB version, i.e., temples.

The red pomegranate has long been a symbol of sexuality and appears in relation to Inanna on a vase from Uruk (c. 3100 BCE). The pomegranate has an ancient history of being used as an aphrodisiac but also as a prophylactic, used as such by the Greek Persephone, who *chose* not to become a mother. The insinuation may be that Nitocris's cheeks are flushed due to some degree of sexual behaviour, i.e., to demonstrate her married and thus sexually-active status.

One of the first signs of pregnancy for many women, however, is the sudden appearance of a red/spotty face. While one version of this hormonal change is deemed a healthy pregnancy glow and makes a woman seem flushed with colour quite uniformly, there is another, more common, that causes acne. The multiple red seeds within the halved (and rounded) pomegranate would aptly represent such a condition. (This could be further support for a female author who would probably have experienced this herself.)

The other option is to understand the noun *raqqah* as a person's temple; this is its translation in *Strong's* and its only other appearance in the HB is in Judg 4:21, where the indomitable Jael kills the enemy soldier Sisera by hammering a tent-peg through his temple. The pomegranate here in the Song evokes Sisera's temples reddened by his spilt blood. Linked to this is the word *pelach,* meaning cleavage (translated as "halves"), from the verb *palach,* to cleave, pierce through, split open, etc.; this is further support for the allusion to Jael hammering the tent-peg into Sisera's temple (splitting his head open).

The previous lines of the Song refer to Nitocris's hair resembling goats; the word used for goat is *ez,* which stems from *azaz,* meaning to be stout/strong, to harden, to prevail, etc. This sounds like Jael's character but what is more, her name in Hebrew is the masculine noun *ya'al,* which indicates a mountain-goat (or ibex, i.e., one of Ishtar's animals).

Jael lures the Canaanite general/king into her tent, where she tends to him, relaxes (drugs?) him, and then murders him. This is a woman of foreign extraction, employed in the service of Israel, so she is praised and made an honorary Israelite but she is, nonetheless, a foreign woman, whose name suggests the stalwart constitution of wild goats, who seduces a ruler, only to overwhelm him when he is in a weakened state. Early audiences would begin to realise the pattern by now; things are not going to go well for Nabonidus!

Though Nitocris will not physically murder the king, she does use every trick in her repertoire to 'ensnare' Nabonidus while he is intoxicated (by her). She has the resolution, the intensity of Jael, and the allusion to an almost masculine sense of mission is intentional, evoking the androgynous, war-like Ishtar.

Finally, the veil is mentioned a second time, reminding us that all this clandestine talk of pregnancy is done so in the context of marriage.

NECKLACE (4:4)

For Ishtar, the neck is one of her most powerful body-parts, for this is where she wears the all-important necklaces. Preparing to enter the underworld, she puts lapis-lazuli beads around her neck as part of her royal regalia (*ETCSL t.1.4.1,* §14–19), which represents her magical prowess; she also wears the necklace of prostitution (*ETCSL t.4.07.4,* §109–15).

Ishtar is referred to as the "tower among great rulers,"[5] and weapons and shields are displayed on towers in war (*ETCSL t.2.4.2.b,* §A1–4; *t.4.27.04,* §7–13). She is known for her lust for battle, for blood, for victories; she "soaks her mace / in blood and gore / smashes heads ... / all

---

[5] Betty De Shong Meador, *Inanna: Lady of Largest Heart: Poems of the Sumerian High Priestess Enheduanna* (University of Texas Press, 2000), 117.

day."[6] She is known for her many lovers, all of whom perish or go mad. The towering neck of the goddess, then, metaphorically adorned with the trophies of her conquests (warriors in a battle for her love), just as kings placed their trophies on the walls of their palaces (1 Kgs 10:15–17), seems an apt interpretation of the shields in the Song, hanging on the tower.

Of all the flattery spouting from the lips of Nabonidus, this is the second most damning, for the king identifies the Egyptian idolater with the most sacred concept known to the Israelites (especially those returning from Babylon), besides that of Yahweh (and yes, he does go that far, too), i.e., the heritage of the house of David.[7] He is obscuring the line between true Israelite and alien, between captor and captive, between king and kingdom.

Nitocris, now in possession of those necklaces and trinkets with which the king had originally planned to subdue, tame, or control her (i.e., the bridle and the ornaments of Song 1), is now using them to her own advantage. One stratagem of ancient warfare is to effectively make an opponent *blind*, either by forcing them to march into the sun, or by reflecting light off the shields to stop them in their tracks; the allusion is a sinister one. The incapacitated king loses his power to the queen, who wears his defeat like a trophy; she is bedazzling, blinding to him. In fact, by Song 4:9, Nabonidus himself acknowledges that the shimmering jewels of her necklace have "ravished" him, thus reiterating her overall hypnotic effect.

We are again reminded of Nitocris's Egyptian heritage, for the necklace worn by ancient Egyptian royalty is called a *wesekh* collar, made of many small beads in horizontal rows, i.e., "built in courses." There is often a counterpoise that hangs down the back, called a *mankhet*, which means "that which lives," i.e., has energy. This is reminiscent of the energy-imbued *seshed* band/ribbon/cord hanging down Min's back (yet again). As an Egyptian princess, Nitocris would certainly have these to wear for special occasions. Similarly, Hathor's *menet*-necklace is profoundly significant, cultically; it possesses great sexual energy and is associated with fertility and the magical transference of power.

SEX WHILST PREGNANT (4:5–7)

The obvious repetition of "until the shadows flee," first heard in 2:16–17, is significant because in the earlier instance, it was the young bride urging the king to forgo his duties and remain with her (as in the tale about Bathya

---

[6] Meador, 120.

[7] There is a possible significance in the fact that "tower of David" can also be understood as "ziggurat of the beloved," which then links into the stories of Solomon and his amassed treasures ("shields"), his seven-staged, adorned throne, and his pseudonym, Jedidiah.

fooling Solomon with jewels sewn to the canopy), to enjoy the pleasures of her "cleft mountains" (breasts). Nabonidus, blindly repeating his mistress's speech, reveals that he is her student, but also that he is steadily descending into her 'snare', from which there is only a descent into Sheol (Prov 7:27). He is becoming more and more like the doomed Tammuz.

BREASTS AND WAR

The word for "gazelle," *tsebiyyah*, is the feminine of *tsbiy*, so this is obviously a female animal; *tsbiy*, however, stems from *tsabah*, which has meanings of to swell, to fight, become turgid and, most interestingly, to array an army against. Here is a beautiful woman, arrayed in daunting, powerful jewels (that can serve as weapons, as we soon see), and with breasts that evoke the image of battle. It is as if she is poised, ready for war. Before Ishtar descends into the underworld, she prepares herself for battle, gathering her powers and placing "twin egg-shaped beads on her breast" (*ETCSL t.1.4.1*, §20–5).

The word for "fawn" is *opher*, which refers to a dusty colour (used only in the Song); this stems from *aphar*, to throw dust. We have encountered dust in the context of the "litter of Solomon" on the horizon, coming back from Egypt. It is from that moment the nature of the Song becomes more bellicose, with the goddess' masculine/warlike nature becoming increasingly noticeable. Ishtar's fury is renowned and the imagery of dust in her wake is relatively common: "He gave me the stormwind and he gave me the dust cloud (*ETCSL t.4.07.6*, §4–13).

The twins are *male* here, and by referring to them as fawns, we can assume that these male twins are young, i.e., little. Strangely, even this has a link to Ishtar in her warlike mode. In the constellation known by the Babylonians as the Great Twins, (Gemini), lies a pair of lesser twinned stars, known as the Little Twins; both were thought to be omens of war. An omen pertaining to the Little Twins reads: "If Venus—the Little Twins stand toward her front: the land will altogether p[erish]."[8] With the "young/little twins" most definitely on Venus's (Ishtar's, therefore Nitocris's) "front," this is certainly intended as a bad sign, for it links to the "bereaved" (i.e., "perish") reference in the context of "twins" in 4:2.

Feeding "among the lilies" (i.e., lotuses) is a euphemism for sex, as mentioned earlier. There is an ancient Egyptian motif, however, referred to as the "nursing gazelle," wherein a fawn is shown suckling its mother while she eats lotus plants. The juxtaposition of the gazelle and a marshland is counter-intuitive, for gazelles are not indigenous to swampy areas; the motif,

---

[8] David Edwin Pingree and Erica Reiner, *Babylonian Planetary Omens* (Netherlands: Undena Publications, 1975), 127.

therefore, is deemed by scholars to refer to birth/nursing.[9] Nitocris's breasts are, it seems, praised as being perfect for nursing.

MOUNTAIN AND HILL
Mountains and hills are symbolic of a woman's reproductive organs, i.e., pudendum and/or womb (often signified by the same word in Mesopotamian texts). In this particular context, the king says he will "hasten to" these body parts, so the womb does not seem apt (why would he rush to her belly?). He hastens to her genitals. The "mountain of myrrh" is thus the site of bleeding (pubic mound and vulva), and the "hill of frankincense" probably her clitoris.

FERTILITY IDOL 1
Looking at this entire scenario and the body descriptions, we see Nabonidus attempting to learn the ways of his foreign wife's cultic practices, just as we are told of Solomon in the Talmud (Shabbath 56.2; 1 Kgs 11:7–8). He has already shown that he is repeating her words, and now he is emulating the construction of an idol; this is the first of three such objects in the Song. He begins with the head (eyes, hair, teeth, lips, etc.), moves down to the neck, and then to the breasts. At this point, he seems to get side-tracked; suddenly the simple delights of her features fall victim to the more visceral delights of her sexual body-parts. She is left with no legs, no feet; she is purely a sexual object. Though already pregnant, Nitocris still proves irresistible and must succumb to the king's advances; this fleeting allusion to their sexual union will prove highly significant. There is archaeological evidence indicating that Egyptian fertility idols *were* often made with the legs/feet omitted because it was "thought important to include only the parts of the body needed for the conception and rearing of children."[10]

The king's idol has seven stages, i.e., seven "Your ..." statements. The Hebrew gematria of seven is significant; the seventh Hebrew letter is *zayin*, which means crown, and thus relates symbolically to the king but also to Nitocris, who is made Queen in Song 4:8. Other terms that have the same gematria (seven) include: "to lose oneself," "to be undone," and "to bring to ruin."[11] There is also a link to the Seven Hathors, a collection of spirits

---

[9] Åsa Strandberg, *The Gazelle in Ancient Egyptian Art: Image and Meaning*, Uppsala Studies in Egyptology 6, (Uppsala University: Department of Archaeology and Ancient History, 2009), 148–52, https://www.diva-portal.org/smash/get/diva2:232265/ FULLTEXT01.pdf.

[10] Geraldine Pinch *Egyptian Mythology* (Oxford: Oxford University Press, 2004), 126.

[11] Gematria phrases throughout this analysis are from Bill Heidrick, "Hebrew Gematria," http://www.billheidrick.com/works/hgemat.htm.

invoked in erotic spells and most often appearing in connection with women giving birth.

NO FLAW?

The king sees his lover as though she were perfect. He does not see the "flaw" in his wife that will lead him down a daunting and dangerous path. It is an allusion to the descent to come and a clear sign of the king's relative weakness (or figurative blindness). Beauty and apparent perfection are the perfect disguise for the "harlot," the wayward woman up to no good; this is how the early Jews would have seen it. The author of the Song places on the king's lips a declaration that is, itself, flawed, ironic, perhaps even sarcastic. Nitocris's flaw, however, is not exposed immediately; it is the cumulative effect of her behaviour and her choices.

Nitocris is called "beautiful" (*yapheh*) many times in the Song (more often translated as "fair"). In the Egyptian context, Hathor is the goddess of beauty and is *called* The Beautiful One; in her temple at Dendera she is referred to as "the perfect sister of Osiris." Ishtar, especially as Nanaya, is also called "the beautiful one."

The idea of physical perfection is one of the basic tenets of the Israelite priesthood, i.e., Lev 21:17–23 describes how no one with certain physical blemishes can serve as a priest or enter a sacred space. The same word, *mum* (blemish), is used in both Leviticus 21 and here, in Song 4:7. The Mesopotamians and the Egyptians had similar physical purity concerns for those who entered or served in sacred spaces, and we must remember that Nitocris was First Prophet of Amun-Re before marrying Nabonidus; she has always been expected to be the "perfect" mother of the new *entu*, so she has to be (deemed) flawless.

One could interpret this seven-tiered construct of the king's idol as depicting Nitocris *as* a temple, i.e., a ziggurat; from the perspective of her potentially becoming pregnant with the *entu*, this makes her entire body a temple of Life and thus worthy of worship (as mentioned earlier, Mesopotamian temples symbolically mirror the reproductive anatomy of the female body): an Egyptian funerary text describes the temple at Karnak as "a beautiful woman, her hair braided and falling upon her beautiful breasts in the Hathoric ideal," anticipating the sexual union with the deity.[12]

> *The temple towered upwards in full grandeur,*
> *unparalleled in fearsomeness and radiance.*
> *ETCSL t.2.1.7, §1182–1202*

---

[12] John Coleman Darnell, "Hathor Returns to Medamûd," *Studien zur Altägyptischen Kultur* 22 (1995): 47–94, here 60–2.

With no stabilizing base, however (i.e., the idol has no feet), the temple is weakened, it is a folly, doomed to fail, so this seemingly positive praise turns out to be another portent of doom, which is realised shortly.

ILLICIT WORSHIP

Mountains and hills have another significance; they represent the "high places" of illicit worship, such as in Isa 65:7 and Hos 4:3. Thus, the king, in hastening to the altar of Nitocris's sexuality, reveals his 'idolatry'; he is all but worshipping at *her* high places. Recalling the link to Mount Gerizim and the sacrificial connotations of her inviting him to revel in her breasts (Song 2:17), one must appreciate how powerful this ominous symbolism is. The sense of doom is augmented by the inclusion of frankincense and myrrh, mentioned in 3:6, in the context of sacrifice and looming danger ("death").

DEIFICATION (4:8)

Nabonidus is beside himself with joy that Nitocris is pregnant and, as promised in the treaty with her father, makes Nitocris Queen, i.e., *primary* Queen. This is what she has wanted all along but it has come at a cost, for she now has to give up her sacred duty to the Elixir Rubeus. Nabonidus is not concerned with this, as yet. He sees the portended *entu* within his grasp, which means the gods have looked favourably upon him and his plan.

GODS AND DEMI-GODS

Pope asserts that "a number of critics have found [Song 4:8] incomprehensible and utterly disconcerting," and that it only really makes sense if we see the woman as the "goddess, Lady of the Steppe, Mountain Mother, and Mistress of the Beasts."[13]

Ishtar is identified with mountains. She lives there: "The great queen of heaven ... dwelling on the peaks of the bright mountains ..." (*ETCSL t.1.8.2.3*, §227–235). She learns about sex up a mountain: "... let me ride with you ... to the mountains of cedars .... I am unfamiliar with sexual intercourse ..." (*ETCSL t.4.32.f*, §35–8).

Although the common translation is "come with me *from* Lebanon," Pope suggests the "rendering '*to* Lebanon' is possible but there is no clear warrant here to choose that sense";[14] but what if there were? If we read the male voice as saying, "Come with me *to* Lebanon. / Look from the peak ...," so much more can be gleaned. Song 4:8 is not just about making Nitocris Queen; it is also about making Nabonidus a god.

---

[13] Marvin H. Pope, *Song of Songs: A New Translation with Introduction and Commentary* (New York: Doubleday, 1977), 476–7.

[14] Pope, 474.

LEBANON

There are two male figures who are associated with Lebanon: Tammuz (as the Phoenician Adonis) and Gilgamesh. Adonis is born, lives, and dies in Lebanon; Gilgamesh and his friend Enkidu go to Lebanon to kill the guardian of the cedar forest, Humbaba. Mourning the demise of Enkidu, Gilgamesh goes on a spiritual sojourn to this netherworld, in search of an understanding of death. The mountains of Lebanon, then, despite being known as the dwelling place of gods, are also the netherworld, i.e., the land of death.

Lebanon lay in the heart of Phoenician territory and was land once belonging to King Hiram of Tyre. Just below the great River Euphrates, the boundary came to represent the 'us-and-them' distinction, when lands acquired there were lost and Damascus became an enemy. The land "beyond the river" was always a little mysterious, mistrusted; after all, both Assyria and Babylon lay in this general direction, i.e., both had held Israel captive. In just about all the early references to Lebanon, the area is depicted only in terms of its amazing cedar forests but in the Song, and especially in Isaiah (which I consider contemporaneous), we begin to see a change.

The cedars of Lebanon (along with the "oaks of Bashan") become, in Isaiah, the representative of all who are "proud and lofty" (Isa 2:12) and in need of humbling, a now familiar theme. The passage goes on to make reference to the worship of idols, to the hiding of the ungodly in the "caverns of the rocks and the clefts in the crags" (2:21). By Isa 10:34, Lebanon's symbolic "majestic trees" are fated to be hacked down, brought low. By 33:9, it is a land overcome by its own iniquities. Jeremiah continues on this theme, with the prophet warning of impending doom for Lebanon's ungodly ways (Jer 22:20–23).

The mountainous regions mentioned here in 4:8 also prove fascinating. Just as in the Epic of Gilgamesh, which has the delineation of heaven, earth, and underworld, so here, three distinct realms are named: Amana, Senir, and Hermon.

AMANA

Indirectly referred to in 2 Kgs 5:12, Amana is seen as the source of the Abana/Amana River; the name is roughly translated as "a covenant." The verb *aman* (to establish, confirm, support) most often alludes to the constancy or continuity of a person's name (1 Chr 17:24), or *his house or dynasty* (1 Sam 2:35).

In the treaty between Pharaoh Rameses II and the Hittites, the pharaoh calls himself "Rea-mashesha mai Amana, the great king, the king of the land of Egypt"; Pritchard notes that this title is "Egyptian in cuneiform characters meaning 'Ramses beloved of Amon'."[15] Thus, the Babylonian name Amana equates to Amon/Amun. Nitocris is First Prophet of Amun-Re. She is established, confirmed, supported as Queen, by Nabonidus, who makes a treaty, a covenant, with Ahmose III, the king of the land of Egypt.

Perhaps even more intriguingly, *aman* is sometimes used in the sense of caring for or *carrying a child* (Num 11:12, Ruth 4:16, 2 Kgs 10:1). This echoes the establishment of a *house/dynasty* (1 Sam 2:35).

Nabonidus finds himself in the Amanus Mountains in his third year, i.e., the year he leaves Babylon (Nab Chr 1.11–22). He is said to have cut huge swathes of cedar from the mountains of Lebanon and Amanus (just like Gilgamesh does), sending 1050 massive tree trunks back to Babylon, to be used in the rebuilding of the Ebabbar temple in Sippar.[16]

SENIR AND HERMON

Senir and Hermon represent the same place. Senir is the Amorite name, while Hermon is the accepted Hebrew name. So why use both? My theory is that the author of the Song wishes to emphasise the number three (Amana, Senir, Hermon), i.e., to emulate the three mountainous regions in Gilgamesh's story, and to highlight the fact that Mount Hermon has three peaks.

The word *shenir/senir* means to be pointed, which is apt for a mountain peak. Here, it could also be a play on *shen*, which designated Nitocris's teeth; from *shanan*, meaning to sharpen. Recall that *shen* also means to teach diligently, or inculcate. This was seen in terms of Nitocris's voice, her chanting, her 'idolatry', and her teaching Nabonidus the chants to her idols, i.e., it implies a high place (for worship).

Hermon is *chermon* in Hebrew, meaning abrupt, stemming from *charam*, to seclude, e.g., via banishment, to devote, e.g., to religious purposes, to make accursed, to consecrate. Mount Hermon is renowned for being the tallest of the Canaanite high places (Judg 3:3; 1 Chr 5:23); one of its three peaks is called Baal-Hermon, the sacred mountain of Baal and his consort Ashtoreth, i.e., Ishtar.

In terms of Nabonidus and Nitocris, the insinuation is that the king, steadily building his new kingdom in Arabia, gradually setting things up in expectation of a daughter and thus the new priestly 'dynasty', seems to be proving himself just as the VA depicts him. He is, according to the author of the Song, attempting to make himself a god, even if only a demi-god, like Gilgamesh and Tammuz. He is seen to be setting himself up on the sacred

---

[15] J. B. Pritchard, *Ancient Near Eastern Texts Relating to the Old Testament with Supplement* (United States: Princeton University Press, 2016), 202 note 1.
[16] Josette Elayi, *The History of Phoenicia* (United States: Lockwood Press, 2018), 211.

mountain, i.e., as Baal, Lord of the mountain, with Nitocris as Lady of the mountain. Hand in hand they can look down at the world below, self-deified, self-assured.

Just as Nabonidus is accused, in a roundabout way, of attempting to steal the Tablet of Destinies from Enlil (for which his penance is banishment), so he is accused of the next step, i.e., usurping the throne of the "Great Mountain" Enlil (*ETCSL t.1.1.3*, §1–16); that is, apotheosis. Compare this: "My bride, come forth … I shall bring you to the house of my god. I shall get you to lie down before my god and … you shall sit with me in my god's seat of honour!" (*ETCSL t.4.08.29*, §C9–13). The context of this quotation is the post-marriage transfer of the bride Ishtar, to Tammuz's house. He affirms: "I have not carried you off to be my slave girl!" and reassures her that she will have everything she wants and more than even his own mother and sister. In other words, he makes her his Queen and gives her the seat of honour next to him, before the gods.

> *Upon a high and lofty mountain you have set your bed,*
> *and there you went up to offer sacrifice.*
> Isa 57:7

This reminds us of the worry Ahmose has, according to Herodotus (*Hist.* 3.1–3), concerning the possible fate of his daughter, should she be sent to marry the foreign king. Nabonidus, however, seems to provide everything for Nitocris, to ensure he honours her status and his side of the treaty; in return for conceiving, she is given supremacy at court.

The allusions to Adonis-Tammuz and Gilgamesh, however, remind us that Nabonidus is in a very precarious situation. He is rapidly becoming Nitocris's ensnared gazelle and his fate is becoming more and more akin to that of the two heroes. The tension builds for the audience who, in the Song's earliest rendition, would have been well aware of the meaning of this verse, both mythologically and historically—it is only we, literally thousands of years later and far removed, who struggle!

Nabonidus figuratively takes his new Queen, his *pregnant* queen, up to the peaks of the mountains, the home of the gods, to the high places. While he is demonstrating his desire to learn all he can about his Egyptian bride's religion, Nabonidus is not just looking down at his kingdom from on high, he is unwittingly gazing into the abyss, the looming underworld. The reference to Lebanon and its mountain peaks, therefore, is an allusion to the ultimate fate of Nabonidus, hinted at throughout the Song, i.e., to follow both Adonis-Tammuz and Gilgamesh to the land of no return, unless he changes his ways.

QUEEN ISHTAR

Queen Nitocris ascends the mountains as her avatar, Ishtar. The early Mesopotamian audiences of the Song may not relate to the Egyptian symbolism here but they would comprehend that Nitocris is being deified alongside her "beloved." They would know that Ishtar's iconic beasts include both lions and leopards: "The mistress, a leopard among the Anuna gods, full of pride" (*ETCSL t.4.07.3*, §73–9); "A leopard of the hills ... (*ETCSL t.4.07.3*, §18–28); "your seat is set upon a lion and a leopard" (*ETCSL t.4.07.4*, §22–36).

ONE EYE, ONE JEWEL (4:9)

The word for "ravished" in this verse is *labab*, which also means, amazingly, to make cakes *and* to be wise (from *labiybah*); it can also mean to 'get a mind', or to encourage (as denominative from *lebab*, inner man, mind, will, heart). Most interpreters suggest this phrase in the Song implies a sense of overwhelming attraction, infatuation, etc., but it can also have a more sinister understanding, for *labab* can *also* mean to stultify. In Gen 31:26, *lebab* is used to convey deception (to steal the mind); in Job 11:12 it denotes the empty mind; and in Job 27:6, one's conscience. The word *labab* is used elsewhere only in 2 Sam 13:8, where it is used twice in a single sentence. The Song uses *labab* twice in short succession, suggesting a potential echo/parallel of 2 Sam 13:8, where we find the second, *virginal* Tamar, i.e., King David's daughter.

The young Tamar is requested by her brother to bake and bring two cakes for him to eat; she does so and is, for her kindness, raped. She is then thrown out onto the street. Tearing her long robe, described by G. Wright as her "sacred robe (of the hierodule of Ishtar),"[17] she places it on her head, i.e., as a veil. Thus, both Tamars are treated erroneously as illicit sexual objects by men who should be protecting them, i.e., Tamar in Genesis has sex with her father-in-law, and Tamar in 2 Samuel, with her brother. I suggest this is why we get the phrase "my sister, my bride" first at *this* particular juncture in the Song, i.e., to point us in the direction of the sister in 2 Samuel's Tamar precedent.[18]

The point is that the virginal Tamar is so obviously *violated*. She physically mourns the loss of her virginity by throwing ashes on her head, and she dons a veil to mark herself as both in mourning and deflowered. She is a broken woman. So, the use of *labab* in the Song strongly suggests

---

[17] G. Wright, "Dumuzi at the Court of David," *Numen*, 28.1 (1981): 54–63.

[18] The identification of sister with bride is common enough in the Bible, e.g., Gen 12:12–13; 20:2; Add Esth 15:9; Tob 5:20; 1 Cor 9:5, and is prolific in Near Eastern texts.

Nabonidus is feeling violated in some way. Nitocris has proven to be indomitable, unrelenting, persuasive, and seemingly omnipresent. He is breaking down, becoming confused, weakening, but at the same time, he is becoming angry with her (and this is played out soon).[19] His mind is ravaged; she has overstepped the line and is gradually overtaking what little is left of his strength and sense.

The king is "ravished" (stultified) not by "one glance" of the woman's eyes but by *"one* eye" and the numeral here is *masculine*. Pope argues that despite many attempts to explain this away, it still seems a very odd thing to say, unless we are talking about a goddess; he cites figurines of Ishtar, found at Tell Brak in Syria, which have multiple eyes.[20] An ancient eye god did exist and was later assimilated into the Babylonian god Ea but the eye iconography gradually disappeared; no image of a one-eyed deity, however, has ever been found. There is, I suggest an alternative understanding of this phrase that might fit the analysis of the Song so far.

One consideration, for instance, is the most ancient and prevalent form of occult magnetism, i.e., the Evil Eye, the Art of Fascination, or Binding by the Look. Seen as powerful energy emanating from the eye of the one with intent, the Evil Eye seems to possess its target, making him/her subject to the evil intentions of the one who looks. Nitocris, however, has not displayed any animosity toward Nabonidus, so this does not seem the best interpretation. There is a far more apt understanding that brings Nitocris's Egyptian heritage into play, especially her role as the First Prophet of Amun-Re.

EYE OF RE

In Egyptian mythology there are two well-known "eyes", i.e., the Eye of Horus and the Eye of Re. They are polar opposites in nature. The Eye of Horus came first, historically, and represents the moon and its phases. During a battle, Horus loses his left eye but Thoth magically heals it; the various stages of injury and healing echo the moon's waxing and waning. It becomes a magical talisman of protection. The Eye of Re is another matter.

Re loses his children, so he sends out his right eye in search of them. This eye is personified (predominantly) by Hathor. There are various twists to the myth but basically, Hathor, as the Eye of Re, travels the land in search of the missing children; she ends up killing many people when she takes on the form of a lioness, her avatar, Sekhmet, who is impetuous, dangerous, warlike. Eventually, Re calls her home and she is greeted with much

---

[19] Pope (479) relates that some scholars have argued for the term *laban* to be identified with the Akkadian *labābu*, which conveys a sense of "rage" and "insanity" in a sexual context.

[20] Pope, 481. See images of these figurines on 456.

partying, drinking, etc., and becomes her kindly, mothering Hathor-self again. The Eye of Re thus becomes identified with rage, wrath, anger, bloodlust, etc., and is often depicted with a red pupil to reflect the heat/flame of its passions.

The Eye of Re is terrifying; it is the wrath of the gods in a single eye. It represents the power of Egypt itself, for the hieroglyphic sign for Egypt is the eye-sign; Hathor, as The Beautiful One, is likewise represented with an eye-sign. Although Hathor is female, she takes on the masculine warring aspect, as Ishtar does, and she represents the masculine solar deity, which may seem the rationale for the numeral in "one eye" being masculine. However, both the Egyptian and the Hebrew words for "eye" are feminine, so it is the author's use of gender manipulation here in the Song that proves the key to understanding the phrase, i.e., it is deliberately indicating hidden meaning (and what could be more "hidden" than the occult nature of Amun-Re?).

It is highly probable that Nitocris, as First Prophet, wears an amulet of the Eye of Re on her beaded collar; it becomes the "one jewel" that dominates her "necklace" and the one symbol that puts fear into the king's heart. It represents the power of the solar deity, the power of Egypt, i.e., a symbolic antithesis of Nabonidus's Babylonian, lunar-based religion. This allusion serves to foreshadow the significance of Hathor in Song 7, and underscores the element of spiritual battle that has already entered the narrative.

...hidden jewel and sparkling / I spread terror ....[21]

TURNING POINT (4:10–11)

From these verses, the depiction of Nitocris and the tone of the Song undergo a drastic shift. She is no longer the blushing new bride in awe of the mighty king, hoping to keep him happy at arm's length, while still expecting to get her hands on the crown. She is carrying his child and has, therefore, stopped menstruating. There is no Elixir. Nabonidus is not yet fully aware of the profundity of the Elixir Rubeus, so he seems unconcerned; he has what he wants. He repeats Nitocris's words from 1:2 ("Your *dod* is better than wine"); this repetition is something he is *expected* to do as part of his initiate training, as any student would. Back then, however, it was Nitocris attempting to distract the king from penetrative sex, using the ultimate lure of hidden wisdom to protect her blood-rite. Her attempt has been in vain; Nabonidus declares that her *dod*, i.e., her pregnancy, is far more important than the Elixir (the blend of "wine" and "spices").

---

[21] Meador, 97.

HONEY LIPS

When the king mentions her lips, there is deeper meaning. The Hebrew reads "drip/drop as honeycomb." Recall that in discussing Nitocris's (oral) lips, the implied reference was to her seductive speech. The author of the Song alludes to speech again here, for, as Prov 5:3–5 declares, "the lips of a loose/strange woman drip honey, and her speech is smoother than oil ... her feet go down to death (Sheol)."

> *...with words that were softer than oil, but in fact were drawn swords.*
> Ps 55:21

> *...call insight your intimate friend, that [it] may keep you*
> *from the loose woman ... with her smooth words.*
> Prov 7:4–5

This negative perception of Nitocris is augmented by the reference to "honey and milk" being *under her tongue*, for this is a sign of "cursing and deceit and oppression ... mischief and iniquity" (Ps 10:7; Job 20:12). The honey and milk are mentioned below, in terms of their cultic significance but here, they are a clear reversal of Exod 3:8, 17, etc., i.e., the "land of milk and honey" as the Promised Land. It once again reveals Nabonidus (as Solomon, in the Jewish context) to be not in his right senses; his mind is not as it should be, his wisdom affected, his fundamental bond with his kingdom topsy-turvy.

The sensuous nature of dripping honey is a prominent feature of Sumerian cultic hymns and poems pertaining to Inanna, conveying a highly sexual, opulent, luxurious atmosphere: "She chooses that which drips with honey and puts it on her face" (*ETCSL t.4.08.20*, §11–24); "The brother brought you into his house and had you lie down on a bed dripping with honey" (*ETCSL t.4.08.0*, §4–11).

MILK

In Mesopotamian culture, milk is a symbol of the benevolence of the gods and the productivity of the land. It is used as an offering to the gods, as its value is so high to the people: "May the food offerings, wine, and milk that you bring ...." (*ETCSL t.2.5.5.3*, §33–52).

Milk, as a euphemism, is strongly linked to the sexual attraction of Inanna and Dumuzi during their courtship: "... and smeared milk and honey on it. The youth is gentle towards his spouse ..." (*ETCSL t.4.08.23*, §39–44); "He laid his hands on my holy vulva / He smoothed my black boat with cream / He quickened my narrow boat with milk ...."[22] Dumuzi is the master

---

[22] Diane Wolkstein and Samuel Noah Kramer, *Inanna, Queen of Heaven: Her*

of the milk churns: "The plenty of Dumuzi's holy butter churn, whose butter is the butter of all the world …. Its milk is the milk of all the world …" (*ETCSL t.1.8.2.2*, §155–9). Upon his death, the churns are toppled over and no milk flows (*ETCSL t.1.4.3*, §256–60).

Milk can also carry the venom of an angry goddess: "Whoever eats … Inanna's food and milk of death will not last …" (*ETCSL t.4.07.3*, §39–48).

It is also wise to recall that Jael gives Sisera milk (e.g., strong-tasting goat's milk), instead of water, probably to disguise the potion she puts into it, to drug him before piercing his temple (Judg 4:19). The milk itself then becomes a symbol of deceit, for Jael feigned hospitality for nefarious purposes.

AROMATIC OILS

The scent of the queen's garments is likened to that of Lebanon, i.e., cedar oil, the fragrance of the gods, thereby reiterating the deification scene up on the Lebanese mountains. In the discussion of Song 3:6, scent was considered the most important offering to the gods, i.e., *reyach*, the 'odour of soothing'; it therefore suggests *sacrifice*, strengthening the escalating allusions to capture, the cutting up of sacrificial animals upon the mountains, etc., that have already painted a vivid picture of Nabonidus's fate. This theme continues through Song 6.

The term for "oils," *shemen*, is predominantly used to refer to sacerdotal or royal anointing/libation oils, and is a reminder of Song 1:3, where "anointing oils" are mentioned. However, there is a subtle play on words here, for *shemen* stems from *shamen*, which means to grow fat and although this can have the connotation of arrogance (Deut 32:15) or wickedness (Jer 5:28), which would serve as another camouflaged insult, I think it is a further suggestion that Nitocris is pregnant, for instance: "Has she become pregnant without intercourse? Has she become fat without eating?"[23]

MISCARRIAGE (4:12–15)

Many have suggested the idea that "locked" implies the woman of the Song is a virgin, as in Arabic, a woman who loses her virginity is deemed "open." As discussed earlier, however, a woman menstruating (virgin or not) is also considered "open."

Stories and Hymns from Sumer (New York: Harper and Row, 1983), 44.

[23] Sumerian/Babylonian proverb cited by Marten Stol, *Birth in Babylonia and the Bible: Its Mediterranean Setting*, Cuneiform Monographs 14, eds. T. Abusch, et al. (Groningen: Styx Publications, 2000), 1.

The Hebrew text reads, "a garden (en)closed," "a spring shut up," and "a fountain sealed." The first two use the same word for "enclosed/shut up," i.e., the verb *na'al*, and this actually means to furnish with sandals (by association, to enclose or fasten up, etc.). An odd little detail, perhaps, but the subtle sandal allusion here is a precursor to stronger allusion in Song 7:1, i.e., as a reference to miscarriage. In the Talmud, prayers offered up during pregnancy include this one: "Within the first three days a man should pray that the seed should not putrefy; from the third to the fortieth day, he should pray that the child should be a male; from the fortieth day to three months, he should pray that it should not be a sandal ..." (Berakoth 60a). The sandal is "a kind of abortion resembling a flat-shaped fish (*foetus compressus*)."[24] It would seem that the queen's pregnancy will not extend beyond the first trimester.

The phrasing "garden enclosed" is thus understood to be Nitocris's vulva etc., being (officially) off limits. Her "spring shut up" is the cessation of her periods. The "fountain sealed," using *chatham,* to seal up, make an end, stop, implies the resulting lack of the Elixir.

The word for "channel" is *shelach,* literally translated as "plants" in the KJV. Ishtar refers to her own genitals, and those of Tammuz (and Gilgamesh for that matter), in terms of plants, fruit, tree trunks, etc.: "I poured out plants from my womb / I placed plants before him. / ... The plants and herbs in his field are ripe."[25] The word *shelach,* however, also means a missile of attack, e.g., a spear, or perhaps an arrow (befitting Ishtar, who is the divine archer). Nitocris's missile of attack would appear to be her monthly cycle; she will use this weapon to manipulate, capture, and conquer the king.

The Mesopotamians perceived the physiological processes as following direct routes, e.g., from mouth to anus, through "rivers" and "canals." The queen's "channel" is her reproductive "canal," i.e., her birth-canal, or vagina. It is described in terms of a plurality of red pomegranates, and the Hebrew term translated as "orchard" is *pardes,* which describes an enclosed space, usually in order to preserve what is inside, i.e., in this context, the "fruit" (*peri*) of the womb (Gen 30:2). Thus, the "garden enclosed" *suggests* the "fruit" is being protected but this soon becomes a matter of contention.

There are references in ancient Egyptian papyri that preserve "enchantments to prevent 'the flood' ... (i.e., spontaneous abortion) due to its abundant bleeding."[26] The imagery of not just one pomegranate but an

---

[24] Stol, *Birth in Babylonia,* 18, n. 95. See also Niddah 31a.
[25] Wolkstein and Kramer, 40.
[26] Veiga, 461.

orchard of them suggests a "flood" of red "juice" through the queen's "channel." In the ancient incantation texts this "gynaecological haemorrhage" is referred to as "a carnelian river" or "canal."[27]

Nitocris, then, is miscarrying. What should have been protected is not. This idea lies behind the author's slur, "Your vagina/womb is a wilderness." The queen's pregnancy ends in disaster; if it is a natural and regretful incident, why be so callous? I submit it is because the author knows it is induced. An aborted foetus in the first trimester could be a "sandal"; Niddah 31a states that sex during the first three months of pregnancy is a primary cause for a "sandal" miscarriage. Therefore, it seems to be suggested that Nitocris has allowed the king to have intercourse with her, i.e., she has failed to protect the "fruit" of her womb. This union seems to be alluded to in Song 4:6, where Nabonidus cuts short his praise of the pregnant Nitocris, to "hasten" to her nether regions.

The phrase "choicest fruits" is, in the HB, *megedim peri*, or precious thing/fruit; the flush of blood (pomegranates) flowing down the queen's channel is accompanied by the precious fruit, i.e., the child (foetus). This confirms the miscarriage but I think there are two levels of meaning here, i.e., both the aborted foetus *and* womb-blood are "precious things," depending on who is speaking (the author or Nitocris), which becomes clearer later.

The menstrual blood ingested ritually is considered the most powerful concoction, created by the gods in the vessel of the womb, containing the concentrated Life force. It is certainly considered most "precious." The reference to "trees of frankincense and myrrh," which are considered sources of divine/celestial menstrual/womb blood[28] and the "spices," *combined*, is another affirmation of the miscarriage, but also a foreshadowing of the Elixir Rubeus proper.

TIMELINE

In 2:11 the "winter is past" phrase implied that it was spring; in 4:15, we see flowing streams from the mountains of Lebanon. Spring floods from the melting snow on the mountain peaks are vital to the fecundity of the arid earth of the plains and are mentioned often in the Sumerian texts. Two

---

[27] "Similar references to carnelian rivers and canals appear in medical incantations to stop menorrhagia": Scott B. Noegel, "Scarlet and Harlots: Seeing Red in the Hebrew Bible," *Hebrew Union College Annual* 87 (2016) 1–47, here 29. https://faculty.washington.edu/snoegel/PDFs/articles/noegel-scarlet-harlots-HUCA-87-2016.pdf.

[28] Elliott Wise, "An 'Odor of Sanctity': The Iconography, Magic, and Ritual of Egyptian Incense," *Studia Antiqua* 7.1 (2009): 67–80, here 71.

springs have now gone by, and there have been two *hieros gamos* allusions; it is now c. 547 BCE, which supports the theory that the death of Adad-guppi coincides with the events of 3:11. A table of the Timeline of the Song appears in the Appendix.

HERBAL 'REMEDIES'

The plants mentioned here are all, barring frankincense, mentioned in pairs, as if they are *used* together this way for some reason. Nard (spikenard), for instance, is listed in unison with henna, but then again with saffron. All, *without exception*, have a history of being used as medicines for the relief of abdominal pains, menstrual cramps, painful or heavy periods, or the general shifting of "blockages." Some help with premenstrual tension, while some help to regulate menses. Calamus, for instance, is not only an aphrodisiac, called the Venus plant, it is also used to calm period cramps, and if used in higher dosage, can trigger abortion. Myrrh and nard purge the uterus.

Honey and natron (natural sodium carbonate) served as a barrier and spermicide, and "pulverised pomegranate mixed with gall nut" was used as a contraceptive pessary; aloe and myrrh combined had contraceptive benefits but could also abort a pregnancy.[29] It may very well be that the pairing of henna and nard, and nard with saffron, were combinations known to women, or to men of medicine, but it certainly acts as an indication that what we are dealing with here is not just a collection of nice-smelling herbs.

Henna was mentioned back in 1:14, but this was in the context of the king being likened to the protective (spikey) nature of the plant. In this new context it takes on new meaning. Henna is intrinsically linked to menstruation, the marriage ritual, and conception, in many cultures. It is also linked, via this route, to the Evil Eye and/or demons. An apparent loss of fertility was often put down to the woman or the man having somehow been affected by the Evil Eye, and the blood of menstruating women, who were considered "open," was said to attract demons, so Persian women, for instance, would use complex henna tattoos to ensnare the demons who could take advantage of their compromised condition.

The term saffron is commonly applied to the ground stigmas and style of the *Crocus sativus* but it can just as legitimately be applied to the plant itself, and in the ancient Language of Flowers, saffron means, perhaps inauspiciously, "beware of excess (pleasures)." The Phoenicians, from the second millennium BCE to the first century CE, flavoured small round cakes with saffron, which were eaten in honour of the fertility goddess, Astarte, the Queen of Heaven (recall the "raisin cakes" of Song 2:5; see Jer 7:18).

---

[29] William H. Robertson, *An Illustrated History of Contraception: A concise Account of the Quest for Fertility Control* (Camforth: Parthenon, 1990), 24–28.

The earliest known reference to saffron being used medically in Mesopotamia comes from the library of Assurbanipal (668–627 BCE), where it is said to reduce menstrual/urinary pain and also regulate menses but it, too, was often used as contraception (i.e., abortion).

In early rabbinic texts, both contraception and abortion are discussed at length and a certain "drug of uprooting" was known to cause miscarriage; the word "drug" however, was "more frequently and generally [rendered] 'aromatic plant'."[30] Women who could "regulate their reproductive activities" were considered witches and a "danger to society"; such women could "either stop or 'open' a womb by witchcraft."[31]

> *May your spices be scattered and may the wind blow away the saffron*
> *you hold in your hands for the practising of sorcery.*
> P'sachim 110.2

Some of the prescriptions advised in the Mesopotamian diagnostic texts were to "provoke uterine bleeding," thereby "interrupting an undesirable early-term pregnancy": "You prepare (this) mixture for a woman [..., or] for a woman who is locked (lit. turned back) regarding her fluids, [or for a woman who] does not get (lit. see) [her menstrual period?], to make it appear."[32] (Note that the idea here of being "locked" pertains to a lack of menses).

An early miscarriage was seen in terms of the "water" flowing out; this "seems to refer to the amniotic fluid, which is said to flow out—very likely describing a preterm or premature rupture of the foetal membranes."[33]

> *If a woman has been given herbs of hate-(magic) to eat (and because of*
> *this) 'fluids' flow abundantly from her vagina ....*[34]

There is a Babylonian spell to stop the excessive flow of a woman's (womb) blood, referred to as "the waters" that need damming up, i.e., a flood: "Carnelian colour is her blood. In the carnelian branch canal, will they dry up the waters [with] a carnelian *mirtu*-tool .... *Ada-ru*-wood, and lapis

---

[30] Athalya Brenner, The Intercourse of Knowledge: On Gendering Desire and 'Sexuality' in the Hebrew Bible (Leiden: Brill, 1997), 81.

[31] Brenner, 86–9 and note 122.

[32] Ulrike Steinert, "Leakage and Retention of Fluids: The Body Imagery of Incantations and Rituals" in "Fluids, Rivers, and Vessels: Metaphors and Body Concepts in Mesopotamian Gynaecological Texts," *Le Journal des Medecines Cuneiformes* 22 (2013): 1–23, here §1, https://www.ncbi.nlm.nih.gov /pmc/articles/PMC3791376/.

[33] Steinert, "Fluids," §1.

[34] Steinert, "Fluids," §1.

lazuli, will dam up the canal; *ashlu*-rush will dry up the waters."[35]

FOUNTAINS AND STREAMS

The word for "fountain" is *mayan*, i.e., spring, and this stems from *ayin*, eye, which can mean a physical eye, but given the context here, it probably means a source (of a spring). This is depicted in direct connection with the queen's "garden," i.e., her genitals/womb. The intimate relationship between the "garden," the "living water," and the "flowing streams," all point to the Sumerian depiction of menstruation, conception, and birth—or miscarriage/abortion in this case. There is, however, a pun here, a play on words subtly included by the author on a level over the king's head, for Nitocris herself is the "source" of "living waters," the fountain of Life-affirming blood, i.e., the Elixir. In esoteric circles the word *ayin* pertains to the source, or fountain of wisdom within the pineal gland, i.e., the inner third eye, and it is this part of the brain the ingestion of ritual the Elixir Rubeus is said to affect, on a chemical, or alchemical level.[36]

Interestingly, the numerical value of the Hebrew letter *ayin* is seventy. In gematria, there are two significant words sharing this value: *yayin* (wine), as 10+10+50) and *sohd* (secret), being 60+6+4.[37]

The Sumerian word for "to be pregnant" literally means to pour water/semen into the womb; in cuneiform, "pregnant" is a combination of belly and water signs, and the sign *A* means both water and semen/offspring. The womb is seen as a vessel, filled with waters that sustain and nurture Life (e.g., blood and/or amniotic fluid), whereas the phrase "waters of life" often indicates semen.[38]

TRY AGAIN

The Hebrew for "from Lebanon" can be translated as "of whiteness," thus making a potential reference to semen (in this context), which is most commonly referred to in the Babylonian medical texts as "white matter" or "white substance," and as being poured, flowing, even flooding. An incantation to aid pregnancy reads: "'My meadow becomes blocked again

---

[35] Joann Scurlock, "Medicine and Healing Magic," in *Women in the Ancient Near East: A Sourcebook*, ed. Mark Chavalas (United Kingdom: Taylor & Francis, 2013), 101–143, here 110. In the Draconian Tradition of pre-Eighteenth Dynasty Egypt, menstrual blood was symbolised by "water," i.e., both being Life-giving fluids (Kenneth Grant, *Cults of the Shadow* [London: Frederick Muller Ltd., 1975], 56).

[36] Gardner, 186.

[37] "The Hebrew Alphabet: The Letter Ayin," Hebrew Today, https://hebrewtoday.com/alphabet/the-letter-ain-%D7%A2/.

[38] Stol, Birth in Babylonia, 4–5.

and again, (although) he filled [(it) with a flood] of water.' The incantation further speaks of the woman's 'dikes,' implying blockage as an explanation for failed conception *despite sufficient intercourse* (emphasis mine)."[39]

In other words, Song 4:15 suggests that time has passed since the miscarriage and the king is keen to try again.[40] Nitocris's "garden fountain" (her menses) and her "well of living water" (her womb) are again ready, he supposes, for *his* "streams of whiteness." The vessel of the womb is where, according to ancient wisdom, the two substances, menstrual blood and semen, are "mixed" to create a baby. Nabonidus cannot understand why she is not conceiving again, given his sexual prowess and consistency.

Nitocris, however, has other ideas. She never wanted the pregnancy; her religious duties as First Prophet of Amun-Re, and potentially as God's Hand, take precedence. She has, it seems, returned from Egypt, having consulted with Ankhnesneferibre on the topic of contraception and perhaps gained wisdom (i.e., the art of women) concerning how to deal with the possibility of an undesirable pregnancy. She uses the herbs and potions to protect *her* "precious thing" (her blood) but when she realises they have not worked as contraceptives, she both continues with the potions *and* allows the king access to her in the hope, presumably, that sex will 'dislodge' the foetus. There is no way we can know which tactic finally does the trick but either way, the author of the Song is adamant that Nitocris is to blame for the miscarriage and, as such, is deserving of her slur/curse.

The loss of Nabonidus's child is intentional but what is more, there is seemingly no regret or sadness shown by Nitocris. This is an important clue to understanding the author's jaded depiction of the foreign Queen of Babylon.

MAGIC (4:16)

Nitocris calls upon the powers of the winds to help her secure the king. She uses the word *ur*, i.e., awake—the same word she uses to adjure the daughters of Jerusalem not to stir up love too soon. The same word is used for both Nitocris's trance or meditative state in Song 5:2 (and it is in the temple at Ur where such practices are conducted, in a context of awakening knowledge, therefore this may be an intended homonymic pun), and also for the moment she says "I awakened you," in Song 8:5. In her command of and to the winds, Nitocris seizes control of the situation. She is formidable now—she has demonstrated the power of her Egyptian heritage, she has been made (Number One) Queen, and now *she* (like Persephone) decides

---

[39] Steinert, "Concepts," 315, note 82.

[40] For an example of how the nine months of conception-pregnancy is truncated into just a few lines in Mesopotamian literature, see Stol, *Birth in Babylonia,* 6.

whether or not she will have a child.

The Hebrew text reads, "... blow upon my garden so that its spices/perfume may flow out," with the word for "flow out" being *nazal*, predominantly used in the context of floods and streams (e.g., Exod 15:8; Ps 78:16; Prov 5:15), which brings us back to the notion of menstruation and miscarriage. The queen seems to be using her magic upon herself, commanding the winds to blow away the effects of the miscarriage (to flow out of her body, along with the aromatic herbs and spices she has used), and this notion does have a precedent in an anti-witchcraft ritual from Mesopotamia: "Let your favourable wind blow towards me so that the sicknesses may flee ...."[41] This 'blowing away' of the rejected pregnancy leaves Nitocris mentally and physically free to continue her own agenda. She directs the winds to send the scent of her menstrual blood to the king, to draw him further into her "dark" and secretive world, i.e., the realm of occult mysteries and the Elixir Rubeus. Had she given birth, her blood would not be deemed suitable for the rite.

CARDINAL POINTS

Nitocris calls on the *northerly* and *southerly* winds. This is important, as to the Jewish mind the primary directions are East and West, being the orientation of the temple in Jerusalem, while to an Egyptian, North and South represent the Upper and Lower lands of the Nile Valley. In the Book of the Dead, the winds are associated with deities: Osiris with the Northwind, Re with the Southwind. Power over the winds is granted to Re's daughter, Hathor. Amun-Re (the deity to whom Nitocris is First Prophet/high priest) is *the* god of Wind. Thus, Nitocris, again demonstrating a symbolic link with Hathor, is commanding the sacred winds of Amun-Re, calling upon him to assist her in manipulating the king.

From a Mesopotamian perspective, too, North and South are the principal cardinal points; the great Processional Way in Babylon runs from North to South, from Marduk's temple to the Ishtar Gate. The winds mentioned in cuneiform texts are also predominantly northern and southern, i.e., the northern wind "dwells" in the cool mountains and brings "vigour to the Land" (*ETCSL t.2.1.7*, §294–305), while the southern wind is harsh, malevolent/evil and destructive (*ETCSL t.1.3.5*, §B16–23). The ancient god Enlil is Lord Wind. Ishtar is often depicted controlling the North and South winds, demonstrating the power of her fury: "She let the south wind pass across, she let the north wind pass across" (*ETCSL t.1.3.3*, §239–55).

The North and South winds of the Song are an ingenious construct,

---

[41] Tzvi Abusch and Daniel Schwemer, *Corpus of Mesopotamian Anti-Witchcraft Rituals: Volume One*, in *Ancient Magic and Divination*, 8.1, ed. Tzvi Abusch, et al., (Leiden: Brill, 2011), Text 8.6, line 51, 330.

reminding us that Babylon and Egypt, despite many similarities, have always been diametrically opposed, at odds. This also seems to portend the fate of Nabonidus and Nitocris, on a personal level.

CHOICEST FRUITS

The garden motif is employed in a sexual context in the Song and as this is such a common theme in the Sumerian texts, it hardly needs further explanation.

The inclusion of eating the "choicest fruits" at the end of 4:16 is not just a euphemism for enjoying her body sexually (with "eat" being used as it was in the tale of Inanna and Utu "eating," up on the mountain). It echoes 4:13's use of the phrase, i.e., in a context of offspring but also the Elixir Rubeus. This is a vital turning point and one that sets the fate of the royal couple, and it is a sinister and disturbing reference, for this is the moment the die is cast; the king is about to surrender to the influence of his Egyptian bride, the "daughter of Pharaoh." This will lay the foundation of the Solomon/Ashmedai legend, and the biblical castigations of the king (Solomon) as an idolater and miscreant.

With respect to the "choicest fruit" being a reference to the miscarried baby, I refer you to Deut 28:53–7. Moses divides the tribes between Mount Gerizim and Mount Ebal; the former "for the blessing of the people," the latter "for the curse" (Deut 27:11–13). Amongst the long list of curses, for those who fail to obey the "statutes" of Yahweh, is a curse that the people will suffer at the hands of a great enemy and will thereby be driven to ruin and starvation: "... you will eat the fruit of your womb, the flesh of your own sons and daughters ..." (Deut 28:53). Solomon, recall, is chastised for not observing "what the Lord commanded"; he has not kept the "covenant" and the "statutes" (1 Kgs 11:10–11), and has turned his heart to idolatry and foreign women. Moses makes it clear that if those who anger God "return" with a "circumcise[d] ... heart," God will make them "abundantly prosperous ... in the fruit of [their] body ... livestock ... [and] soil" (Deut 30:9).

The allusion to Moses's curse foreshadows Solomon's (and thus Nabonidus's) fall; it is not a literal eating of a baby (probably, but recall the Phibionites, who emulate Nitocris as she appears in the Song; they allegedly consume unwanted foetuses), but in the king's case, it is consumption of the blood that is Life-giving—to the Jewish mind, this is anathema (Lev 17:13–14).[42]

---

[42] There is also a strange account of a mother eating her unborn child in the lyrics of a Mesopotamian inscribed magic-bowl, pertaining to the infertility demoness Bguzan-Lilith. Christa Müller-Kessler, "The Story of Bguzan-Lilit, Daughter of Zanay-Lilit," *JAOS* 116.2 (1996): 185–95, here 190, v.21.

5. WHAT IS HIDDEN

The summoning of the winds is a conscious effort to begin the king's spiritual training, and to introduce him to the Elixir. So far, Nabonidus has merely shown that he can listen and repeat, and make a basic fertility idol. In this chapter, Nabonidus becomes Nitocris's official protégée.

> *The wind ... will rest upon him,*
> *The wind of wisdom and of understanding,*
> *The wind of counsel and might,*
> *The wind of ... knowledge ...*
> Isa 11:2

INITIATION (5:1)

The chant-like repetition in this verse, i.e., "I come ... I gather ... I eat ... I drink ..." suggests that Nabonidus is performing some sort of ritual. The heady scent of Nitocris's "precious thing," her blood, has been magically (symbolically) wafted in his direction; he cannot resist. First, he responds by dutifully coming to the queen's side, to his "garden," i.e., to *her* sexual "garden." His words are not in the same tone as the gushing flattery of 4:1–5; they are now sombre and resolute.

The next few lines contain ingredients that are mentioned in the king's description of Nitocris in 4:10–11, i.e., milk, honey, wine, myrrh, spices. The three mixtures in Song 5:1 are:

★ *Myrrh with spices*
    Liquid myrrh is a euphemism for womb-blood, and the spices are additives to make the Elixir palatable or to boost its hallucinogenic properties.

★ *Honeycomb and honey*
    Bees, Veronica Goodchild asserts, "point to the 'key' of knowledge of the mysteries and hidden wisdom that leads to immortality." She adds: "The ancient European lineage of bee shamanism—*The Path of Pollen*—is deeply inspired by the

wisdom of the womb as the seat of oracular knowing."[1]

Said to be created from the tears of the solar god Re, bees are connected with the goddess Neith, the veiled goddess whose statue in Sais bears the message that no man has looked beneath her veil, i.e., it may be to the female-controlled rituals that this veil alludes. Recall that "veil" is also a euphemism for the hymen, e.g., the veil Ishtar celebrates at the moment a woman loses her virginity; that no man has *transgressed* this barrier suggests complete autonomy (sexually) for the Neith worshipper. As Nitocris is a priestess within the Sais-based kingdom, and the daughter of the "son of Neith," it cannot be denied that she would be influenced by this, providing a further rationale for why she does not wish to become pregnant. The veil implies secrecy, and probably initiation into the cult.

The first king of Egypt, Menes, bore the title "The Beekeeper" as did every pharaoh thereafter. The pharaoh had complete control over the production of honey, and "the royal and ritual word for bee (*dsr.t*) was taboo to the vulgar"; it was a secret concealed in the Holy of Holies.[2]

Thus, I suggest the honey/honeycomb in this verse refers to an occult initiation ritual involving the secret world of priestly women and their hidden arts.[3]

★ *Wine and milk: the Elixir Rubeus*

This is the ritualistic imbibing of menstrual blood ("wine") and semen (the "milk" of the male). This is most certainly the "cup full of abominations" referred to in Rev 17:4.

Symbolically "partaking of an ithyphallic god's ejaculum as it spills over lotus flowers and libation vases … allowed priests to revive and refresh themselves with truth

---

[1] Veronica Goodchild, "Sacred Bees: Some Cultural, Mythic, and Symbolic Considerations (2018), 1–11, here 2, http://www.veronicagoodchild.com/wordpress/wp-content/uploads /2018/04/sacredbees-042018.pdf.

[2] Hugh W. Nibley, "Symbolism of the Bee: The Deseret Connection" (2015), https://oneclimbs.com /2013/03/25/symbolism-of-the-bee-the-deseret-connection-by-hugh-w-nibley/.

[3] Intriguingly, in Old Babylonia, "honeycomb" was another name for the placenta, used in the context of the birth goddess (Marten Stol, *Birth in Babylonia and the Bible: Its Mediterranean Setting*, Cuneiform Monographs 14, eds. T. Abusch, et al. (Groningen: Styx Publications, 2000), 125 note 98. The subtle link to an all-female ritual soon after the miscarriage might well suggest a placenta-based rite of some sort the king was privy to.

(*maat*), wisdom, and joy." A young initiate experiences "ecstatic exhilaration upon drinking the sacramental beverage" and is convinced that he had become one with Amun-Re and had all the secrets of the netherworld revealed to him.[4] Recall, too, the comment earlier (Part One, Chapter 1), that Neith produces "two kinds of stimulating drugs" as part of her occult repertoire;[5] it is possible this is emulated by the female First Prophet and daughter of Neith, Nitocris.

The key to immortality is deemed to be in the ingestion of divine efflux, both male and female. It may be that Nabonidus is partaking of these substances in the hopes of experiencing something beyond the physical realm (i.e., a psychedelic trip), or perhaps he has hopes for immortality.

In reviewing what has been seen of the king thus far, we know he is listening to Nitocris, for he echoes her several times (e.g., the "lily" of 2:2; the "shadows flee" phrase of 4:6, etc.), like a student repeating what he has learned. In Song 2:14 he says: "Let me hear your voice, for your voice is sweet," implying that he is actively seeking instruction from one he sees as enlightened. In 5:1, he responds directly to Nitocris's occult instruction by coming to the "garden." The power of the spoken word is central to ancient Egyptian beliefs, especially in the context of priestly ritual, and the Song demonstrates this on several occasions.

Nitocris, no longer pregnant, is motivated to distract the king from attempting another impregnation by convincing him of the wisdom he could attain if he converts to, or at least learns, the tenets of her religion. Like Hathor offering the initiate her *menet* necklace of sexual energies, the queen tempts the king (while he is emotionally/psychologically compromised, i.e., a recipe for disaster), with the prospect of full initiation into her occult world.

Song 5:1, therefore, is a sign that Nabonidus has accepted the challenge; he "gathers" his myrrh and spice, the "spiced wine," or intoxicating Elixir Rubeus (he "gathers" again in 6:2, also in a sexual/elixir context); he has entered into the labyrinthine honeycomb of mysteries and has taken part in the most sacred re-enactments of the divine Creation. He is an initiate.

Of significance is the fact that the verb "to swallow," as used in the Book of the Dead, came to mean "to know." This is understood to be a

---

[4] J. Andrew McDonald, "Influences of Egyptian Lotus Symbolism and Ritualistic Practices on Sacral Tree Worship in the Fertile Crescent from 1500 BCE to 200 CE," *Religions* 9, 256 (2018): 1–27, here 17–18.

[5] Edward P. Butler, "Neith," Henadology: Philosophy and Theology, https://henadology.wordpress .com/theology/netjeru/neith/.

specifically Egyptian development within the magical sphere. Inscriptions on Ankhnesneferibre's sarcophagus include "an address to deified 'Perception' (Sia) as 'the Great Swallower'."[6] This may be further evidence for the connection between the Elixir and the God's Hand. King Nabonidus ingests, he "swallows," therefore, he "knows" (in theory).

The distant rumble of approaching doom can be heard in the final phrase of 5:1, for here we learn that the king, once ambivalent, is now fully engaged in the practices Nitocris has revealed to him. The pleasures of initiation soon outweigh any potential wisdom acquired, however, and the cherished secrecy of the divine path soon falls into open revelry. This will become even more evident in the analysis of Song 8.

ALL AND SUNDRY

This is the moment of the king's long-awaited descent into a Sheol of his own making. He has turned Nitocris's gift of potential enlightenment into an orgiastic free-for-all. Men of the kingdom are called to "imbibe deeply," to "become intoxicated" (employing the verb *shakar*). The NRSV suggests intoxication "with love" but the Hebrew reads "drink deeply *beloved ones*," using the now familiar *dodi* but in the *plural*; the king has cheapened *dodi* by applying it to anyone who partakes of the Elixir (recall, for him it is a reference to his being Nitocris's protégée). As he had done in the making of his idol of Nitocris, the king does not complete his task. Like a child getting bored with homework, he is soon distracted and chooses the path of instant gratification.

Proverbs 5 offers a very clear parallel to this situation, though reversed and blaming the artful woman, whose "lips drip with honey." The speaker claims he failed to learn fully from his teachers (i.e., to complete the initiation, in our context), that he succumbed to "intoxication," debauchery, etc., only to bring down upon himself "ruin in the public assembly." He claims to have been "ensnared" by the "toils of [his] sin" and lack of discipline.

WISDOM

Nabonidus's ambition for wisdom and, by association, his initiation into Nitocris's occult Egyptian religion, is immortalised in the mockery of the VA (5.3):

> It was he who once stood up in the assembly to praise himself, saying: "I am wise, I know, I have seen what is hidden. ... I have seen secret things. The god Ilteri has made me see a vision; he has

---

[6] Robert Kreich Ritner, *The Mechanics of Ancient Egyptian Magical Practice*, ed. Thomas A. Holland, SAOC 54 (Chicago: University of Chicago, 1993), 106–7.

shown me everything. I am aware of a wisdom which greatly surpasses even that of the series of insights which Adapa has composed!"

Note that this is also where the Tayma version of Sîn is alluded to, i.e., "Ilteri"; this suggests Nabonidus's quest for insight *is* rooted in his experiences in Tayma. In Nab 47 (3.0–4), after a lacuna of eight lines and just before his fateful omen that it is time to leave Tayma, comes the phrase, "… my path did not stop with the diviner or the dream-interpreter …," further suggesting his quest for occult wisdom peaked during his stay there, and surpassed anything available to him in Babylonia. The VA's paraphrasing of Nabonidus's boast is echoed, almost verbatim, in the HB (note the mention of "madness" and his failure to succeed):

> I said to myself, "I have acquired great wisdom, surpassing all who were over Jerusalem before me; and my mind has had great experience of wisdom and knowledge." And I applied my mind to know wisdom and to know madness and folly. I perceived that this is … but a chasing after wind.
>
> Eccl 1:1–17

Nabonidus seeks wisdom from Nitocris, he is keen to learn but his own hubris and perhaps his more mundane, visceral nature prevents him from attaining the *dod*, the "love" that is eternal Life. Things are not much better for Nitocris, for she has used her knowledge, status, and experience to seduce the king, not into her bed but into her cult. She has done so for her own ulterior motives and as such, she has probably broken vows, tainted her own spirit (from her Egyptian perspective), and cheapened the sacred. As one of the two wombs of Song 2:1, she is the blood-giving womb; this is her raison d'etre (i.e., not to be the child-bearing womb), so to preserve her womb for service to her god, she must exploit the "precious thing" itself.

GOD'S HAND

Nitocris's role as First Prophet of Amun-Re is fact. That she was Adoratrice and/or God's Hand is debated. With the repeated allusions to "hand" we find in the Nabonidus (Solomon)/Nitocris story, I suggest she is either God's Hand at the time of the treaty (recall that there are no depictions of Nitocris II at Karnak, suggesting she left Egypt before her ceremonial image was added), or she takes on the role, symbolically, in her isolated and somewhat desperate situation. In a way, she appropriates the God's Hand prestige, knowledge, and power to get the king where she wants him. This may well be a harbinger of *her* ultimate fall.

SACRED SPACE (5:2–3)

This is the second instance of Nitocris apparently exhibiting the ability to "sleep" but "not dream" (i.e., her heart was "awake"), as mentioned in the discussion of Song 3:1. Kenneth Grant, in describing the ancient rituals associated with the mystical feminine blood rites, suggests the Adept priestesses would ultimately become seers or oracles, i.e., they knew how to sublimate the sexual energy in order to empower their innate third eye and thus, it was inferred, they could 'see' with their womb.[7]

ATTEMPTED ACCESS

Nitocris is now in a rather different headspace and is more mature, experienced not only in the sexual act but in the reality of living with this king. Her need to restrict his access to her body has led her to become more introverted and isolated; she is in her chamber in deep meditation, during the quiet of the night. She is communing with her deity when the king, like a drunken marauder, interrupts her silent concentration. He arrives sexually aroused, i.e., his "head is wet with dew … with the drops of the night" but there is, of course, a plurality of meaning here.[8] On one level of interpretation, he arrives ready to create the Elixir; he has the "dew" (the "milk"), she must supply the blood ("wine"). He is impatient, earnest, possibly addicted.

On another level, recall that in the interpretation of the tree-dream offered to Nabonidus in Dan 4:25 (and 5:21), the king is fated to become mad, i.e., to wander as an animal, "bathed with the dew of heaven." At this stage in the Song, the king *is* losing himself. He is becoming infatuated with the rituals and the sexual gratification of the Elixir Rubeus rite and is losing all sense of proportion and dignity. This is a direct parallel to Daniel's warning, suggesting both the author of the Song and that of Daniel had the same recollection of Nabonidus (Daniel advises the king in Tayma, where he witnesses the king's behaviour first-hand [see Prayer of Nabonidus 4Q242, where Tayma is called "Temen"]).

Beaulieu draws attention to the fact that Nabonidus's plan for the *entu*-ship at Ur is met with derision in Babylon, where it is, for some reason, deemed "inappropriate"; Nabonidus is accused, in R Chr 3.5–10 of "unwittingly" or "ignorantly" manhandling the sacred tablets, i.e., of being "impious" and a bit 'rough around the edges.'[9] This is exactly how the king

---

[7] Kenneth Grant, *Cults of the Shadow* (London: Frederick Muller Ltd., 1975), 11.

[8] On dew as a euphemism for semen, see W. M. Clarke, "The God in the Dew," *L'Antiquité Classique* 43.1 (1974): 57–73, especially 66–73.

[9] Paul-Alain Beaulieu, *The Reign of Nabonidus King of Babylon 556–539 B.C.* (New Haven: Yale University Press, 1989), 129–31.

in the Song comes across; he is not a brute but he is not versed in the gentler forms of love. He is a soldier, a very physically-orientated man. Although he attempts to learn, to acquire wisdom, he stumbles and gets frustrated. In this scene, his impious behaviour and his coarseness are revealed.

Nitocris has disrobed and is assumed to be naked, suggesting she is taking on the role of the goddess, i.e., Ishtar, whose natural and most iconic state is nakedness. The scene is clearly set at night and thus alludes to hidden, or occult behaviour.

PURITY

As First Prophet of Amun-Re, Nitocris was head of the entire Egyptian cultus. She was subject to the same cultic preparations, the same rules and regulations regarding the temple, and the same ritual training as any other high priest before her. The First Prophet immediately before her, of course, was Ankhnesneferibre. This is the person Nitocris strives to emulate; this is the woman alluded to in Song 1:6, 3:4 and 8:2. Awareness of the need for purity would have been instilled in Nitocris as soon as she could comprehend. Purity is vital to the efficacy of sacred rituals; the delineation between purity and cosmic order, and impurity and primordial chaos, is profoundly significant. The priests, therefore, constitute the frontline of defence against imbalance, against the infringement of divine sanctity, especially at times of ritual, where the Creation aspect is most potent. The Egyptian term for (an ordinary) "priest" (*wab*) means "a pure one"; in Song 7:9, Nitocris is given the epithet, "the pure one."

Nitocris is acting in her priestly aspect at night because she worships Amun-Re, the solar deity, i.e., the morning purification ritual always takes place *before* sunrise. Although "purification" is not mentioned directly, the imagery of the scene, especially now the pervasive theme of menstruation is recognised, points to the possibility that she had disrobed to bathe because she is menstruating. The Egyptian word for menstruation (*hsmn*) *means* purification.

The queen's feet are mentioned as being clean because this is one of the most vital elements of purification, and one that is mundanely logical, for ritual bathing is performed whilst standing in a tank of shallow water, often on a stone platform (presumably, so the sullied water can drain from the body before one steps out). The feet that make contact with hallowed ground must be pure. Lev 15:28–30 suggests no such ritualistic bathing is required by a (Jewish) woman after menses but in Mesopotamia, recall, a girl's menarche is celebrated as a spiritual and cultural ascension, and her feet are ceremonially bathed; it may be that each month thereafter such women performed the ritual for themselves, in private. The postexilic Jews shun the practice maintained by both Egyptians and Babylonians.

Just like the cella within the *giparu* in Ur, the priestess has a designated area for performing her sacred rituals. The king, technically impure because he has had a "nocturnal emission" (Deut 23:10), imposes not only on her performance of these rituals but on the sanctity of her private space.

HUBRIS

In the tale "Setne and the Book of Thoth (Setne 1)," the son of Pharaoh Merneptah develops an unhealthy obsessional ...

> ...desire to possess the Book of Thoth. ... The main theme of this Demotic narrative is the inevitable failure of any human endeavour to get hold of divine knowledge for reasons of sheer curiosity. ... The division between the divine and human spheres should be respected and maintained. ... It clearly shows that transgressing the spatial rule blurs the established oppositions and, as a consequence, is doomed to bring trouble.[10]

This is the understanding we have of Nabonidus, whose zeal to learn occult matters, to prove himself superior, leads him to eventual ruin, for he fails to complete his training, fails to fully contemplate Nitocris's teachings, and has now failed to acknowledge the sacred space of the very one he is looking to for wisdom (a little knowledge is a dangerous thing). It is also reminiscent of his metaphorical stealing of Enlil's Tablet of Destinies, which was, I argue, the (symbolic) cause for his original banishment, i.e., his nature is consistent in the Song, the Book of Daniel, and the Babylonian inscriptions.

ADDICTION (5:4)

The king is psychologically affected by the Elixir he has been introduced to. He is becoming addicted and wants more of this mind-bending experience. He forces his way into Nitocris's private space when she is naked, assuming he can take whatever he wishes from her. Thrusting "his hand into the opening" was commonly considered to mean he puts his hand through an aperture in the door to gain access but, as most scholars now agree, it is a sexual metaphor.

MOLESTED?

The Hebrew noun *chor* is employed, signifying a hole or cave, both common

---

[10] Jacco Dieleman, *Priests, Tongues, and Rites: The London-Leiden Magical Manuscripts and Translation in Egyptian Ritual* (100–300 CE) (Leiden: Brill, 2005), 229–30.

euphemisms for the vagina. In describing the occult Elixir Rubeus ritual, Nicholas de Vere suggests that a man desirous of drinking a woman's menstrual blood directly, would first stimulate her using his fingers on the "roof of her mouth," i.e., "the uppermost wall of the 'canal' nearest the opening of the vagina ...."[11] The "roof of the mouth" is alluded to in Song 7, again in a context of drinking the Elixir. However, the king does not get this far.

Nabonidus is *willing* to force himself on Nitocris, to demand access to her "precious thing," i.e., her menstrual blood. His first words, "open to me" are, in the HB, "open *for* me," and are indicative of her condition, i.e., where to be "open" can equate to menstrual bleeding. Therefore, we could read here, "bleed for me."[12] It is possible that the queen's knowledge of the medicinal plants that trigger uterine bleeding, such as those that led to her miscarriage, are routinely used by her to keep the flow of blood as constant as possible. Such a treatment of her body would be detrimental over time but it could explain why the king seems to act as though she would always have blood 'on tap' for him.

Nitocris is not delighted, nor aroused, nor yearning. She is perturbed. Her "inmost being" is her belly, her womb, using the noun *meeh* (Isa 49:1, Ps 71:6, and Ruth 1:11). "Yearned" is translated from the verb *hamah*, which has rather a negative connotation, as it suggests growling, roaring, becoming disturbed, groaning in distress. Nitocris, therefore, is upset, annoyed at the king's presumption. She knows she has taken Nabonidus too deep and too quickly into the mysteries; he just cannot handle the responsibility or appreciate their profundity. He has come to her like a "madman" (as was deemed his fate by Daniel) but she cannot fully blame him; she should not have tried to win him over with promises of enlightenment via the blood-rite.

> *Babylon was a golden cup in the LORD's hand, making all the earth drunken; the nations drank of her wine; therefore the nations went mad.*
> Jer 51:7

NO FAIRY TALE
The king, in his ignorant, addictive stupor, ironically declares Nitocris "blameless." ("my perfect one," with the adjective *tam*). She is not, however.

---

[11] Nicholas de Vere, *The Dragon Legacy: The Secret History of an Ancient Bloodline* (San Diego, CA: The Book Tree, 2004), 382.

[12] In the Book of the Dead, the word to denote "to bleed" has a root connection with the term for "opening," so bleeding and opening could be synonymous to an Egyptian (H. Clay Trumbull, *The Blood Covenant: A Primitive Rite and its Bearings on Scripture*, [Philadelphia: John D. Wattles, 1893], 84).

She has lied to the king about her contraception and abortion, and has compromised her own purity and priestly status in attempting to distract, or convert him. The point is, the king is blissfully ignorant of this "flaw" (remember Song 4:7), and this is reiterated in Song 6:9, a most significant moment in the Song.

In one myth of Inanna, Utu tells Dumuzi that when nightfall comes, he will "draw the bolt from the door" for him, so he can be with the goddess (*ETCSL t.4.08.25*, §9–23). "Open the house, my lady!" Dumuzi calls. Inanna bathes, adorns her body with various jewels, opens the door (to her body), and the couple kiss and embrace (*ETCSL t.4.08.29*, §B11–23). This is what early audiences of the Song would perhaps be expecting, but the reality is not so perfect.

COVENANT OR CAPTURE? (5:5)

Nitocris has been purifying herself, meditating; her privacy shattered, her ablutions all but nullified, she resentfully agrees to "open" for the king. She feels obliged, responsible. The "handles of the bolt" phrase is a metaphor for her labia, where the "bolt" is her vulva; it is a commonly expressed, figurative lock on the woman's body.[13] With bloody fingers Nitocris reluctantly opens her labia and thus removes the perceived obstacle. She is at the point of despair with him, however.

The word to suggest "liquid" myrrh is the verb *abar*, to pass over/through/by/on (Song 2:11; 3:4). A better word to indicate fluid, or "liquid myrrh" would be *deror*, indicating something flowing, and this is used in Exod 30:23 in connection with the priestly sacred anointing oils ("take the finest spices: of liquid myrrh …"). The author of the Song clearly wishes to convey a specific meaning here, e.g., a link to the original blood-covenant in Exod 12:6–27, where *abar* is used to describe the original "pass over" blood ritual. This, too, was done at night. Blood signifies Life and binds those who share it. In Exod 23:32–3, however, the Israelites are told concerning the "inhabitants of the land" they are to acquire: "You shall make no covenant with them and their gods. … they will make you sin against me; for if you worship their gods, it will surely be a snare for you." The connection to the Song's themes of idol worship and the queen's ensnaring ways is obvious.

---

[13] A Babylonian incantation recited as a child is born, says: "She has spoken to the doorbolt: You are released. Removed are the locks, the doors are thrown aside": Marten Stol, *Birth in Babylonia and the Bible: Its Mediterranean Setting*, Cuneiform Monographs 14, ed. T. Abusch, et. al., (Groningen: Styx Publications, 2000), 11.

THE QUEEN'S DESCENT (5:6–7)

Nabonidus, in his deranged state, does not wait for Nitocris to prepare herself. He turns away and storms off in a fit of pique. Her "soul" (using the noun *nephesh*, i.e., breath) has "failed" her (using the verb *yatsa*, to go or come out), in that she suddenly feels utterly exasperated; her breath "goes out." She is deflated, fuming, and in a vexed sigh (or scream) she vents her frustration with the king. There is a lingering doubt, however, as to whether or not the king actually molests Nitocris. The "hand" in the "hole" imagery seems to be merely predictive, showing *intention*, for the subsequent action suggests it was not followed through. This will prove significant.

This scene bears a striking resemblance to the Mesopotamian tale of Gilgamesh and Siduri:

> Siduri sits in the garden.... She is covered in a veil ... she sees Gilgamesh coming towards her ... despair in his heart ... she barred her gate against him with the cross-bar and shot home the bolt. But Gilgamesh...lodged his foot in the gate.... "I will break in your door and burst in your gate, for I am Gilgamesh...."[14]

Siduri is also in the middle of a sacred ritual (preparing her "wine" in a "golden bowl," for the gods). Gilgamesh has been wandering in an emotional turmoil, just like Nabonidus. He also attempts to force his way in but then leaves. The point of such a precedent is that both the Epic and the Song employ the same imagery and both continue with a descent of the main character into the nether/underworld.

The most famous mythological descent, of course, is Ishtar's. As a petulant and somewhat arrogant young goddess, Ishtar decides to visit the underworld home of her sister, Erishkigal. She arrays herself in all her royal finery, paints kohl on her eyes, and arms herself with selected powers and talismans. When she reaches the gate of the underworld, she is forced to strip naked, surrender everything she has brought with her, and succumb to humiliation and violence. She is killed. Eventually, the deity Enki ensures her resurrection and she is allowed to return to the earth. In her stead, however, her husband Tammuz must descend into the abyss for half of the year.

The pattern of 'seeking and finding' is presented in the myths of Isis searching for Osiris's body parts, and also Ishtar's searching for Tammuz, who runs away when he realises what is to become of him. Although both goddesses do find their respective men, in both these legends the death of the lover/husband/king is central to the story; in the Song the king is not

---

[14] N. K. Sandars, *The Epic of Gilgamesh*, rev. ed. (London: Penguin, 1972), 100–1.

killed, i.e., death is replaced by madness.

SENTINELS 2

The first time Nitocris had sought the king after his retreat from her (in Song 3:1), she behaved petulantly, hunting him down, for all to witness. His whereabouts was given away by the city guards. This second time, she is distraught; she truly wishes to find the king, for in such a mood he might reject her. Her position as Queen could be at risk and she might lose everything, so she runs out again, back into the streets, to seek him out.

Nitocris says, "I called him," using the verb *qara*, which can have the connotation of commanding or summoning. Is she demanding the king return to her to explain himself (unlike the coy invitation to return in Song 2:17)? This verb, *qara*, is also used in 1 Kgs 18:20–9, where Elijah is confronting the Baal worshippers and tells them to call out to their god, in a bid to prove the superiority of Yahweh over Baal. Later, in Song 8, the king is subtly linked to Baal. Might this be the suggestion, again, of a battle between the deities of Nitocris and of Nabonidus? In the context of 1 Kings 18, Jezebel is the high priestess of the opposing deity (on Mount Carmel), i.e., a woman who figures significantly in discussions to follow. Meditating, blood-letting, and the calling out but receiving "no answer" motif are all mirrored there.

The guards Nabonidus has placed around him are here performing their duty, keeping the king safe as he wanders the streets at night. Perhaps Nitocris stumbles across them but the context would suggest they actively seek her out; they *find* (*matsa*) her. The king, it would seem, has reissued his order for her to be denied access to him; he knew she would follow, so he has set his men against her.

The sentinels, once just as manipulated by her charms as the king, once able to flirt with her and let her go on her way, now offer a new challenge to the woman who has allowed matters to get out of control. The men, as too the king, have had time to retrench. She descends into her own underworld, her own Sheol, in her desperate pursuit of the king through the dark city streets. She is beaten and wounded. Such action in the HB is almost exclusively reserved for the smiting of enemies. Nitocris is now considered as such.

Taking away the queen's mantle is one of the most significant things these guards could have done. The mantle is signified by the term *radid*, which means a large body-veil (not just a face/head veil), and thus it 'covers her nakedness'; by its removal, she is exposed and degraded but there is a direct correlation here to the diatribe of Isa 3:18–26, the same passage discussed in the analysis of Song 3:11: "... the Lord will take away the finery ... of the ... robes and mantles ... and the veils ... and instead of a rich robe, a binding of sackcloth; instead of beauty, shame. ... ravaged, she shall sit upon the ground." This was Isaiah's rejection of the gynocentric cultus that the "daughters of Zion" represented; they were "haughty," "wanton" and "mincing" and needed to be brought low.

An immediate repetition of a word is one of the author's scribal techniques, to point the audience to a parallel elsewhere in the HB (which, I posit, is predominantly contemporaneous; it may be that books not in the canon also served as precedents or parallels). There are but two examples of an immediate repetition of "sentinels" in the HB, i.e., Ps 130:6 and Isa 21:11–12. The "oracle concerning Dumah" of Isa 21:11–12 is only a few lines long but it is filled with potential substantiation for the descent theme here. Dumah means a deathly silence (Ps 94:17; Ps 115:17). The scene is set during the Babylonian captivity; Isaiah is on a watch-tower, and it is night, i.e., the time of demons and terrors. Someone asks if there is any hope of deliverance from the night, the darkness, and the alarms it brings. The setting in the Song here is, indeed, the night; there are watchmen/sentinels guarding the city (walls); there is an air of doom and despair.

Even in the name, Dumah, i.e., silence, there is, for those following the goddess theme in the Song, an allusion to one of the most suppressive aspects of her descent before she is killed, that is, she is ordered to stay silent (seven times): "Be silent ... a divine power of the underworld has been fulfilled ... you must not open your mouth against the rites of the underworld" (*ETCSL t.1.4.1*, §129–33). Nitocris stays silent; she does not tell Nabonidus about the attack.

This is not the end of Isaiah 21 for us, as the passage concerning Dumah is nestled, significantly, between the castigation of Babylon, including a potential reference to the festivities the day before the Persians enter the city (21:5; see Daniel 5), the calm oasis of Tayma (21:14), *and* the damnation of Kedar (perhaps signifying a mutual source/experience). Recall, too, that the VA paints Nabonidus as one "seized by misfortunes" (1.5), and it has been shown that he often refers to anxiety, ominous dreams, etc. This seems to fit the doom and gloom of Isa 21:11–12.

Nabonidus seems to be unusually concerned about his safety. He is depicted in the Song as being surrounded by bodyguards; he appoints guards to protect him when he leaves Babylon (Nab 47, 1.30–1); and he makes peaceful Tayma a fortress: "He made the town beautiful, built there a palace like the palace in Babylon. He also built walls for the fortification of the town and he surrounded the town with sentinels" (VA 2.8).[15]

---

[15] In 1 Kgs 10:18–21, Solomon's throne is described as having twelve lion statues guarding the six steps leading to his throne, which also had one on either side. To a Mesopotamian king, of course, the lion is a symbol of power and ritual protection; it also symbolises Ishtar. Lions and/or sphinxes flank the Pharaoh's throne/dais

In Isaiah 47, Babylon is depicted as the rejected, humiliated "virgin daughter," who is told: "... remove your veil, strip off your robe .... Your nakedness shall be uncovered, and your shame shall be seen. Sit in silence, and go into darkness ..." (Isa 47:2–3, 5). This is what happens to Ishtar; she is forced to remove all her clothing and regalia, to stay silent, and to subjugate herself, in the dust. This chapter of Isaiah ridicules Chaldea's reliance on magic, omens, and astrology; now Nitocris is seen to be similarly rejected. "The Targum employs the Aramaic expression *npqt br* (lit. 'a woman who goes outside')" as the standard term for "prostitute,"[16] providing, perhaps, an insight into how this woman running through the streets would have been perceived by early Jewish audiences (if not the guards themselves).

With that in mind, Psalm 130 can be seen to have relevance in that it is a supplication to the deity from "the depths" for redemption, for salvation.

HERODOTUS

In Herodotus's account of the marriage of Nitetis to Cambyses (*Hist.* 3.1–3), the Persian king is said to be made angry "some time afterwards" by his new bride revealing to him who she actually is, i.e., the (alleged) daughter of Apries. If it is possible (as most historians now agree) that Herodotus may not always be precise, might we see, instead, Nabonidus becoming frustrated with Nitocris? She has lost a child, is not conceiving again, is keeping her distance sexually, and is beginning to drive him (quite literally) insane with her inculcation and her Elixir. Would this not be potential justification for the foreign king to be "angry" with his bride "some time" after the wedding?

POINT OF NO RETURN (5:8)

Continuing with the Descent of Ishtar allusion, the Song echoes the goddess' instructions to her minister, Ninshubur, just prior to abandoning the world for the underworld. The faithful servant is told to go and *tell*, i.e., to make it known to the gods that the goddess has descended, and to ascertain that they will not leave her to perish.

THE BIG LIE

Nitocris descends into the dark streets without any preparation, however, and succumbs to the violence that awaits her, only *then* adjuring the

---

(which is probably where Nabonidus gets the idea) and represent Sekhmet, Hathor's menacing avatar. Could this be part of the perceived weakness, the emasculation, of the king, i.e., hiding behind his powerful wife?

[16] Esther Marie Menn, *Judah and Tamar (Genesis 38) in Ancient Jewish Exegesis: Studies in Literary Form and Hermeneutics* (Leiden: Brill, 1997), 65.

"daughters" to tell the king she is "faint with love." This is in order to remind him (and us) of the first time she had said this, back in Song 2:5. The term employed for "faint" is *chalah*, and this has many meanings, including weak, sick, beseech, be sorry (which is possible), wounded (this is clearly true), etc.

In the context of 2:5, the idea of the queen being in a weakened state after much sexual attention from the king seems fitting but to simply transfer that interpretation to the new context is not helpful, for everything has changed. Surely, though, like Enki in the Descent myth, Nabonidus will have pity and save Nitocris, as he had protected her when she first came to court. The king, however, does not come to her rescue.

I suggest there is another potential interpretation to be gleaned from the declaration "I am faint with love," within this current context. In Song 2, the queen is "taken" by the king, sexually, and within a few verses he is urging her to get pregnant (i.e., the "little foxes"). So, "I am faint with love" is linked to the concept of sex and procreation, not lovesickness. In Song 5:8, Nitocris repeats the words in the context of just having angered a volatile Nabonidus, who has taken himself away. She has had a miscarriage, and has attempted to dissuade him from trying again by introducing him to the sacred rituals of her religion. She has just been accosted by the guards and humiliated. Suddenly, she gets an idea. "Tell him I am pregnant!" she instructs the "daughters of Jerusalem." This is not as big a leap of the imagination as you think, for the Hebrew word for "faint" (*chalah*), can also be used in the context of *feigned* sickness (e.g., 2 Sam 13:5–6, in the scene prior to the rape of Tamar), and as a "woman in travail" (giving birth, as per Jer 4:31).

A potential allusion to 2 Sam 11:5 is suggested. Bathsheba, Solomon's mother, has sex with David just after her purification period after menses. She declares (using *harah*, pregnant): "I am pregnant!" She, too, loses her first child.

Whether the king actually witnessed Nitocris menstruating when he burst in on her is uncertain, for it is not clear if he ever got that close to her, physically; it may be that he mistook her nocturnal reticence for feminine defiance (shades of Vashti?), which is why he stormed off to find another source. With the rest of the Song yet to be discussed, I ask that you suppress your scepticism until Nitocris's ultimate plan is exposed.

Nitocris knows how to get the king's attention but has she made this declaration in time? She *is* menstruating, so of course she is *not* pregnant. It is a ploy. Thus, the queen's deception and the king's ignorance are perpetuated, and this sets the foundation for the rest of the Song and its convoluted tale.

JEALOUS "DAUGHTERS" (5:9)

The "daughters of Jerusalem" are young women who have begun menses; they are part of the harem, other potential "vineyards" (which make "wine"); they also love (*aheb*) the king. No doubt fully aware of the queen's behaviour and the king's predicament, and lacking any respect for this foreign upstart, they mock her. What makes the king so special, if she can so easily flit from one beloved to another? There is such a sense of sarcasm here ("O *fairest* among women"), of spite, that one can imagine the women gathered together, feeling superior and rather self-satisfied, having seen Nitocris demeaned and humiliated.

Why would they accuse Nitocris of having more than one beloved? There is a reminder, here, of the queen's admission to having been "gazed" upon, in Song 1:6, where she felt she had to apologise for her sexually-orientated role as, it is supposed, God's Hand. Their words, however, are more directly linked to Song 5:1, where the king had called other men (i.e., the "beloved ones") to "imbibe deeply." He has made his wife no better than a prostitute, providing access to her sacred Elixir to a select, elite group. This is strong grounds for the later rabbinic obsession with the alleged lasciviousness of foreign women (especially sacerdotal women), *and* the Ashmedai and Samson legends pertaining to a leader wanting to engage in sex with menstruants. It also serves to reinforce the pressure and anxiety Nitocris is experiencing by this point. There will be further discussion on this 'pimping out' of the king's women later in this analysis.

The queen isolates herself, retreating to her own space, to conduct true, Egyptian magic, or *heka*. She makes an idol, a poppet, to manipulate the king into her (alleged) snare once and for all but also, to present him as an offering to Amun-Re.

IDOL/POPPET (5:10–16)

In Sumerian/Akkadian poetry personal attributes (especially of deities) are invoked, and descriptions of their power or influence are laced with metaphors and similes. Ishtar, for instance, might be called a "wild bull," or "wood-clamp." She is "unveiled clear light" and she wears "brilliance." Thus, what is depicted in the following verses of the Song is series of items that represent the king on some personal, symbolic level (now mostly lost to us).

Gilgamesh's body is also fashioned by the hand of a goddess. Although fragmented, the legible lines of a tablet telling this myth refer "to his stature, body, foot, leg, thumb, cheeks, locks and height—that is, his handsome and powerful body from bottom to top."[17] This proves to be highly significant, for although this is the reverse sequence to the queen's figurine, it is the same as that alluded to in the worship of Nitocris in Song 7. The point is, there is evidence for an accepted tradition, or sequential format (i.e., from bottom to top) for such a procedure, and because there is variation to this in the Song, we need to understand why.

NINE

There are nine individual references to "His ..." in Song 5:11–16. The ninth letter of the Hebrew alphabet is *tet*, and this corresponds, in gematria, to conception and the nine months of pregnancy (the eighth letter, *chet*, represents marriage).[18] Other terms with the value of nine include: "to rise, be high," "exalted, majestic"; "to be haughty"; "pride"; "ungodly," "to act covertly"; "to deceive"; and "the *hollow* (empty) belly"!

There are also nine deities (*neturu*) that make up the Egyptian Ennead; each represents, metaphorically, an aspect of the 'body' of Amun-Re. Correspondingly, there are nine aspects to the human, i.e., one physical (the body), eight spiritual (the soul/mind).

RADIANT AND RUDDY

In Sumerian literature, radiance is *bestowed* upon the king via the crown, granted to him by the gods, specifically Ishtar, who has the final say regarding the new king: "When I am radiant in the holy crown like a brilliance that is renewed daily ... I lift my head high" (*ETCSL t.2.4.2.b*, §A5–8). Tammuz, Ishtar's first king, is also described as radiant: "... radiant in the temple and on earth!" (*ETCSL t.4.07.7*, §52–65). This radiance is, therefore, another sign that Nabonidus has been deified.

Solomon's father, King David "was ruddy" (1 Sam 16:12; 17:12). Scott Noegel suggests this ruddy colour is symbolic of male fertility; "the sanguine colour indexed fertility in males in much the same way that blood signalled female fecundity," making the king the "male counterpart to [the woman's] 'scarlet lips'."[19] This helps to affirm the Song's focus on fertility and procreation.

The ruddy countenance .... She conferred attractiveness on his beauty.
She made charm approach the colourful statue.

---

[17] John R. Maier, *Gilgamesh and the Great Goddess of Uruk*, (SUNY Brockport eBooks digital commons: 2018), 225.

[18] Rabbi Aaron L. Raskin "Tet: The Ninth Letter of the Hebrew Alphabet," https://www.chabad.org/library/article_cdo/aid/137081/jewish/Tet.htm.

[19] Scott B. Noegel, "Scarlet and Harlots: Seeing Red in the Hebrew Bible," *Hebrew Union College Annual* 87 (2016): 1–47, here 31.

She erected the statue for him ....
ETCSL t.2.8.3.1, §1–8

"Ruddy" is translated from *adom* (*adam*), meaning to be (made) red, or showing blood (in the face, e.g., after drinking or exertion, etc.). There may be wordplay on the idea of being angry (red-faced); this has a bearing on the discussion of the eclipse in Song 6. We have just witnessed the king's anger/derangement in Song 5:4–5.

The life of the flesh is in the blood ....
Lev 17:11

Perhaps Nitocris uses her own (menstrual) blood, mixed with earth, to emulate the Creation aspect in the ritual, and to make this version of the king uniquely *hers*.

STATUE

Head: "This statue was huge, its brilliance extraordinary.... The head ... was of fine gold ..." (Dan 2:31–2). Daniel interprets King Nabonidus's dream and tells him in no uncertain terms, "*you* are the head of gold" (2:38), so the king builds a large statue and orders everyone in the kingdom to worship it, i.e., it is a cultic idol (3:5). The VA (1.5–8) also insinuates that Nabonidus enforces the worship of his idol of Sîn upon a bemused nation.

Gold is deemed by the Egyptians to be the earthly incarnation of the gods, i.e., the *flesh* of the gods, which is why it figures so heavily in their ritualistic practices. Reflecting the rays of the sun, gold links the idol/statue to Amun-Re, and imbues both the inanimate object and its subject with divine essence. Nitocris is again invoking the powers of the solar deity in her ritual.

Hair: In the story of the Great Flood, An, Enlil, Enki, and Ninhursaga create "the black-headed people" (*ETCSL t.1.7.4,* §A10–14). This is how the Sumerians refer to themselves. Their hair, as evidenced by many reliefs and statues, is thick and wavy.

Ishtar adores Tammuz's hair, and he becomes identifiable by it: "My one distinguished by a shock of hair ... a shock of hair like a palm tree! ... (*ETCSL t.4.08.25,* §34–47). Gilgamesh is known as "the lord with the very black beard" (*ETCSL t. 1.8.1.2,* §A5–11).

Nitocris is black, with all its accompanying connotations; the king is now described in terms of blackness but this is probably the figurative blackness of spirit being alluded to. From the early Jewish perspective, he is becoming more and more a reflection of Nitocris; he is, effectively, her creation, the amalgamation of her moods, her tricks, her lies, her magic, her blood.

Eyes: In the narrative "Lugalbanda and the Anzu Bird," the bird that later steals the Tablet of Destinies is described as: "Bird with sparkling eyes ... you frolic as you bathe in a pool" (*ETCSL t.1.8.2.2*, §111–31). This could be subtle reference to Nabonidus and the sin of his hubris, discussed earlier.

As a priestess, as a woman of magical insight, this could also suggest Nitocris is ritually/symbolically "gazing" at the king's soul through the windows of his own eyes; the doves may be an imagined reflection in his eyes of *her*, the dove. This adds to the sense of intoxication or mesmerisation that was hinted at earlier.

The same word for the "waters," *mayim*, is also used in Song 4:15, and in Prov 5:15–16; in both contexts the waters are representative of fertility/sexuality. Although "milk" is probably used to refer to the whites of the eyes, it seems too simple; we cannot ignore the allusion to the king's milk, i.e., semen, especially as it appears in unison with waters of fertility, in which case the reference may allude to his third eye, also, which is being opened by the Elixir Rubeus, i.e., the blend of milk and "waters" (blood).

Cheeks: The Hebrew noun *lechi* suggests jaw and/or the cheek, which means Nitocris is probably describing his beard. The ornately designed beards seen in depictions of Mesopotamian kings and deities incorporate plaits and angular cuts, to give an almost solid appearance. This might well tally with the more precise translation here of "banks or towers" (*migdal* or *migdalah*) of "scented herbs," i.e., an almost block-like mass of hair, scented with oils. The NRSV reads "beds of spices" but this phrase is used in Song 6:2 to refer to a woman's genitals; this could make the reverence here another allusion to the king's penchant for cunnilingus.

Ishtar says of Tammuz (who is the beard, personified): "My lapis lazuli beard .... My beard mottled like lapis lazuli!" (*ETCSL t.4.08.25*, §34–47).

Lips: The word for "distil," i.e., *nataph*, is the same in both 4:11 and 5:13b, and means drip/dripping. The line here reads, "dripping with liquid myrrh," which is a direct echo of Song 5:5 and Nitocris's dripping hands as she rises to let the king access her for the Elixir Rubeus rite. The king's lips are now said to be lilies dripping with the same fluid; recalling the Sumerian/Akkadian perception of the direct "canal" through the woman's body from mouth to vulva, one has to assume this to be a sexual pun, where the lilies are in/on the king's mouth, again accentuating cunnilingus at the time of menstruation. Nitocris is highlighting this as part of the king's initiation/education. The sacred blood-rite is intended only for the most elite, e.g., the priests and the king/pharaoh; this supposedly makes them one with the gods.

The queen, therefore, intends that her image of the king reflects him as her subservient, obedient student, with his eyes reflecting her as the "dove," his mouth dripping with the blood that has come from her sacred 'crimson lips'.

In the Book of the Dead, an initiated scribe offers *maat* and as part of his preparation to enter the sacred space, he declares he has brought with him "the myrrh of women ...,"[20] i.e., menstrual blood.

Arms: The king's arms are also of gold, suggesting that his *skin* is gold, marking him as deified. Mesopotamian cult statues are adorned with multiple jewels (precious and semi-precious stones) and these are considered an aspect of the deity's divinity; they are not merely adornment but are considered integral to the efficacy of any ritual involving such statues (e.g., during the Akitu festival). A cultic statue is thus a conglomeration of sacred objects that have known symbolic meaning and/or magical/divine properties peculiar to the deity.

Body: Ishtar says of Tammuz: "My ivory figurine, my golden figure! My object fashioned by a skilled carpenter! My one worked on by a skilled metal worker!" (*ETCSL t.4.08.25*, §34–47).

According to 1 Kgs 10:18, Solomon's throne was made of ivory, overlaid with gold. It was "covered with fine gold from Ophir, studded with beryls, inlaid with marble, and jewelled with emeralds, and rubies, and pearls, and all manner of gems."[21] It represented but one aspect of the king's supposed sin against God, as it overtly demonstrated his desire for riches: "Apart from having married a Gentile ... the king transgressed two other biblical laws. He kept many horses (recall Nitocris being likened to a mare in Song 1:9–11), which a Jewish king ought not to do, and, what the law holds in equal abhorrence, he amassed much silver and gold."[22]

Ivory, though fairly common in Egypt, was imported into Palestine every three years (1 Kgs 10:22) and was reserved exclusively for royalty (1 Kgs 22:39 and Ps 45:8). There is also an "ivory" link to the idolatrous practices of Samaria in Amos 3:15, where it is warned that the "houses of

---

[20] Muata Ashby, *The Forty-two Precepts of Maat, the Philosophy of Righteous Action, and the Ancient Egyptian Wisdom Texts* (Miami: Sema Institute of Yoga, 1998), 109.

[21] "The Throne of Solomon," Legends of the Jews, 4.5 (110), https://www.sefaria.org /Legends_of_the_Jews.4.5.105?lang=bi.

[22] "The Marriage of Solomon," Legends of the Jews, 4.5, (22), https://www.sefaria.org /Legends_of_the_Jews.4.5.105?lang=bi.

ivory," i.e., the shrines with their cultic statuary, "shall perish". The jewel-encrusted ivory "body" thus represents the man as king (on the throne), but also, as sinner.

The term for "sapphires," *sappir*, may in fact mean lapis lazuli, as the NRSV note "i" suggests (see also Exod 28:18, note "o"). Lapis is one of the most frequently mentioned/used gemstones in Mesopotamia from the earliest traditions of Inanna, who first strings her beads about her neck, to the building of the Ishtar Gate in Babylon. To an Egyptian princess/priestess, of course, lapis is the stone of the gods, a symbol of the heavens, a representation of wisdom and truth. The word *sappir* comes from *caphar*, meaning to score, inscribe, enumerate, and the Mesopotamian Tablet of Destinies is said to be an inscribed tablet of lapis lazuli.

Legs: The legs are depicted in terms of architectural "pillars" (*ammud*) and this is an echo of Song 3:10 and the pillars of the king's Egyptian-style palanquin. Alabaster (calcite) is predominantly an Egyptian export, named after Albastron, where it is found. Nitocris probably perceives Nabonidus's kingdom (in Tayma) as being founded on the wealth of Egypt, through the treaty and bride price arranged by her father.

Ishtar says to Tammuz: "My holy statuette .... My alabaster statuette adorned with a lapis-lazuli jewel, your charms are lovely" (*ETCSL t.4.08.02*, §27–32).

Feet: Unlike Nabonidus's fertility idol of Nitocris, her figure does have feet, or "bases"; these are also of gold, thereby making the object begin and end with gold. The overall impression is one of a golden statue (with inlay and ornamentation), with flesh the colour of the gods' flesh; it reminds us of the golden statue in Daniel, and of Ishtar's golden figure of Tammuz.

In Daniel's description of the statue the king dreams about, the thighs are bronze, the legs (calves) iron, and the feet a blend of iron and clay (Dan 2:32–3); it lacks stability, its feet symbolising weakness. This weakness is described in terms of a mixed marriage; though "they mix with one another in marriage ... they will not hold together, just as iron does not mix with clay" (Dan 2:43). If the various substances each represent a kingdom, as Daniel explains, which kingdom is the iron, and which the clay? I posit that in his remark, Daniel is revealing his concern for the marriage of Nabonidus to Nitocris, i.e., it is not the king who is the iron, but the Egyptian queen! We learn later that Daniel is not enamoured with Nabonidus, and it seems fitting he should see this strange, troubled king as the "clay" that is both malleable and weak (even though he flatters Nabonidus initially by claiming he is the head of gold).

Appearance: The king's "appearance" is likened to the tall, impressive trees for which Lebanon is famous but remember, Lebanon has very well-attested negative connotations. It represents the king's enforcement of labour among his own people, and the house in which his personal treasures are kept secure; it symbolises everything "proud and lofty" and in need of humbling (Isa 2:12); it reflects the idolatry of sinners and the doom of nations that turn against God. It is the netherworld for both Gilgamesh and Adonis-Tammuz.

Speech: The finishing touch, once the idol is complete, is this declaration concerning the king's speech, his *words*. The sweetness of these words is described as *mamthaqqim* and the only other place in the HB this term is used is in Neh 8:10, where the context is the reading of new laws that include the segregation of those in mixed marriages. However, *mamthaqqim* stems from *mathoq*, used in the previously mentioned passage in Job that pertained to the honey under Nitocris's tongue, in Song 4:11, i.e., "Though wickedness is sweet in their mouth, though they hide it under their tongues" (Job 20:12). So, once again, the king is depicted in reference to the queen; he reflects her eyes, he repeats her words, now his words are deceptively "sweet" as hers had been. This is a tactic by the author to warn the audience that all is not as it appears.

Speech, in the Sumerian texts, is deemed something powerful, important, a gift from the gods, i.e., Ishtar is given the *me* of "women's speech" (*ETCSL t.1.1.3*, §424–36); she takes also "forthright speech, deceitful speech, grandiloquent speech" (*ETCSL t.1.3.1*, §F31–2).

MAAT

Idols, both Mesopotamian and Egyptian, are deemed living entities and, in order to inspire them with divine spirit, which then serves as a direct channel to the deity, they have to undergo a sacred ritual known as "the opening (or 'washing') of the mouth." This involves much incense, libations, and anointings; the robing and embellishment of the idol; and, in Egypt, the ritualistic offering of *maat*, the philosophical ideal of justice, order, balance, truth, and morality, often phrased as "What is Right" (physically represented by a small statue of the goddess Maat).

> *Hear, for I will speak noble things,*
> *and from my lips will come what is right;*
> *for my mouth will utter truth ...*
> Prov 8:6–7a

Although offering *maat* is essentially a ritual for the reigning king, the later God's Wives, up to and including Ankhnesneferibre, are depicted at Karnak presenting *maat* to Amun-Re; this is seen as a sign of the women's high status and independence. Nitocris would have witnessed this ritual first hand. In her lonely and unique position now, she emulates her cultic mother, adapting the ceremony to fit her needs.

Recall that the link between *maat* and the veracity of a soul is the weighing of the heart after death and the judgement of *maat kheru*, or True of Voice, i.e., of being found innocent of wrongful deeds, etc.; this does not seem to tally with the depiction of the king thus far. Perhaps naively, he says things that are not "true" and he has proven disrespectful of the divine path to enlightenment. I suggest, therefore, the author of the Song is hinting at a more sinister reason behind the making of this idol/poppet, i.e., the ultimate (symbolic) capture of the king as Nitocris's prey, which is a constant theme throughout the Song. The subtle allusion to the judgement in the afterlife reiterates the sacrificial/Sheol motif.[23]

There is an ancient Egyptian ritual that combines *maat* with the name of the king, creating a dual presentation to the god that represents the entire nation, i.e., the nation and its ruler are offered up to Amun-Re.[24] Nitocris, by providing this idol/poppet with an identity, i.e., "This is my beloved," is not merely offering up the king to Amun-Re, she is offering up his entire kingdom—as a ritual sacrifice? This is red-flag moment for the early audiences of the Song, this is the fate, so they are led to believe, of any nation whose leader is weak, idolatrous, and influenced by a (foreign) woman.

FRIEND

Finally, Nitocris is finished creating her idol/poppet. All the ideals are represented and wrapped up in one potent package that is "altogether desirable"; desirable to the gods, that is. She announces its completion with a slightly acerbic and superior snub: "O '*daughters* of Jerusalem'."

The Hebrew term for "friend" is that used by Nabonidus to refer to Nitocris, i.e., *rea*, which generally means a companion, fellow. It is not an overtly sexual or romantic term. There is a formality to the notion of "friend," however, especially within royal spheres, for it does appear as a title, both official and honorific, in ancient Mesopotamia and Egypt, usually in the context of marriage. As explained earlier, the concept of *dod* in the Song is profoundly more significant than generally considered; it pertains to the ultimate, divine love, peace, and truth, i.e., a person's relationship with cosmic harmony. As the *dodi*, or beloved, the king is singled out as Nitocris's protégée, the initiate, i.e., her cultic "companion." Therefore,

---

[23] See the Supplemental Note "Ankhnesneferibre and Nitocris II: A Question of Filiation" on Academia.edu, especially § "The Osiris."

[24] Emily Teeter, *The Presentation of Maat: Ritual and Legitimacy in Ancient Egypt*, Studies in Ancient Oriental Civilization 57 (Chicago: Oriental Institute of the University of Chicago, 1997), 77–8.

Nitocris, in offering this figurine up to her god, is saying: "This is the one I am teaching; this is a representation of the one I am married to." She is offering up his identity, making sure the gods know precisely who this poppet is for.

Note the "This is ..." closing statement, which was discussed earlier, in connection with the Phibionite liturgical practices.

TWO WOMEN, ONE KING

The queen is not physically *making* a true cultic statue, despite the apparent richness of the constituent parts (this would be the responsibility of "master craftsmen"). What she creates in her cella, in her sacred space, is probably a clay, crudely-shaped humanoid object, embellished with broken beads, the king's hair, an old ivory pin, etc. It is a magical poppet, imbued with her intention toward the king. The sequence of her construction of the object, i.e., from top to bottom, is thus a sign that it is *not* a cultic statue, even though the rest of the imagery might suggest that it is. It is topsy-turvy, just like the "honey and milk" of Song 4:11, which demonstrated the king's apparent lack of judgement and a degree of falling away from orthodoxy. The sequence is reversed from the norm to highlight the *magical* process; it also echoes Nabonidus's idol of Nitocris, constructed from top to bottom, further emphasizing their occult, idolatrous relationship.

There is a Babylonian prayer in which a king is tormented by a woman who makes a poppet of him, leaving him with "discord ... anxiety ... terror ... loss of sleep ...": She "made figurines of me and took my measurements, / Collected dust grains from my footprints, took up my spittle, / Plucked out a lock of hair, cut off a piece of my clothing ...."[25] An ancient Egyptian poem tells of a young man who protests that a "girl has lassoed him with her hair, caught him with her eye, restrained him with her necklace, and branded him with her seal. These metaphors are all equivalent to magical techniques."[26] They are also remarkably akin to what is said of Nitocris in the Song.

The presentation of the king as cultic idol in the Song may be an indication that Nabonidus attempts to re-establish the ancient "cult of the king," which would be an unsurprising parallel to the resurgence of the *entu*-priesthood at Ur. The statue becomes a significant object in not only the VA's admonition of the strange idol of Sîn but also in R Chr 3.29–4.5, which describes Nabonidus renovating the dilapidated statue of Sargon; it stood inside Ebabbar, the temple of Shamash in Sippar, and received offerings,

---

[25] Benjamin R. Foster, *From Distant Days: Myths, Tales, and Poetry of Ancient Mesopotamia* (Bethesda: CDL Press; 1995), 262–4.

[26] Geraldine Pinch, *Magic in Ancient Egypt* (London: British Museum Press, 1994), 124.

thereby affirming its status as a cult statue of a deified king. Nabonidus does not stop there, for he openly declares: "I securely placed an inscription of mine and an image of my royal majesty in the presence of the god Shamash and the goddess Aya ..." (Nab 26, 1.33–2.1; Nab 24, 2.7b–10a). By conferring sanctity upon a royal image, it necessarily becomes a focus of worship and respect, and the authority of that person, assuming deified status, is unquestioned.

The parallel depictions, i.e., the ceremonial statue and the crude occult figurine, represent the perception of the king from two different people, i.e., the latter reflects Nitocris's now jaded view of the king, representing her alleged desire to make him her "captive," while the former points to the author's perspective, something that must await a later discussion.

6. Fruit of the Moon

Taunting (6:1)

The women taunt the isolated queen: "Where is your beloved, *now*?" Their offer to help look for him is not a sign of sisterly solidarity but a dare, intended to expose Nitocris's rejection.

The term for "turned," here, is the verb *panah*, which has a general understanding of turning away, aside, askance, etc., and this is in contrast to *saba*, which had been used in 2:17, where Nitocris had told the king to "turn" and come back to bed, i.e., to turn *toward* her, as he was already leaving. Thus, the gloating women, aware that the king has had enough of her antics, urge the queen to disclose where Nabonidus has gone, believing she does not know, and must be humiliated again when they tell her—but she is unabated and has a powerful answer for them.

Other Lilies (6:2–3)

The king goes *down* to "his garden"; the term for "garden" is *gan*, here used in the (masculine) singular, meaning an enclosure, hence its use to define the reproductive parts of the body (i.e., the "plants" of Ishtar; the enclosed space of the vagina/womb). A king's harem is an enclosed society, where the females are kept in isolation from the rest of the court. Nabonidus, I submit, "goes down" to his harem; the phrase is significant, as it is a play on words, forming an inclusio with 6:11, explained at that juncture.

Nabonidus has gone "to gather lilies." Up to this point, only Nitocris has been openly described as a "lily/lotus" (Song 2:1), and the sexual union of the royal couple was couched in terms of the king grazing amongst the lilies/lotuses (where the plural was a poetic necessity, to make the allusion work, but also a reference to the entirety of a woman's genitalia). Nabonidus, in "gathering" lilies, is having sex with his other women, i.e., the (plural) "beds of spices." He "grazes" in the "gardens."

Nitocris has already told the "daughters" and the king that she is pregnant. It would be most natural for the king to enjoy his other women once his pregnant wife is off-limits (considering what seems to have happened the first time). If she were to make any kind of fuss, it would give the game away, so she openly declares that she knows precisely where

Nabonidus is and what he is doing. Between the lines, however, the king is seeking not just sex but a substitute Elixir (this becomes clear later); Nitocris cannot provide it now, and he is effectively addicted, so he seeks it elsewhere, not comprehending that the *source* of the Elixir Rubeus is as significant as its alleged psychological effects. The idea of "going down" is repeated in Song 7 and is a euphemism, once again, for cunnilingus.

This is a turning point in Nabonidus's story, for his new "desire" begins to overshadow his original "desire" (for the *entu*), and this affirms his symbolic fall. As the king descends, the queen ascends, just as with Ishtar and Tammuz.

Nitocris's response to the catty "daughters" reminds them that she is now (supposedly) carrying the king's special child; she demands respect. At this point, however, her plan is not fully thought through. She had panicked, earlier, when she declared herself pregnant, but soon she will have to provide the king with this alleged child. She cannot risk feigning another 'miscarriage'.

ROYAL PRECEDENT

There is a well-known Sumerian tale of Dumuzi suddenly deciding to leave Inanna alone, in order to find sexual pleasure elsewhere; he sees it as a magnanimous action: "Wife, I am going to bring flowing water to the arid place. I am going to look after my spacious cattle-pen. I am going to find out the condition of the holy sheepfold. I am going to feed my sheep" (*ETCSL t.4.08.28*, §1–20).

BATTLE FRONT (6:4–5A)

"Beautiful," as we learned earlier, is translated from the Hebrew *yapheh*, from *yaphah*, to be bright, to deck oneself out in order to become beautiful. It has the connotation of being over the top, gaudy, dazzling. It may not be such a compliment, especially given the early Jewish tradition of insinuating cultic prostitution for such women; it is almost the antithesis of the Akkadian notion of "beautiful," which is signifies godliness.

Tirzah is the name of both a woman and the northern capital of Israel but as it is here coupled with Jerusalem, the latter is probably implied. Tirzah was the northern capital under Jeroboam, who had fled to Egypt for sanctuary until Solomon was dead (1 Kgs 11:26–12:2). This region later became known as Samaria, nemesis of the Judeans, so the mere link to Solomon's rebellious prefect suggests a dubious and somewhat sinister allusion in the Song. Its "beauty" belies its alleged 'heathen' practices and its perceived ungodliness (yet another misconception by the king). The influence of anti-Samaritanism on the language of the Song is a constant theme to be considered, suggesting a postexilic context for its construction.

The name Tirzah is taken from the root *ratsah*, which means to be pleased with, to satisfy a debt, to pardon; perhaps this is intended as a reference to the deal with Ahmose and/or Nitocris's public pardon for her supposedly idolatrous practices (i.e., the king's "banner"). There may also be an intended play on the word *ratsach*, which means to kill, to dash to pieces, to slay; while an odd inference if the Song is taken to be a love-poem, when you take into consideration all the allusions to hunting, battle, ensnaring, etc., and the themes of madness and the underworld, it should not be so surprising. It also helps to emphasise the imagery of the queen being "terrible as an army," in the next line.

The name Jerusalem, though assumed to be the most Hebrew/Jewish of any in the Bible, has Ugaritic/Canaanite origins that predate the Israelites.[1] It can mean dual, in allusion to the two large hills in the area; having its roots in *yara/yarah*, to shoot, throw forward, e.g., as in throwing a weapon; it also suggests battle, which seems at odds with the tradition that the name means "founded on peace." In the Song, Jerusalem is a pseudonym for Tayma (e.g., the "daughters of Jerusalem" represent the young women of the harem in Tayma who worship the king as Tammuz).

The word for "terrible" is the Hebrew adjective *ayom*. It appears in only one other place in the HB, i.e., Hab 1:7, where it refers to the Chaldeans who are "dread and fearsome," sent by an avenging God to a nation that has fallen by the wayside. It therefore brings the Song's queen to the fore as a force to be reckoned with, i.e., a force as daunting as Babylonia itself.

Then there is *emah*, a word from the same root as *ayom*, used only in Job 39:20 and 41:14; it means "terror, fright, dread" but can also mean "an idol," as in a *feared* idol. In Job, the word appears in contexts of battle; the first reference is to the snorting of a horse as it charges into battle, with the noise of weapons (arrows, spears, and javelins) and trumpets around it. The second, is to the Leviathan, the beast who consumes Job; its teeth are said to be like "shields in rows, shut up closely as with a seal" (Job 41:15).

The "terrible" nature of the queen's presence is just like Job's rattling, charging horses, for she is decked out with all her jewels and finery, her feminine weapons at the ready. Like the Leviathan's mouth, the entrance to Hell for Job, with teeth as shields sealed together, so Nitocris's necklace is

---

[1] "Most likely, the original name, that sounded something like Urusalimum or Ursalimmu, meant Foundation of Salem, the latter being a known Ugaritic god" (Abarim, https://www.abarim-publications.com /Meaning /Jerusalem.html). Significantly, James Meek argued that the name Urusalima appears in a Mesopotamian god list, i.e., "Shulamanitu is the title of Ishtar of Urasalima" ("Canticles and the Tammuz Cult," *The American Journal of Semitic Languages and Literatures* 39.1 (1922): 1–14, here 7, note 1). See also the discussion of the Shulammite from Song 7.

(earlier) compared to shields on the wall, i.e., her body, the entrance to Sheol for Nabonidus. She is the wrath of God, the divinely imposed vengeance on a king who has fallen from grace.

This juxtaposition of the northern and southern capitals, clearly post-dates the accepted dating of Solomon as king (and thus has significant bearing on the dating of the Song) but for the purposes of this current investigation, it plays with the imagery of Nitocris, the warrior goddess-incarnate, standing with one foot in each realm, seizing control of the kingdom; clad in her armour, her bow and arrow in hand, she is awesome, terrifying. This is no mere flattery—this is war. If this is how Nitocris is remembered by those who knew her, it might also have influenced Herodotus's perception of her as a powerful ruler and defender of the city (*Hist.* 1.185–7).

It has been suggested that in the ancient Near East, new "mothers are ascribed with warrior status" and that pregnancy and childbirth are considered a "battle front."[2] Those who see Nitocris as the new mother see her as this impenetrable wall (as she later calls herself) of strength, a powerful and daunting woman who is facing the battle head-on. To those who see Nitocris as the author sees her, and as we are beginning to understand her, she is facing a battle of a different kind.

Nitocris's war is not about motherhood but about spiritual veracity; she has compromised her religious ideals in a bid to protect them. She is feigning a pregnancy, in order to keep the Elixir safe, knowing all the while she can never return to being the "fountain" once she has supposedly "given birth." Perhaps she has dreams of returning to Karnak one day, to her role as God's Hand; perhaps the winds will blow everything away, again. I would argue that since the events of Song 5:2–8, she has begun to see Nabonidus as an adversary; once, she thought him just ignorant, just uncouth, but now he has ridden roughshod over her most precious blood-rite, inviting all and sundry to partake, going to non-sacerdotal women for his fix; she can no longer see him as anything but her rival. The conflict of their respective lunar and solar-based religions is mirrored in their private relationship.

TERRIBLE

Such dread is a staple element of Near Eastern praise poems to the gods, and this is significant because this scene is rebuilding the queen's idyllic reputation in the king's eyes; she is once again his goddess (for he believes she is again bearing his child), and as the verses continue, we see her imposing and awe-inspiring depiction increase in intensity.

---

[2] Janice P. De-Whyte, "Wom(b)an: A Cultural-Narrative Reading of the Hebrew Bible Barrenness Narratives" (PhD diss., McMaster Divinity College, Ontario, 2014), 191.

... you are imbued with a terrible great awesomeness ...
your praise and renown are such as to unleash awe and terror!
ETCSL t.2.5.2.1, §25–8

Ishtar in her warlike guise is, perhaps, the most terrible in the true sense, that is, she is terrifying but inspires awe and respect: "When humanity comes before you in awed silence at the terrifying radiance and tempest, you grasp the most terrible of all the divine powers" (*ETCSL t.4.07.2*, §20–33). Around the Eanna, Ishtar's holy temple, are erected many impressive banners, illustrating the importance and authority of the goddess (*ETCSL t.4.08.30*, §1–7).

BANNERS
In Song 2:4, the king set a symbolic "banner" (*dagal*) over the queen in an effort to clarify her position in the court; it was not a sign of battle in that context but of protection, identity, and status. In Song 6, the context has changed to one of conflict; the only other use of *dagal* in the HB is in Ps 20:5, where it also appears in a context of conflict, and there is an intriguing twist in 20:4, which reads: "May he grant you your heart's desire, / and fulfil all your plans." There are two "plans" in the Song: Nabonidus's plan (his "desire") for the *entu* priesthood, and Nitocris's plan to evade pregnancy, whilst retaining her status as Queen. In terms of the ever-increasing tension between the king and queen, the battle imagery is profoundly suitable.

TURN AWAY
Nitocris's eyes were a delight to Nabonidus in 4:1 but by 6:5 he cannot bear to make eye contact. The king has fallen for the ruse and believes Nitocris carries his longed-for child but he is a broken man. He knows the cause of his unrest at night, of his uneasy conscience. In a pitiful plea to Nitocris, the mesmeric, intense, and unrelenting priestess, he begs her to stop the fascination, divert the power of her gaze, for he is conquered. The Hebrew word for "overcome" is *rahab*, which can mean to behave self-proudly but also, to capture. This anticipates the imagery of the "captive" king in Song 7:5.

NO LIPS (6:5B–7)
Notice how Song 6:5b (i.e., "Your hair is like a flock of goats ..."), up to and including 6:7, is an almost verbatim repetition of 4:1b–3, with one exception. The "crimson lips" that allude to the visible evidence of her menstruation, are not mentioned. Nitocris cannot both perform the Elixir Rubeus rite *and* be pregnant; she is not revealing her blood now. Nabonidus assumes that she is no longer bleeding because she is pregnant again. It is

149

the author's way of reminding us that the king is ignorant of Nitocris's conniving.

Recalling the discussion of Song 4:2, where the context of sheep-shearing was proposed for this metaphor of the teeth, it has been argued by J. C. Geoghegan that sheep-shearing in the HB is used as a "backdrop—both literary and actual—for events in Israel's past, involving the repayment of debts or the righting of wrongs"; the scenes all have consequences for the throne, in that they provide a narrative context for the "emergence of the royal clan."[3] He discusses four episodes involving sheep-shearing, three of which have already proven significant in the Song's analysis: Genesis 31 (Jacob, Leah and Rachel); Genesis 38 (Judah and Tamar); and 2 Samuel 13 (the rape of Tamar; the fourth is 1 Samuel 25, in connection with David). In the Song, we have allusions to both Tamar characters, the idea of two women and pregnancy, and the concept of making amends, or putting things right, which will be a theme in the next few verses. There is also the underlying notion of the dawn of a new "royal clan" (in terms of the *entu*-ship).

A NUMBERS THEORY (6:8–9A)

This is a very strange passage as it uses numbers in such a mundane level as to be suspicious, especially in such a symbolic, complex song/poem. It is my conjecture that these numbers represent something far more profound, and I offer the following discussion as a starting point for further investigations. The numbers given are sixty (queens), eighty (concubines), and one (Nitocris).

The Jewish Virtual Library states:

> The use of letters to signify numbers was known to the Babylonians and the Greeks. The first use of gematria occurs in an inscription of Sargon II (727–707 BCE) which states that the king built the wall of Khorsabad 16,283 cubits long to correspond with the numerical value of his name. "The use of gematria … was widespread in the literature of the Magi and among interpreters of dreams in the Hellenistic world.[4]

Gematria has been mentioned already, i.e., with respect to the sixty soldiers surrounding the king on his return from afar (Song 3:7), i.e., equating to the sixty queens. The number sixty is represented by the fifteenth letter of the Hebrew alphabet, *samech*, and has meanings that relate to

---

[3] Jeffrey C. Geoghegan, "Israelite Sheepshearing and David's Rise to Power," *Biblica* 87 (2006) 55–63, here 55.
[4] "Gematria," *Jewish Virtual Library*, https://www.jewishvirtuallibrary.org/gematria-2.

marriage, the full moon, and by extension, Ishtar/Venus.

The number eighty relates to the seventeenth letter of the Hebrew alphabet, *pey*, which means mouth. Its significance pertains to the power of speech but it might also pertain to the sexual mouth, i.e., the vagina, especially as "lust/passion" also has the gematria of eighty. This would correspond to the sexually-active women of the harem. Other words or phrases that have this gematria include "throne; banner; priesthood; to ensnare; and perfection or complete." The phrase in Song 6:9, "my perfect one," uses the Hebrew word *tam*, meaning complete; Nitocris is considered complete as a woman, i.e., pregnant.

The queens, who are married to the king, are given the number that relates to marriage, and the concubines, the sexual companions who probably whisper sweet nothings to the king, are given the number pertaining to their sexual organs and their words. Nitocris is depicted in terms of her reproductive organs and as having powerful words. It *could* then follow that Nitocris is still considered no better than these concubines (as another disguised slur)—a fate both she and her father (Ahmose) are adamant will not be the case. She appears to the king, however, as on a pedestal; she stands apart from both the queens and the concubines, i.e., she is "the *only* one."

The other women are represented by the fifteenth and the seventeenth Hebrew letters and this becomes: 15 + 17 = 32. The phrase "only one" has a gematria of 32, so she is 'worth' all the other women, combined. Nitocris is represented as "one" *twice* (i.e., "perfect one" and "only one"), using the word *echad*. This makes it 32 + 1 + 1 = 34. The gematria of Babylon is 34. An ominous portent?

The term *echad* is made up of three letters: *dalet, khet, aleph.* It can mean "first," i.e., Nitocris is now granted the status of primary Queen, which is what she wanted all along. The word can also mean the numeral one, as used in gematria, and this has repercussions for the king in the Song, for the number one represents Yahweh/God. Back in 4:8, the king and queen became self-deified, represented in a mountain-top apotheosis; now, because Nitocris has finally become pregnant again (he thinks), the king takes things to an even higher level of aggrandisement (than raising her above the House of David), i.e., he raises her above the glory of God. She is his idol once more, his hand-chosen, awesome goddess; she has become the *only* "one."

The three letters of *echad* ("one"), i.e., *aleph* (gematria of one) representing God; *khet* (gematria of eight) abundant life and reproduction; and *dalet* (gematria of four) motherhood, associated with the four mothers of the HB, i.e., Sarah, Rebekah, Rachel, and Leah, who all suffer from barrenness, combine as 1 + 8 + 4 = 13. The gematria of thirteen is fascinating, for it includes: "Yah is Father" (Iah ≈ the lunar deity ≈ Sîn is

Father); beloved; water (recall the "living water" of 4:15); to devise, plot, or mutter (as an enchanter); to have sex, especially "excessively"; to long for; to rejoice. In a single word, *echad*, the author of the Song potentially encapsulates everything that has happened thus far in Nitocris's tormented struggle with pregnancy and "love," with the final outcome being, to the king at least, a longed-for cause of celebration.

PURE ONE (6:9B–C)

In Song 4:2, the author uses *mum* to indicate a (physical or moral) blemish (i.e., a lack thereof) but in 6:9, the word employed is *bar*, meaning pure, i.e., "pure [one] of her mother ..." (without *echad*, suggesting, perhaps, that to include it would interfere with the symbolic gematria).

Egyptian *wab* priests are "the pure ones"; these are ordinary priests, low in the hierarchy, who perform tasks at the behest of their superiors.[5] Perhaps this is intended as another slur on Nitocris's self-importance, but it does help to identify her as a priestess. The accolade is given in direct relation to her "mother," i.e., a clear indication of Nitocris being a priestess within the sphere of the temple at Karnak, serving alongside Ankhnesneferibre.

The concept of purity is also inextricably linked with ritual and holiness in the Mesopotamian texts. It relates to the holy perfection of the deities, the temples, the ritual purification rites, or the ritually pure kings, priests, diviners: "... purification priest of An, who is fitted for pure prayers rites ... (*ETCSL t.2.6.9.5*, §1–7); "I am a ritually pure interpreter of omens (*ETCSL t.2.4.2.02*, §131–49).

Feminine powers, the art of women, pass from mother to daughter through the ages, unbroken, unstifled, and unfathomable. The queen is now leaving the realm of the petulant, fickle, Ishtar and is being portrayed more and more in the context of the mothering Egyptian Hathor. She shifts from being the virginal "daughter of Pharaoh" to being the epitome of the Mother Goddess in all her glory. A precedent has been created that will follow through to the final verses of the Song, where the concept of the art of women, in all its mysterious forms, is seen being handed down from Nitocris to the "little sister" and this, for the budding Jewish nation, is most certainly a cause for concern.

SYCOPHANTS (6:9D–E)

The maidens are the "daughters of Jerusalem," the ones who also "love" the

---

[5] Nitocris's title is First Prophet of Amun-Re (High Priest); it is highly unlikely the author can devise a subtle pun based on that!

king, and who have seen Nitocris as the disruptive foreign interloper, seizing the king, the crown, the kingdom, but failing to provide the monarch with what he most desires, i.e., a daughter.

The term for "happy" in this verse is *ashar*, meaning to go straight, or advance, and, more appropriately for this current context, to set right, which may suggest they see the queen as now towing the line and behaving as expected. It is often translated in the HB, however, as "blessed," i.e., as in the blessed event (birth). I suggest there is an intended allusion to Rachel and Leah that is further exploited in Song 7:10–13.

In Gen 29:21–30:24, Rachel and Leah go through their respective issues concerning becoming pregnant. Leah, the one less loved, has many sons but then reaches menopause, while Rachel, the younger, more beautiful sister (whom Jacob says he loves) is apparently barren. Both employ the use of a handmaid (or *shifkhah*) to produce children for their husbands: "And Leah said, 'Happy am I! For the women will call me happy ...'" (Gen 30:13).

The "daughters" in the Song, the ones most at odds with the queen, suddenly "see" Nitocris in a new light; they, in unison, attest to her pregnancy with their seemingly sycophantic praise. It would appear Nitocris has succeeded in duping the entire court (or has she?).

SHINING ONE

For "praised" there is *halal*, to shine. One might overlook this simple word but it represents a profound transition from the Song prior to this, and the Song after. Up to this point, the queen has had as an avatar the indomitable Ishtar, mirroring her impetuousness, youthful, sexual intensity, and her warlike nature. From this *exact* point, from this very word, *halal*, the queen's avatar blossoms, transforming into the mothering Shining One, i.e., Hathor. This does not mean that Ishtar is redundant now; it simply means that the queen takes on the symbolic attributes of the Egyptian goddess, who (unlike Ishtar) is known for her role as mother.

HAIL HATHOR (6:10)

In Song 3, the litter of Solomon, the smoke and the dust, etc., brought to mind the arrival of Tammuz in his marriage chariot, and revealed links to a descent into Egypt and, for the first time, a link to Hathor. It was a question concerning something at a distance, not recognised, impending, daunting perhaps; it reflected an apprehension of things to come.

Now, the question relates to something far more specific and much more intimidating. The court had seen the queen in all her glory, on the day she took the crown and was glorified on the mountains of Lebanon (Song 4:8)—but that was nothing compared to this moment, for now the queen is the goddess made manifest. In her finest hour, when she has convinced everyone that she has provided the king with his child, she *becomes* the Shining One and all that power is displayed, as she stands triumphant, looking down at her people, for that is what the Hebrew *shaqaph* means, i.e., not looking "forth" but looking *down*, from above—from the heavens.

The reference to the "dawn" alludes to Hathor as the solar goddess, the Eye of Re, rising at dawn (and also to Ishtar as Venus, but less visually dramatic). It is important to remember that in the Song, it is not only the king who experiences a form of descent (i.e., into madness); the queen endured her own descent in Song 5. She ran through the streets unprotected by the king's "banner." Ridiculed, tormented, demeaned, she came through the other side, like Ishtar returning from the depths, i.e., more mature, wiser, and more powerful. *This* is now Nitocris's moment of ascension; as the dawn sun/star rises in all its glory, so does the queen.

The fact that those asking the question, "Who is that ... ?" need to ask it at all, gives credence to the interpretation here that a drastic transformation has occurred, i.e., the queen is, in effect, unrecognizable. She puts on a good act.

ANOTHER 13 ULŪLŪ ECLIPSE

The powerful combination of lunar and solar metaphors at the height of the queen's glorification is, I suggest, indicative of an eclipse marking the (long-awaited) birth of the historical Ennigaldi-Nanna. I have posited that the 554 BCE eclipse set Nabonidus off on his sojourn through Arabia. As the Song does have its own consistent timeline (see Timeline in the Appendix), both solar and lunar eclipses for the period were researched to discern any potential link to the date already deduced for this stage of the Song, i.e., 545 BCE. There is one lunar eclipse that potentially resolves some longstanding issues surrounding not only Nabonidus and his daughter's dedication cylinder, but also the strange description of the idol of Sîn in the VA.

The two eclipses, for which full information is available in NASA's Lunar Eclipse database,[6] can be compared from an astronomical perspective:

554 BCE (03495): The eclipse began at 01:45 and ended below the horizon, at 07:09, i.e., it "set while eclipsed" (as stated in Nab 34, 1.8–10). The umbral magnitude, i.e., the percentage of the moon darkened by the earth's shadow, was 83.5 per cent. It

---

[6] Details pertain to Baghdad, Iraq (Latitude: 33° 21' 00" N, Longitude: 44° 25' 00" E), some fifty miles from Babylon and cross-referenced with several sites in Saudi Arabia, i.e., as observed from Tayma (Eclipse Predictions by Fred Espenak and Chris O'Byrne (NASA's GSFC), https: //eclipse.gsfc.nasa.gov/JLEX/JLEX-AS.html. For a schematic see https://eclipse.gsfc.nasa.gov/5MCLEmap/-0599--0500/LE-0544-09-16P.gif.

took place on 26 September, or 13 Ulūlū, during the morning watch.

545 BCE (03518): The eclipse began just before midnight, at 23:54,[7] and ended at 04:38 fully visible throughout. It had 29 per cent of its surface darkened. It took place on 16 September, i.e., also 13 Ulūlū, and also during the morning watch.

Nabonidus, recall, was ridiculed in the VA (5.4) for getting things wrong with the series omens and for devising the most abominable idol of Sîn. Michalowski suggested it was the word *inbu*, or "fruit," usually used to describe the new moon crescent, that was wrong, because in order to have a lunar eclipse, the moon must be in its full stage.[8]

What I suggest is that with the 545 BCE eclipse, 29% of the moon in shadow could equate to about the same surface area as a crescent moon, just convex instead of concave. It is only a *small* portion of the moon that is eclipsed, that is the point, so *inbu*/fruit *is* appropriate ("fruit" relates to offspring, i.e., the new moon is 'reborn' as a crescent).[9] Sîn is normally equated with the *full* moon; on the cylinder itself (Nab 34, 1.4–7), Sîn is called "lord of the crown" or "disk," so it is clear Nabonidus wants to make a distinction, i.e., it is not the fuller crown that is eclipsed in this second event but the diminutive "fruit."

In the VA (1.7), the idol of Sîn Nabonidus makes is described as having the "appearance ... of the eclipsed moon," and yet it took human form, with a gesturing hand, and with hair (i.e., that fell down its back, to the ground; might there have been a *seshed* band?); its "face turned hostile" when the king worshipped it (1.8). How can a humanoid figure possibly resemble a partially-shadowed moon?

Beaulieu comments on the depiction of a perceived "man in the

---

[7] There are discrepancies of several minutes between the various catalogue entries, for both eclipses, depending on the source cited, the inherent error margins for calculations, etc. The 545 BCE eclipse is listed elsewhere as 15 September but as it began so close to midnight, the bulk of the event is listed as 16 September. Also, it must be remembered that Babylonian nocturnal timekeeping was based on "watches"; a discrepancy of a few moments would have been impossible to discern.

[8] Piotr Michalowski, "The Doors of the Past," *Eretz-Israel: Archaeological, Historical and Geographical Studies* (2003): 136–52, here 145.

[9] The word *inbi*/*inbu* ("fruit") is also used in Mesopotamian literature as a euphemism for the penis, *implying* procreation. It is used proudly by Ishtar in the Epic of Gilgamesh, when she urges him to give her his "fruit." Ronald A. Veenker, "Forbidden Fruit: Ancient Near Eastern Sexual Metaphors," *Hebrew Union College Annual* 70/71 (1999): 57–73, here 59.

moon" (possibly meant to be the god Nabu fighting a lion) who, during a lunar eclipse that *sets eclipsed*, is said to retain Earth's shadow on his *feet*, thus making them look dirty (i.e., a ruddy colour).[10] This is anthropomorphised and becomes an emotional state of the moon, i.e., it is seen as being distressed somehow, revealing its distemper via the darkening of its features.[11] The northern quadrant of the moon relates to Akkad (Babylon); Nabu is represented as a full human figure on the left of the moon, with his face appearing in the northern quadrant. I suggest that in this second (545 BCE) eclipse it is his face that turns/remains red from Earth's shadow (and the image of the passage of the eclipse on the NASA website confirms this).[12] Nabonidus's statue is probably given a red face (which no one would have seen on an idol before) and this appears as "hostile," or aggressive, to the incoming Persians.[13]

Beaulieu admits that something is amiss regarding the eclipse and that the king probably twisted the interpretation to suit his own plans. Apparently, Nabonidus visits Ur in 555 BCE, ostensibly for preparation of some "project," e.g., the *entu*-priesthood.[14] If we accept the 554 BCE eclipse as the one pertaining to the dedication of his daughter to the new temple of Sîn at Ur, this would give the king only a year to complete all the clearing, designing, and building, and all the preparations for the priesthood itself (Nab 34, 1.26–2.7). It is not enough time. If, however, the 545 BCE eclipse is taken as the one that mark's the birth of Ennigaldi, the king has several years to prepare Ur (whether he visits there in person or not), whilst living in Tayma.

---

[10] Paul-Alain Beaulieu, "The Babylonian Man in the Moon," *Journal of Cuneiform Studies* 51 (1999): 91–99, here 93.

[11] Francesca Rochberg, "Personifications and Metaphors in Babylonian Celestial Omina," *Journal of the American Oriental Society* 116.3 (1996): 475–85, here 479.

[12] See diagram at https://eclipse.gsfc.nasa.gov/5MCLEmap/-0599--0500/LE-0544-09-16P.gif. Cf. the illustration in Beaulieu, "Man in the Moon," 92.

[13] The idea of the moon being distressed is expanded upon with the myth that demons are responsible for this darkening and emotional stress (Rochberg, 479); the Persians might have misunderstood the concept and applied this to the idol of Sîn *himself* "becoming like a demon." The red colour of household idols seems to be a common phenomenon, according to Wis 13:14, but not for cultic statues. Esarhaddon describes fashioning a crown of "red gold" for a cultic statue he was renovating, which was never done before; pure gold was used for the "skin" of such statues (Christopher Walker and Michael B. Dick, "The Induction of the Cult Image in Ancient Mesopotamia: The Mesopotamian *mis pî* Ritual," in *Born in Heaven, Made on Earth: The Making of the Cult Image in the Ancient Near East*, ed. Michael B. Dick [Winona Lake: Eisenbrauns,1999], 55–122, here 64–6).

[14] Paul-Alain Beaulieu, *The Reign of Nabonidus King of Babylon 556–539 B.C.* (London: Yale University Press, 1989), 129.

The Song, therefore, presents a calendrical matrix for its narrative, with a 13 Ulūlū eclipse in the year 545 BCE, set in a context of the birth of a special child (the "fruit"). The two eclipses, one starting Nabonidus's physical and spiritual sojourn, and one (effectively) ending it, must have seemed to the king as a divine confirmation of his plan, of Sin's "desire," and thus immutable, regardless of any human omens of doom.

The inscription on Ennigaldi's cylinder (Nab 34) can be interpreted to include *both* events, i.e., the "setting" of the 554 BCE eclipse *and* the "fruit" of the 545 BCE eclipse; this would undoubtedly seem to the (blinkered) astrologers as if the king had made a mistake. The idol of Sîn certainly seems to have a visual/symbolic correlation with the 545 BCE eclipse, and hints at Nabonidus's strange new method of conflating various concepts into his design of the idol. For the Song, the first eclipse is not as important as the second because it occurs before Nitocris is introduced (and therefore before the author begins the tale), so it is not mentioned. The event of the *entu*'s birth is central to the Song's narrative, so it is apt that the 13 Ulūlū eclipse in the year of her arrival is recorded.

THANKS ISHTAR

The two main inscriptions pertaining to Nabonidus repairing or improving the temples of Ishtar fall in his seventh and ninth-to-eleventh regnal years; the former in the king's own words (Nab 10, 2.10b–13), the latter an estimate by scholars.[15] That is, the year of the treaty with Ahmose, the formalised plan to re-establish the *entu*-priesthood at Ur, and the "Dream Omen" (549 BCE); and just after Ennigaldi is born in Tayma (c.545 BCE). Might these be "please" and "thank you" gestures to the goddess?

FLASHBACK (6:11–12)

For "orchard," is the Hebrew noun *ginnah*, which is the feminine form of *gan* that was used to describe the king's "garden" in Song 6:2. This suggests the "nut orchard," or "nut garden," is a feminine place, i.e., a place of women (in Song 4:13, the "orchard" was mentioned in connection with the miscarriage, i.e., also a feminine context).

The term for "nut" is *egoz*, which is more specifically a walnut; this is the only instance in the HB of this term. There is an Ugaritic hymn to Ningal, the consort of Nanna/Sîn and the mother of Ishtar, that says: "I sing the goddesses … / Who go down to the walnut (grove)"; a "walnut grove …

---

[15] Frauke Weiershäuser and Jamie Novotny, *The Royal Inscriptions of Amēl-Marduk (561–560 BC), Neriglissar (559–556 BC), and Nabonidus (555–539 BC), Kings of Babylon*, The Royal Inscriptions of the Neo-Babylonian Empire, Vol. 2 (University Park: Eisenbrauns, 2020), 104; Beaulieu, *The Reign of Nabonidus*, 32.

surrounds the shrine of Adonis at Afqa," in Lebanon.[16]

The symbolic (Jewish) history of the walnut pertains predominantly to marriage, sex, and pregnancy: "What does an embryo resemble when it is in its mother's bowels? A nut floating in a bowl of water" (Niddah 31a). In the Baraita de-Niddah, the walnut's multiple layers represent the hymen, protecting virginity; the four inner chambers represent the four female reproductive organs (as perceived in Niddah 17b); and the nut, as a whole represents the male glans penis, and/or the testicles.[17] This was seen as a divine mystery and deliberated in a text by Rabbi Eleazar of Worms (1176–1238 CE) called "The Secret of the Nut," which expounded the esoteric connection between the Song's mention of the nut/walnut and the vision of the divine chariot in Ezekiel 1 (of course, we have a chariot mentioned in Song 6:12). Basically, the idea was that both female and male energies "united in the Godhead," and this was signified by the feminine terminology for the chariot or "divine throne."[18] If Eleazar's "Secret of the Nut" was instigated by his understanding of Song 6:11, then we must acknowledge that the topics of the queen's menstrual cycle and womb, and the basic tenets of her *dod*-based religious perspective, are fundamental to an understanding of the Song.

FRUIT

The Hebrew term used in 6:11 for "green" is *eb*, and this can mean freshness (as in new growth) but it can also mean fruit. This is interesting because we have just had the eclipse scene, where the fruit is a central consideration; the Akkadian cognate of *eb* is *inbu*,[19] the very word used on the cylinder (Nab 34).

CHARIOT

In 1 Kgs 10:26, the masculine noun *rekeb* is used to denote a military chariot. The Song's author intentionally feminises the chariot (*merkabah*) reflecting *her* gender perhaps, and the intimate connection she would have with the context (compared to a male author), i.e., childbirth and motherhood. If we consider, however, that much of the Song's original audience is Canaanite, i.e., those who follow the Ugaritic Baal/Astarte religion (the local versions of Ishtar and Tammuz), perhaps the reference is directly related to their understanding of the mythology. Astarte is also a deity within the Egyptian

---

[16] Marvin H. Pope, *Song of Songs, The Anchor Bible* (New York: Doubleday, 1977), 577.

[17] Sharon Faye Koren, *Forsaken: The Menstruant in Medieval Jewish Mysticism* (Hanover: Brandeis University Press, 2011), 56–7.

[18] Koren, 58.

[19] Pope, 582.

pantheon, where she is even more a war-faring goddess, referred to as the Mistress of the Horses, Lady of the Chariot. Thus, the reference may be another intended conflation, to reiterate the queen's Egyptian heritage (and her warlike nature) but also, to maintain the interest of the locals.

There is also a potential link to the constellation of the Chariot, known to us now as Auriga, which is depicted as a shepherd carrying two kids and the reins of a chariot. "The constellation is especially prominent in the winter and spring months, a time when shepherds traditionally spent nights out in the fields with their flocks."[20] The constellation is thus symbolically linked to Tammuz, the shepherd, the bringer of spring, and participant in the *hieros gamos*. The third and final sacred marriage allusion begins with the very next verse.

> *Enlil stepped onto the chariot and embraced*
> *Mother Ninlil, his spouse.*
> *ETCSL t.2.5.4.09, §66–81*

AMMINADAB?

Some consider the words *ammi nadib* to be the name, Amminadab (Exod 6:23; Num 1:7; Ruth 4:19). The verb *nadab* connotes a volunteering for war (Judg 5:2) or other service (2 Chr 17:16), but most often for donating goods to the temple (1 Chr 29:5, Ezra 1:4). The queen has just made a profound transition from irresponsible, petulant youth, to mature, seemingly domesticated mother. She has been depicted in "battle mode" for some time now, so the allusion is apt. Of course, the *entu* will be given up to the temple, in due course. This seems enough to justify the use of *nadib*, perhaps, but I suggest there is more to be gleaned from this choice of phrasing.

The noun *am* (people) stems from the verb *amam*, meaning to darken and figuratively, to make secret. It is like going right back to the beginning of the Song and Nitocris's alleged darkness. The insinuation of secrecy is highly significant, for there are many secrets in the Song: Nitocris's contraceptives and intended abortion are kept a secret from her husband; she does not seem to want to tell the king about her being bullied by the guards, or ridiculed by the "daughters"; and now there is the fake pregnancy.

In addition, with the use of *ammi nadib* (in this format), coming so soon after the query "Who is that …?" and in the context of one "looking down" points us (as a proper noun may not) to a parallel in Ps 113:5–9:

> …who looks far down on the heavens and the earth?
> He raises the poor from the dust …

---

[20] Adam Mann, "Auriga constellation: Facts about the charioteer," (2020), https://www.space.com /auriga-constellation.html.

to make them sit with princes,
with the princes of his people.
He gives the barren woman a home,
making her the joyous mother of children.

Song 6:11–12, then, acts as a flashback, providing an explanation for the previous scene of Nitocris's amazing transformation and ascent. It provides the truth of the matter. This technique allows for the momentum of her ascension to be unbroken, intensifying the notion of a whirlwind of circumstances (e.g., "Before I was aware ...") that sweep her upward, from her descent and humiliation, her spontaneous declaration of pregnancy, through the making of the idol, and then being heralded as a mother goddess. We get swept along, too, which is one of the most powerful aspects of the Song as a whole, i.e., allowing us to fall for everything she says and does, so we experience what the king experiences. Therein lies a lesson.

Nitocris, from the moment the king burst in on her as she was meditating in a purified state, has seen the king as an adversary. She is intent on retaining her position as Queen, and on preventing any further sexual harassment. In a moment of frustration and fear she had declared herself pregnant (Song 5:8), and since then she has kept close to her chest the fact that under her clothing there is no rounded belly, no breasts enlarging with milk. The king is diverted by his other women, seeing what he wants to see, and the entire over-enthusiastic scene in Song 6:5–9, echoing his delight when she *was* pregnant in 4:1–7, confirms that he is oblivious to her trickery. He does not see clearly any longer.

DOWN IN THE VALLEY

The truth of the matter is that Nitocris has devised to find a child she can pass off as her own, i.e., a child of one of the king's many other "lilies."

The king "goes down" to "gather lilies," and the queen goes "*down*" to the "nut orchard" because, on a mundane level, both seem to allude to the same notion—the abode of women, i.e., in the latter case, those he has impregnated. Beyond the palace and the city, in the countryside, where the green vegetation grows, i.e., where Life grows, the "nut orchard" reflects, perhaps, a designated place where concubines that become pregnant are sent for their confinement. Nitocris goes down "to see" but the verb *raah* has many applications, including to inspect, or select, which supports the idea that she has gone to this "nut garden" for a purpose, not just to admire the flora.

The Hebrew noun *nachal* is employed for "valley," whereas in Song 2:1 it is *emeq* (i.e., a vale), so the author is making a distinction. *Nachal* is a stream, or a winter torrent that cuts through the land, making a valley. In Song 4 flooding waters and streams were understood in relation to the pregnancy, the miscarriage, and the king's multiple efforts at impregnation. In the tale of Samson in Judg 16:4, Delilah is seen to come the "valley of Sorek" and *nachal* is used there, also; this was interpreted (in Part One, Chapter 3) in terms of allusions to menstruation, therefore to the woman's womb/genitalia.

Note the inclusion of blossoms, buds, and pomegranates, all in the plural, again identifying the "nut orchard" as a collective, i.e., the place of a group of women. These are said to be the objects of the queen's attention. In both Egyptian and Mesopotamian iconography, the lotus bud-and-blossom motif "is widely recognised as a symbol of rebirth and immortal life."[21] Hathor, in giving life to Horus "presents lotus buds" from her body, representing the birth of the "proverbial scion of the sun."[22] Childbirth is thus implied, here in the Song. The third element often depicted in Egyptian art is the fruit set between the bud and the blossom. This denotes the father (to a Mesopotamian mind, Tammuz/Nabonidus, the "bud"), mother (the blossom of the lotus, Ishtar/Nitocris), and the *inbu* (fruit/offspring).

Nitocris's plan is daring but it seems to be working, for everyone is under the impression she is the mother of the king's child, who still remains down in the valley, ostensibly with her wet-nurse (but in reality, with her natural mother). All too soon, however, the "truth" nearly comes to light in an unexpected way.

---

[21] J. Andrew McDonald, "Botanical Determination of the Middle Eastern Tree of Life," *Economic Botany* 56.2 (2002): 113–29, here 117.
[22] McDonald, "Botanical Determination," 124–5.

7. DELECTABLE DECEIVER

HIEROS GAMOS 3: GOD'S HAND, RETURN! (6:13)

Hathor, as the itinerant Eye of Re, travels deep into the far south-eastern desert; when the time comes for her to return to Re, her worshippers implore her to "Come! Come!" i.e., *twice*, in a well-known song, intended to convince her to hurry back to Egypt, where she belongs. Her people wish to adore her and have prepared a welcoming festival in her honour, called the Festival of Drunkenness, during which there is much dancing, drinking, and a very broadminded enjoyment of all manner of pornographic and lewd behaviour. The return of Hathor anticipates the *hieros gamos*, coinciding "with the coming of the god and their union at the entrance of the temple, the place of ... celebration and inebriation."[1]

Hathor is, like Ishtar, the goddess of sexuality but she is also, unlike Ishtar, the goddess of birthing, i.e., creation. In this capacity, she is known as "the Hand of God," that is, God's Hand (the Egyptian, *dtr*). I posit that this complex incorporation of Hathoric allusions into the Song, apart from telling us Nitocris is Egyptian, and even apart from the fact that it positions her in a pregnancy/motherhood context, deliberately points to the identification of Nitocris *as* God's Hand, confirming the suspicion declared in the analysis of Song 5, and thereby making her truly her mother's (i.e., God's Hand, Ankhnesneferibre's) cultic daughter.

The emissaries hint, in a sardonic manner, at the miraculous birth of the child, from the once apparently barren Nitocris (i.e., after the miscarriage she fails to get pregnant again quickly, a combination which would classify her as barren).

The context of Hathor and her return from Nubia to Egypt also serves as a partial calendrical clue in the Song. The Festival of Drunkenness takes place on the twentieth day of the first month of the Egyptian year, Thoth (i.e., roughly 11 September to 10 October). It is now c.544 BCE (20 Thoth equates to 30 September in this year).

---

[1] John Coleman Darnell, "Hathor Returns to Medamûd," *Studien Zur Altägyptischen Kultur* 22 (1995): 47–94, here 59.

TURN!

The Festival of Drunkenness is known for its dancing, which Hathor is said to enjoy more than anything. Here, in 6:13, the imperative *shuvi*, is used, i.e., turn or return. In the Masoretic Text, it is *sovi*, revolve, spin, from *savav*, to turn around, i.e., as if in a dance, which, of course, is mentioned in the subsequent sentence.

Remember that the use of Hathoric symbolism does not preclude the consistency of Ishtar allusions. Ishtar is dubbed the "dancing one" in the Great Prayer to Ishtar; she dances the "whirl like a man"; "the Akkadian word for this whirling dance is *gushtu*, a pun on Ishtar's name Gushea" and, like the famous Whirling Dervishes, it was normally associated with men.[2] Moreover, as the goddess who dons armour and relishes in the gory, exciting mayhem that is war, she is honoured for her "dance"—her dance of war: "… heroic lady, fit for battle, who, as the heroine of the battleground, makes the troops dance the dance of Inanna" (*ETCSL t.1.8.2.3*, §281–93). With the association of motherhood and battle discussed earlier, this could be quite an ominous portent.

LOOKING

The word for "look," *chazah*, is unique to 6:13 and suggests rather more than mere visual contact; it means to gaze at, to contemplate, have a vision of, etc., and is linked to the notion of prophecy. It can suggest an ecstatic state, and the Arabic form of this implies "seeing" with an inner vision, as an astrologer/diviner. In the following verses, we see a group of people (men) gazing upon Nitocris as if she were an idol, and we learn that they do, indeed, have an uncanny insight ("inner vision"). What follows is a debauched, veritable assault on the queen (veiled in idol-worship imagery), which is in keeping with the Egyptian festivities upon Hathor's return. Their gaze makes Nitocris uncomfortable, however, for it touches a nerve. She is no longer in the Egyptian camp, and has never been truly accepted into the king's camp.

It was once said of Inanna: "You never grow weary with admirers looking at you" (*ETCSL t.1.1.3*, §445–50); now Nitocris has matured, such scrutiny of *her* has become wearisome.

SHULAMMITE

The traditional understanding of "Shulammite" is that it is the feminine of "Solomon." I railed against this seemingly simplistic explanation for years, only to end up thinking it is correct!

Shulammite has intriguing cultic roots, i.e., Albright argued that the

---

[2] Rivkah Harris, "Inanna-Ištar as Paradox and a Coincidence of Opposites," *History of Religions* 30.3 (1991): 261–78, here 267, note 31; 275.

name represents "the goddess [Ishtar] belonging to Shulman";[3] Meek asserted that the similar Shulmanitu is to be equated with "Ishtar of Urusilima," a Babylonian city.[4] However, I posit that there has to be specific meaning within the context of the narrative itself.

The Hebrew term, *shulammith*, is derived from *shalem*, and thereby has the same etymology as "Solomon," i.e., to be complete, whole, make restitution/amends. For Nabonidus, the pseudonym "Solomon" pointed to his penance for stealing the Tablet of Destinies (figuratively); his restitution is dictated by Daniel (in Daniel 4). For Nitocris, restitution comes in the form of the feigned pregnancy; this is how she fulfils her 'penance' for making the king mad (she takes away his first child, takes away his senses, but then 'restores' them). The Song, therefore, provides corresponding epithets for both parties, based on their respective quests to make amends. This binds them; it sets them up as the two parties in the "peace-making" processes, the adversaries "dancing" around each other in a battle of wills and philosophies.

That *shulammith* is spoken by a certain group of people is significant, for it implies they not only know Nitocris, they also know what she has been up to; this is substantiated in the next verses. The Egyptian visitors use the epithet disparagingly, not as a form of praise.

DANCE OF MAHANAIM

In Gen 32:2, the place where Jacob meets the "angels of God" is called Mahanaim, which is taken to mean "two camps" (see NRSV note "i"). This is often noted to be the source of the allusion in the Song but there is no satisfying reintegration into the narrative. I always contend that when relying on intertextual connections for interpretation, the entire context of a passage must be taken into consideration, not just the one sentence that seems obvious.

In Gen 32:9, for instance, God tells Jacob to go home: "Return to your country and to your kindred ...." This sets the context for the ensuing scenario, i.e., one of personal transformation. Jacob, intent on making amends for past wrongs, is revealed in his moment of ascension; he is raised up, given a figurative seat of honour, and receives his commission name, Israel. This is what has just happened to Nitocris; the people in the Song are saying to Nitocris, "Return to your homeland, to us, your kindred." The "dance" she speaks of, via its relation to Mahanaim of Gen 32:2, relates directly to the men's perception of her as "the Shulammite," i.e., the one who has seemingly made amends, has been declared blameless, etc. It then

---

[3] Marvin H. Pope, *Song of Songs: A New Translation with Introduction and Commentary* (New York: Doubleday, 1977), 599.

[4] James Meek, "Canticles and the Tammuz Cult," *American Journal of Semitic Languages and Literature* 39.1 (1922):1–14, here, 7, note 1.

follows that Nitocris's situation with the men should, in some way, emulate that of Jacob.

When you take a closer look at what Jacob does at Mahanaim, you see that he is hedging his bets, i.e., he splits his community and all the livestock into "two companies," so that if one group gets killed in battle, the other will remain safe. Nitocris is hedging her bets here, too; she is playing a dangerous game in the hope that she can retain her position as Queen and eventually secure her rightful place in the new temple at Ur; if she can satisfy the conditions of her father's treaty, retain her physical isolation from the king, and still give Nabonidus what he wants, she can live with her choices (perhaps).

The "insight" of these men is yet to be demonstrated but Nitocris's strange question starts the ball rolling; if she had stayed silent, perhaps things would have gone a different way but her Ishtar-like overconfidence puts her in the most precarious position. She asks, in effect: "What do you see when you look at me? In order to make things right (i.e., not just for her husband, but for her father and the treaty), I have to put on this performance," i.e., the "dance" that is ultimately a battle of the two camps—his and hers, physical and spiritual, solar and lunar.

EMISSARIES

I suggest these people are emissaries sent by Ahmose, to see how Nitocris is being cared for, i.e., to judge whether Nabonidus is living up to his part of the bargain. As news reaches him that she has had a child, the pharaoh, perhaps, feels the need to have eyes and ears in Nabonidus's court. A well-known precedent exists in Amarna Letter EA 4:4–14 (cuneiform correspondence between Amenhotep III and various kingdom leaders). Kadashman-Enlil I, the Kassite King of Babylon (c.1374–60 BCE), is keen to receive one of the pharaoh's daughters as a wife but Amenhotep explains that he never allows his daughters to marry foreigners. Famously, Kadashman settles for any beautiful woman and much gold, but the not so famous aspect of the story is the continued conversation between the rulers. Amenhotep has already married Kadashman-Enlil's sister and tells him his sister is not being treated as a concubine, as the previous envoys had falsely intimated, offering to let a suitable eunuch come and inspect her surroundings.

It is feasible that the emissaries of Song 7 are the ones responsible for the rumours that end up being immortalised in Herodotus's *Histories*, concerning not only Nitetis and her "angry" husband, the foreign king (3.1–3), but also Ahmose's legitimate concern about the status of the woman he sends as part of the treaty of 549 BCE.

SANDALS AND THIGHS (7:1)

In Song 7:1–9, the Egyptian visitors pay homage to the Queen of Babylon using sexually-charged metaphors and suggestive, probably wine-induced innuendo befitting the Festival of Drunkenness.

The apparent song of praise in Song 7:1–9 contains symbolic references to everything the queen has done, from her early miscarriage to her final entrapment of the king, and its superficially flattering language belies a sobering incentive for this tribute.

SANDALS

In Song 5:10–16 Nitocris began her idol of the king with the head and worked her way down. These men, although her Egyptian kindred, start from the feet and work upward. I have argued that the queen's magical poppet is portrayed as inverted to reveal its occult, magical nature, thereby illustrating its potentially sinister ramifications for the Jewish nation. The Egyptian men create an idol with their words, in the manner a cultic idol would be made, i.e., from the bottom up, with strong feet/bases, a lifelike body, and a head that is central to the "opening of the mouth" ceremony, upon completion. Recall, too, the creation of Gilgamesh by the goddess was performed "from bottom to top."

We, the audience, know the secret of Nitocris's unwillingness to conceive, of her misuse of contraceptives, and of her pregnancy deception. The king and his harem, however, do not, but *somehow* her own people, these visiting men, seem cognisant of everything she has done; they exhibit an uncanny insight into the most intimate and personal aspects of her life. In an uncomfortable demonstration, in response to her question, the queen is subjected to an uncanny account of her nature and her actions.

By mentioning sandals, the men instantly alert Nitocris to their less than reverential intentions. Recall that "sandal" is the name (in Mesopotamia) given to a certain type of aborted foetus. It would have been public knowledge that the queen had lost a child (as the king had openly declared her pregnancy), so this is not really "insight"; it is, however, their opening gambit. They have hit a nerve and have her attention.

The Song's author foresees the inevitable fall of Nabonidus to the foreign woman but she can appreciate that this has worked both ways. Nitocris has been taken away from everything she knew and loved, perhaps "dragged" away against her will (as Song 1:4 could suggest), and her own people may see the marriage in much the same light as their Jewish counterparts. Perhaps, on one level, the sandals represent domesticity and ownership, as the bridle imagery had done, earlier in Song 1:10–11. It may be that the men are attempting to play on Nitocris's strong sense of independence, of being in control, i.e., the sandals become symbolic of the dominance of the Babylonian (or, in the case of Solomon, the Hebrew) culture, supposedly restraining her, forcing her to conform.

From a cultic perspective, however, sandals are given high status: Ishtar "chooses ornate sandals and puts them on her toes" (*ETCSL t.4.08.20*, §11–24). In the tale of their courtship, the goddess decrees the fate of Tammuz, affirming his kingship; he is deemed "fit" to "race on the road with the holy sceptre in [his] hand / And the holy sandals on [his] feet."[5] Sandals represent the warrior goddess; as the "whirlwind warrior," Inanna "goes out running / strapping on her sandals."[6] The sandal is deemed a living entity in its own right and performs certain actions in Ishtar's temple at Uruk. It "rises" in the presence of the gods and goddesses, and is escorted to the sacred bed-chamber by the divine "daughters of Uruk and An, where it is ceremoniously placed on a stool.[7]

In Egypt, the God's Wife, Ankhnesneferibre, is depicted at Karnak wearing sandals as part of her official cultic regalia; she also appears on her sarcophagus with well-made sandals, attesting to her status. As the First Prophet of Amun-Re, Nitocris surely wore sandals (of papyrus) while initiating but her queenly sandals are probably leather, finely decorated and ornamental. Perhaps this is a backhanded compliment, suggesting she has been 'bought' and has therefore lost her sacerdotal status, in favour of a very earthly station.

PRINCESS/GODDESS

The Hebrew words used here for "queenly maiden" are *bath* (daughter) and *nadiyb* (inclined, generous, noble), a term used in Song 6:12, recall. The KJV is closer to the truth with its "prince's daughter" translation, for Nitocris is, indeed, a royal princess. The fact that she is called a daughter and not a wife or companion, is significant, for this is a subtle allusion to her identity as the cultic daughter of Ankhnesneferibre, and the "daughter of Pharaoh."

In the myths of Ishtar, the goddess is hailed in just these terms: "… you are unmatched among the Great Princes …" (*ETCSL t.1.3.5*, §D61–2); "The great princely scion …" (*ETCSL t.1.3.1*, §H206–17). Ningal, Ishtar's mother, is likewise depicted as "the woman of princely seed" (*ETCSL*

---

[5] Diane Wolkstein and Samuel Noah Kramer, *Inanna, Queen of Heaven: Her Stories and Hymns from Sumer* (New York: Harper and Row, 1983), 45. Also, E. Douglas Van Buren asserts that sandals were a symbol of royalty ("The Sacred Marriage in Early Times in Mesopotamia," *Orientalia*, NOVA Series, 13 (1944): 1–72, here 10).
[6] Betty De Shong Meador, "Lady of Largest Heart," in *Inanna: Lady of Largest Heart: Poems of the Sumerian High Priestess Enheduanna* (Austin: University of Texas Press, 2000), 118.
[7] Beatrice L. Goff, "The Role of Amulets in Mesopotamian Ritual Texts," *Journal of the Warburg and Courtauld Institutes* 19.1/2 (1956): 1–39, here 9.

t.2.4.1.6, §36–44), reiterating the mother-daughter element. The greater gods are called "princes," their powers are the "princely powers"; the Sumerian Nanna, Enki, and An are all given the title of Prince, and each, in one myth or other, is portrayed as Inanna's father. So, again, Nitocris's presentation as the avatar of the Mesopotamian goddess is maintained, even within the Egyptian context, here; this is a sign of a very skilful author who wishes to keep the attention of her audiences, who are probably not Egyptian.

THIGHS

Rounded thighs have long been a symbol of female sexuality, fertility, and strength in childbearing. For "rounded," the Hebrew noun employed is *chammuq*, used in the HB only here in the Song, and translated as "curves." This is generally understood to be the gentle curve of her outer thighs. *Chammuq* stems from the verb *chamaq*, to turn away, which is used in Song 5:6, to indicate that the king had turned away from the queen and had left. The only other place in the HB where the verb *chamaq* is used is in Jer 31:22, i.e., "How long will you *waver*, / O faithless daughter?" The men are hinting at Nitocris's constant hot and cold treatment of the king, her teasing him with seduction and then shutting him out. Jer 31:21 also contains a familiar cry: "Return, O virgin Israel, / return to these your cities," and elsewhere are found "vineyards," "dancing," "sentinels," "fruit," "Zion," fatherhood, the death of children, and even "thigh," all in a context of forgiveness and restoration of one who admits fault and puts things right.

In the KJV, *chammuq* is translated as, "joints." The joints of a woman's thighs? I suggest this is a reference to the tops of her *inner* thighs, where the natural fullness of a young woman's flesh *turns* to join her genital area, i.e., the 'joints' between legs and pubis. The 'turning away' of the fleshy thigh, to form the iconic feminine "v" is more apt given the context, where the Egyptian men are intoxicated, revelling, and performing their sacred duty by using pornographic imagery. The gentle curve of the queen's outer thigh just does not fit the tone.

A poem of Ishtar reads: "Into your vulva, where you put your trust, / As if it were your precious jewel in front of you."[8] Body jewels, in the form of precious and semi-precious stones, are an aspect of the sacred couple's sexual attraction: Tammuz "brings to the maiden ... a heap of stones to choose from. ... She chooses the buttocks beads ... the head stones ... bright alabaster and puts it on her thighs (*ETCSL t.4.08.20*, §8–24); "He of the *shuba* jewels ... is indeed ploughing with the *shuba* jewels! ... May the large jewels among his jewels be on our holy breast!" (*ETCSL t.4.08.09*, §25–35).

---

[8] Benjamin R. Foster, *From Distant Days: Myths, Tales, and Poetry of Ancient Mesopotamia* (Bethesda: CDL Press, 1995), a:3–4, 377.

MASTER CRAFTSMAN

The idea of the queen being depicted in Song 7 as an idol, a sculpture, or figurine, is further emphasised by the mention of the "master craftsman," and this can relate to either a deity, e.g., "... through their intricate craftsmanship, the Enki and Ninki deities have perfected the divine powers with their righteousness ..." (*ETCSL t.4.13.08*, §B7–9); or, as the priest in charge of "opening the mouth" of the statues, who is called "craftsman of the great gods" (*ETCSL t.2.6.9.2*, §9–20). It may also identify those skilled artists who actually manufacture the cultic idols for the temples. It undeniably pertains to cultic statues.

NAVEL AND BELLY (7:2)

There has been much debate about whether or not the reference to her navel implies Nitocris's vulva. As I have committed to rendering the bejewelled "joints" (of the thighs) as the external genital area, I have another suggestion for the combined rendering of "navel" and "belly."

The Hebrew noun *shorer* designates the navel and this is said to come from *sharar*, meaning twisting, in reference to the umbilical cord; the word *shor* is used in Ezek 16:4, where Jerusalem is said to be the offspring of mixed parentage, and "abhorred" from the day of "her" birth, the umbilical cord left uncut. The allusion could not be clearer; the men in Song 7 are insulting the potential offspring of the mixed marriage, i.e., neither Egyptian nor Babylonian, therefore not wanted by either camp. This is why Nitocris's navel does not lack ("never lacks" is misleading) "mixed wine." As mentioned earlier, in terms of female reproduction, wine is equated with blood (Mishnah Niddah 9:11), so the reference here is to mixed *blood*. The root word *sharar* actually means hostile, or enemy, which fits the context, from the Egyptians' perspective.

BASIN

The "goblet" or "bowl" is indicated by *aggan*, and this word is used in only two other places in the HB, namely, Isa 22:24 (translated as vessel) and Exod 24:6 (basin). Isaiah uses the term in the context of offspring/descendants, while in Exodus, the context is that of the blood-covenant, so both seem to be potential targets of an allusion, i.e., to the womb, as a vessel (for the blood of procreation, and the "fruit" of mixed blood).

Ancient Near Eastern perceptions of conception are founded on a belief that a woman's womb serves as a *vessel* for *mixing* the male semen and the female blood, the latter of which is deemed to be the woman's contribution to conception. Recall the king's words in Song 4:15, which speak of his generous supply of "living water" that he 'fills' her with.

So, I would argue that "navel" relates to the internal reproductive organs (vagina and uterus), as it implies the umbilical cord, which is attached to a foetus within; the rounded "belly" (*beten*) therefore, becomes the outward sign of what is (supposedly) within. There is really no problem with this sequence, i.e., "joints" as pudendum/vulva; then via that route to the supposed child in the womb; then praising the (presumed) resulting fullness.

To the ancient Near Eastern mind, the vessel, or basin, is almost certainly an *internal* organ, i.e., Ishtar prepares herself for a sexual encounter with her lover, Dumuzi: "'Plough in my genitals, man of my heart!'" ... bathed her holy hips ... holy ... the holy basin ...." (*ETCSL t.4.08.16*, §B31–4). She bathes her intimate areas but the text is fragmented and leaves the tantalizing "holy basin" to our imagination; as she has already washed her hips, and there follows another body part, which is probably her vulva, perhaps the rest of the sentence may pertain to being ready to receive Tammuz's much-cherished "milk" into her "basin" (hence vagina/womb), as in this parallel (where her "churn" equates to her vessel/basin): "Let the milk of the goat flow in my sheepfold. / Fill my holy churn with honey cheese."[9] In other words, Ishtar washes her vagina. In her yearly bathing ritual (in Ulūlū), the goddess reaffirms her virginity (whatever she has been up to), so a cleansing of the vagina (e.g., by douching), seems appropriate.

WHEAT

In the HB, wheat is associated with pregnancy on at least two occasions, i.e., in the books of Genesis and Ruth. It is during the wheat harvest that Leah allows Rachel, who is desperate to conceive, to lay with Jacob one more time in exchange for Reuben's mandrakes (Genesis 30). In the Book of Ruth, the wheat fields and the threshing floor become synonymous with sexual attraction and fulfilment, as Ruth, the foreigner, makes clear her intention to marry and conceive. Nitocris is described here in the language of fertility, and in Mesopotamia and Egypt the first and foremost sign of fertility is abundant wheat, i.e., grain. In the Sumerian literature, even the notion of a "heap" becomes synonymous with plenty, abundance, etc.: "The fertile arable tracts shall grow dappled grain for you; grain piles shall be heaped up for you" (*ETCSL t.2.5.4.02*, §43–60). Ishtar herself is likened to a heap of grain: "Maiden, colourful as a pile of grain, fit for the king ... colourful as a pile of grain" (*ETCSL t.4.08.18*, §A1–8). The oldest known pregnancy test is that of a women urinating on wheat, i.e., if it sprouts, she is pregnant; might this be another of the men's obscure hints?

LOTUS FENCE

The very clear fertility goddess imagery is linked all the more to Nitocris by

---

[9] Diane Wolkstein and Samuel Noah Kramer, *Inanna, Queen of Heaven: Her Stories and Hymns from Sumer* (New York: Harper and Row, 1983), 39.

the mention of the ring of "lilies" which adorns the place where Nabonidus "pastures his flock"; they draw attention to the site of fertilization, the womb. Her belly is symbolically crowned by a circle of lotuses, as the child is a girl. She, like her mother, and the other wombs of the king's intimate acquaintance, is represented by this gender-biased bed of flowers.[10]

This circle of lotuses is defined by the word *sug*, which means a protective fence; why would her belly/womb need protection, if the context here is not one of pregnancy? In ancient Egypt the womb was seen as a protective container: "17 Coffin Texts Spell 148 thus informs us: 'It is in my uterus that he (Re-Atum) has tied a protective circle around him (Horus) (because) he (Re-Atum) knows that that is the heir of Osiris.'"[11] As the representation of Hathor, in the eyes of her Egyptian visitors, the symbolic circle of lotuses on Nitocris's alluded-to bump emulates this "protective circle." Again, however, this proves to be more an accusation than a suggestion of praise or endearment, for while she was once the protector of the young "vineyards," she has since failed to protect the one child she did conceive, and has also failed to protect the Elixir, i.e., the womb-blood.

FERTILITY IDOL 2: PARODY

The emissaries arrive in Tayma a year after Ennigaldi is born (if we follow the internal chronology) but they praise Nitocris *as if* she is pregnant; their focus on her body, her reproductive qualities, suggests she is being worshipped as a fertility idol, as Hathor would be upon her return. They have just alluded to her genitals and her inner "vessel" and now they expound upon her *supposedly* fuller belly. This entire scenario, however, is a parody (within the parody of the Song itself). While superficially creating a living idol of Nitocris, making her appear to be their cherished fertility goddess, the resulting depiction of the queen is far from what one might expect. They toy with her in a most denigrating way.

I argue that it is the author's personal perspective that fills these next few verses with the venom they exude but that must await the appropriate discussion (Part Two, Chapter 9).

---

[10] Irit Ziffer states: "The lily pattern representing female genitals is used in stones resembling pregnant women found at Deir el-Medina," in "Western Asiatic Tree-Goddesses," *Ägypten Und Levante / Egypt and the Levant* 20 (2010): 411–30, here 415.

[11] Martin Pehal and Markéta Preininger Svobodová, "Death and the Right Fluids: Perspectives from Egyptology and Anthropology," *Journal of Ancient Egyptian Interconnections* 17 (2018): 114–136, here 116.

NO NURSING BREASTS (7:3)

This is a partial repetition of Song 4:5, following the upward movement of the men's gaze but without the final phrase, "that feed among the lilies." As noted in the analysis of Song 4:5, this metaphor was used to allude to Nitocris as an expectant mother, i.e., her breasts were fit for nursing the child she carried. Just as with the omission of the "crimson lips" from the king's praise in Song 6:6–7, which indicated the (assumed) absence of menses, the omission of the "nursing gazelle" indicates the emissaries are aware of Nitocris's ruse. They know she has never nursed a baby.

CITIES (7:4)

A luxury product, ivory was reserved for the elite/royalty. In Amos 3:15, ivory is directly linked to idolatrous practices in Samaria, where the temples of ivory are ordered destroyed. Thus, ivory relates to postexilic Samaria, royalty, sex, and idolatry.

The reference to the tower also echoes the description of Nitocris's neck as the "tower of David" in 4:4. It anticipates her own reference to herself as a "wall" with "towers" in 8:10, i.e., just like the Ishtar Gate. The tower is a symbol of strength, fortitude.

Heshbon is not a place one would expect to see identified with a woman's attributes, e.g., "fire came out from Heshbon" (Num 21:28); "posterity perished" (21:30); "the fields of Heshbon languish" (Isa 16:8); "In Heshbon they planned evil" (Jer 48:2). It is a city that is really only known for being conquered, and it may be that this is meant to reflect Nitocris's apparent submission to the king. There is, however, a much more profound meaning being employed here, for the masculine noun *heshbon* suggests a thing thought up, invented, while the verb *hashab* means to contemplate or devise, especially in terms of wisdom or knowledge. The name, therefore, is used in the Song as a pun, telling the audience that there is more going on here than meets the eye, i.e., the thing thought up is Nitocris's entire plan, from the abortion, to the initiation, to the fake pregnancy—it is all a thing devised.

As for the pools of Heshbon, the area itself was renowned for its rich water supply: "For even the waters of Nimrim have become desolate" (Jer 48:34). Jeremiah's invective against Moab reveals the drying up of Heshbon's waters, i.e., they no longer support life. This could be a comment not only on the queen's (self-induced) inability to conceive again, but also on the "drying up" of the Elixir, for once she declared herself pregnant this stopped.

Bath-rabbim means "daughter of Rabbah," the city. Much as the ladies of the court are called "daughters of Jerusalem," so Nitocris is referred to in terms of her affiliation with a city; but why Rabbah? In Jer 49:3–4 "daughters of Rabbah" are paired with the inhabitants of Heshbon in a diatribe against their haughtiness, believing they are invincible. To the Egyptian visitors, the queen must seem self-assured in all her finery and sandals; perhaps they allude to her arrogance, her hubris, in thinking she can get away with deceiving the king and his court. In Jer 49:4, we read: "Your strength is ebbing, / O faithless daughter." The men, clearly trying to manipulate Nitocris's sense of duty, are warning her that she has been unfaithful to her own kind, her own religion, even though they are aware of her duty to Ahmose and the treaty. They have their own agendum.

The name Bath-rabbim is traditionally translated as "daughter of the multitudes." It has been suggested that Daughter of [City] names can refer to an individual or a city, usually a capital, and these cities are often linked to a patron god or goddess, which results in a possible translation of "daughter" as "goddess."[12] The meaning then would be: Goddess of the Peoples, or Goddess of the Capital. Bath-rabbim has a gate (Song 7:4); the capital city Babylon has a gate intrinsically linked to a goddess, i.e., the Gate of Ishtar. Both Ishtar and Hathor are known as "goddess of the people, of the multitudes." The Ishtar Gate, of course, may have a link to Nitocris via Herodotus's *Histories* (1.187), as discussed (so this may serve as a foreshadowing of the queen's fate, debated in the Epilogue). Bath-rabbim may also have a connection to Song 8:11's "Baal-hamon."

As for Lebanon, the diatribe against the Lebanese city of Tyre in Ezek 26:7–29:23 is extensive and vitriolic, almost unnecessarily so; it is a now familiar tale of conceit before a fall, of "perfection ... wisdom ... (and) beauty" (28:12) gone bad, resulting in the devastation of the nation. Damascus, an oasis plain, has a history of Egyptian rule.

Thus, we see Nitocris in terms of her towering position, looking *down* her Egyptian nose, as it were, from the heights of the mountains of Lebanon, upon which she was deified (Song 4:8). She has become, for the early Jews, the personification of everything the post-Babylon generation abhors, and is the (unwitting) embodiment of cities known for their idolatrous ways and apparent self-importance. The emissaries to Tayma become the active voice of this disdain.

PURPLE HAIR (7:5)

Mount Carmel has been recorded as a sacred site in Egyptian texts as far back as the sixteenth century BCE. Its name means garden/orchard and it is

---

[12] Magnar Kartveit, *Rejoice, Dear Zion!: Hebrew Construct Phrases with "Daughter" and "Virgin" as Nomen Regens* (Berlin: De Gruyter, 2013), here, 3, 8, 22.

referred to as lush and abundant, in passages such as Jer 50:19, Amos 1:2, etc. In Niddah 21a, the "wine" (blood) of Sharon is compared to the "wine" (blood) of Carmel, thereby personifying both regions as women in menses.

JEZEBEL

In 1 Kgs 18:19, we meet a familiar woman on Mount Carmel: Jezebel, daughter of the King of Tyre, i.e., a princess, whose ancestors were the Sidonians, one of the "foreign" peoples Solomon supposedly married into (1 Kgs 11:1). She is depicted as a powerful and determined woman with a mind of her own, something, as we have seen, that is not welcome in the new, postexilic Judaism. Her sway over her husband Ahab parallels that of the rabbis' Bathya over Solomon, for as soon as she is Queen, Jezebel ensures there are high places for her deities, right in the heart of his kingdom (1 Kgs 16:31–33). Ahab, like Solomon, is remembered as a pivotal character in the decline of Israel.

In 1 Kgs 21:8–16, Jezebel assumes the role of regent, usurping the power of her husband, whom she belittles; using his name and his royal seals, she devises a plan to trick Naboth out of his vineyard, i.e., by getting him executed on false charges. We see her taking the pose of Kilili, in 2 Kgs 9:30, i.e., "Jezebel … painted her eyes, and adorned her head, and looked out of the window." In many ways, Jezebel is a parallel to Nitocris; even her violent and degrading end, being thrown from a window, has a potential link to the historical Nitocris (see the Epilogue).

CARMEL OR CRIMSON?

Pope provides an alternative understanding, proposed by several other interpreters, i.e., that it is not the mountain of Carmel the Song alludes to, but the word *karmil*, meaning crimson; he states that dying hair with henna was prevalent and that a statuette of Ishtar was discovered at Mari, with a red-coloured head, proposing that the "divine ideal of feminine beauty may have had dyed hair."[13]

PURPLE

In 4:1 and 6:5, the noun *sear* was used to represent the woman's black, coarse curls, which I suggested related to her pubic hair, not her head of hair. Here, though, we have the term *dallah*, which suggests a thread, or something dangling down. The term for "purple" (*argaman*) is often used in conjunction with scarlet/crimson (Exod 35:25) but can also mean a reddish-purple ("reddish like purple," *ETCSL t.1.6.2*, §168–86). Again, we have an allusion to the "crimson cord," the red cords/ribbons/threads hanging from the head, the symbol of sexual energy/menstrual blood, and a link back to

---

[13] Pope, 629–30.

Amun-Re/Min, i.e., a reminder to the queen of her roots in the temple at Karnak, to her potential role as God's Hand.

By the time of Pliny the Elder (23/24–79 CE), menstrual blood was known in some circles as Saturn's Blood, where the name Saturn is partially derived from the Sumerian word for womb (shA-TUR): "One important characteristic of Saturn's Blood was that it was the colour and consistency of pitch. The ancients saw a close relationship between this substance and menstrual blood, apparently believing that it was the earth's equivalent of human menses."[14] In a form of homeopathy, pitch, taken with wine and castor oil, was yet another remedy for female reproductive problems, called "strangulations of the womb"; the Greek first century CE physician Pedanius Dioscorides, commented that "Judean bitumen is the best … 'it shines like purple'."[15]

A woman who wears a veil in the street when she is not permitted to, the Assyrian Code tells us, must endure a severe beating and have bitumen, or pitch, poured over her head as punishment, in a parody of her veiling. Here then, do the Egyptian visitors reveal that they know the queen has suffered public humiliation, perhaps implying that when she ran out into the streets (in Song 5:6–7) and was assaulted, she somehow deserved it? Was she, between the lines of the Song, symbolically beaten and so-covered in shameful "purple" (bitumen)? Or, are they hinting that she was menstruating when she left the house and that was why she was accosted? This would be proof that she had lied to Nabonidus about being pregnant.

CAPTIVE

Following on from this, the men make a direct reference to the entrapment of the king with the word "captive," or *asar*, to tie, bind, imprison. This is not a lover's captivation by the charms of his woman; this is quite sinister.

The woman's "tresses" are represented by *rahat,* meaning to hollow out, i.e., a trough, and appears elsewhere in the HB only in Gen 30:38, 41 and Exod 2:16. Each instance relates to a watering hole or well, in the context of marriage and/or reproduction. Troughs in the ancient Near East come in three main forms: bread troughs, watering troughs (for animals), and *birthing* troughs (for humans). The name of the Mesopotamian mouth-opening ritual for idols is called *mīs pî,* to give birth, and the terminology used to describe the act of fashioning cultic statues/idols also means to give birth.[16] The final stages of this ritual involve the imagery of childbirth, with

---

[14] John M. Allegro, *The Sacred Mushroom and the Cross: A Study of the Nature and Origins of Christianity Within the Fertility Cults of the Ancient Near East* (Garden City, NY: Doubleday, 1970), 40.

[15] Allegro, 40.

[16] Christopher Walker and Michael B. Dick, "The Induction of the Cult Image in

the statue being placed in a wooden *trough*, set upon traditional birthing bricks, filled with either Enki's "waters of incantation" (i.e., his semen), or representational blood (birth blood). The men are, it seems, claiming the king has been ensnared by the queen's magic (i.e., the poppet/statue) and her so-called pregnancy. They have guessed her plan.

The Egyptian men's song of praise is, therefore: 1) an initial plea for Nitocris to come back to Egypt, 2) a parodic representation of a fertility icon, and 3) a complex attack on the Egyptian princess, raising the spectre of her miscarriage and her subsequent descent, alluding to the daughter that she has *not* conceived, and the breasts that have never nursed. It is almost as if the men are taunting her. This is why they give her the epithet of Shulammite; it is accusatory, not honorific, i.e., she has not truly made amends, just as the king was not True of Voice (i.e., his "speech" is not so "sweet"), nor has she truly made restitution, as we see later; *everything* is a sham.

Compare the context of the word, *asar* (to tie, bind, imprison) in Song 7:5 to that of Eccl 8:26, where the same word is used: "I found more bitter than death the woman who is a trap, whose heart is snares and nets, whose hands are *fetters* ... the sinner is taken by her." Those who enter into a blood-covenant via assimilation (e.g., ingestion) are said to wear armbands known as "fetters"[17] (and this idea is alluded to again in Song 8), so it may be that the men also know that the queen has used the intoxicating effects of the Elixir to ravage the king's mind and thereby subdue him (*à la* Jael). I suggest that in the subsequent verses of Song 7 there is a definite possibility that the envoys imply they *could* take what they know back to Nitocris's unsuspecting father, which would be detrimental to all concerned.

There is a remarkable echo here of a scene in "The Exaltation of Inanna," a poem written by Enheduanna, daughter of King Sargon (c.2334–2279 BCE), the first known *entu* of Nanna (Sîn) at Ur, Chief Astronomer, and the first ever *known* author. Composer of multiple temple hymns and praise poems, her most famous work is "The Exaltation," in which she recounts the tale of being ousted by the lecherous Lugal-ane, a local ruler who supposedly makes sexual advances toward her in the temple, during a revolt. She describes her repulsion: "he wipes his spit-soaked hand / on my honey sweet mouth."[18] In the end, she is reinstated, but the image of the sullied *entu*, her body and her sacred space raped, reminds us of Song 5 and Nabonidus's unwelcome advances within the queen's personal cella. Now,

---

Ancient Mesopotamia: The Mesopotamian *mīs pî* Ritual," in Michael B. Dick, *Born in Heaven*, 55–122, here 116.

[17] H. Clay Trumbull, *The Blood Covenant: A Primitive Rite and its Bearings on Scripture*, (Philadelphia: John D. Wattles, 1893), 81. Herodotus describes this "oath" ceremony "among the Syths" (*Hist.* 4.70).

[18] Meador, 175.

in Song 7, Nitocris is confronted by a group of men who act in a similar fashion; they press Nitocris into a corner, making her feel uneasy. They are becoming oppressive and insalubrious.

DELECTABLE (7:6)

In the next few verses, the men from Egypt show their true colours. They have a deal for Nitocris. This both serves to help identify them in a historical sense, and reaffirms that Nitocris is the vessel of the Elixir Rubeus.

FAIR AND PLEASANT

The verb *yaphah* means to be fair, beautiful, and is used eight times in the HB. In Ps 45:2 (the same Psalm that depicts a royal marriage and is often discussed in relation to the Song), the term relates to a king. It appears twice in the Song, i.e., in 4:10, where it is used to describe the queen's *dod* (her pregnancy), and here in 7:6. By alluding to Nitocris's actual pregnancy, which she intentionally ended in order to protect the Elixir, the emissaries reveal more of their uncanny "insight," and demonstrate their understanding of *dod*. This is a clue to their identity, i.e., in an Egyptian cultic context, only a select few know the significance of what the Song calls *dod*.

The term *yaphah* also appears *twice* in both Jeremiah and Ezekiel, which may be an intended intertextual pointer. In Jer 4:10, God chastises Jerusalem for wearing crimson, for beautifying herself (shamefully); her "lovers despise" her ("despise" in Song 8:1), and there is mention of giving birth. In Jer 10:4, Israel is admonished for worshipping idols. Ezek 16:13 has the context of Jerusalem as the mixed-race daughter whom no-one wants, who is granted protection and all the riches and trappings of queendom; but the woman takes her beauty for granted and not only plays "the whore," but "slaughters the children." Finally, in Ezek 31:7, there is a tirade against "Pharaoh king of Egypt," in which the beauty and prestige of Egypt is brought low, for it is deemed to be too proud and ambitious, setting itself too high; a parallel to Daniel's explanation of Nabonidus's tree-dream follows.

The Hebrew for "pleasant" is the verb *naem*, which can also mean delightful, lovely, sweet. The idea of sweetness in the Sumerian texts is also widespread and used in many contexts, including the sweetness of food (honey, fruit, etc.,), which seems to be a very important aspect of their diet and rituals, but also the sweetness of people and deities, most especially the sexual "sweetness" between Ishtar and Tammuz: "...let me do the sweetest things to you ... let us enjoy over and over your allure, the sweet thing" (*ETCSL t.2.4.4.2*, §9–14).

177

TASTY

The noun *taanug*, used for "*delectable* maiden," means a luxury, an exquisite delight, i.e., something beyond the norm. This takes on new meaning now we are aware of Nitocris's role as the blood-giving womb; she, or rather her "precious thing" (her blood) truly is delectable to those who crave its properties.

PALM TREE (7:7–8A)

Ishtar is the Lady of the Date Clusters; she lives in Eanna, the House of the Date Clusters. The early depictions of Inanna of Uruk saw her as the goddess of the storehouse of dates; her marriage to Dumuzi takes place in the storehouse; Dumuzi is referred to as "the power in the single great bud of the date palm."[19] The tall palm tree is the most represented tree in Mesopotamian art and appears in many depictions of Ishtar, and in her later manifestation as Artemis, she is portrayed as a palm tree laden with dates, like breasts.

In the courtyard of the palace of Zimri-Lim, at Mari, named the Court of the Palm, there once stood a single palm tree.[20] These, like grapevines, are notoriously difficult to grow in Mesopotamia, due to the climate, so a single specimen could only have been grown in the cosseted royal garden, making it a central focus of symbolic import. On the walls surrounding the courtyard is a depiction of the king's investiture, where Inanna is the central figure, portrayed in her warrior status, performing her role as the maker of kings ("To give the crown, the throne and the royal sceptre is yours, Inanna" [*ETCSL t.4.07.3*, §133–54]). There is also a palm tree laden with date clusters; climbing the tree are two men, arms reaching upward to pick the dates. Ziffer suggests that in the Song, the "branches, the objects he lusts to lay hold of, are the date palm [spadices] with fruit. Hebrew: *sansinnim*, Akkadian: *sissinu*, Sumerian: AN, a wordplay on Ishtar's Sumerian counterpart's name: *in-an-na(k)*."[21] This gives the Song's portrayal of the lusty male speaker a solid cultic context, but it is Dumuzi who is the (official) date gatherer: "He who gathers the dates for holy Inanna" (*ETCSL t.4.08.20*, §1–10). In the context of the Song, the man is assuming he can usurp this intimate position.

In keeping with the Song's employment of Hathor-related mythology, the date palm is also sacred to Hathor. The Book of the Dead reads: "In a

---

[19] Thorkild Jacobsen, *Toward the Image of Tammuz and Other Essays on Mesopotamian Religion*, ed. William L. Moran (Cambridge: Harvard University Press, 1970), 24; 27.

[20] Ziffer, 417–23.

[21] Ziffer, 423.

clean place shall I sit on the ground. Beneath the foliage of a date palm of the goddess Hathor ....”; like the lotus, the date palm is an emblem of Amun-Re and thus becomes sacred to his daughter—a palm grove surrounded the Hathor sanctuary at Denderah (Upper Egypt).[22]

The Hebrew word for “palm tree” is *tamar*, a word discussed previously in the context of the two women in the HB called Tamar (Gen 38:11–23; 2 Sam 13:15–22). The “stately” aspect of the reference to the palm tree is derived from the word *qomah*, meaning height, and this stems from the verb *qum*, to rise, which has a plethora of applications but generally means to rise in status, to become greater, to be appointed, etc., which suits the context here. Nitocris has, indeed, been made greater, by virtue of becoming Queen, being deified, and then by becoming mother to the *entu*. From the original term, however, this could be an interesting affirmation of Herodotus’s description of Nitetis (Nitocris), who is said to be “*tall* and beautiful” (*Hist.* 3.1).

The palm tree is a factor of Solomon’s temple decoration in 1 Kgs 6:29–35 and in the prophet’s vision of the new temple in Ezek 40:16, 22, 26. Van Buren states that palm tree representations (naturalistic in early days and stylised later) “decorated the temples of Sîn, Shamash, and Ningal at Dûr Sarrukin .... They were emblems of fertility ... representing the goddess” as the “divine bride ....”[23]

In the HB, the only female judge of Israel, Deborah (whose name means Bee; perhaps a remnant of another rendition of the Nabonidus/Nitocris tale that emphasised the Egyptian influence; see the discussion concerning the author, in Chapter 9), sits beneath a palm tree (Judg 4:5). In Sir 24:14, Wisdom (feminine) is said to have grown tall like the “palm tree in En-gedi.”

FEMININE VOICE

Nitocris is faced with men who see her as a sexual object; one claims the right to grab a quick feel. Although this episode is founded on the Festival of Drunkenness allusions, where pornographic and lewd behaviour is expected, there is nothing devout or respectful, or divinely inspired about these advances. The man speaking is a letch, just like Lugal-ane. Would a male author have included this scene knowing, undoubtedly, the precursor of Enheduanna’s “Exaltation”?

---

[22] “The Date Palm in Ancient History, Part 1,” Ancientfoods (2011), https://ancientfoods. wordpress.com/2011/08/15/the-date-palm-in-ancient-history-part1/.

[23] Van Buren, 13–14.

SEX (7:8)

The men speak of sex. They anticipate Nitocris's voluptuous breasts, i.e., more-than-a-handful that a "cluster" suggests. They speak of the smell of sex, i.e., the remaining scent of intimacy that they find intoxicating. Apples are one of Ishtar's fruits: "You are she who creates apples in their clusters" (*ETCSL t.4.07.a*, §23–9); she calls her lover, "… my first-class fruitful apple tree" (*ETCSL t.4.08.05*, §1–4); and in a love song, the male voice yearns: "May … the apple tree be in my hand," i.e., clearly a euphemism for his penis (*ETCSL t.2.4.2.26*, §B10–19). Climbing the tree and eating the fruit is a reference to the Eden myth; even the woman's breath smelling of apples implies, on a visceral level, that she has already eaten the fruit of carnal knowledge.

By the time we get to these last few lines, the men have become oppressive, gazing upon Nitocris no longer as worshippers but as lustful usurpers; they wish to own her, seize her, control her, to oust the king from his role as Tammuz. By their behaviour, they infer that she has become no better than Tamar (the "palm"), i.e., a prostitute, and if she is not going to return, i.e., to be their sacred priestess, she deserves what she gets. There is a hint of the sentinels' attitude here, too, for they also treated her with respect to begin with (Song 3:3), only to succumb to ridicule and violence later (5:7).

ANGER

The term for "breath" in this verse is *af*, which is used in the HB sometimes as nose, nostril, face, but *only* in this passage of the Song is it translated as breath; in the vast majority of instances, it relates to anger (stemming from *anaph*, to be angry). We already know that the king has tried to avert Nitocris's gaze; he has sought refuge away from her. He set the guards against her but, most significantly, he became angry with her for failing to give him the Elixir when he demanded it. This put her entire situation in jeopardy, so she devised her plan to placate him. Here, though, the men seem to be suggesting that they are willing to expose her scheming ways (recall the allusion to deceit in the reference to honey being "under her tongue" in Song 4:11; perhaps that makes more sense now). Her entire life is held to ransom, just as Enheduanna's was. In this context, the use of *af* for breath is also seen as a pun on the king's anger; she will need to offer up her apple-scented breath (her sexuality) to these Egyptian men, if she hopes to assuage the king's anger. Thus, the tale of the woman of the Song begins with the anger of men and comes to a close with the same theme—but there is a twist coming!

This is the fourth use of *reyach*, the 'odour of soothing', a term used consistently throughout the Song to insinuate a context of sacrifice; here, the womb-blood itself becomes Nitocris's would-be (enforced) placating sacrifice.

ELIXIR RANSOM (7:9)

The Hebrew word used to suggest "kisses" in 7:9 is *chek*, i.e., the palate, *roof of the mouth*, gums. It is used also in Song 2:3 (in the context of taste) and 5:16 (in the context of speech). It does not mean the *lips* of the mouth (*saphah*, as in Song 4:11 and 5:13, for instance). Back in 2:3, Nitocris had declared that she enjoyed *the taste* of the king's "fruit"; it was an unabashed sexual statement, echoing the kneeling of Ishtar beneath her "apple-tree," Tammuz, i.e., oral sex. In discussing 5:4, it was mentioned that in the context of the Elixir the "roof of the mouth" is a euphemism for the vagina; here in Song 7, *chek* becomes a double entendre, uniting mouth with genitals, as is common in Mesopotamian texts.[24]

The "best wine" of course, is Nitocris's sacred menstrual blood; the men imagine it flowing from her vagina, over their teeth, and down their throats. The NRSV's note "q" suggests the Hebrew should read, "down for my lover," a distinct representation of cunnilingus. Also, the Hebrew uses *dod* here, i.e., as *dodi*, not "lover" but "beloved," i.e., the men also seem to be aware of the "beloved" relationship with the Elixir, strengthening the intimation that they are connected to Nitocris's ritualistic sphere. It also suggests they know she has made Nabonidus her protégée.

To the contemporaneous Jewish mind, this places Nitocris most certainly in the category of the alleged female "temple prostitute." This idea has a bearing on the discussion of 8:2.

NINE

The men's symbolic idol of Nitocris contains nine "your" statements pertaining to her body (as similes or metaphors), mirroring the queen's nine "his" statements for the king's idol, suggesting they may have similar cultural perceptions. Recall that the gematria of nine is predominantly related to pregnancy but also includes words/phrases such as "to rise, be high; "exalted, majestic"; "to be haughty"; "pride"; "ungodly," "to act

---

[24] Pope suggests that "the palate belongs to the female" and that "the context suggests oral activity beyond mere verbal communication ... the revisers tended to resist erotic language.... The modern reader, however, scarcely needs to have the language ... clarified by paraphrase" (638–9). See also Swami Ram Charran, who tells of a Tibetan woman, Lady Yeshe Tsogyal, revered as a "female Buddha" (c. 800 BCE), whose name (in part) means "Wisdom," and who practised tantric yoga at its highest level: she wrote of having a vision of a "red naked woman" lifting up her vulva, in order that her menstrual blood be consumed (in *Sexual Death* [N.p.: Lulu Press, 2012], 281).

covertly"; "to deceive"; and "the hollow belly" (e.g., of conjurers, but a very subtle allusion perhaps, in this instance, to there being no pregnancy). Nine is also the number of the Ennead, i.e., the deities as aspects of the body of Amun-Re; the men are reminding Nitocris of who/what she is.

SLEEPERS

In the NRSV, note "r" suggests "gliding over lips and teeth" is rendered "the lips of sleepers" in the Greek, Syriac, and Vulgate versions. The allusion here is to the spiritual awakening facilitated by the Elixir, about which Nitocris is attempting to teach the king. In order to be awakened, one must first be 'asleep'. Thus, the men not only comprehend *dod*, and *dodi*, they also know the qualities ascribed to Nitocris's blood and they wish to share in the feast, like the other "beloved ones" (in Song 5:1). This is the price for their silence.

DESIRE (7:10)

On the surface, it seems as if Nitocris is trying to convince us all that the king and she are inseparable and devoted to one another but there is something quite profound in her statement. The use of *tesuqah* (desire) calls attention to itself, since this particular word occurs at only two other points in the HB, e.g., in Gen 3:16 God says to Eve: "... your desire shall be for your husband ... and he shall rule over you"; this is a punishment for her assuming independence by listening to the serpent and eating the prohibited fruit. Basically, the woman must be controlled by the man because she is the embodiment of the *yeser*, that sexual demon the rabbis fear lurks behind every woman's veil.

In Gen 4:7, on the other hand, we read that sin's "desire is for you but you must master it." This is spoken to Cain when he becomes angry that his meagre offering to God is not accepted; he gives with the wrong spirit, he is stingy in his offering, and he is petulant. God warns Cain that if he does not act well, sin will be his downfall; he must learn to conquer sin. Unfortunately, Cain's response is to lash out in a fit of pique and kill his brother, Able. Recall the fate of the man who raped Ishtar; his actions are immortalised in a song that is sung forever, thus keeping his sin alive, his guilt permanently in the minds of his descendants. Cain is kept in his inner torment for eternity, not by the words of a beautiful song, but by a "mark" that keeps him from getting killed, i.e., he must forever face the consequences of his actions.

Nabonidus has been angry, has behaved impetuously and wrongly; from the early Jews' perspective, he (as Solomon) is in a precarious position, i.e., on the precipice of his self-made Sheol. He has a choice now; either he puts the past behind him, changes his ways, and chooses Yahweh, or he falls into the snare Nitocris has supposedly set, and effectively loses his soul (this understanding is vehemently reiterated in Song 8).

As the Song draws to a close, we are reminded of Nabonidus's "desire," the desire mocked in the VA, i.e., for the new temple of Sîn at Ur, and the dream-interpreting *entu* who would bring to life all his ambitions of returning the kingdom to its glory days. This desire, however, is ultimately overtaken by that for the Elixir Rubeus, which takes the king on a rocky road to infamy. Like Cain, Nabonidus is warned by Daniel that for his sin of hubris he will be banished, to "wander." It is highly probable that the VA's sarcastic allusion to Nabonidus's "desire" was a tongue-in-cheek dig at the man's more, shall we say, biological desire, i.e., an in-joke amongst those composing the text. This seems more plausible when Song 8 is discussed.

The broader context of Gen 4:7 pertains not only to Nabonidus but also to Nitocris. Cain offers God "*an* offering of the fruit of the ground," whereas Able offers up his *first*-fruit, the choicest of all his flock. Nitocris is saying one thing, i.e., "Leave me alone, for I am loyal to my husband and he wants only me," while the inference seems to be that she is no better than Cain, holding back the first-fruits, i.e., refusing to bear a child. In the very next verse, the already familiar concept of the first-fruits is reiterated. (This is from the perspective of the author, not the emissaries, which becomes clear later.)

PROOF OF *DOD* (7:11–12)

FIELD

In ancient Near Eastern terminology, a fertile woman is referred to as a field, while an infertile woman (in Hebrew) is a stony field (*galmuda*), i.e., hard, barren (Isa 49:21). The Sumerian/Babylonian *naditu*, the sacred temple-women who are to remain childless, are known as "abandoned fields."

> *Seek a fertile field within the whole plain,*
> *and sow it with your own seed,*
> *trusting in your fine stock.*
> Sir 26:20

The Hebrew noun for "field," i.e., *sadeh*, is used in the oath/adjuration Nitocris speaks when telling the "daughters of Jerusalem" not to awaken love too early, i.e., in Song 2:7 and 3:5. This word *sadeh* suggests a plain, i.e., flat land, as opposed to mountains. The royal couple is portrayed as being deified upon the mountains of Lebanon; Nitocris is described as looking down her nose at those beneath her; the king and the queen both "go down" to somewhere that is connected to the conception of the child. The pattern continues here, i.e., Nitocris urges her beloved to come with her, *down* to the villages, to the countryside abode of the woman who has born the child. It is time to collect the king's daughter from the supposed wet-nurse.

VILLAGE

The Hebrew word for "village" is *kaphar*, which, due to its similarity to *kopher*, or henna, has led some interpreters to see this as a reference to the lovers finding a place to be together amongst the henna bushes that were mentioned in Song 1:14! As noted earlier, henna bushes are notoriously barbed and certainly not the idyllic site for a romantic tryst. Instead, I suggest there is an intentional play on words here.

The word *kaphar* (village) stems from *kaphar*, meaning to cover (specifically with bitumen), but more significantly, to expiate, to placate, make atonement, pacify, and reconcile. Covering a building with bitumen implies a *protective* structure (against the elements), hence the idea of a house/village; but note that the Song has only just alluded to Nitocris's (possible) bitumen-related (i.e., the "purple" of 7:5) humiliation by being on the streets (in 5:7). The king has been angry with her but here she is seen to be attempting to make amends by bringing him to the one thing that will pacify him and bring about a reconciliation, i.e., his daughter. The entire depiction of the men attempting to 'blackmail' Nitocris gives us the impetus and the emotional platform for this scene. The fact that she suggests lodging in the area suggests the site is not so close to the palace that they could return the same day.

FIRST FRUIT

In the final sentence of 7:12, is the verb *nathan* (to give), which has multiple meanings and applications, indicating more a giving personally, a handing to, but it also signifies to yield produce, fruit, etc., especially of the land; this is how it is used in Lev 25:19 ("the land will yield its fruit"); 26:4 ("the trees of the field shall yield their fruit"); *and* here, in Song 7:12. Nitocris speaks of going down to the countryside to introduce the king to the "fruit" (child) of the "field/vineyard" (the mother/wet-nurse, i.e., the plural here corresponds to the "nut *orchard*" to form an inclusio with 6:11); at that moment, she will give (hand to) the king his daughter. This is why the queen does not need to respond any further to the leering men. She has already secured a complete reversal of their allusion to Cain and the intended insult, i.e., she *is* bringing the first fruit, just in a different way.

Nitocris says: "There (or then) I will give you my *dod*." The first two uses of *dod* attributed to the queen are said by the king when she first gets pregnant (Song 4:10); now, in Song 7, she has supposedly gone full term and produced offspring, so this third instance of the queen's *dod* pertains to the same theme, i.e., pregnancy/birth. The *dod* Nitocris knows is self-sacrificing, altruistic; she is teaching by example the wisdom Nabonidus (her *dodi*, her "beloved" student) had sought but has failed to master. This is why the word *dod* is not used anywhere else; it is too special a concept and its unique significance is only appreciated within the context of Nitocris's Egyptian religion, the royal couple's personal relationship, and menstrual blood. This final use of *dod* from the queen's lips tips the balance in her favour, for Nabonidus does not mention it again; it is the ultimate gesture— again, unreciprocated.

SACRIFICIAL INCLUSIO

The verb *nathan* (to give) was used in Song 1:12, along with *reyach* ('odour of soothing'); this was interpreted in terms of Nitocris, almost immediately upon her arrival, beginning to formulate her plan to keep the king at bay, i.e., to make him (according to the author) her sacrifice, a theme permeating the entire text. The next time we see *nathan* used, in 7:12, her ruse, her 'plan', is completed with the presentation of the child; we see *reyach* again here, too. The offering up of her *dod*, in the form of the king's daughter, is the greatest sacrifice Nitocris can make, for she will never be able to return to being the source of the Elixir. This proves far greater a sacrifice than potentially providing the Elixir to a group of rowdy men!

SECOND WIFE?

Had Nitocris chosen to solve her predicament via surrogacy, she would be subject to the requirements of Mesopotamian family law, which are quite complex. It would be an embarrassing and unwelcome intervention into her private life and could mean, perhaps, that she would lose her primary queenly status.

Mesopotamian men are legally permitted to secure another woman to ensure children, if a wife is unable to conceive within three years of marriage. This surrogate is referred to as a "slave" simply to denote her status in comparison to the (chief) wife but is legally considered a spouse, and has a relatively high status and certain rights. Everything is done according to contract, with inheritance laws and the welfare of the family as the prime focus. Nitocris, of course, has circumvented the public shame of being considered barren, and has sidestepped the legalities by simply pretending she has given birth (amongst her trusted female attendants) and left the child with this woman of the "villages" to nurse. There is, however, cause to return to the idea of the second wife, later.

Even kings both gave daughters for adoption and adopted them, sometimes in order to legitimate a concubine's child but in the Song, Nabonidus is unaware of his queen's scheme and believes the child to be hers.

GOING EARLY

The king and queen go early to the "vineyards" (again, in the plural, reaffirming the 'place of several women' idea). Nitocris is urging the king to make haste because she wishes to extricate herself from the busy, cosmopolitan city of Tayma, where tongues wag, rumours and gossip are rife, and anyone, like the emissaries from Egypt, can cause trouble. Just as she had said "let us make haste" in Song 1:4, and had spirited him away to Egypt to ensure his undivided attention in Song 3:4, so she seems to gather him up and whisk him off to the country. She is forthright and masterful but her motives become even clearer once the mandrakes are explained, below.

The reference to budding and flowering is to accentuate the idea of the resultant fruit, for no henna or lilies are mentioned, only grapes and pomegranates. The same noun, *semadar*, [grape] blossom, appears in Song 2:13, 15, in connection with Nabonidus's suggestion that the time was ripe for getting pregnant; the two scenarios are thus thematically linked.

Infant mortality in Mesopotamia is high; a child is deemed viable (outside the womb) at the age of one,[25] so waiting until Ennigaldi is proven viable before formally declaring her the *entu* is prudent. Nitocris and Nabonidus go to see whether the little girl is blossoming, growing; they settle in the country, until her first birthday, perhaps.

This return to the bucolic idyll of vegetation and the open countryside is a reminder of the couple's beginnings, i.e., as the representations of Ishtar and Tammuz in their green bower.

OLD AND NEW (7:13)

MANDRAKES

Mandrakes are profoundly linked to Hathor, in the tale of the roaming Eye of Re, where she is brought back to her mothering self after a bout of reckless behaviour, thanks to the soporific effects of the mandrake-beer Re tricks her with. In New Kingdom love poetry, the fruit of the mandrake is often associated with lotus flowers, and Hathor, recall, is the lotus.

In an Eighteenth Dynasty funerary banquet scene, a group of women are depicted smelling mandrake fruits; this has led scholars to suggest the mandrake was seen as a symbol of regeneration/rebirth brought about exclusively by women in some obscure ritual.[26] This could suggest that

---

[25] Jonathan Valk "'They Enjoy Syrup and Ghee at Tables of Silver and Gold': Infant Loss in Ancient Mesopotamia," *Journal of the Economic and Social History of the Orient* 59 (2016) 695-749, here 696.

[26] Emanuele Casini, "Rethinking the Multifaceted Aspects of Mandrake in Ancient

Nitocris and the mother have colluded, for the queen already knows about the scented mandrakes and merely tells the king.

An Arabic story "reflects the belief from the ... Harran area that a child could be born from the mandrake."[27] Similarly, the mandrake was known in Syrio-Arabic as the "soul giver" and in Aramaic as the "giver of life."[28]

SMELL

The focus in the Song is not upon ingesting or applying any derivative of the plant for medicinal or aphrodisiacal purposes; it is on the *scent*. The perfume of the mandrake was sought out in a field experiment by Fleisher and Fleisher, who found flowering mandrakes in spring only out in the fields (of Palestine) away from cultivated land, echoing the Song's context of going out to the countryside:

> The smell is perceptible only when the berries are fully ripe. Even slightly green fruits emit no odour. The berries are thin skinned and very juicy, and like small tomatoes ... they can be kept fresh only for a very short time. The smell of over-ripe fruits soon loses freshness, becoming heavy and unpleasant.[29]

There is, therefore, a very small window of opportunity to witness and enjoy the scent of the fruit, i.e., when it is "fully ripe." This would be known to many more people in ancient, rural Palestine, than to audiences today. I suggest the Song's author is using this knowledge to indicate that the queen is urging Nabonidus to make haste, to strike while the iron is hot, for the child, she urges, *is* "fully ripe"—she is viable.

The disturbing encounter with the men from Egypt has made Nitocris feel uneasy; she wants to set things in motion, to start her new life in Ur, in a temple setting she is familiar with. She takes control, again.

TALISMANS

Recall that "choicest fruits," in the Song, relates to Nitocris's menstrual

---

Egypt," *Egitto e Vicino Oriente* 41 (2018): 101–16, here 110–11.

[27] Marten Stol, *Birth in Babylonia and the Bible: Its Mediterranean Setting,* Cuneiform Monographs 14, ed. T. Abusch, et. Al., (Groningen: Styx Publications, 2000), 55.

[28] Amots Dafni, et al., "In Search of Traces of the Mandrake Myth – The Etymological, Historical, and Ethnobotanical Roots of Its Vernacular Names," *Journal of Ethnobiology Ethnomedicine* 17.68 (2021), https://doi.org/10.1186/s13002-021-00494-5.

[29] Alexander Fleisher and Zhenia Fleisher, "The Fragrance of Biblical Mandrake," *Economic Botany* 48.3 (1994): 243-251, here 248.

blood and/or the foetus. There has to be a meaningful connection to the same phrase in this scene, where the women place offerings above their doors.

Throughout the ancient world and still today in some places, there is a semi-religious, superstitious fascination with, and deep respect for the placenta and/or the umbilical cord.[30] Beliefs pertaining to the placenta include that it is the mother, sibling, or double of the foetus. In Mesopotamia, the placenta is considered female.[31] Practices include ceremonial washing, burying, or drying/preserving, in order to assure a felicitous life for the youngster. The ancient Egyptians deem the placenta the stillborn "twin" of the child, serving as the seat of the (external) *ka*, one of the two souls a person is said to have (the other being the internal *ba*).[32] The spirit of the placenta is thus considered an integral aspect of the identity and fate of the person (see 1 Sam 25:29 and the "bundle of the living," which some ascribe to the placenta). Perhaps this might have a bearing on the "twins" aspect of the teeth metaphor in Song 4:2 and 6:6.

The Egyptians insist that the placenta must be buried with the deceased, for the *ka*, having left the body upon death, must find its repose within the placenta again, "to ensure the integrity of the burial and facilitate … resurrection."[33] In the meantime, however, the placenta and/or the stump of the umbilical cord becomes a talisman, a revered relic, especially in the case of the pharaoh, whose placenta and umbilical stump are emblazoned on a banner (and probably preserved in a reliquary) and ceremoniously paraded.[34]

Marten Stol suggests that in Babylonia the afterbirth is often buried, or cast into a flowing river, but that "sometimes it is preserved in a jar or hung in a tree or at the doorpost to ward off evil."[35] In such accounts, the act of "hiding" the talisman is emphasised, and this is how the verb *tsaphan* is translated, i.e., not "laid up" (i.e., "I have laid up for you") but hidden, or stored as a treasure. Therefore, I suggest, what we are seeing in the Song here is Nitocris employing probably the umbilical cord of her first "sandal" miscarriage/abortion as a talisman, hung high on the doorpost. The mother

---

[30] For a broad perspective see E. Croft Long, "The Placenta in Lore and Legend," *Bulletin of the Medical Library Association* 51.2 (1963): 233–241.

[31] Stol, *Birth in Babylonia*, 144 note 207.

[32] Aylward M. Blackman, "The Pharaoh's Placenta and the Moon-God Khons," *Journal of Egyptian Archaeology* 3.4 (1916): 235–49, here 239–40.

[33] Glennise West, *The Tekenu and Ancient Egyptian Funerary Ritual* (Oxford: Archaeopress, Egyptology 23, 2019), 17.

[34] Aylward M. Blackman, "Some Remarks on an Emblem upon the Head of an Ancient Egyptian Birth-Goddess," *Journal of Egyptian Archaeology* 3.2/3 (1916): 199–206, here 203–4.

[35] Stol, *Birth in Babylonia*, 145.

of the new child does likewise, placing the new child's cord above her door. (The plural "our doors" is qualified by the previous indication that the royal couple are staying in the vicinity.)

To the early Jewish audience, this scene might provide a reminder of the first Passover, in Exod 11:7, where the blood of the lamb is painted onto the doorposts and lintels of the houses (plural) to protect the Israelites from the plagues sent to destroy Egypt. Nitocris may also smear her sacred blood, and the mother her birth-blood, above their respective doors.

DEDICATION?

In the comparison of Solomon and Nabonidus in Part One, Chapter 2, it was suggested that the building/dedication schedule for Solomon's temple in 1 King 6–8 paralleled that of Nabonidus's stay in Tayma.[36] It is said in 1 Kings that Solomon completes the temple in year eleven, builds his "own house" over thirteen years (1 Kgs 7:1), and dedicates the temple in the "seventh month," Tishrei (1 Kgs 8:2). Most interpreters suggest this is a delay of *eleven* months (even though the HB does not designate a year for this date, unlike the other dates mentioned) and have great difficulty explaining why this would have happened. Perhaps, however, it was just *one* month's delay, i.e., Ennigaldi's birth falls in the sixth month (Ulūlū), so she, metaphorically the "temple" Nabonidus has been 'building', is dedicated as soon as she is proven viable (a month after her first birthday).

If this is the time of the formal dedication of the new *entu* (not mentioned by the Song's author because it would validate Nabonidus), it may be why the emissaries have chosen such a moment to confront Nitocris, i.e., at the peak of the king's plan, with much to lose and much public humiliation should the truth come out. The Festival of Drunkenness is on 20 Thoth, or 30 September, making it also within the Hebrew month of Tishrei (in the Song's chronology, 544 BCE, i.e., one month after the girl's first birthday). The king's "own house" (the *entu*-dynasty) is formally accomplished in the thirteenth year, when the little girl is formally presented at the temple in Ur (and thus the clay cylinder, Nab 34, is created post-543 BCE).

So, the couple "go early" to visit the *nearly* one-year-old child and reside in the village until she is proven viable; the dedication takes place once all is deemed favourable; the family leaves Tayma in Nabonidus's thirteenth regnal year. It could be that 17 Tishritu, 543 BCE is the "propitious" anniversary of the dedication ceremony (departure delayed until the girl is old enough to travel such a distance, i.e., is weaned, at about two years of age, which is still young by Babylonian standards but feasible).

---

[36] See Supplemental Note "Ziv, Bul, and Ethanim" (at the end of the book).

8. LITTLE SISTER

BROTHER (8:1)

For the king to nurse at her mother's breast means, in the Song, to have grown up in Egypt, or even to be part of Nitocris's temple/priestly milieu. The couple would have the same norms, the same cultural ideals. They could enjoy a convivial relationship without all the political and racial complications; if she "met him outside" she would not be considered a prostitute to be reprimanded and humiliated; she could kiss him, as his "sister" (kin).

If Nitocris had been just a concubine, or a passing fancy, she would have been added to the list of the king's conquests and that would be that. Because she is deemed so special, so different and exotic, the other women of the court scorn and ridicule her. They are jealous and "despise" her being there, and this is really the first out and out statement from Nitocris's own lips that confirms the author's constant, but somewhat implicit inference to such contempt.

Of course, the entire Ishtar/Tammuz mythology is based on their brother/sister relationship. There are, however, other uses of the "brother" motif in the Sumerian literature, such as to depict a (social) group, a band of brothers: "... he can help me find the place to which the troops ...are going, Anzud can put me on the track of my brothers" (*ETCSL t.1.8.2.2*, §1–27); "... join the city-dwellers .... Go at once to the black-headed people, your brothers!" (*ETCSL t.1.3.3*, §177–84).

HOUSE OF THE MOTHER (8:2)

Nitocris's cultic mother is the incumbent God's Wife, Ankhnesneferibre, so her "house" is the temple at Karnak. That the NRSV's translation of the next line, i.e., "into the chamber of the one who bore me" differs profoundly from the Hebrew, is significant. The HB has: "... the house of my mother; she who used to teach me." Thus, the mother-daughter cultic relationship (in the context of God's Wife, Adoratrice, and God's Hand) within the Temple of Karnak is reiterated.

190

CONTROL

Yet again, Nitocris is taking control of the king and his actions. In Song 1:4, she tells the king to "make haste" as they depart for Tayma; in 3:4 she takes him (almost by force) to Egypt; in 4:16 she uses magic to get him to come to her; 5:10–16 lures him into her occult world; and in 7:11 she instigates the move to the "villages." She is now declaring that, in her ideal world, she would *lead* him to her "mother's house"; the use of the verb *nahag* places the king, once more, in the passive position.

SPICED POMEGRANATE WINE (8:2B)

Nitocris has already given her blood to the king, so why would being in Egypt make any difference? Perhaps it is because she thinks that under the tutelage of Ankhnesneferibre, under the auspices of the priesthood, the temple structure, even the pharaoh, Nabonidus would understand the Elixir and would experience *dod*. The phrasing here is more "I would *make* you drink" or "I would *cause you* to drink"; again, a submissive king and a dominant queen are implied.[1] Also, the Hebrew has the *singular* "pomegranate," which proves important. The spiced wine is *equated* with the juice of the pomegranate; recall Song 4:13 and the pomegranate juice that indicated the flow of blood through Nitocris's "channel." The "juice of the pomegranate," the "spiced wine," is her sacred womb-blood.

THE SCENT OF BLOOD

Menstrual blood has its own distinct aroma and this, as Bertrand and Bertrand suggest, is our first olfactory experience as we are born; it has a primal, visceral quality that can inspire strong emotion, catharsis, and intensified sexual experiences.[2] For a man, the aromatic menstrual blood is an "olfactory emotional bridge that invites him into his ... spiritual rebirth into sacred sexual union ...."[3]

It is possible that the heady scent of this blood is accentuated by various herbal extracts, e.g., "spices"; some may serve as entheogens (hallucinogens). The spices here link back to Song 4:14 and their original use in the context of female herbal wisdom and uterine blood, i.e., the miscarriage/abortion.

---

[1] The name Vashti (Book of Esther), without the "V" (which is not a letter of the Hebrew alphabet, see Abarim entry on "Vashti") seems to be based on *sheti*, meaning "a drinking," from the verb *shata*, to drink. This has no direct significance to the presentation of Queen Vashti, so could this be another allusion to the self-possessed Queen Nitocris and her Elixir, from a different source?
[2] Seren Bertrand and Azra Bertrand, *Womb Awakening: Initiatory Wisdom from the Creatrix of All Life* (Rochester: Bear & Co., 2017), PDF version, 406–7.
[3] Bertrand, 408.

MOTHER'S SONS

Women have long been recognised as the repositories of herbal wisdom but we must remember that the blood-rite we now call the Elixir Rubeus ideally exists in the context of an elite priesthood and royalty together, in a setting so sacred and clandestine, none but those performing the ceremony could witness it. The more esoteric the priests make it, the more mysterious the rite, the more power is seen to be inherent and this power is vital to the priesthood.

I have claimed it is the Karnak priests who are "passionate" about Nitocris in Song 1:6; it may well be that it is these same priests who are the emissaries of Song 7, encouraging her to return to her true 'duty' and, when she refuses (claiming she must perform this "dance," i.e., to maintain her father's treaty and her sanctity), they turn nasty, for they are losing a major source of their power. This may also help to substantiate the theory that Nitocris was God's Hand before leaving to marry Nabonidus, i.e., there is no subsequent God's Hand or First Prophet on record, meaning she was probably not replaced. The priests do not have a substitute. (A further discussion concerning Ankhnesneferibre's role as God's Hand can be found in the Supplemental Note, "Ankhnesneferibre and Nitocris II," on Academia.edu.)

RESIGNING HERSELF (8:3–4)

EMBRACE

Back in Song 2:6–7, Nitocris was already aware that she wanted something the king was unable to reciprocate; she longed for the all-important ritual "embrace" of the *hieros gamos* and, therefore, exclusivity. This was not forthcoming, at least not until she got pregnant.

Nabonidus has partaken of Nitocris's "precious thing," her blood, and has been struggling to fulfil his side of the bargain, i.e., to learn and become enlightened. The earthly, royal embrace Nitocris once longed for, however, is now replaced with the notion of a more mature embrace, i.e., that which is ritually performed within the Holy of Holies of the temple (e.g., at Karnak), and considered "preparation for entrance into the presence of the gods."[4] In the discussion of 2:6, we saw that the king's hand *"was* under her head," but the final embrace did not occur (i.e., the sexual aspect was fulfilled but the subsequent formal dedication to each other was not); the translation from the Hebrew of 8:3, however, reads: "His left hand *would* be under my head, and his right hand *would* embrace me," suggesting, perhaps,

---

[4] Stephen D. Ricks, "The Sacred Embrace and the Sacred Handclasp in Ancient Mediterranean Religions," *Interpreter: A Journal of Latter-day Saint Faith and Scholarship* 37 (2020): 319–330, here 323.

that the couple are no longer physically together at all, for both phrases are now conditional.

A blood-covenant demands a complete surrender of one to the other, obliterating any concept of individuality: "The measure of one's love may, indeed ... be tested by the measure of his [/her] yielded blood."[5] Nabonidus has not surrendered his own blood, nor has he committed to the symbolic embrace; he has not reached this level of understanding.

ADJURATION

This is the third of three adjurations spoken by Nitocris to the "daughters," i.e., the maidens who also love (*aheb*) the king (Song 2:7; 3:5). In the first two instances, the sexual nature of the charge not to "awaken love" is conveyed via the hinds and does of the field, and by the use of *ahabah* (e.g., mundane/sexual love). The queen was, then, telling the young girls not to rush into sexual union, for she knows there is something more worthy of attainment, i.e., *dod*. In the first two adjurations, she tells the girls: "*Do not do it.*" In the third, her tone has changed with time and experience. Now she says: "*Why do it?*" (i.e., using the interrogative *mah/meh*). Nitocris is now jaded, disappointed, and cynical. "Why bother?" she seems to suggest, "When that is all there is," especially if the man is not ready, or willing, to aspire to anything more. Nitocris's entire existence and belief system is called into question if she is unable to pursue the *dod* she lives for.

DESERT AND LEANING (8:5A–B)

In Song 3:6, the "coming up" phrase was related to the king and queen and their entourage coming back from Egypt. Here, the family dynamic has changed and Nitocris, ever the instigator, has hurried the king along, to free herself from the incriminating gaze of the envoys from Egypt. Arriving elsewhere, Nitocris is not immediately recognised. There is a connotation of "ascending" with the verb *alah* (used also in Song 3:6), indicating that the family travels toward a more exalted place (Jer 31:6, where the "going up" is to a communion with the divine, and Ezra 1:3, where the Jews are permitted to "go up" to Jerusalem, even though they travel southward).

Nabonidus leaves the desert oasis at Tayma on 17 Tishritu, 543 BCE (H2, 2.11–14), according to a positive omen (about ten years after first leaving Babylon for Arabia), and although it is commonly believed the king returns to Babylon, there is no record in the Chronicle of him doing so. I therefore submit that the family unit, including Nitocris and Ennigaldi, heads straight for the sacred ziggurat at Ur, where the temple and *giparu* have been

---

[5] H. Clay Trumbull, *The Blood Covenant: A Primitive Rite and its Bearings on Scripture*, (Philadelphia: John D. Wattles, 1893), 116.

prepared for the new *entu* of Sîn. Thus, it makes sense for Nitocris to appear unfamiliar to those watching their arrival, for the queen has only lived in Tayma, not Babylonia.

FEIGNING

In Mesopotamia, a weaned child is taken care of by a woman called a *taritu*, literally "she who is taking the child with her," one "who guides"; a child of this age is called a "guided one."[6] The wet-nurse becomes a dry-nurse, or nursemaid, and in some circumstances is granted the familiar/intimate title of "mother." A young child, weary of walking, would be carried in a special shawl tied at the woman's shoulder, so the infant sits upon her hip. This would be, I suggest, how Nitocris is being depicted arriving with Ennigaldi astride her hip, as she herself leans upon the king for support, thus the two females are, in effect, a single entity.

> *I shall lean against you ... as against a wood of cypresses.*
> *ETCSL t.4.08.06*, §37–44

This is a symbolic arrival scene; it is highly probable that the royal couple arrive in splendour while the child is looked after by her biological mother, whom the king understands is his daughter's wet-nurse/nanny (but see the discussion in Part Two, Chapter 9).

AWAKENING (8:5C–E)

The concept of awakening here is linked to the three previous adjurations, which employ the same word, *ur*, to awaken, arouse, incite; the link is *ahabah*, the same sexual/mundane love that the queen warned the girls about awakening too soon. She is guilty of it herself. She has toyed with Nabonidus's lust, manipulated his sexual drives, teased him with delights beyond the norm, and now she must pay the consequences. She must live a lie. Emulating Ishtar kneeling under *her* "apple tree," Tammuz (a euphemism for penis, recall), Nitocris knows she is responsible for the king's crazed behaviour and carnal addictions. She has orchestrated this entire situation.

LABOUR

The word for "labour," *chabal*, can mean to travail, bear, but it can also mean to bind, pledge, take captive, snare, destroy, spoil, ruin. Apply any one of

---

[6] Marten Stol, *Birth in Babylonia and the Bible: Its Mediterranean Setting*, Cuneiform Monographs 14, ed. T. Abusch, et. Al., (Groningen: Styx Publications, 2000), 188.

these words to what now know of the Song and you get a completely different understanding of this verse. For instance, the binding/pledge idea can relate to the blood-giving covenant; "captive" is directly mentioned in the emissaries' taunting of the queen; the metaphorical snare is a running motif throughout; "destroy, spoil, ruin" relate to the king's desire for "little foxes" in Song 2:15 and to the subsequent miscarriage.

The reference to Nabonidus's mother and the imagery of her giving birth to him is not intended literally. This is an inclusio formed with the similar imagery in Song 3:4, where Nitocris refers to her own mother "who bore" her. The emphasis on the two mothers highlights the two mother-countries, reiterating the chasm between the Egyptian princess/priest and the Babylonian king, i.e., the former is born and nurtured under the Sun (Amun-Re), taught (Song 8:2) by her cultic mother, Ankhnesneferibre, indoctrinated into the mysteries of Neith, and devoted to maintaining the purity and sanctity of her religion, rituals, etc. This is her inheritance, her birth right. Nabonidus's inheritance is his own mother's religion, i.e., he is born and nurtured under the Moon (Sîn). He is driven by "desire" on various levels; he wants, he takes. This final face-to-face clashing of the two ideologies ends the royal couple's relationship once and for all. They are diametrically opposed. Each is a product of their respective cultures.

The two-mothers construct also alludes to there being two mothers within the Song's immediate context: Nitocris as official mother, and the hidden, biological mother of the child.

DON'T SIT UNDER THE APPLE TREE
When Ishtar ascends from the underworld, she goes in search of Tammuz, only to find him sitting, in all his glory, under "the great apple tree," oblivious to the travailing of the goddess; she commits herself, though with a heavy heart, to his demise (*ETCSL t.1.4.1*, §348–358). The apple tree thus becomes a portent of doom, a symbol of the fall, of karma (hence the Eden myth).

SEAL (8:6)

Most see this "seal" in terms of a signet ring, suggesting it should be on the hand, not the arm. In the ritual of blood-covenanting, however, a blood-soaked talisman, a representation of that covenant, is worn in a small leather case upon the arm, i.e., as "fetters," mentioned previously. To the Jews, of course, the outward symbol of their blood-covenant is the phylacteries worn on the hand (perhaps the main reason for the difficulty in accepting "arm" in the Song) and the head/neck (Deut 11:18–19; Ps 3:1, 3; Prov 6:20–21).

It may be from this very line in the Song that the esoteric Seal of Solomon was first devised, e.g., the two triangles, male and female, interlocked but diametrically opposed. The rabbis' tale of Ashmedai, and the king's supposed need to protect himself (seal himself off) from another encounter with the demon who toyed with his soul, might well be the inspiration for this occult symbol.

The word for "heart" is the noun *leb*, meaning the inner being, mind, will; the heart, both in Mesopotamia and Egypt, is the seat of knowledge, wisdom, and Life. Nitocris is not saying this in a romantic way; she is saying, in effect: "Set this reminder on your arm as my 'fetter'—ponder on its meaning and learn from it." The symbolic seal both closes the relationship between them and seals the fate of the king. Nitocris is closing the book on her and Nabonidus, sealing it shut.

FUTILITY OF *AHABAH* (8:6B–7A)

Nitocris has learned about divine love (*dod*) in the context of her Egyptian upbringing. She has learned about sexual love (*ahabah*) from an aging, emotionally stifled, easily distracted, offspring-focused foreigner. She does everything she can to bring the king closer to her way of thinking and feeling. He does not seem to be interested beyond a titivating curiosity and a physical addiction to certain stimuli.

DEATH AND SHEOL

The noun *qinah,* although commonly translated as jealousy, or envy, can also suggest ardour or zeal. This is related to the king's version of love (*ahabah*), the mundane, visceral, physical love reflected in his haste to have sex, his need to procreate, his ardent non-sacerdotal desire for the Elixir Rubeus, and his readiness to lay with many women. This type of love is *qasheh* i.e., as cruel, hard, difficult, fierce, intense, relentless as "the grave." For "grave," the HB uses *sheol,* i.e., not the physical space occupied by the body in the ground but the underworld, the place of torment and judgement. This is the motif of impending doom that is woven through the entire Song, suggesting the king's idea of love will bring him nothing but torment; it will lead him down to Sheol. It will never conquer Death, for (to Nitocris) it *is* a form of death. She understands the difference. She has come to see the king as spiritually lost.

FLAME, FIRE, QUENCH

The noun employed to suggest "raging flame" is *shalhebeth* but it appears in the text as *shalhebethyah*, i.e., "flame of Yah" (recall that Yah is identical to Iah, the Egyptian lunar deity worshipped by Ahmose). Ezek 20:47–8 and Job 15:30 are the only other places *shalhebeth* is used but without the *-yah* suffix, suggesting it is added by the Song's author to convey meaning peculiar to this tale. The Song twice uses the image of a flame, and the waters that might "quench" it. In Ezekiel there are two references to both flame (using *shalhebeth*) and water; it may be, therefore, that the author of Ezekiel and the author of the Song have a similar perspective, one drawing on the other, so this needs closer examination.

The context of the passage in Ezekiel 20 is one of a warning against "the forest of Negeb"; the Negeb is a desert, whose name means 'a parched place'. In ancient times, this was deemed to be the desert far to the south of Jerusalem, i.e., in the area of Kedar, where the oasis (forest?) of Tayma is situated. Once again, therefore, there is an oblique allusion to Nitocris (the one who is "black as the tents of Kedar" and who lives in Tayma), in the context of a spiritual fall.

The Song uses the noun *resheph* to suggest the "flame" of passion, jealousy, etc.; it can also mean flashing, or something like a bolt of lightning, or an arrow flashing through the air. Bolts of lightning are usually a sign of God's anger, and flames/fire are seen as part of God's arsenal (Ezek 22:31); the arrow is angry Ishtar's weapon. The portents of doom and the allusions to the fall and to retribution are thus maintained.

The Hebrew noun for "fire" here is *esh*, and this is used widely in the HB to denote the "fire of God," usually in the context of anger, punishment, or warning. It is the word used in 1 Kgs 18:38, where Jezebel and Elijah have the standoff in the temple, to see whose deity is strongest, i.e., a contest of fire, where the water does not extinguish (quench) the flames. The connection to Jezebel and this scenario has already proven significant.

The link to Hathor, however, is also enlightening, for in her guise as Sekhmet, the Mighty One, her weapon is often her fiery breath; this then translates, in some myths, to the fire-spitting serpent that takes the place of the missing Eye of Re. Thus, a reference to "flashing fire" within the context of someone just depicted as Hathor, must bring to mind the power and dread of the supreme deity. There is a fitting reference to the rage and bloodlust of Hathor/Sekhmet as the divine Eye:

> The eye of Re
> … is powerful against you.
> She devours you,
> … In this her name
> 'Devouring Flame'.[7]

There are, as with many other verses, several layers of meaning to this powerful declaration in Song 8. Nitocris has been attempting to teach Nabonidus about *dod*; he has demonstrated his subjugation to the power of

---

[7] Alison Roberts, *Hathor Rising: The Serpent Power of Ancient Egypt* (Rottingdean: Northgate, 1995), 9. Quoting *Papyrus Bremner-Rhind* 25, 2–4; see note 6 (173).

the Eye (Song 4:9) but he is also at the spiritual level of those who prefer *ahabah* to *dod* (i.e., they prefer sex to enlightenment). The "devouring flame" (in the quotation above) is the destructive, merciless Hathor/Sekhmet, the embodiment of the wrath of Re. This is how Nitocris is remembered. She is the divine tool for vengeance, the indomitable force sent by God to bring Nabonidus to his fate; she is the "daughter of Pharaoh" who makes Solomon an idolater and who sows the seeds for the (future) fall of Israel. She becomes the "raging flame," the intense, inescapable force that (in the eyes of the early Jews) brings down both king and country.

It should be noted that the overall context of sexual love (*ahabah*) and ardour/passion/jealousy/envy, etc. (*qinah*), is one that does not sit well with Nitocris, who has constantly attempted to keep herself at arm's length from the king since her miscarriage. She was infatuated, had her head turned, was curious, perhaps, to begin with, but her sentiments throughout most of the Song do not include sexual jealousy. When she runs through the streets after Nabonidus, there are mitigating circumstances. When he leaves her to be with his other women, she accepts it. Even when the king becomes an adversary, and she manipulates him with her magic, she never comes across as vindictive, irrational, or overly suspicious; such base emotions serve to *restrict* enlightenment. I suggest, therefore, that the jealousy, the raging flame of passion, the burning fire, the envy, are all attributable to the author of the Song, not to Queen Nitocris.

-*YAH*

So, why does the author add the suffix -*yah* to *shalhebeth*? I suggest it has something to do with the date of the Song, in that Yah/Iah was some sort of transitional name for the deity that was later to become Yahweh (again, I support an exilic/postexilic date for the creation of the entire HB), i.e., an amalgamation of various influences, both Egyptian and Mesopotamian. The author of the Song uses Yah to denote "the fire of God" in a way that is familiar to her various audiences. It speaks to almost everyone; Babylonian, Egyptian, Jew (e.g., the Egyptian Iah, and the early Mesopotamian Aa, Â, or Ai).[8] The "I am who I am" of Exod 3:14, suggests a degree of cultural ambiguity during this time of upheaval. "It may well be that ... the name of the god of the Levites as it appeared in their cult cry Hallelu Yah was the true name of the Semitic god in all his local forms ...."[9] This is why the name Yahweh is missing from the Song; the concept of deity, of a supreme Life force, however, is at the core of the entire narrative.

---

[8] Donald A. Mackenzie, *Myths of Babylon and Assyria* (London: Gresham Publishing, 1915), 301.

[9] Robert Briffault, *The Mothers: The Matriarchal Theory of Social Origins*, Vol. 3 (London: George Allen & Unwin, 1927), 110.

That *-yah* relates to the moon god is a direct connection to the historical situation; Nabonidus is an avid worshipper of Sîn, the lunar deity, and Nitocris is the daughter of Ahmose, the lunar deity incarnate. It makes perfect sense to have this suggestion of retribution, of divine anger, couched in lunar-deity terms, for this is what Nabonidus would comprehend, what he would fear most—if he were in his right mind. It may also be another clue to the identity of the author, as we shall see.

DESPISED (8:7B)

Back in Song 8:1, Nitocris had imagined what it would be like if the king had been her kinsman; she could kiss him openly, as a brother, and she could share with him the wonders of her religion, with impunity. Instead, in Nabonidus's kingdom, she is mocked, attacked, and "despised" (using the verb *buz*).

Here, in Song 8:7b, the HB emphasises the masculine, i.e., "if *a man* would give ..." and "*he* would be despised." Nabonidus would be "despised" (by the gods?) if he were to attempt to buy "love" (*ahabah*) with all his profound and famous wealth. The sheer strength of this contempt is literally double that of anything Nitocris has experienced; the word *buz* is used twice (i.e., "*utterly* scorned" in the NRSV).

Nabonidus is investing far too much of his being, his time, his influence, etc., on this mundane aspect of love. As will be seen shortly, he takes his penchant for the Elixir to an entirely new level, and this is certainly not done in the sense of respecting *dod*, or even Nitocris herself; he places a value on the Elixir that makes it base, a parody of its true nature. This castigation of someone who would pay for *ahabah* (sexual love, in this context) does two things: a) it brings to mind Nitocris's words at the very beginning of the Song, in 1:2 (i.e., "... *dod* is better than wine"), hinting that the king would not sacrifice much at all to receive the blessings of *dod*, but he would sell his soul for the hallucinogenic blood drink, and b) it foreshadows Song 8:11–12.

The wealth of the king is hinted at in Song 3:6–10 and is linked to his dealings with Egypt, presumably as part of the treaty and marriage agreement. We know from elsewhere in the HB that Solomon's wealth is a conspicuous aspect of his depiction, and that this was seen by the rabbis as one of the reasons for his fall from grace.

TEMPLE TALK (8:8)

Suddenly, there is another "we" reference. The queen is not speaking to the "daughters of Jerusalem" now, for she is in another place and they are never mentioned again. The "we" now pertains to another group of women, i.e., in the temple; an inclusio is thus formed with the group of women Nitocris was responsible for in Song 1:6 (the "vineyards"). In a way, things have come full circle—but now the queen is far more mature and knowledgeable, and now *she* is in charge.

SORORITY

Nitocris and the young Ennigaldi-Nanna have settled at Ur. The child is too young to take on anything more than a symbolic role, so the First Prophet of Amun-Re serves as the acting *entu*. This is where she has wanted to be, i.e., in her own space, independent, away from the gaze of oppressive men, surrounded by women who are there to support her, free to perform her priestly responsibilities. It is a far cry from Karnak, but she is willing to make the most of it. It is to these sacerdotal women that she speaks concerning the "little sister"; Ennigaldi is the youngest of many sisters (i.e., in the sorority of the *giparu*). That she "has no breasts" is a stark reminder of how young and vulnerable she is.

The early *entus,* centuries before, were expected to be celibate. It would seem this stemmed from the epic "Atrahasis," i.e., the legend of the Flood, where an edict is pronounced in an attempt to reduce the population of the earth: "Establish *Ugbabtu*-women, *Entu*-women, and *Igishitu*-women, / And let them be taboo and so stop childbirth."[10] This ideal was broadly interpreted, however, and at least two historical records prove it was not even generally believed that the *entus* were chaste, i.e., the legend that King Sargon's mother was an *entu* who bore him in secret, and the fact that it was suggested, in a (late) liver omen, that the *entus* should engage in anal sex in order to prevent pregnancy.[11] Recall that the inherited attitude toward the long-defunct, sexually-orientated cultus at Ur was one of ridicule and disparagement. It is also known that the *entus* were permitted to marry, so long as they were faithful to their husbands and did not bear children.[12]

So, this brings us back to little Ennigaldi-Nanna, and the day she is "spoken for." Nitocris, in the Song, has drawn a line under her life with the King of Babylon; she has had a difficult time trying to maintain her religious and physical purity and now she attempts to safeguard that of the youngest member of the new order. She must make another plan to protect Ennigaldi from men like the king, like the emissaries, like the legendary Lugal-ane. She may well have to be married, one day, but with Nitocris's experience and the other women's assistance, Ennigaldi will learn how to cope and how

---

[10] W. G. Lambert and A. R. Millard, *Atrahasis: The Babylonian Story of the Flood* (Oxford: Clarendon Press, 1969), 103 (3.7: 6–8).
[11] Marten Stol, *Women in the Ancient Near East*, trans., Helen and Mervyn Richardson (Berlin: De Gruyter, 2016), 571–2.
[12] Stol, *Birth in Babylonia*, 172.

to protect both herself and what is deemed sacred. This is a case of "learn by my mistakes."

In terms of the sanctity of ritual space, it is noteworthy that in Nab 34 (2.20–8), the king, on setting up the new *entu*-priesthood at Ur makes the only truly significant changes to the extant cultus of Babylonia; only at Ur, he removes from the priesthood and the entire temple staff the burden of corvée labour and other non-sacerdotal responsibilities, for the sole purpose of keeping everyone and everything "pure." It would seem that his run-in with Nitocris over purity issues also results in a case of learning from mistakes! No doubt Nitocris, previously First Prophet and now acting *entu*, demands this overhaul of the temple setup.

FAREWELL HATHOR

The Hathor-related mythology is spent, having served its purpose. The queen now returns to the Ishtar-related parallels for the last few lines of the Song. This may substantiate the idea that Nitocris is now in Babylonia, having severed her link to her quasi-Egyptian life in Tayma (but not her religion), and now resolved to make the most of her new situation at Ur.

WALL VS. DOOR (8:9–10B)

WALL

The wall in Mesopotamian texts is understood as the great edifice that surrounds and protects the city and acts as an earthly representation of the protection of the gods (*ETCSL t.2.4.4.4*, §22–28; *t.2.5.4.01*, §236–50; *t.4.27.02*, §1–3). Inanna is described as "a young woman who was as high as the heavens and as broad as the earth. She was firmly set as the base of a wall" (*ETCSL t.2.1.4*, §12–24).

It is because Nitocris compares this wall to herself, especially in relation to her breasts as towers, that the metaphor becomes clear. If the "little sister" grows up to be a wall, she is going to grow up a strong, independent woman, and she will be equipped with "a battlement of silver." She will, in essence, become like the warlike Ishtar, as Nitocris had once been. This, in turn, reminds us of the Ishtar Gate, which has both crenulation and towers, and this may be a *very* subtle allusion to the fate of Nitocris, which must await the Epilogue.

The word for "battlements" is the noun *tirah* (which can also mean encampment, echoing the "dance of Mahanaim" in Song 6:13), stemming from the same (unknown) root as *tur*, which means a row, as in a course of building-stones. This could be a play on the tower-like neck built "in courses" and/or the necklace Nitocris once wore, that overwhelmed the king, in Song 4:4, 9.

The combination of the wall, battlements, and towers can be seen in light of the so-called "mural crown" worn by a Neo-Assyrian queen in a banquet scene (relief) from Ashurbanipal's (668–627 BCE) North Palace at Nineveh; the crown is designed as a fortified city wall. Given that Nabonidus "recognised Ashurbanipal's renown and influence in no uncertain way," and Adad-guppi was likely of Assyrian/Aramaean descent,[13] a comment from Frances Pinnock regarding the mural crown proves intriguing. She claims that the crenelated crown served as a political statement of "female power" that potentially had its roots in "the Aramaean principalities of Syria, and, in particular, of women included in the royal harems, [who] played an important role in the elaboration of the overall image of … Assyrian imperial power…."[14] So, it may just be that such a crown was yet another of Nabonidus's revival projects, and one to which Nitocris was drawn for its strong symbolism of feminine authority.[15] The Assyrian crown was gold but Ennigaldi is officially the *entu* of Sîn, the Moon God, so silver would undoubtedly be more appropriate.

Door

The Song contrasts the wall and the door, i.e., Ennigaldi can grow up to be one or the other. The opposite of a wall that is strong, defensive, a protective barricade, is a door that can be used repeatedly, opened or closed according to anyone's will, walked through, or even blocked off. It does not have lookout towers, it cannot withstand much force, and it certainly cannot protect (for long) what is behind it. In a Mesopotamian poem, a man demonstrates his sexual dominance over a woman by saying: "I walk right through you like a flimsy door, I span you like a doorway."[16]

In ancient Near Eastern texts, the door is another euphemism for a woman's vulva/vagina, often used in the context of childbirth, e.g., an ancient incantation refers to "the door of the baby" and "the door of women

---

[13] Raymond Philip Dougherty, *Nabonidus and Belshazzar: A Study of the Closing Events of the Neo-Babylonian Empire* (Eugene: Wipf & Stock, 2008), 18–27, here 24. See also Frauke Weiershäuser and Jamie Novotny, *The Royal Inscriptions of Amēl-Marduk (561–560 BC), Neriglissar (559–556 BC), and Nabonidus (555–539 BC), Kings of Babylon*, The Royal Inscriptions of the Neo-Babylonian Empire, Vol. 2 (University Park: Eisenbrauns, 2020), 4.

[14] Frances Pinnock, "A City of Gold for the Queen: Some Thoughts about the Mural Crown of Assyrian Queens," *Multa per Aequora* 2, eds. Marco Cavalieri and Cristina Boschetti (Belgium: Presses universitaires de Louvain, 2018): 731–52, here 744.

[15] Although the primary evidence for the mural crown comes from Nineveh, there are other examples from Anatolian, Ugaritic, and Akkadian sources. See Pinnock, 737–8.

[16] Benjamin R. Foster, in *From Distant Days: Myths, Tales, and Poetry of Ancient Mesopotamia* (Bethesda: CDL Press, 1995), 341.

giving birth";[17] "The bolt is lowered, the door is closed ... the opening of the womb is blocked" describes a difficult birth.[18] In rabbinic literature, a woman's body is often discussed in "house" metaphors, where "the 'door' into a woman's body" signifies the vagina.[19] In Egyptian texts, the vulva is considered "the exterior door of the womb to which medical prescriptions are applied."[20]

The concept of the door in this verse, then, relates to the perception of a relatively weak, utilitarian, constantly available, sexual female; the wall, on the other hand alludes to an indomitable, confident, self-sufficient woman, whose defences are secure, whose wisdom and experience (her heart, therefore her breast) serve as her watchtowers.

ENNIGALDI

If the little girl grows up to be a wall, she will inherit the crown of feminine fortification and authority, and her battlements will shine like the shields on Nitocris's neck(lace) that once bedazzled the king. She will be Ishtar in all her regalia, in all her magnificence. Back in Song 7:2, the emissaries had described the queen's belly as being encircled with a protective "fence" of lilies, and I suggested that this (despite its negative connotations within that context) foreshadowed Nitocris's "I was a wall" reference here, in Song 8; the "fence" is a diminutive version of a wall. We already know which path the child will take.

If, however, the girl should prove less formidable than Nitocris, i.e., should become a "door," the women will (effectively) board her up, lock her up, seal her away, i.e., using the verb *tsuwr* (to confine, bind, besiege). They will not allow her to make the same mistakes. Although Nitocris sees herself as a wall, having stood her ground with the king as much as she could, the reality of the situation seems to be that she felt she had been *treated* like a door. Her blood-rite had been all but abused, taken for granted, shared around, making her feel like a prostitute. She will not allow this little girl to experience that.

Ennigaldi's surroundings, this imagined barricade protecting her from the world, is, of course, made from the very best cedar, Tammuz's symbolic

---

[17] Stol, *Birth in Babylonia*, 206.

[18] Stol, *Birth in Babylonia*, 130.

[19] Sharon Faye Koren, *Forsaken: The Menstruant in Medieval Jewish Mysticism* (Hanover: Brandeis University Press, 2011), 73.

[20] Paula Veiga, "To Prevent, Treat and Cure Love in Ancient Egypt. Aspects of Sexual Medicine and Practice in Ancient Egypt," *Proceedings of the II International Congress for Young Egyptologists*, Lisboa, November 2009 (Centro de História, Faculdade de Letras da Universidade de Lisboa, 2010): 453–465, here 456.

tree, i.e., the 'royal' tree. Her enclosure of sacred, sweet-smelling cedar is intended to convey the idea not only of royalty but also of a temple; the ziggurat's construction includes the huge trunks of cedars from Lebanon (e.g., Nab 28, 3.1–3), and the temple Solomon builds in 1 Kings 6 is lined with cedar. She will be locked away, protected by a veritable temple constructed around her. *She* will not have anyone forcing himself upon her or contaminating her pure, sacred space!

PEACE (8:10C–D)

The Hebrew for "brings" (*matsa*) more accurately means finds, discovers, or attains. Nitocris has been Nabonidus's inspiration and mentor; she has shown him many hidden things and he is so affected, his enthusiasm is immortalised in the VA. For "peace," the noun is *shalom*, i.e., completeness, soundness, welfare. While "brings" could allude to the peace treaty, for which Nitocris is the price that is intended to bring stability and ensure the welfare of the nation, the allusion does not really fit the overall theme of the Song, least of all at this juncture. I submit that the "peace" referred to here is the cosmic, transcendental, complete peace that is the goal of every initiate into her religion. One can easily imagine Nitocris, like a Scheherazade figure, teaching the curious and eager Nabonidus, assuring him that all his angst and "troubles" will fade away, if he aspires to (discovers, attains) this "peace," as she has. She, just like the Arabian storyteller, uses what she knows to hold the king at bay.[21]

A reminder of both "Solomon" and the "Shulammite" epithets seems apt, here, for these suggested an ongoing battle between the two parties, and of apparently making restitution for their previous actions. Both were deceptive. The king had looked to Nitocris for guidance to make his case (regarding his penance) with the gods; she *was* his path to peace once, but no longer.

The only other place in the HB where the concepts of "tower" and "peace" merge so clearly, is 2 Kgs 9:17, 22, where Jezebel is once again the focus: "What peace can there be, so long as the many whoredoms and sorceries of your mother Jezebel continue?" This is the ideology of the post-Babylon generation, i.e., there can be no peace or safety for Jerusalem until the dangerous, foreign women are removed. The Song thus emphasises Nabonidus's supposedly foolhardy trust in Nitocris and her 'misleading' cultic influence. The parallel to Jezebel is actually more significant than at first it may seem, so I shall return to it in the Epilogue.

---

[21] See Supplemental Note "Alternative Tales of Nabonidus and Nitocris."

BLOOD MONEY (8:11)

NABONIDUS

"Baal-hamon" is a pun. The first part, *baal* means lord, owner, husband, leader. The second part, *hamon*, suggests a tumult, uproar, multitude, commotion, etc., such as much noise emanating from a great crowd. Together, the two words can be understood as "lord/leader of a very noisy people."

The combination of a leading figure and the word *hamon* appears in one other place in the HB, i.e., Gen 17:5, where Abram receives his commission name, Abraham; he is called the "father of many nations." I posit, therefore, that Baal-hamon is a symbolic pseudonym for Nabonidus in the Song; by referring to a place rather than a person, a link can be made to Babylon/Mesopotamia, thereby disassociating the king from Jerusalem (and a fictional Solomon) entirely. Nabonidus's name is considered by the author as "empty," unworthy of being spoken or remembered, and "Solomon" is a pseudonym paired with "Shulammite" in the Song, so "Baal-hamon" comes as close to identifying Nabonidus as one can get, without actually mentioning his name.

Nabonidus refers to himself as "the [shepherd] of all (four) quarters (of the world and) rule[r] over the entirety of the black-headed (people), all humankind" (Nab 1, 2.12–16); and "... great king, strong king, *king of the world*, king of Babylon, king of the four quarters" (Nab 28, 1.1–6). The Flood myth, "Atrahasis," tells of the origins of humankind in the crucible of Life, Mesopotamia; the symbolic power and religious centre of this world is Babylon. Nabonidus is thus represented in the Song as Baal-hamon, the lord/leader of the noisy, tumultuous city of Babylon. It should be noted that the supreme god of Babylon is often referred to as Baal (or Bêl), as his real name is unspoken, so again, the connection to Babylon is iterated (the king in the Song is deified *and* his true name is unspoken).

Baal-hamon is therefore symbolically linked to Bath-rabbim, "daughter/goddess of the multitudes," attributed to Nitocris in Song 7:4.

In "Atrahasis," Enlil, disturbed by the incessant noise of the ever-increasing population on the earth, is determined to alleviate the problem by obliterating humanity, sending a plague, a famine, a drought, and then "the Flood" (none of which work, so the gods devise Death and Infertility as the means to restrict humanity):

Twelve hundred years had not yet passed ...
And the peoples multiplied.
... The god got disturbed by their uproar.

… "The noise of mankind has become too intense for me …."[22]

The Song is, in this one sentence, speaking directly of Nabonidus, and is focussing our attention no longer on what happened in Tayma, but in Babylon itself. What then follows?

VINEYARD
This "vineyard" the king "had" in Babylon must, if following the Song's hitherto consistent understanding of the term (i.e., as female sexuality), refer to a woman or a collective seen as a singular entity/institution (e.g., many "vines"). There is no indication this is Nitocris (see the Epilogue). I think the rest of this verse unequivocally refers to the 'pimping out' of the Elixir rite in the temple at Babylon, i.e., the very same practice mentioned by Herodotus (*Hist.* 1.199) in somewhat tempered terms.

Herodotus speaks of "prostitution" in the temple of Aphrodite being reprehensible (*Hist.* 1.199) yet, in 1.196, he praises Babylonians for their ingenious practice of getting their daughters to earn a dowry via prostitution! Early translators of Herodotus's works had a "…tendency to adopt translations that entail pejorative insinuations about the morality of Near Eastern cultures in antiquity"; it has since been argued that Herodotus had issue only with the fact that these alleged "prostitutes" were not servants within the sphere of the cult of Ishtar, but ordinary women from all social statuses, both single and married.[23] According to Westenholz, there were strict delineations between women who served as cultic "professionals," whose sexuality was governed by codes of practice, and those who earned their living as non-cultic, unregulated sex-workers.[24] In other words, what Herodotus describes is a very different *type* of practice to anything familiar in circa 543–39 BCE Babylon.

The NRSV's "everyone" may be politically correct today but it hides the fact that an intentionally masculine noun is employed here, i.e., *ish*, meaning every *man* (and note how in Song 1:6, Nitocris is supposedly the sole "keeper" of several vineyards, yet here there are many "keepers" to one vineyard). Men have to pay one thousand pieces of silver to partake of the "fruit," i.e., in this context not the fruit of the womb as a child, but the fruit of sexuality, the fruit that is also the "precious thing." In discussing the

---

[22] W. G. Lambert and A. R. Millard, *Atrahasis: The Babylonian Story of the Flood* (Oxford: Clarendon Press, 1969), 67 (K3399+3934[s] obv. 3), 7.352–9.

[23] Eva Anagnostou-Laoutides and Michael B. Charles, "Herodotus on Sacred Marriage and Sacred Prostitution at Babylon," *Kernos* 31 (2018), Online 2020, 9–37, here §20, doi: https://doi.org/10.4000 /kernos.2653.

[24] Joan Goodnick Westenholz, "Tamar, Qĕdēšā, Qadištu, and Sacred Prostitution in Mesopotamia," *The Harvard Theological Review* 82.3 (1989): 245–65, here 251.

king's "fruit" in Song 2:3 (i.e., as a euphemism for his penis), I mentioned the two interchangeable Akkadian words for "fruit," *kuzbu* and *inbu*, as a female sexual references; it is evident from many sources that one term in Sumerian/Akkadian can have many translations, depending on the context. Also, in the discussion of Song 4:13, the phrase "choicest fruits" was understood to be both the aborted foetus *and* the ensuing flow of blood, depending on the perspective taken (e.g., Nitocris's or the author's). Therefore, here, the focus of attention is the woman's (or the collective's) genitals *and* menstrual blood.

I have no difficulty imagining Nabonidus's addiction to the Elixir being turned into a large-scale, unique exploitation of the country's young women, leading to confused rumours that found their way out of Babylon to Herodotus years later. I think this may also be one of the reasons for the scoffing in the VA of the king's "desire."

HERODOTUS'S "PROSTITUTION"

Calling it the "most shameful custom," Herodotus's account (1.199) describes a form of temple-based prostitution whereby every woman must sell herself to a man for a piece of "silver" once in her lifetime. These women, I suggest, are nubile women, i.e., menstruating women, either virgins or married women without children, for they wear the cord/ribbon down the back of their heads, the *seshed* band of Min, the "crimson cord" of the Song. They are physically linked by another "cord," making them, in effect, a single unit, i.e., a winding flow of red gold, of potential Elixir Rubeus. In Bar 6:42–3, the same situation is referred to:

> And the women, with cords around them, sit along the passageways .... When one of them is led off by one of the passers-by and is taken to bed by him, she derides the woman next to her, because she was not as attractive and her cord was not broken.

The breaking of the cord is thus highly symbolic, for it not only confirms the women are linked, to represent a united collective, but it demands a forceful action by the man upon the woman, i.e., he must *break* her away. For the virgins, especially, this is an allusion to the breaking of the hymen and the special, purest womb-blood that would be the most sought after, hence the allusion, in both sources, to the fact that the young, beautiful girls get taken first, while the "ugly" ones have to wait (though one would think this was standard human nature, so why mention it, unless a deeper significance is intended?).

Nabonidus, on returning to Babylon from Tayma, sets up his own quasi-sacred business in the temple, selling (or "leasing," i.e., giving at a price) the women's menstrual blood. It is not that far a leap from his inviting "friends" to partake of Nitocris's "wine" back in Song 5:1. He makes it into a money-making venture, the likes of which, probably, were never seen before in Babylon, like his unorthodox religious zeal for Sîn and the strange chimera of an idol that confuses and angers many (the sentiment of Song 8:7b might be remembered here, for we have the procurement of *ahabah* for cash; all those who partake are thus potentially "despised"). Nabonidus is proving to be a law completely unto himself. This must surely be inspiration for the women-loving, money-mad, retrograde, Solomon![25]

Beaulieu suggests that the VA's account of Nabonidus appropriating the Esagila (temple) in Babylon for Sîn seems to be his only attempt to do so, i.e., Uruk and Sippar are not interfered with.[26] The king and the Babylonian (Marduk) priesthood are pitted against each other; it is possible that the introduction of this new "prostitution" is one of the reforms the incumbent priests consider foreign, improper, and impious. It would also make sense for the temple at Ur to be avoided in this regard, despite its heritage as a sexually-orientated temple, as Nabonidus's daughter is there, and so is Nitocris, who is now adamant such a future is not for Ennigaldi. The king takes his pleasure elsewhere, as is his way.

ONE THOUSAND

Keeping with the apparent use of gematria in the Song, we must attempt to understand what is significant about the "one thousand" mentioned here. There is a possible intertextual reference to Solomon's seven hundred "princesses" (wives) and three hundred "concubines" in 1 Kgs 11:3, which would fit the notion of the vineyard/woman context here.

If we break the "one thousand" down into manageable portions, however, which can represent letters of the alphabet, we can then use these to prise out any potential hidden meaning. Using the numbers 100+200+300+400 instead, we arrive at the four Hebrew letters *kuf, resh,*

---

[25] Recall Samson's burning of three hundred foxes in Judges 15, i.e., he destroys the Philistines' "fields" and "vineyards"—their *women*. Is this a subtle reference to the Elixir prostitution ring? Herodotus (*Hist.* 1.199) says of the women being forced to go with any man who pays with silver, that once they have performed their duty, they go home, "and from that time forth no gift however great will prevail" with them. That is, they feel abused, raped, tainted, vowing never to let it happen again. They are "ruined," like poor young Tamar. Was Nabonidus's 'madness' implicit in the tale of Samson's bizarre outburst?

[26] Paul-Alain Beaulieu, *The Reign of Nabonidus King of Babylon 556–539 B.C.* (New Haven: Yale University Press, 1989), 219. This may suggest that Herodotus, yet again, gets his wires crossed, assuming that such practices would be fitting for a "temple of Aphrodite" (Ishtar).

shin, and *tav*. [27]

★ **kuf (100)** represents "unholy thoughts, profane speech and evil actions." These negative qualities are represented by the form of the *kuf*, i.e., "long left leg plunges beneath the letter's baseline. It represents one who ventures below the acceptable, an individual who violates the circumscribed boundaries of the Torah."

★ **resh (200)** means "poor," i.e., in knowledge/wisdom. "There is no poor person except he who is poor in knowledge" (Nedarim 41a) .... He is spiritually bereft; the poorest of the poor."

★ **shin (300)** The letter itself means "monkey" and thus represents the base, animalistic elements of humanity, but with a *potential* for making amends for mistakes or lack of knowledge.

★ **tav (400)** is the word for "truth" (Shabbos 104a); it represents the universal concepts of Life and Death. It "represents humankind's ultimate destination, the culmination of our Divine service to perfect the world."

Perhaps the inferences do not need much explaining, as the journey of the king throughout the Song is now a clear reflection of each of these symbolic letters. Nabonidus, a base, animalistic man, focussed on attaining wealth, luxuries, and secret knowledge he can boast about, fails to live up to Nitocris's expectations as an initiate; he does not succeed in making amends for his "sin" of hubris. She pities him and sees him as a lost soul, despite his attempts. She knows *dod* is lost to him.

The past tense of "Solomon *had* a vineyard ..." reflects a shift in time and location; this is spoken with hindsight, i.e., the "vineyard" is no longer extant (a sign that the Song is, indeed, written after the fall of Babylon).

One curious little fact: The Egyptian hieroglyph for the numeral 1000 is the lotus (lily), the symbol in the Song for women's genitals and/or their wombs.

"MY OWN" (8:12)

Nitocris has removed herself from the king's influence, on a personal level. She no longer lives with him. She has, supposedly, given birth, so her menstrual blood is no longer appropriate for the Elixir; it is a thing of the past. Her own "vineyard" here forms another inclusio, i.e., with Song 1:6.

---

[27] Information from Rabbi Aaron L. Raskin, "Letters of Light: The Meaning of the Hebrew Alphabet," Chabad.org, https://www.chabad.org/library/article_cdo/aid/137068/jewish/Letters-of-Light.htm.

So her sexuality, her womb, begins the Song's tale, and ends it. Finally, she can keep her own body to herself and honour Amun-Re in peace and quiet, in the privacy of the *giparu* (or her own palace). Like Siduri, preparing her blood/wine in a golden bowl as an offering to the gods, Nitocris can continue to treat her blood as sacred, in the sanctity of her own temple. It is quite possible Nabonidus never sees her again in an intimate way, so he would be none the wiser.

The "one thousand" reference is repeated, i.e., the king can make all the money he wants from his venture but it merely confirms the denigration and ignorance expressed in the gematria, i.e., it will never give him Life, Love, or Peace. She wants no part in it.

What of the "two hundred" in the same sentence? On one level, I think there is an intentional allusion to the "Atrahasis" story, with its temporal delineations of "twelve hundred years" (1000 + 200); it serves as a reiteration of the subtle allusion to Nabonidus as the leader of the "noisy peoples" (i.e., the world). It may also suggest that the keepers add on another fee of two hundred pieces of silver, which they pocket for themselves; these would probably be the Nabonidus-loyal priests of the temple (in Babylon, not Ur) responsible for organizing the women.[28] In this regard, we are then compelled to recall that the gematria of 200 (*resh*) suggests those lacking in wisdom, "spiritually bereft; the poorest of the poor." No more need be said.

Nitocris's distant and somewhat acerbic tone here echoes that of her defiant declaration to the "daughters" after finishing her idol of the king (in Song 5:16, i.e., "O *daughters* of Jerusalem"): "*You*, O Solomon" sounds less than loving, now.

GARDEN DWELLERS (8:13)

The verb *yashab* means to dwell, remain, sit; I suggest the "remain" aspect is more fitting in this context. The queen has just declared how the base, animalistic, un-awakened people (i.e., those who choose the path of *ahabah*, not *dod*) are doomed to failure, to spiritual death. She carries on in this frame of mind, i.e., "You who remain (passively) in the gardens" means those who do not aspire to anything more, e.g., enlightenment, where "gardens," of course, refers to physical, mundane, sexuality.

---

[28] W. Wittekindt, in the 1930s, advocated for a cultic interpretation of the Song and saw the "keepers" as "eunuchs who supervised the hierodules"; the reference to money changing hands he saw as "payment" for services rendered during the sacred rites. See Marvin H. Pope, *Song of Songs: A New Translation with Introduction and Commentary* (New York: Doubleday, 1977), 689.

COMPANIONS

The "companions" form yet another inclusio, this time with the king's "companions" of Song 1:7, whom I discussed in terms of being akin to Tammuz worshippers. Here, the queen (like Ishtar) has her own "worshippers," women who serve as priestesses, i.e., the ones who are honour-bound to protect their "little sister." If we see the queen as once again the avatar of Ishtar, Hathor having been relegated after the feigned pregnancy, we can see Nitocris in all her glory once more. She stands proud, independent, wise, and in complete control, calling to her followers to take heed, to listen for the voices struggling to be heard from the dark recesses of the "gardens." Through her associates she will "hear" the voices asking for wisdom.

THE SOUND OF TRUTH

Back in Song 2:14, Nabonidus had said to Nitocris "Let me hear your voice": yet another inclusio is created by this line in 8:13. The former was linked to the king's perception of Nitocris as an Adept, an enlightened one, offering him insights into the greatest mysteries. Now, that offer, in contrast to the king's open invitation to men of the kingdom to partake of her Elixir (5:1), is one that demands personal agency. Those who seek wisdom must come to Nitocris, must use their voice and ask, must *want* transcendence.

Like the Adams and Eves in every little Eden suddenly realizing that perhaps eating of the tree of knowledge means more than just carnality, their cries of "teach me!" are like the scent of cedar to the gods. Nitocris is, once again, leaving the door open to anyone wishing to learn. This time, though, it will be done *her* way.

In discussing the Pyramid Texts, Susan Morrow defines one inscription from the North wall: "Ma'a herw *the truth is vibration, sound*: The truth has a voice. ... the vibration of truth that is the goal of a life."[29]

GO AND PLAY! (8:14)

In her ultimate performance, Nitocris, Queen, First Prophet, and *entu*, "black and beautiful," powerful and formidable, raises her chin, looks down her "tower of Lebanon" nose and laughs at the king and his new, pointless venture. "Run away!" she says to the king (i.e., using the verb *berah*, to flee, run away, bolt), as if he were a child, "run away and play!" Only his play is upon the "mountains of spices," the genitalia of other women. She shakes off the king like a robe that ill-suits, mockingly encouraging him to carry on playing the "stag," the sexual conqueror (though forever the target of the

---

[29] Susan Brind Morrow, *The Dawning Moon of the Mind: Unlocking the Pyramid Text,* (New York: Farrar, Straus and Giroux, 2015), 215.

huntress, thanks to his proclivities). She has no further need of him. Like Ishtar, she belongs to no man.

9. THE ART OF A WOMAN

The Song of Solomon is penned by a woman. She is an eyewitness to the events in Tayma, i.e., the marriage and shenanigans of the royal couple as they battle to find a peaceful compromise. She appears to know the intimate and private sphere of the queen as only a personal maid or companion can. She writes from the perspective of Nitocris because she understands the feminine domain, the courtly province, the harem. Highly intelligent and a skilled scribe, she is no common servant; I propose she is a woman of high standing in her own right, and that she is the "other woman" of the Song, i.e., it is *she* who "loved" (*aheb*) the king.

THE OTHER WIFE

I have asserted that Bithiah and Mered of 1 Chronicles 4 are alternative depictions of Nabonidus and Nitocris. If Nitocris could not or did not wish to become pregnant herself, e.g., due to her apparent devotion to her role as God's Hand and 'perpetual fountain' of the Elixir Rubeus, how could she be mentioned in 1 Chronicles as having a daughter and two sons?

1 Chr 4:18 employs *harah* to indicate that Bithiah "conceived and bore" her daughter Miriam (the firstborn); *harah* is used throughout the HB to mean conceive but it can also mean contrive or devise, i.e., to conceive *of* (e.g., Isa 59:13, in the context of falsehoods). The words "and bore" are not in 1 Chr 4:18 (see note "v" in the NRSV), intimating that Bithiah might not have given birth to her children (leaving "conceived" hanging, without "bore" could be a hint at her first pregnancy). This seems to be a confirmation of my claim that there is another woman who bears Ennigaldi. The Bithiah of 1 Chronicles (and thus our Nitocris) "conceived (of)" but Mered's second "wife" (i.e., the "field" of Song 7) "bore" (i.e., *yalad*, to give birth, bring forth, beget). Quite a pronounced difference.

Note that this second wife, though ostensibly a Judean, is not given the honour of a name in the NSRV and yet Bithiah, the Egyptian, is. Here, we must investigate the Hebrew word used to denote this second wife: *yehudiyyah*. This *can* be used as a name, not merely an adjective (meaning Jewish/Judean), i.e., Jehudijah. The name means Praise Yah/Iah (*yada*, to praise; the plural noun *huyyedot* means "songs of praise"; see Ps 146, especially v.10). The word *yehudiyyah*, therefore, can mean Praise the Moon God. It also relates to the noun *yad*, or hand, thereby linking it, intimately, with Jedidiah, the so-called divine name of Solomon. The name Jedidiah, recall, is derived from the verb *yadad*, to love, i.e., sexually. So, the supposedly descriptive name of Mered's second wife does seem to be a composite or euphemistic name; the subtle allusion to "songs of praise" proves uncanny.

Bithiah's two sons (remember Ishtar has two sons, yet she is never 'pregnant') are called Shammai and Ishbah. The former means "desolation" and the latter means "praise/praising"; this could suggest the author of 1 Chronicles knew the relationship between the queen, whose "womb was a wilderness" (desolation) and the woman known for her songs of praise, that resulted in Ennigaldi (Miriam).

I argue, therefore, that the historical person behind the name Jehudijah is not only the mother of Nabonidus's daughter, Ennigaldi (and, apparently, other children), she is also the author of the Song of Solomon. The name could well have been devised in order to link her to the King of Babylon (i.e., as Jedidiah) for eternity, paralleling the Song's pairing of Solomon and Shulammite, and Baal-hamon and Bath-rabbim. This is but one account of her in the HB, however. As I suggest the Song is written very soon after the dispensation of Cyrus, and probably has its roots in the migration itself, there could have been several discrete factions aware of Nitocris's 'companion', especially those from Ur, who would have seen her in the context of the temple. Each of these factions might have a unique perspective, or recollection of the events surrounding Nabonidus and Nitocris, hence the alternative renditions in the story of Samson and Solomon, for instance. If they knew Jehudijah, they possibly called her by another name.

TEMPLE SERVANTS

Ezra 2:55–8 lists those families who travelled to Jerusalem; the "descendants of Solomon's servants" are mentioned. If Solomon is based on Nabonidus, this would entail "Nabonidus's servants." The phrase "temple servants" is translated from *nethinim*; this is explained by the *Jewish Encyclopedia* as pertaining to the lowest of the low amongst the returnees, i.e., they were potentially considered "descendants of the Ḳedeshot, or sacred prostitutes"; "both the Septuagint and Josephus refer to the Nethinim as 'Hieroduli'," which seems to confirm this notion.[1] They were strictly prohibited from marrying Israelites.

Therefore, there *are* female temple priestesses and attendants who

---

[1] Joseph Jacobs, "Nethinim," *The Jewish Encyclopedia*, https://www. jewishencyclopedia.com/articles /11451-nethinim.

leave Babylon with the Jews. They are probably the clergy and devotees of Sîn, i.e., Nabonidus's clergy (i.e., "Solomon's servants"), who deem it a safer option to leave than remain in Babylon to face the consequences. By the time of Ezra, with an increasingly anti-Solomon (Nabonidus) sentiment, these women are clearly *personae non gratae*. Ezra 2:58 states that there were "three hundred and ninety-two" such servants. The gematria of 300, 90, and 2, although just one of many combinations possible, *can* equate to: "crimson cloth" (300) + "they are defiled" (90) + "house" (2): "The temple prostitutes who defile the house/temple with their menstruation." (Compare Ezra 9:11: Israel is considered *niddah* [unclean] due to the "abominations" of the indigenous peoples.)

At the time of the exodus from Babylon, could a woman have the necessary skills to write a complicated and multi-layered work such as the Song? She would have to master the required ritualistic knowledge (i.e., of incantations, idol-making, Elixir ceremonies, etc.), and have intimate access to the queen, possibly as her confident, learning the more intimate details of her relationship with the king. She would have to be able to read and write Aramaic and/or Hebrew but also either Sumerian or Akkadian, to appreciate the Enheduanna poetry and allusions to Babylonian mythology and contemporaneous inscriptions.

Taking a closer look at Ezra's account of the three hundred and ninety-two returnees from "Solomon's" temple, we notice that one of those mentioned is a certain Hasophereth (in Neh 7:57 the name is recorded as Sophereth). This is a feminine proper noun, i.e., a woman's name, meaning "the scribe."[2] This confirms that at least one woman on the journey was, indeed, in a high enough position to earn the title of "scribe," and to be immortalised, however obscurely, in the record of those who enter the promised land in the new era.

This brings to mind the previous discussion about Huldah of 2 Kings 22, who is apparently a temple-woman but who is sought out for advice in the very early stages of the development of the new settlement. She is given a derogatory name (in hindsight) but is found living in Jerusalem in the Mishneh (Second Quarter in the NRSV; 2 Kgs 22:14), as a teacher. Recall that her husband's name, Shallum is from the same etymological root (*shalem*) as "Solomon," making Huldah, possibly, an alternative rendition of Mered's second wife, Jehudijah. With this in mind, we might understand Song 8:11–14 as being more the author's voice than Nitocris's, having become *the* scribal/wise woman of the time; Jehudijah could be placing herself in Nitocris's stead, rising from the "shadow" she had lived under for

---

[2] Meir Bar-Ilan, *Some Jewish Women in Antiquity*, Brown Judaic Studies 317, ed., Shaye J. D. Cohen (Atlanta: Scholar's Press, 1998), 36.

years.

When Leonard Woolly excavated the *giparu* at Ur in the 1920s, where Jehudijah and Ennigaldi would have lived (perhaps not Nitocris, for she, though acting *entu*, was still Queen), he discovered a small collection of artefacts with museum-like labels on them (Nabonidus was an archaeologist at heart and perhaps shared his enthusiasm with his young daughter who collected objects in emulation of her father). Next door to the "museum," he found a vast collection of used clay tablets, upon which were written practice sentences, several beginning with the same letter or syllable, as though teaching the alphabet. On one tablet he found the inscription "Property of the boys' class"; from this he surmised Ennigaldi must have kept a school.[3] Ennigaldi, however, was about six years old when Babylon fell, so it was not she who ran the school; more likely, it was Jehudijah.

Perhaps the reference to Jehudijah working as a teacher, in 2 Kings, alludes to her previous role as a teacher within the school at Ur, which she continues when she settles in Jerusalem. There are about four years between the inauguration of the *entu* and the fall of Babylon, allowing Jehudijah time enough to hone skills already possessed, perhaps, and to learn more of the various cultural nuances that appear in the Song. I therefore submit that Hasophereth, Huldah, and Jehudijah are pseudonyms of the same woman, from various sources, each preserving the idea of an important woman once close to the king, and who was identified as the most memorable of the migrating group's wise-women. Of course, this did not last long, with the new patriarchal Judaism quickly growing and the old, feminine-dominated cultic practices of the past being hastily and thoroughly rejected.

This woman was later seen (e.g., by Ezra) as someone to be ashamed of, to be ridiculed and put down. She represents the three hundred and ninety-two temple servants who had left Babylon for fear of retribution by the Marduk priests, only to be denigrated by the new Jewish priests. The strength of her legacy, however, is something that cannot be ignored, even though the HB's male authors attempt to hide her identity.

EVERYONE LOVES A CODE

As if fully aware of this new incentive for diminishing the female voice, Jehudijah has made sure her identity is never erased from the record; she has inserted it into the Song in a very simple, yet almost undetectable way; only by understanding the Song as an account of Nabonidus and his life in Tayma can the author's "signature" be recognised.

Solomon's name is used seven times in the Song (i.e., 1:1, 5; 3:7, 9, 11; 8:11, 12); this follows the pattern of 2–3–2, in that his name appears

---

[3] Leonard Woolly, *Ur of the Chaldees* (London: Herbert Press, 1982), 251.

twice close together at the beginning, then three times in the middle, then twice again at the end. This is a simple code. If we consider the numerical values of the second and third letters of the Hebrew alphabet, i.e., *bet* and *gimmel*, we find something rather fascinating. The letter *bet* (gematria of 2) means house, and this is alluded to twice; *gimmel* (gematria of 3) is used once, and its meaning is nourish (until ripe), wean. Recall the focus on the mandrakes' scent in Song 7:13, which occurs very briefly, when the "fruit" is "fully ripe."

The author, therefore, inserts into the narrative two references to a house, once at the beginning, and once at the end of the narrative. Who is it that nourishes and weans the "fruit"/child until Nitocris and Nabonidus take her (when she is "ripe")? The woman of the "nut orchard," the fertile "field," the "lily" down in the valley. The letter with a gematria of 7 (i.e., 2+3+2) is *zayin*, and this means a crown. Jehudijah is, I submit, claiming to be associated with the crown, King Nabonidus; *she* is the biological mother of Ennigaldi, and she lives (as nanny) first in one of the palaces (house) in Tayma, and then in Ur (house/temple)[4] with Nitocris and the girl.

I had considered that this woman might have been a personal companion to Nitocris, sent along with her when she first left Egypt to marry Nabonidus (she most certainly would have had at least one). Due to the name Jehudijah being theophoric, and pertaining to an Egyptian deity (Iah), *combined* with the adjectival interpretation, "Jewish," however, it is possible that she was a lady from an elite family in Tayma, the cosmopolitan city where Egyptians and Jews were known to mingle, i.e., an Egyptian Jew. As such, she could certainly have learned to read and write Aramaic/Hebrew, and would probably be a devotee of Ilteri, the Tayma version of Sîn. Her use of the -*yah* suffix in *shalhebethyah* (i.e., "the "flame of Yah" of Song 8:6) may indicate a degree of Egyptian heritage but it is certainly an indication of an association with lunar worship that she would have shared in common with the king, unlike Nitocris.

It is quite plausible such a woman ranked high in the harem and would have been one of the gathered "lilies" of Song 6:2. Nabonidus probably made many women pregnant and these were dutifully sent somewhere, e.g., to the "villages," to give birth, not to be seen again until the children were presented to him, later. Perhaps this is why Nitocris can so easily carry out her plan without alerting the king's suspicion.

---

[4] Ziggurats were often called "House." Clinton Briar, "Sunshine and Shadowplay: An Archaeoastronomical Study of Dūr Kurigalzu" (2019): 10, https://www.academia.edu/45577518/.

JEALOUSY

If such a woman is the author of the Song, I argue it is *her* voice, *her* emotional reactions, not the queen's, that are found in the more visceral, longing, and pitiful scenes. *She* was the one who suffered the pangs of unrequited love, for the king was besotted with Nitocris, not her. She can say with a sigh, "rightly do they love you" (Song 1:4), knowing that she secretly wished his hands could embrace *her* (e.g., 2:6). It is probably by *her* loving hands that the purple seat of the wedding chariot was made; this would be the closest she could get to him, before Song 6 and the other "lilies" episode. This would make her one of the snide, jealous, lovesick "daughters of Jerusalem" (Song 2:10), i.e., one in the king's harem at Tayma. It is she who subtly declares, between the lines of 2:1, "*I* am the one who loves the king."

This angst, this passion stemming from unrequited love, and subjugation to a foreign woman who is so clearly deceiving everyone, breeds a level of contempt that rivals that of Enheduanna's for Lugal-ane, and even of Ishtar's for Shu-kale-tuda, who had raped her (*ETCSL, t.1.3.3*, §290–310). The Song becomes a parody of an exaltation poem, for it uses superficial imagery to lure its audience into a false sense of admiration for this supposedly beautiful and much-loved queen, but scratch the surface and you find a constant spitting of venom; truly, the pangs of jealousy *are* a fierce flame! Jehudijah had always loved (*aheb*) Nabonidus, and probably agrees to Nitocris's adoption of her child in a bid to get closer to him, within the court. If 1 Chronicles 4 does bear witness to the second wife of Nabonidus, it is clear she gets her wish.

Jehudijah places herself on a par with Nitocris from the very start, i.e., the "other" womb of Song 2:1, though the subsequent drama suggests she must tolerate living under her shadow. Although she voices her disdain for her Egyptian rival, as most women would, she retains an element of historicity, of "truth," that is impressive, especially with respect to Nitocris's struggle to maintain her own religious ideals, her purity, and her ultimate independence. Nevertheless, Jehudijah includes in the Song the most damning insult of the time, when she declares to the world that Nitocris is barren: "Your vagina/womb is a wilderness" (Song 4:3a).

As the child-bearing womb, Jehudijah is indignant. Nitocris's disinterest in becoming pregnant, but worse, her (apparently) blatant disregard for the child she loses, makes her all but inhuman to the "lily from the valleys" that was never allowed to reveal her true identity or feelings to *her* "beloved." With hindsight, perhaps, she realises he would never have reciprocated.

The Song bears witness to the vehemence and the frustration the author had felt, for years. I suggest it is once she is taken on as the wet-nurse/nanny for the child, having to watch the king praise Nitocris so much, knowing all along it is sheer deception, that the scales fall from Jehudijah's eyes and she begins to see Nabonidus for who and what he is. This is why she starts the Song's depiction of the king with the eternal damnation, "Your name is empty," making everything else that follows fundamentally about Nitocris and her.

HIDDEN LOVE

Song 2:1's "I am the one who loves the king" interpretation was based on the author's subtle employment of *chabab*, the rare word for a form of love, unique within the Song, and used elsewhere only in Deut 33:3, as a word for God's love for his people. A first reaction might be to assume this would refer to Nitocris, and her concept of *dod* but I think not.

The verb *chabab* is hidden within another word; when you look at the etymology of *chabab*, you find that it is closely linked to *chabah*, to withdraw/hide, and this, *Strong's* suggests, can mean to "hide in the bosom." Jehudijah is claiming, from the very start of her tale, that her love was secret, i.e., she cherished it, held it close to her heart. She loved from afar (just as the "daughters" did, and told Nitocris to do, in Song 1:7–8); such an unrequited love, however, often decays with time and resentment takes its place. Jehudijah's voice can be heard in the scathing account of love and jealousy in Song 8:6–7, for this is *her* child, *her* experience.[5] The description of the 'unrecognised' female leaning on her beloved in Song 8:5 takes on another level of meaning, perhaps.

STATUE

It is due to this resentment, ironically, that Nitocris's poppet in Song 5 is depicted as a cultic statue of the king. While the Egyptian priestess probably works her magic on a crude, clay representation of the king for her own supposedly nefarious purposes, Jehudijah describes Nabonidus in terms of his royalty, his high status, and even his deification, making his subsequent fall even more pronounced. It is as if she is building him up, expressing how she had once envisioned him in all his finery, as *her* fantasy, *her* idol. She uses this as a weapon of words, adding impetus to her initial curse, i.e., it is not only the king's name that is "empty" but the kingdom he represents, and

---

[5] Queen Tahpenes of 1 Kings 11 may be significant to the historicity of the Song; the LXX version of the name includes a potential allusion to the Egyptian God's Hand, as mentioned, but also, Tahpenes's sister gives birth to a son called Genubath, but the queen takes the child as her own and has him live with her in the palace. Genubath means stolen. See also Supplemental Note "Tahpenes and Hadad: Nabonidus and his Alter Ego?" (at the end of the book).

even his assumed exaltation as a demi-god. It will all come to nothing (as in Daniel 5; this demonstrates hindsight and therefore a postexilic perspective). With allusions to his mesmerisation by Nitocris and his penchant for the Elixir, and then to death and the underworld, Jehudijah's portrayal of the king as a statue (something with no feelings) serves as an act of vengeance and anticipates a similar treatment for Nitocris, in Song 7.

WISDOM?

It makes sense, then, for the one example in the HB canon of Solomon's supposed "wisdom" that is meant to impress "all Israel" (1 Kgs 3:16–28) is a story of two mothers vying for one child. The child is a boy (i.e., expected to be of more significance to the early Jews) but note that the two women are living together in the same "house"; both are "prostitutes" (of course); one gives birth before the other (reduced timeframe to fit the allegory) but 'carelessly' kills her baby; this woman shows no mothering instinct or remorse, while the true mother is said to have compassion that "burns" within her. This is an allusion to the historical situation of an unwitting Nabonidus and these two women, Nitocris and Jehudijah, I am certain.

I do wonder, however, if there is not an element of feminine bonding that takes place between Jehudijah and her nemesis, her mistress, Nitocris, at least on some level. They share the responsibility for Ennigaldi and Song 8 does seem most determined and unanimous. The one element in the Song that speaks to this possible mutual acceptance is the image of the two women placing the umbilical cords over their doors, as protection for the new child. Not only is this the one and only thing Nitocris does (of her own volition) in the Song that intimately involves someone other than the king, it demonstrates that the otherwise castigated and insulted Queen Nitocris did, indeed, have a conscience about the abortion (for she kept the umbilical cord), and Jehudijah grants her that.

WRITER OF SONGS

Animosity for Nabonidus and his devotees builds amongst his dissenters in post-invasion Babylon. Jehudijah and Ennigaldi leave with the first Jews to travel through the desert toward Jerusalem, resting at the place that is remembered for their visit, i.e., the Conduit of the Infidel's Daughter. Intriguingly, not far south of the site of the Conduit is a town called "Hulda" (the masculine form, of course), potentially affirming the theory proposed earlier that it is a pseudonym for Jehudijah. She is later tarred (by Ezra) with the same brush as the "temple prostitutes," thanks to Nabonidus's notorious "desire" for the Elixir Rubeus, but it is probable she was never a biological source for the famous "spiced wine," as she had given birth.

Jehudijah imbues the Song with clues to her existence and enough information to tell future generations exactly who this Song is about and even when they lived. It is Jehudijah's voice that (quite literally) cries out in the wilderness: "Come to *me!*" (Song 8:13). Through her character, Nitocris, she calls to anyone who wants to learn, for she has all but taken Nitocris's place; she has learned enough to step into the high priestess' sandals. What better vengeance for a life in the shadows than to rise to your mistress' station and surpass her? It is said that the earth trembles and cannot bear up under "an unloved woman when she gets a husband, / and a maid when she succeeds her mistress" (Prov 30:22–23)!

As a skilled writer of "songs of praise," it may be that Jehudijah, a student of Enheduanna's poetic style, the "rose of Sharon" and the "lily of the valleys," is indirectly responsible for the curious headings to several of the Psalms, i.e., Ps 45 ("according to Lilies"); Ps 60 ("according to the Lily of the Covenant"); Ps 69 ("according to Lilies"); Ps 80 ("on Lilies; a Covenant"). Although it is often assumed such subtitles are related to the format or style of the music to which these songs were ritually performed,[6] I like to think they pertain to the formally-recognised school or style of "the Lily," i.e., derived from the writer of the Song of Solomon. Perhaps Ezra, who resented having to attribute any praise to such a female, felt it necessary to make her part of the historical record, given her standing and popularity, and thus referred to her obliquely as Hasophereth, "the scribe." She has found recognition under several guises within the canon, as has Nitocris, both leaving their indelible mark on those who knew them; both fading into obscurity to those who followed.

The Song itself turns out to be a parody of the praise poems written and sung for Mesopotamian kings, such as King Shulgi (c. 2094–46 BCE), who ruled at Ur. Shulgi's praise poem is filled with instructions on how his every good deed, his strength, wisdom, benevolence, good looks, etc., are to be preserved for posterity in songs: "I am a hero! Let them appropriately acknowledge my fame! … Let them tell in song a perfect recital of all my praiseworthy deeds" (*ETCSL c.2.4.2.03*C, 18–20). Jehudijah might once have loved Nabonidus but her subsequent scorn is as vicious and damning as the "raging flame" of 8:6.

The author of this complex and multi-dimensional Song still has a powerful voice, despite attempts to hush her. Although she retains a venomous resentment toward both Nitocris and Nabonidus, as an Egyptian

---

[6] William L. Holladay, *The Psalms Through Three Thousand Years: Prayerbook of a Cloud of Witnesses* (Minneapolis, MN: Fortress Press, 1995), 73–4; "Lessons from the Psalm Inscriptions: Titles of Description," Ken Puls Music Blog (2014), http://kenpulsmusic.com /blog/2014/12/lessons-from-the-psalm-inscriptions-titles-of-description/.

Jew, Jehudijah does, in the end, see Nitocris's spiritual quest as worthy of emulating. She sings the song of Nabonidus and Nitocris in order to keep them from resting in peace; this is her curse. The profound and "hidden" *dod*, the peace, love, and truth of the divine, makes her Song sweet ... and thus it is sung forever.

EPILOGUE

Certain lines of investigation revealed during the initial research for this book fascinated me but fell beyond the scope of a focused study, so these are discussed in the Supplemental Notes section, as I consider them platforms for future investigations. A few themes, however, do require a little more attention, to provide closure to the current analysis.

DANIEL AND THE MADNESS OF KING NABONIDUS

There are subtle clues in both the Neo-Babylonian texts and the HB that suggest Nabonidus was, indeed, mentally unstable during the latter part of his reign.

Daniel is sent for to attend the king, who complains: "… my fantasies in bed and the visions of my head terrified me" (Dan 4:5). This probably coincides with the king's "alarms by night" in Song 3:8, where his relationship with Nitocris begins to take on a more sinister tone. Although the Elixir rite is yet to become manifest in the narrative of the Song, the king is clearly already perturbed and deeply affected by his bride's influence on him (e.g., by Song 4:9 he already feels "ravished" and overwhelmed).

Just before the "writing on the wall" scene of Daniel 5, we see Nabonidus acting in just the same way he is depicted in Song 8, i.e., inviting all and sundry to partake of "wine" in a drunken parody of sacredness, i.e., by having them drink from the holy vessels of the Jewish temple. The "lords" (the friends, or "beloveds" of Song 5:1), wives, and concubines are all there. The male party-goers number one thousand, i.e., another parallel to the Song's "thousand pieces of silver" (8:11) and to Solomon's thousand wives and concubines (1 Kgs 11:3). There is, therefore, one piece of silver for every female (as in *Hist.* 1.199); an allusion to the "prostitution" in the temple of Babylon? The revelry takes place in the context of idol worship (Dan 5:4).

At this point (Dan 5:5–6), it is the king *alone* who notices the hand, writing its ominous words on the wall. No one else seems to see what he is seeing. I suggest he is having a hallucination brought on by his over-indulging in the Elixir. When he orders all the diviners and magicians to come and decipher the writing, they are unable, not because the script is illegible or foreign, but because *they do not see* what he sees, i.e., there is no script there! He has already offered a huge reward for the interpretation of his vision, so obviously everyone comes running (5:7–8) but when they look, they just see a wall and probably some shadows caused by the lamp, which is so obviously mentioned in 5:5 to help us understand the scene. It is a simple case of "The Emperor's New Clothes"; everyone is afraid to offend the king. They are all yes-men who wish to enjoy their luxurious, lucrative positions at court. They simply claim to be unable to decipher the strange shadows.

At this point Nitocris, the "queen" of Dan 5:10–12, steps in to suggest Daniel be called for. Daniel has already advised the king with respect to the tree-dream of Daniel 4 and the ensuing seven-year banishment, where there is a subtle insinuation that the king's fate will be influenced by his mixed-marriage. In the current scene, Daniel seems to take advantage of Nabonidus's compromised mental state; he refers back to his previous omen of rejection and madness (Dan 5:20–1), telling the king in no uncertain terms, now, that he has not learned from his mistakes, from his punishment, i.e., he is still arrogant and self-absorbed. He has not made restitution; he has proven no better than Nebuchadnezzar. Claiming he can see (read) the "writing," Daniel interprets it, according to his own agenda; Nabonidus's kingdom will be forfeit—it will fall and be divided up, i.e., the very fate of Solomon and his kingdom. It is possible that "the queen" calls for Daniel because the two (or perhaps three, if we include Belshazzar; see Supplemental Note "A Cuckolded King?" at the end of the book) are in cahoots, attempting to put an end to his unsavoury antics.

Thus, the alleged madness of King Nabonidus does have a potential foundation in Daniel's account of his communications with the king (in Tayma). In the VA, also, the king's proclivity to hallucinations is hinted at in the much damaged fourth column: "… 'the king is mad' can be discerned … Nabonidus had some kind of hallucinatory vision …."[1] When we remember the king's manic, addict-like behaviour toward his wife in Song 5:2–6, these external examples of the same idea (the Book of Daniel, the VA, and the rabbinic legend of Ashmedai) do seem to suggest the last King of Babylon was psychologically susceptible for much of his reign, and certainly rather disturbed by the end of it.[2]

---

[1] See the translation notes, "The Verse Account of Nabonidus," Livius, https://www.livius.org/sources/ content/anet/verse-account-of-nabonidus/.

[2] The queen says to the king "Do not let your thoughts terrify you or your face grow pale" (Dan 5:10); this is an echo of Nabonidus's own words concerning his frequent bouts of self-doubt (or fear), e.g., " I became frightened, worried, (and) anxious, and my face was haggard."(Nab 28, 1.30–2).

THE DEATH OF NITOCRIS

In Nab Chr 2.13–15a is a potential reference to the death of Nitocris within days of the invasion of Cyrus and his armies. We know, from Herodotus (*Hist.* 1.187) that a legend claims she put her tomb in "one of the principal gateways" of Babylon; having argued this to be highly unlikely, I do have one theory about how such a rumour might have begun.[3] I think Nitocris falls from the Ishtar Gate and is killed. It could possibly be that she commits suicide rather than be subjected to the soldiers' unsympathetic attentions (as Enheduanna was); with Nabonidus gone, she would have had no legal protector. Suicide, not as uncommon a tactic as might be supposed,[4] would have had the same overall effect of making the site impure to the Zoroastrian Persians (for a while), and would be adequately sensational to leave its mark.

There is an alternative scenario, however. It is highly unlikely that Nabonidus's Queen would have been allowed to wander through the city unattended once Babylon had been seized. I posit that she is *thrown* from the Gate. Nitocris, to the Babylonians, is just the foreign wife of a king they had become indifferent to; to the incoming Persians, she is a prisoner—and an Egyptian one at that, which does not bode well, given the Persians have their eye on Egypt. It has been popular to suggest the "[wife] of the king" mentioned in the Chronicle was Cyrus' wife, Cassandane;[5] the substantiation always falls to Herodotus's brief mention of the "great mourning" throughout the Persian kingdom for Cyrus's beloved wife (*Hist.* 2.1). Yet, the Chronicle is a record of the reign of Nabonidus; *he* is "the king" throughout. The mourning period is only in Akkad. It states that on the day after mourning ends, Cambyses goes to the temple and holds the hand of the idol of Nabu, declaring himself King of Babylon. The death of the "queen," therefore, comes before the Persians officially seize the throne. One would think any kowtowing to Cyrus, if his wife is the subject here, would be evident but the Chronicle reference is minimal, dispassionate, reflecting ambivalence at best. Also, Herodotus says Cassandane died during Cyrus's

---

[3] Herodotus might have been confused by the legend that Cyrus's wife Cassandane was buried in the citadel (tower) called Zendan-e Solayman. M. Boyce, "A Tomb for Cassandane," *Orientalia,* Acta Iranica 23 (1984): 67–71.

[4] Ahmad Abo el Magd, "Death Without Dishonour: Suicide as Punishment in the Judicial Sources of the New Kingdom," Minia University, https://www.academia.edu/4749930; Jan Dietrich, "The Meanings of Suicide in the Ancient Near East," *Friends of ASOR,* 6.6 (2018), https://www.asor.org/anetoday/2018 /06/Meanings-of-Suicide.

[5] Frauke Weiershäuser and Jamie Novotny, *The Royal Inscriptions of Amēl-Marduk (561–560 BC), Neriglissar (559–556 BC), and Nabonidus (555–539 BC), Kings of Babylon,* The Royal Inscriptions of the Neo-Babylonian Empire, Vol. 2 (University Park: Eisenbrauns, 2020), 27, note 169.

lifetime, not that such a dramatic event took place literally days after conquering Babylon, which I think would have been emphasised. I support Dougherty's suggestion that it was, instead, Nitocris, Nabonidus's wife, who died so suddenly.[6]

It is possible that subsequent scribes offer a more rounded account of Nitocris' death, i.e., in the execution of Jezebel in 2 Kings 9. Defenestrated and devoured by dogs, Jezebel's skull, feet, and the palms of her hands are symbolically left untouched, probably because these were hennaed, i.e., a sign of priestly status and thus, her inevitable rejection.

In Egyptian mythology, Anubis, the canine god of the underworld, ensures the body of the deceased is intact and ready for its journey to the afterlife. By depicting Nitocris (as Jezebel) being devoured by dogs, the author of 1 Kings suggests she has been abandoned by even her own gods and will never be reborn. It is effectively sending her into eternal darkness, with no reunion with the divine or her family. That her corpse is destined to become "dung on the field" further strengthens the image of a resurrection denied. This done, "no one can say, 'This is Jezebel'" (2 Kgs 9:37), i.e., she becomes nameless, unremembered, a desolation (the name Jezebel means "not honoured"). Link this with the vandalised tombs of Ahmose's family at the time of the Egyptian conquest (525 BCE),[7] and we may be seeing Nitocris (as echoed in Jezebel) being made an example, i.e., of what awaits Egypt.

A PHARAOH MOURNS?

Ahmose III inexplicably changes the law of the land sometime around 537 BCE; that is, just after the fall of Babylon and the death of his daughter, Nitocris. Whereas previous marriage arrangements/contracts were the responsibility of the groom and the bride's father, suddenly Ahmose makes the unprecedented decision to grant the bride the right to be her own legal representative in a contract of marriage.[8] Could this possibly be in response to his feelings about handing over his daughter as part of the treaty with Nabonidus, knowing she did not, initially, wish to go with him, and then lost her life when the Babylonian king evidently did nothing to protect her? Recalling the seal impression that allegedly bears the cartouches of Ahmose

---

[6] Raymond P. Dougherty, *Nabonidus and Belshazzar: A Study of the Closing Events of the Neo-Babylonian Empire* (Oregon: Wipf and Stock Publishers, 2008 [1928]), 175.

[7] See Andrey Bolshakov, "Persians and Egyptians: Cooperation in Vandalism?" in *Offerings to the Discerning Eye*, (Leiden: Brill, 2010), 45–54.

[8] Annalisa Azzoni, "Women and Property in Persian Egypt and Mesopotamia" (paper presented at the Women and Property Conference, Centre for Hellenic Studies, Harvard University, n.d.), 1–28, here 4.

and Nitocris (see Part One, Chapter 1), perhaps it is even more plausible now to consider this a potential posthumous honour for his favourite daughter, the queen of Tayma, Queen of Babylon.

CANONICITY: THE SYMBOLIC *TAV* AND AKIVA'S "HOLY OF HOLIES"

The Song of Solomon was given a specific place in the canon; it is the twenty-second book of the HB. The twenty-second and final letter of the Hebrew alphabet is *tav,* which is described as "an eternal lesson for us. It tells us that if we continue to pursue the instruction of the Torah with humility, then this is *ticheyeh,* life. If, however, we seek this truth through arrogance, it is *tamus*; the antithesis of true living."[9] Recall (from above) that *tav* (gematria of 400) is the word for "truth" (Shabbos 104a) and represents the universal concepts of Life and Death and our quest for spiritual union with the divine.

Thus, *tav* mirrors the entire ethos of the Song, the song of Life and Death. It mirrors the audacity of Nabonidus as he boasts his comprehension of "secret things," yet not getting beyond the first few lessons. It reiterates the declaration in Song 8:6–7 that this type of arrogance, whilst revelling in hedonistic practices, will cut you off from what *is* true, what really *is* Life, and will send you in a downward spiral to Sheol. The Song of Solomon was placed in this position in the canon because it epitomises the struggle to know divine Life and attain universal wisdom. What higher purpose could a text have?

The allegorical interpretation (i.e., God as "husband" and Israel as "wife/lover") advocated by Rabbi Akiva allows for the idea of a *hieros gamos,* i.e., a union between the divine and the "world" (i.e., as king, priestess, initiate, or nation), reaching beyond the mundane, beyond a tale of individuals, to a more esoteric understanding of Life and Death. It appropriates the Egyptian philosophy and transforms it into one for the relatively young Jewish religion. The allegorical view of the Song turns out to be the closest we have to its intended meaning, even though, ironically, this view is now going out of fashion amongst scholars.

Akiva famously declared the Song to be the "Holy of Holies" of the HB (Mishnah Yadayim 3:5). Within the Holy of Holies, legend suggests, lies the Ark of the Covenant. What is the physical, or outward sign of that covenant? Blood. Circumcision. If the Song is to be equated with the inner sanctum, where the original covenant is preserved, the Song itself must be

---

[9] Rabbi Aaron L. Raskin, "Tav: The Twenty-second Letter of the Hebrew Alphabet," Chabad.org, https://www.chabad.org/library/article_cdo/aid/137287/jewish/Tav.htm.

seen as a sanctuary for a covenant (i.e., a blood-covenant). So, there should be a corresponding new circumcision—perhaps now, the circumcision of the heart, rather than the flesh, i.e., as suggested by Jer 9:25–6.

Gen 17:10–14 demands that every male is to be circumcised, in order to demonstrate his inclusion in the covenant. There is no equivalent for women. Although archaeological evidence for the ritual of circumcision goes back to about 3000 BCE, one must suppose the link between Jewish identity and male-only circumcision developed within the exiled community as a way of defining those who were in the 'anti-women/anti-sex' fraternity, i.e., they physically mutilated their members to prove their commitment to the new code (Babylonians themselves did not circumcise). Thus, men could feel included, whilst the women were excluded from this semi-secret society.

The disassociation of male and female, Jew and foreigner, was paramount, i.e., a cleaving of the undesirable from the desirable; the undesirables were predominantly the foreign women and the men who had sex with them. The ritual of mutilating the male child's sexual organ must have served as a vivid and lifelong reminder of the fear of the art of women (deemed so prevalent in Babylonia) and the need to be on one's guard against temptation, i.e., the *yeser*. From the rabbis' perspective, "circumcision serve[d] as a mark of self-control ... sexual sin was the epitome of idolatry and the rejection of God's laws."[10] It has even been suggested that the blood of male circumcision was "the symbolic opposition" to the blood exclusive to females, i.e., of menses, thereby imprinting "androcentric social values onto the body of society."[11]

By exposing the mind to temptation, by illustrating through experience, via a titillating and uncensored exposure to the Song's racier and more sinister themes, e.g., lust, lasciviousness, arrogance, idolatry, etc., the soul is (theoretically) refined and the circumcision of the passions can become the means to purity.[12]

It could be for this reason that centuries ago, the Jews began to read the Song of Solomon during the Passover festival, i.e., to remind them of the context from which the Song arose (the exodus from *Babylon*, not Egypt), the reason for its preservation in the canon (to serve as the new circumcision, severing all contact with the "whore of Babylon"), and its significance to the

---

[10] Matthew Berkowitz, "The Mitzvah of Circumcision" (2000), https://www.jtsa.edu/the-mitzvah-of-circumcision.
[11] Ohr Margalit and Chariklia Tziraki-Segal, "Circumcision: Man's Obligation and Woman's Praxis," *Nashim: A Journal of Jewish Women's Studies & Gender Issues*, 12 (2006): 10–38, here, 11–12.
[12] For a fascinating perspective of the allegorical understanding of the Song, in the context of a celibate clergy, see Stephen D. Moore, "The Song of Songs in the History of Sexuality," *Church History* 69.2 (2000): 328–49, esp. 338–9.

religious aspirations of those who understood its message (to refine the character/soul, in a bid to experience divine wisdom).

In the Zohar, a thousand years after Rabbi Akiva, the Holy of Holies of the temple in Jerusalem was identified as the bed-chamber in the *hieros gamos* of the Shekinah and God. The curtain surrounding the cherubim therein was removed during the festival and the people would witness the two beings intertwined, as lovers, i.e., "the mystery of masculine and feminine together." [13] In the Zohar, several links are made to the Song of Solomon in this context. Rev 22:2–3 hints at a similar reconstitution of the divinely ordained male/female nature of humanity, i.e., when the monthly "curse" of the woman regains its spiritual/healing aspects of old: "... the tree of life with its twelve kinds of fruit, producing its fruit each month; and the leaves of the tree are for the healing of the nations. *Nothing accursed will be found there anymore.*"

FULL CIRCLE

The rabbis had no interest in preserving the story of Jehudijah's heartbreak or revenge; rather, they saw the deeper significance, the influence and underlying truths of the ancient religion she brought with her to the promised land. The scathing curses and insults aimed at both the Babylonian king and the idolatrous "daughter of Pharaoh" suited them nicely, as they served the purpose of educating the masses in the perils of the art of women. As times changed, however, this aspect seemingly fell into obscurity and the allegorical idea was maintained to both justify the Song within the canon and bring its profound truths into the more mainstream Jewish mind-set. As the Romans assimilated the unrelenting force of Christianity so, perhaps, the early postexilic rabbis realised the Song was too powerful and too entrenched to be naysaid, and thus the allegorical interpretation seemed to resolve inherent concerns, without the need to redact, steadily obscuring Jehudijah and her historical account with each generation. In today's multi-cultural and rather more liberal milieu, the original, sometimes dark, sometimes shocking nature of the Song can once again be appreciated (hopefully).

PASSAGE OF THE MOON

One of the fundamental patterns that lies at the heart of all the research undertaken for this book is the constant reference or allusion to the moon.

---

[13] Moshe Weinfeld, "Feminine Features in the Imagery of God in Israel: The Sacred Marriage and the Sacred Tree," *Vetus Testamentum* 46.4 (1996): 515–29, here 518–20.

Sometimes it was this alone that led to astounding discoveries:

⋆ Ankhnesneferibre is the God's Hand and symbolic mother of the moon god, Khonsu.

⋆ Ahmose means The Moon is Born; the pharaoh *is* the deity incarnate, i.e., Ahmose is equated with the moon god, Iah/Yah.

⋆ Nabonidus worships the moon god, Sîn.

⋆ **Nitocris II is Daughter of the Moon** (i.e., daughter of Ahmose III).

⋆ **The names Bithiah (1 Chr 4:17) and Bathya (from the rabbis) both mean Daughter of the Moon.**

⋆ **Bithiah/Bathya is Nitocris, who is depicted in the Song as Ishtar; Ishtar is Daughter of the Moon.**

⋆ Jedidiah can mean Beloved of the Moon God's Hand (perhaps derogatory); Jedidiah is the Song's Solomon, beloved of the queen, who is potentially God's Hand.

⋆ Miriam is the firstborn daughter of Mered and Bithiah; she is Ennigaldi-Nanna, first daughter of Nabonidus and Nitocris. Ennigaldi-Nanna means High Priestess, the Moon God's Desire.

⋆ Ennigaldi is the biological daughter of Jehudijah, which means Praise Yah, i.e., Praise the Moon God.

SUPPLEMENTAL NOTES

1. TAHPENES AND HADAD: NABONIDUS AND HIS ALTER EGO?

This may seem a strange topic to include in an assessment of the Song of Solomon but it is hoped that the following will inspire others, Egyptologists especially, to delve deeper and uncover even more potential connections. I think there is far more to the tale of Hadad and Tahpenes than meets the eye and, at the very least, it may provide further evidence for an exilic/postexilic timeframe for the writing of the HB by placing these two characters firmly in the reign of Ahmose III, Dynasty 26.

When Solomon goes so far as to build high places on the hillside east of the temple in Jerusalem, the king supposedly predetermines his fate. It is *because* of this alleged betrayal, this breaking of the covenant, that adversaries are sent (by God) to weaken Solomon's kingdom, the first of which is Hadad.

Hadad is a royal Edomite. In an echo of Moses's story, Hadad (in 1 Kings 11) is depicted as a child threatened with death along with all the other males of Edom, by King David (11:14–17). He escapes and flees to Egypt where, predictably, he finds favour with the pharaoh and is given a house, land, and an Egyptian bride, i.e., the pharaoh's sister-in-law, the sister of Tahpenes (11:19).

Historically, the Edomites survived the onslaught Nebuchadnezzar II by collaborating with the Babylonians against their own neighbours in Judea.[1] The Edomites became bitter enemies, as Psalm 137 illustrates.[2] The elite Edomites migrated west and settled in Arabia, along the vital trade routes, thereby profiting from the arrangement for nigh on thirty years—until Nabonidus arrived.

---

[1] Eyal ben-eliyahu, "What Links the 'Daughter of Babylon' and 'Sela Edom' in Psalm 137?" *Aram: Trade Routes & Seafaring in the Ancient Near East* 27.1, 2 (2015): 239–44, here 240–1.

[2] Ben-eliyahu (241) provides external evidence of this.

It was not King David (2 Sam 8:13–14) who conquered the Edomites; it was Nabonidus, in c. 551 BCE.[3] Located in the mountains of southern Jordan, as-Sila' (meaning "clefts of the rocks," an Edom toponym) is the rocky fortress at which Nabonidus subdued the Edomite forces. 2 Sam 8:14 states that David put his forces in the area and the people thereafter became his "servants"; the Nabonidus Chronicle mentions the king's "large army" encamping against Edom (1.17–22) and the VA 2.7–9) accuses him of slave labour (e.g., in Tayma). After the conquest, some of the Edomite elite escaped even further west, into the Negev, to re-establish themselves as traders.[4] It is not a huge leap to have them (represented by Hadad) flee even further, i.e., to the relative safety of Egypt, thus proving their adversarial (i.e., Egyptian) nature to the early Jews (especially at a time when the relationship with Egypt was fraught).

Archaeologists have discovered not only a relief left by Nabonidus upon the face of a rock at as-Sila', boasting of his military success there, but also a large stone slab upon which is carved a bull's head, "probably a depiction of the widely worshiped storm god Hadad,"[5] who was a warrior god to the Assyrians, whom Nabonidus admired (see VA 2:4).

In this vein, it is possible, with what we now see of Nabonidus in the Song of Solomon, to argue that Hadad represents the original kernel of the idea of the Demon King Ashmedai, in that Ashmedai is probably invented by the rabbis to help explain the bizarre shift in behaviour of Nabonidus witnessed at his court in Tayma. He, too serves as a foil to the king, becoming his adversary, usurping his place in the kingdom but, symbolically, in his bed, also; this could be why Hadad is said to marry the Egyptian princess (the author knowing full well his immediate readers would understand this as an insulting reference to a betrayed, and thus humiliated Nabonidus; see the short Supplemental Note, "A Cuckolded King?").

The idea of a "substitute king" was discussed (Part One, Chapter 1) in the context of Nabonidus's lunar eclipse but also later, in terms of the legend of Ashmedai; that Hadad's story ends in such an unresolved way, i.e., he simply urges the pharaoh to let him go home (1 Kgs 11:22), does have the same effect of the sudden and unexplained return of the "mad" king to his senses and to his kingdom, in Dan 4:34 and in the Ashmedai story.

It seems as though there is a gradual refining of a theme, a vision, i.e.,

---

[3] For full details of the event read: Bradley L. Crowell, "Nabonidus, As-Sila', and the Beginning of the End of Edom," *Bulletin of the American Schools of Oriental Research*, 348 (2007): 75–88, http://www.jstor.org/stable/25067039.

[4] Crowell, 84.

[5] Glenn J. Corbett, "The Edomite Stronghold of Sela," 2012. https://www.biblicalarchaeology.org/daily/biblical-sites-places/biblical-archaeology-sites/the-edomite-stronghold-of-sela.

from Moses, to Hadad, to Jeroboam, to Solomon. There is a constant echo of the good king/ruler/prince etc., gone bad, so that the expounders of the faith can wag the finger and declare, "he did not respect God," or "he was not worthy and we lost everything." These, at least partially fictitious, men are *designed* to be scapegoats for a nation's bad decisions or bad luck. That each marries a foreign woman (the last three marrying Egyptian princesses—two, at least, supposedly from the same family—is highly unlikely, historically)[6] suggests *this* is the common denominator. It is the foreign (Egyptian) female that seems to be the route of all evil and the route to Sheol for not just the men but their kingdoms, too. Hadad thus becomes an avatar of Nabonidus, i.e., his alter ego.

TAHPANHES (THE CITY) / TAHPENES (THE WOMAN)
The name relates to both a person (1 Kgs 11:18–20) and a place, the latter with variant spellings (Jer 2:16; 43:7–9; 44:1; 46:14; Ezek 30:18).

The City:

★ The place name is often translated as "The mansion of the Nubian," thus suggesting dark skin, and/or a subtle link to its foundation (?) under Pharaoh Taharqa (2 Kings 19:9).[7] It has also been translated as "Head of the Age" or "Beginning of Earth as We Know It" or, intriguingly, "Given of the Serpent."[8]

★ The city is on the eastern front of Lower Egypt, i.e., modern day Tel Defenneh, twenty miles south-west of Pelusium, or the biblical Desert of Sin (Midbar Sîn). It lay close to the trade route between Egypt and Palestine/Mesopotamia, just like Tayma (mentioned in Part Two, Chapter 3). It is the nearest Egyptian town to Palestine; Hebrews and Greeks commune with Egyptians there, just as in Tayma.

★ This could have a bearing on the idea I expound in Part Two, Chapter 9, that after the fall of Babylon, Ennigaldi-Nanna is taken by her biological mother to Jerusalem; the group would most likely follow the trade routes. More importantly, there is an Arabian name connected with the site of Tahpanhes, i.e., *Qasr bint al-Yahudi* or Mansion/Palace of the Jew's Daughter.[9] In Part One, Chapter 2, I mention the Arabic epithet, "Conduit of

---

[6] "And Sousakim gave to Jeroboam Ano the eldest sister of Thekemina his wife, to him as wife; she was great among the king's daughters, and she bore to Jeroboam Abia his son" (3 Reigns, 12:24e, LXX).
[7] "Tahpanhes," *Encyclopedia of the Bible*, https://www.biblegateway.com/resources/encyclopedia-of-the-bible/Tahpanhes.
[8] Abarim-publications.com (see entries for both spellings).
[9] "Tahpanhes," *Encyclopedia of the Bible*; L. Dickerman, in "Mr. Petrie's

the Infidel's Daughter," which I claim to be a reference to Ennigaldi. This would make sense if, indeed, Ennigaldi's mother *was* an Egyptian Jew (Part Two, Chapter 9). Perhaps the two females made it back to Egypt. Did Ahmose demand that his granddaughter be returned after Nitocris's death? He would be unaware of Nitocris's deception but the Arabic legends, based on the events at Tayma, could influence the anecdotal naming of these two sites where Ennigaldi was known to have stayed. Intriguingly, in the tomb of Ahmose's chief wife (Queen Nekhtbastetru) and their son, Ahmose, found at Giza, is the sarcophagus of a mysterious female called Tashentihet, which disappeared from its temporary home at the Cairo School of Medicine "without a trace" before the translation of its inscriptions (in 1891) was fully published.[10] Could this possibly be Ennigaldi-Nanna with her Egyptian name, now deemed part of the family? It would be nice to think so.

✶ In Jer 2:16, Tahpanhes is coupled with Memphis; Ahmose III battles against Apries's armies at Memphis and it becomes his family residence. The Greeks call the site Daphnai (Daphnae) and it is one of the mercenary settlements within Egypt designated for foreign (mostly Greek) fighters (others include Elephantine and the Stratopeda).[11] It was Psametik I who first set up these garrisons. Ahmose moved the soldiers from the Stratopeda (intriguingly roughly translated as "encampments," as there were two main groups of Greeks who were set up opposite each other! Might this be the subject of a contemporaneously 'political' allusion in the Song, i.e., the "two camps" of Song 6:13 NRSV?), to be his own bodyguards at Memphis.

✶ Jer 43:7–8 suggests Tahpanhes is where the Pharaoh has his palace, and where Nebuchadnezzar II is predicted to enthrone himself on Egyptian territory. When Petrie discovered the 'palace' remains, he also found a brick courtyard he identified as Jeremiah's brick pavement.[12] The existence of a 'brick pavement' here is not exclusive, however, for in a more recent archaeological excavation of Memphis,[13] a similar structure was found; it

---

Discoveries at the Biblical Tahpanes," (*The Old and New Testament Student* 10.5 [1890]: 279–81, http://www.jstor.org /stable/3157920) translates this phrase as a plural, to match the "king's daughters" of Jer 43:6, of which Petrie said the Arabic name reminded him.

[10] See Andrey Bolshakov, "Persians and Egyptians: Cooperation in Vandalism?" in *Offerings to the Discerning Eye*, (Leiden: Brill, 2010), 45–54, here 45, note 6.

[11] Denise Demetriou, *Negotiating Identity in the Ancient Mediterranean: The Archaic and Classical Greek Multiethnic Emporia* (Cambridge: Cambridge University Press, 2012), 148.

[12] Dickerman, 280–1.

[13] Maria H. T. Lopes and Sofia Fonseca Braga, "The Apries Palace, Memphis/Kôm Tumân: The First Portuguese Mission in Egypt," *Journal of the American Research*

was probably a standard inclusion for any royal/high-class build, especially in the Delta area, where resources are plentiful.

★ "Some capitals bear the name of king Apries, who was therefore most likely the builder of the palace."[14] This does not preclude (and in fact may support) the possibility that the Hadad-Tahpenes story is set in Ahmose III's reign.

★ "Tahpanhes may be the Hebrew transliteration of *Ṯḥpnḥs* a place mentioned in a Phoenician papyrus letter of the 6th century BCE from Egypt. This text refers to 'Baal-zephon and the gods of Tahpanhes,' from which it is thought that the city must have earlier borne the name of Baalzephon, an Israelite staging post during the exodus (Exod 14:2)."[15]

★ This proves highly intriguing, as I discuss Baal-zaphon in Part Two, Chapter 3, as relating to the inception of the notion of Zion. Baal-zaphon is a cognate of Hadad (or Adad), the Mesopotamian storm god. Hadad is Baal to the Canaanites, and in the Song, Nabonidus is called Baal (to a largely Canaanite audience?).

The Woman:

★ As discussed in Part One, Chapter 1, Tahpenes appears as Thekemina in 1 Kgs 11:19–20 LXX. The etymology of this latter version includes a cryptic insult aimed at the queen, who is deemed a "prostitute."[16] In the Song, Nitocris is constantly the butt of 'prostitute' allusions.

★ Commentators point to the fact that the term for "queen" is unusual here: "*g'birah* is not the usual word for 'queen,' but a title of special honour, used occasionally (1 Kings 15:13; 1 Chronicles 15:16) for the 'queen-mother,' (Cambridge Bible); "… the mistress among the king's wives, as being the principal consort" (K&D).[17]

★ The female name is translated as "She whom the king/palace protects,"[18]

Center in Egypt 47 (2011): 247–58, here 253, http://www.jstor.org/stable/24555396.

[14] Digital Egypt for Universities, "Memphis: The Palace of Apries," University College London (2000), https://www.ucl.ac.uk/museums-static/digitalegypt/memphis/palace.html.

[15] Encyclopedia of the Bible, "Tahpanhes," https://www.biblegateway.com/resources/encyclopedia-of-the-bible/Tahpanhes.

[16] W. F. Albright, "New Light on Early Recensions of the Hebrew Bible," *Bulletin of the American Schools of Oriental Research*, 140 (1955): 27–33, here 32.

[17] See https://biblehub.com/commentaries/1_kings/11-19.htm.

[18] Albright, "Recensions," 32.

a concept that features in the Song, i.e., Nabonidus initially 'protects' Nitocris, publicly, e.g., by symbolically placing his "banner" over her. In fact, the name has also been translated as "standard/banner."[19]

★ Ahmose III's mother (i.e., the "queen mother") is Tasherenese; this made me think of Herodotus's "Nitocris"/"Nitetis" name-play.

★ The Egyptian princess who bears this name in 1 Kings is said to have a "sister," whom Hadad marries (11:19). The noun *acoth* can mean a full sister but it can just as easily mean a half-sister, another relative, a member of a group, etc. It is the same word the king in Song 4:9 uses when he calls Nitocris "sister-bride."

★ If Tahpenes is considered the "prostitute" and the primary wife, this equates to Nitocris as depicted in the Song; the "sister" of Nitocris, in this context, is Nabonidus's second wife (Part Two, Chapter 9).

★ The "sister" of 1 Kings gives birth to a son called "Genubath," which translates as "stolen."[20]

★ In the analysis of the Song, it is discovered that the second wife is the one who bears Nabonidus his children, including Ennigaldi-Nanna. Nitocris claims the child as her own, much to the frustration and disdain of the natural mother, who perhaps sees the child as 'stolen' from her.

★ The verb "wean" is the Hebrew *gamal*, which can mean to deal with, to recompense (and also has the connotation of weaning when "ripe," the same language used in the Song about the new child); this could indicate a deal between Nitocris and the mother.

Some other comments:

★ The correlations between Ahmose and Nabonidus in the tale of Hadad may point to the notion that the Babylonian king was a collaborator, a veritable vassal to Egypt. He (as Solomon) becomes infatuated with Egypt, its wisdom, its wealth, etc. and, as discussed in Part One, Chapter 2, earns the name "Jedidiah" not as some divinely ordained honour but as a sign of his capitulation to Ahmose.

★ The tale of Hadad is very like that of Moses, i.e., Moses is a baby taken by an Egyptian princess; he is accepted into the royal house; he asks the pharaoh permission to leave Egypt.

---

[19] Hitchcock's Dictionary of Bible Names, https://www.biblestudytools.com/dictionaries/hitchcocks-bible-names/tahpenes.html.

[20] See BDB, https://biblehub.com/topical/g/genubath.htm.

★ The story is set in the past but this does not preclude more recent history being the inspiration.

★ The name Hadad comes from the same root as *hedad*, which means shout/shouting (of a multitude);[21] in the Song, Nabonidus is cleverly disguised as "Lord of the noisy multitude" (Part Two, Chapter 8).

★ The name of the deity, Hadad, can also mean sharpness/keen/swift, and this is reflected in his son's name (e.g., in the Enuma Elish), i.e., Girra (Gerra, or Gibil), the god of fire and light, the patron of metallurgists, and a refiner of metals; he maintained the sharp points of weapons.[22]

★ Discoveries from the 6th century BCE Tahpanhes included "many amulets and much rich jewellery and bronze and iron weapons, a piece of scale armour, thousands of arrow heads .... There was also dug up a vast number of minute weights evidently used for weighing precious metals, showing that the manufacture of jewellery was carried on here on a large scale."[23] So, the site known as Tahpanhes affirms at least a symbolic affinity with Hadad and his son (as deities).

★ Thus, Hadad and Genubath (cf. "Hadad and *Gibil*/ Gerra/Girra") of 1 Kings may, in some way as yet not fully understood, represent yet another tangled depiction of Ahmose, Nabonidus, Nitocris, and the second wife.

★ "Note that the form *hdd* also arises when the word *dod*, beloved, is preceded by the definite article *he*."[24] This would help to confirm Hadad as an avatar of Nabonidus/Solomon of the Song!

★ The noun *hida* and the denominative verb *hada* both relate the concept of riddles, which is a strong element of the wisdom tradition. In 1 Kings 10:1 the Queen of Sheba tests Solomon with "hard questions," i.e., riddles. Is the story of Hadad a riddle?

---

[21] See https://biblehub.com/hebrew/1959.htm.
[22] Johanna Tudeau, "Girra (god)," Ancient Mesopotamian Gods and Goddesses, Oracc and the UK Higher Education Academy, 2013, http://oracc.museum.upenn. edu/amgg/listofdeities/girra/.
[23] https://www.biblestudytools.com/dictionary/tahpanhes.
[24] Abarim Publications Biblical Dictionary, "Hadad," https://www.abarim-publications.com/Dictionary/he/he-d-d.html; Osita Iroku, *A Day in the Life of God,* fifth ed. (N.p.: Lulu.com, 2008), 103–5.

2. ZIV, BUL, AND ETHENIM: SOLOMON'S BUILDING SCHEDULE IN 1 KGS 6:37–8:2 AND NABONIDUS'S PLAN TO CREATE HIS "HOUSE" OF THE *ENTU*.

One of the items of evidence, in the bid to prove "Solomon" is a pseudonym for Nabonidus is the very precise dating in 1 Kgs 6:37–7:1 and 8:2 (see Part One, Chapter 2). Solomon is said to have begun the temple in the "fourth year," in the month of Ziv; he completed it in the month of Bul of the "eleventh year"; he took "thirteen years" to complete "his own house"; he delayed the dedication of the temple until the "seventh month," Ethanim.

Ziv

Used in the Bible only in 1 Kgs 6. It is a Hebrew name for the second month in the Hebrew religious calendar, and the eighth month in the civil calendar, i.e., April/May, usually called Iyar.

✭ The word Ziv means "achievement of foundation"; increase (procreation), magnificent (haughty), "bright and beautiful."

✭ The second month of the Babylonian calendar, Aru (with connotations of "blossoming, flowers")[1] is ruled over by Ea, god of the waters of Creation.

✭ The Babylonian city god, Marduk, has a consort called Sarpanitu,[2] who is considered to be a cognate of Ishtar; Sarpanitu means "shining, brilliant one," and Ishtar is the goddess of "increase," the shining one (as Venus), etc.

Bul

✭ Similarly, found only in 1 Kgs 6:38. Bul is the eighth month in the Hebrew religious calendar, second in the civil, i.e., October/November, or Marcheshvan (Cheshvan).

✭ It is of unknown origin but Bul is a) linked to the notion of a "moon god," as the Akkadian term for "eighth month" is *waraḥsamnu*, where the *w-r-ḥ* root means "moon" and, by extension, "month,"[3] and b) (from *Strong's*) it

---

[1] W. Muss-Arnolt, "The Names of the Assyro-Babylonian Months and Their Regents," *Journal of Biblical Literature* 11.1 (1892): 72–94, here 78, https://doi.org/10.2307/3259081.
[2] W. Muss-Arnolt, "The Names of the Assyro-Babylonian Months and Their Regents," *Journal of Biblical Literature* 11.2 (1892): 160–76, here 167. https://doi.org/10.2307/3268813.
[3] See BDB definition on https://biblehub.com/hebrew/945.htm; and https://

238

relates to *buwl* (food/produce); *yebul* (produce of the soil); *yabal* (to conduct, bear along).

★ The Babylonian "eighth month" is Samnu, ruled by Marduk, the city god of Babylon.

Comments: The two months are direct opposites in the calendar, i.e., second religious/eighth civil and eighth religious/second civil. Ziv seems to allude to Marduk's consort Sarpanitu/Ishtar, and Bul seems to allude to Marduk himself. Had the traditional names, Iyar and Cheshvan, been used, this allusion could not be made. The names for these months seem to be invented for this specific context (commentators often suggest these must be more ancient names but they do not suggest a motive for using them only here). There is an etymological connection to a lunar deity. There is a link to the idea of "fruit" (as produce of the land); to the blossoming of flowers; and to the idea of escorting someone along.

Ethanim

★ When the temple is complete, its dedication is inexplicably postponed until Tishrei (September/October), the seventh month of the Hebrew calendar.

★ The seventh month is called Ethanim in 1 Kgs 8:2, during which there is a "festival."

★ This month-name, too, is unique to 1 Kings. The word (according to *Strong's*) means "steady flowings/ permanent brooks."

★ In the Babylonian calendar, this is Tishritu and is ruled by Shamash (the solar deity).

★ The Mesopotamian Akitu festival, in both Ur and Uruk, was traditionally held twice in the calendar year, i.e., in the first month Nisanu (Nisan in the Hebrew calendar), i.e., in spring, and in the seventh, Tishritu (Tishrei) in the autumn; in Babylon, it was celebrated only in Nisanu.

Comments: The Akitu festival was originally the celebration of Sîn's conquest over the sun, Shamash, at the Autumn Equinox; the lunar deity entered the city of Ur as a conquering hero.[4] Nabonidus and his family leave Tayma on 17 Tishritu (Babylonian) / Tishrei (Hebrew); in the Song, it seems they head straight for Ur. This reference to the "festival" in the "seventh

---

dbpedia.org/page/Cheshvan.
[4] "The Akitu Festival," https://www.theishtargate.com/akitu.html.

month" would support an intended allusion (specifically) to Ur, the home of the *entu* priesthood.

Interestingly, one of the primary functions of the Babylonian Akitu festival was to celebrate the authority of Marduk and his conquest over chaos (Tiamat), as well as his marriage to Ishtar; re-enacted by the current king, this served to confirm *his* kingship. As part of the process, Marduk had to undergo a ritual humiliation, a descent into the underworld; Nabonidus underwent his own seven-year penance (humiliation and psychological descent) for his alleged "sin" of hubris (I have argued), until he received the omen that it was time to return to Babylonia (H2, 2.11–14). Recall that Daniel had interpreted the king's tree-dream (Dan 4:19–27) to mean that once Nabonidus had returned what was rightfully the gods' (i.e., the Tablet of Destinies), his "roots" would regrow upon his return from banishment. The Akitu festival plays out Marduk's descent and his liberation by the god Nabu, and on the *seventh* day of the festival Marduk is led in procession into Babylon, i.e., as the conquering hero.

There is, therefore, an apparent creation of names for months that are used solely in connection with Solomon and the temple, only in 1 Kings; these names have meanings and connotations that pertain to themes also in the Song (moon, fruit, flowers, procreation, being taken/escorted, etc.), and thus, to the story of Nabonidus and Nitocris. Creating an allusion to the *hieros gamos* (of Marduk and Sarpanitu/Ishtar) places "Solomon's temple" in a Babylonian context, not a Jewish one. The third month-name relates to the "perennial flowings," i.e., an echo of Nitocris's role in the Song as the "perpetual fountain" (of sacred womb-blood). Of course, as Ishtar/Hathor are her main avatars in the narrative, Nitocris also fits the epithets mentioned above (shining one, magnificent, etc.). It is she who is 'escorted' from Egypt, but then she also escorts the king *to* Egypt.

The constructing of a "temple" might, therefore, be seen as metaphorical, at least on one level; it could pertain to the creation of the *entu* priesthood, which takes the full seven years in Tayma to fulfil. Solomon is said to finish his temple in the eleventh year; Nabonidus's eleventh regnal year is 545 BCE, the year of the second 13 Ulūlū (16 September) lunar eclipse, and the official recognition (date) of Ennigaldi-Nanna's birth, i.e., the creation of the *entu* as 'temple'.

It is as if the author of 1 Kings is trying to provide just enough information to record a historical event not in some legendary ancient Israel, but in the living memories of those he/she was writing for. Just as in the Song, the details are deeply embedded/encoded within the language, only discernible once "Solomon" is replaced with Nabonidus (whose name was not to be mentioned, recall). It is yet another instance of a unique perspective and expression of the history of the Jewish experience of Nabonidus.

TWENTY YEARS

In 1 Kgs 9:10, it is claimed that Solomon gave King Hiram of Tyre one Galilean city for each year spent building the two edifices (the temple and the king's house), which suggests the "seven" and the "thirteen" are simply added together. As elsewhere, it is here suggested that HB numbers are used on more than one level, e.g., as symbolic combinations of gematria pertinent to the narrative.

That the context of 9:10 is an example of Solomon's greed and dishonourable conduct (i.e., like Cain, Solomon gives not what is worthy of Hiram's generosity but what is the minimum he can 'get away with'; he exchanges a hundred and twenty talents of gold for twenty worthless plots of land [see the discussion of Gezer in Part One, Chapter 2]), suggests we are invited to look a bit deeper and discover further meaning. There is no way we can truly know the intentions of such an ancient writer, whose knowledge of the complexities of his/her symbolic language and the contemporaneous historical context eludes us to a degree, but there is a familiar pattern, here, to that within the Song of Solomon, if you use just a little imagination. Yes, there are other phrases with the same gematria that do not fit the storyline of the Song but there are many that do. Can they *all* be just 'coincidence,' or did the author of 1 Kings exploit this linguistic complexity to encode specific meaning?

The seventh letter of the Hebrew alphabet is *zayin*; it has the gematria of seven.[5] Traditionally, the meaning of *zayin* is "crown," "weapon," or "sustain" and there are many stories and examples of later, Jewish explanations. In the context of 1 Kings, however, let us just take the dominant meaning of "crown," as this implies "king." Other concepts having the gematria of seven include: "bring to ruin"; "desire"; and "train."[6] Nabonidus brings himself to ruin by focusing too much on his own desires; in the Song, he is Nitocris's protégée and is thus undergoing training.

The thirteenth Hebrew letter is *mem*, with the gematria of forty, and phrases that have this gematria include: "deceptive"; "Brightness" (as pronoun); "child/offspring"; "to bind/pledge"; "a snare"; "to conceal/hide/be secret" (recall that Solomon is said to reign forty years, in 1 Kgs 11: 42–3 and 2 Chr 9:30). Nitocris in the Song is depicted as being deceptive, as Ishtar she is "Brightness," she is the mother-figure, she binds Nabonidus with her seal/pledge, she is the one who sets a snare, and there is much that is concealed and secretive about her character/actions.

---

[5] Specific letter meanings from Rabbi Aaron L. Raskin, "Letters of Light: The Meaning of the Hebrew Alphabet," https://www.chabad.org/library/ article_cdo/aid/137068/jewish/Letters-of-Light.htm.
[6] All gematria-related phrases from Bill Heidrick, "Hebrew Gematria," http://www.billheidrick.com /works/hgemat.htm.

A gematria of thirteen, on the other hand, suggests "water"; it is therefore symbolic of the waters of Creation. Other phrases with this gematria include "beloved"; "unite"; "enemy"; "anxiety"; and, significantly, "excessive sex or masturbation"! The list also includes "to present as a gift," i.e., to dedicate? Of course, Nabonidus is the "beloved," who unites with the enemy; he is known for being anxious and even better known, at least in the Song, for being excessive in his desire for certain types of sex. He presents Ennigaldi as a gift to Sîn. Intriguingly, the month-name Ziv has a gematria of thirteen.

So, the two strange month-names (*ziv* and *bul*) allude to the union of a king/deity and his queen/consort, with the third name (Ethanim) reminding us of Nitocris's sacred blood and the taking of the child to Ur. I tentatively propose that the "twenty years" reference in 1 Kgs 9:10 unites both "seven" and "thirteen" on a similar, symbolic but higher level.

The eleventh Hebrew letter, with the value of twenty, is *kaf*; this can mean "crown" or "palm." The Hebrew *word* for twenty is *kaf*; when you add up its letters (gematria), you "arrive at 620: *ayin*=70, *shin*=300, *resh*=200, *yud*=10, *mem*=40. 620 is also the gematria of the word *kesser*: *kaf*=20, *tav*=400, *resh*=200. *Kesser* means crown, the ornament placed on the head of a king"; it is…

> …represented by the letter *kaf*—twenty—to teach us that there are two levels, or faculties, within the crown: desire and pleasure, with each faculty containing ten aspects. These aspects are also known as the ten holy Sefiros (spheres), the ten building blocks of Creation. Three of the ten levels reside in the dimension of the intellect— Wisdom, Understanding, and Knowledge—and seven occupy the dimension of the emotions—Love, Fear, Mercy, Victory, Praise (Acknowledgment), Foundation (Bonding), and Sovereignty (Speech). The two faculties of the crown of *kaf*—pleasure and desire—twice encompass the three levels of intellect and seven levels of emotion for a total of twenty levels.[7]

The twentieth letter of the Hebrew alphabet is *resh*, which means poor, evil, or head; it has the gematria of two hundred:

> The *resh*'s two lines represent intellect and speech. Because they are not joined with a *yud*, the speech and intellect of this individual are for his own gratification—they can even degenerate and become corrupt and evil. … In this way he drags his most essential faculties

---

[7] Rabbi Aaron L. Raskin, "Kaf (Chaf): The Eleventh Letter of the Hebrew Alphabet," https://www.chabad.org/library/article_cdo/aid/137083/jewish/Kaf-Chaf.htm.

into the depths of unholiness.[8]

Recalling the interpretation of Song 8:11–12 (Part Two, Chapter 8), and the use of gematria there, which included that of "two hundred," it must be considered uncanny how close this comes to the Song's perception of Nabonidus.

In essence, the number twenty, used to sum up the extent of Solomon's building program ("twenty years") exhibits much of the ideology of Nitocris's Egyptian religion, as depicted within the Song's narrative, i.e., the emphasis on Creation (for Nitocris, the ceremonial Elixir Rubeus rite); the delineation between emotion and intellect (for Nitocris, physical love [*ahabah*] versus divine love [*dod*]); there are seven baser (mundane/physical) levels of Creation (for Nabonidus, this is the extent of his learning; he does not develop beyond the seven levels of his attempted idol [Part Two, Chapter 4]). Each of the ten levels (above) find representation in the Song.

This is not to say every apparent echo or parallel to the Song's use of this symbolism implies that all the other biblical texts were written later than the Song (though the Song does seem to have been written during and/or after the migration from Babylonia); it simply suggests all the works revealing such similarities probably had the same original source of inspiration, and the various authors were probably well aware of what others were writing. I simply contend that there are bound to be more levels of meaning to these numbers and how they were originally used, than merely taking them at face value.

3. ADAD-GUPPI AND THE "GENIUS OF FAVOUR"

The Adad-guppi Stele serves as a propagandistic declaration of divinely-chosen kingship and theological intent. Nabonidus, potentially Assyrian but certainly a usurper, must prove himself a 'true' Babylonian ruler and he does so by insisting the deity Sîn has chosen him to take the crown. Similarly, he writes his mother's epitaph in such a way as to extend this divine sanction to the rebuilding of the temple of Sîn and the anticipated (though not overtly mentioned) revival of the *entu*-priestly order at Ur. It emphasises hereditary piety, duty, and loyalty, and a blessing of *future* offspring.

There are two primary translations of Nab 2001, i.e., Gadd's from

---

[8] Rabbi Aaron L. Raskin, "Resh: The Twentieth Letter of the Hebrew Alphabet," https://www.chabad .org /library/article_cdo/aid/137092/jewish/Resh.htm.

1958 (Nab H1, B),[1] and Weiershäuser and Novotny's from 2020 (Nab 2001).[2] The key term to note in the transliteration is ᵈLAMMA. In Gadd's translation, this sits within a context of enjoying lots of children, seeing descendants flourish, etc.: "... the genius of favour ... which (to be) with me thou hast appointed and they have caused me to attain offspring, with him (too) appoint them" (ii 37–9). The more recent version emphasises the woman's advanced years: "... the good *shedu* (and) the good *lamassu* that you had entrusted to me and who had helped me reach a very old age" (ii 37).

The *shedu* and *lamassu* are generally considered to be male and female (respectively) protective deities and are often described in terms of their familiar Assyrian depictions, i.e., as winged bulls. However, earlier Sumerian/Akkadian renditions of ᵈLAMMA often indicated Lama the goddess, an intercessor deity who is directly linked to Inanna-Ishtar: a pair of Lama stelae once flanked the Ishtar temple (Eanna) at Uruk.[3] Recall that Nabonidus renovates the Ishtar temples at two significant stages in his reign that seem to find an echo in the Song (see Part Two, Chapter 6). She is also seen on an Assyrian seal praying to the heavens for a 'lord's' (king's) offspring to be female![4] W. F. Albright, a peer of Gadd's, also translates ᵈLAMMA as "genius," as it appears in the tale of Gilgamesh and Siduri, claiming Siduri was regarded as "the keeper of the *fruit of life* and the *fountain of life* (emphasis mine). In the incantatory series, Surpu, II, 172, she is called 'goddess of wisdom, genius of Life'...."[5] He goes on to say that this "genius of Life" can also be linked to both the Phoenician Ishtar ("Ba 'alat of Byblos") and the Egyptian Hathor, which suits the context of this current interpretation. As this analysis has revealed the Song's focus on pregnancy, fruit, the "perpetual fountain" (the vessel of the Elixir, i.e., with allusions to Siduri), etc., the subtle reference to Lama, the "genius of favour," the goddess of increase, is uncannily apt.

Significantly, then, both Gadd and Albright render the word

---

[1] C. J. Gadd, "The Harran Inscriptions of Nabonidus," *Anatolian Studies* 8 (1958): 35–92, here 46–53, doi:10.2307/3642415.

[2] Frauke Weiershäuser and Jamie Novotny, *The Royal Inscriptions of Amēl-Marduk (561–560 BC), Neriglissar (559–556 BC), and Nabonidus (555–539 BC), Kings of Babylon*. The Royal Inscriptions of the Neo-Babylonian Empire, Vol. 2 (University Park: Eisenbrauns, 2020), 223–8.

[3] "Stele of the protective goddess Lama, ca. 1307–1282 B.C., Kassite," Met Museum 61.12 https://www.metmuseum.org/art/collection/search/325092.

[4] Gavin White, *Queen of the Night: The Role of the Stars in the Creation of the Child* (London: Solaria Publications, 2014), 99 (Figure 124).

[5] W. F. Albright, "The Goddess of Life and Wisdom," *American Journal of Semitic Languages and Literature* 36.4 (1920): 258–94, here 260.

^dLAMMA as "genius" in a context of "life-giving," i.e., sex and childbearing. Nabonidus is in his sixties, with several sons (Belshazzar is called "the eldest" on several occasions), so surely this warrants further investigation. For all the accuracy and clinical detachment of modern translations, there is still much to be gleaned from the earlier 'poetic' translations that may echo more of the original nuances of the Sumerian/Akkadian mind. Michalowski phrases it well by suggesting Nabonidus uses "highly saturated poetic language" that demands "to be seen in a different light."[6]

Adad-guppi's stele, composed by Nabonidus posthumously, suggests she had performed her last intercession by calling upon the Lama goddess to grant the king his special new child. The stele is probably not created until after Ennigaldi-Nanna's birth, by which time the king can underscore the significance and 'inevitability' of the new priestly order with this seemingly prophetic sanction from his powerful mother.

4. A CUCKOLDED KING?

In one legend of Solomon, he is said to have a daughter called "Kaziah,"[1] a probable play on "Kaššaya," Nebuchadnezzar II's eldest daughter. The name is chosen precisely for this similarity, perhaps, i.e., to *suggest* a Babylonian princess (but note the *-iah* suffix, suggesting Nitocris's Egyptian heritage?). As has been shown throughout this investigation, the use of wordplay, hidden meanings, puns, etc., is a stock-in-trade for the early Jewish writers, and the Song itself has made it clear that none of Nabonidus' immediate family (all except Belshazzar, which is interesting) are granted the privilege of having their own names preserved for posterity after the exodus from Babylon (remember that in 1 Kgs 4:11, 13, Solomon's two daughters are given names that echo the dubious depiction of Nitocris in the Song). It comes as no surprise, therefore, that made-up (i.e., commission) names are provided in these legends; they carry their own significance, once you understand the patterns.

In this legend, Solomon conducts astrological divination (just like Nabonidus) to discern his daughter's future. On learning that she is destined to marry a poor Israelite, the king decides to send Kaziah to live in an isolated tower. Already we can imagine the young Ennigaldi in the tower/ziggurat in Ur, isolated and protected from the outside world. Everyone involved is sworn to secrecy (an aspect that figures much in the

---

[6] Piotr Michalowski, "The Doors of the Past," *Eretz-Israel: Archaeological, Historical and Geographical Studies* (2003): 136–52, here 143.
[1] Angelo Rappaport, *Ancient Israel* Vol. 3 (London: Senate, 1995), 109–11

Song). The young man Kaziah falls for is called Reuben; he is from the town of Akko, which is an ancient, well-known port city (now known as Acre), but was this name *also* chosen for its 'play on words' quality, i.e., for its likeness to "Akkad" (i.e., Babylon)? The character of Reuben in the HB, although the firstborn son of Jacob (just like Belshazzar is Nabonidus's firstborn), forfeits his right of succession because he has sexual relations with his father's concubine, Bilhah (Gen 35:22). "Bilhah" means "terror/calamity"; sounds like Ishtar but also the Bathya of rabbinic lore *and* Nitocris in the Song.

From what we now know of the history of the last years of Babylon under Nabonidus, Belshazzar was nowhere to be seen from the king's thirteenth year onward, i.e., the very year the new family leaves Tayma to return to Babylonia. Once attested quite regularly in missives to and from the king in Tayma, in discussions with merchants, etc., suddenly he disappears from the record; the last thing we learn is that he is given provisions from the storehouse for a long journey, and some have suggested he might have been sent away to lead the army on some distant front.[2]

This might have been a strategic move on Nabonidus's part, as he must have realised his son was not his most avid supporter, preferring to side with the Marduk priests and build his political base in Babylon. On the other hand, if we recall that Daniel employs both "Nebuchadnezzar" and "Belshazzar" to talk about Nabonidus (whose name *must* not be mentioned), we should ask ourselves why does Daniel (alone) choose to name Nabonidus's son? In the discussion about the "writing on the wall" scene in Daniel 5, I hinted at the possibility that Nitocris, Daniel, and Belshazzar might have been in cahoots to rid the nation of Nabonidus (in what might be considered 'gaslighting' today!). It would make sense, in such circumstances, for Daniel not only to mention Belshazzar by name, but to depict him *as* the reigning king. He was probably the son's supporter, and it was almost certainly Belshazzar who pushed for Daniel's promotion (to 'encourage' him to stay on side?).

Perhaps the reason why Belshazzar is sent away just as Nabonidus returns from his life in Tayma—with his special daughter and his exotic, slightly dangerous, highly sexual wife, is because the king either a) doubts his son's political allegiance and is concerned that his influence with the Marduk establishment might interfere with the dedication of Ennigaldi and the plans for the new priesthood at Ur, or b) has suspicions about the relationship between Nitocris and Belshazzar. I do not think this relationship was a sexual one, given Nitocris's determination to avoid intercourse (in the

---

[2] Paul-Alain Beaulieu, *The Reign of Nabonidus King of Babylon 556–539 B.C.* (New haven: Yale, University Press, 1989), 205.

Song); I think it was political.

To the rest of the world, however, the reputation Nitocris had earned whilst in Tayma, her 'foreign' nature and her unbridled Egyptian ways did not earn her respect, or even the benefit of the doubt; she was, as in the Song, probably painted with the same brush as Jezebel and the rumours of illicit meetings with the king's son became rife (e.g., might her night-time excursions, as in Song 3 and 5, have been linked to or interpreted as meetings with Belshazzar, and might this be why the king felt there were 'troubles' brewing and set the guards on her?). She would never have been able to vindicate herself in the face of so much disdain.

5. ALTERNATIVE TALES OF NABONIDUS AND NITOCRIS

The Song of Solomon is far more ingrained into our collective psyche than many would consider. Its themes populate other biblical and non-biblical tales; once you see this repeating pattern of evidence, it is almost impossible to ignore it, and hitherto mysterious or confusing texts seem to take on new meaning.

1. LAYLA AND MAJNUN

As I drew close to finishing the manuscript for *She Brought the Art of Women*, believing the research stage to be at an end, I discovered an early medieval legend that seemed uncannily familiar. I had never heard of it before and as I read the tale, I got goosebumps. The ancient Arabic poem called "Layla and Majnun" by Nezami Ganjawi (1140–1209 CE) tells a story so similar to the one I had just spent years developing, I was not sure whether to laugh or cry! How could I have missed this?

To one who has never read the Song with Nabonidus as the king/lover character before, the parallels do not immediately stand out but once I had a clear perception of the Song as an account of the Babylonian king, his 'intoxicating' wife, and their turbulent and mutually destructive relationship, the similarities proved striking and can only be explained by the fact that Nezami read the Song the same way I do, i.e., as a tale of a doomed union between foreigners, and a "king's" descent into madness.

Nezami was commissioned by a ruler of the Shirvanshah dynasty (in present-day Azerbaijan) to collate a collection of disparate legends and historical details allegedly about a seventh-century Nejdi Bedouin poet, Qays ibn Al-Mulawwah, and Layla bint Mahdi (also known as Layla al-Aamariya), the woman he was besotted with. It is an epic poem with some four thousand verses.

Although I initially feared I had overlooked a previously published link between the Song of Solomon, Nabonidus, and the Arabic poem, I was, almost surprisingly, unable to find any such academic discussion, so the mystery of the parallels between the two works can now be approached from the perspective of this new paradigm.

It will be remembered that the Arabians had a very longstanding legend that Solomon had built Tayma, and that Solomon had just as much a connection to Arabia as to Israel. This, I argued, helped to confirm Solomon was, indeed, Nabonidus, who built up, lived in, and ruled from Tayma for seven years. This connection, and its influence on the literary aftermath, may further elucidate the use of the Arabic *waṣf* in relation to the Song's metaphorical descriptions of the couple's physical traits,[1] i.e., the daring proposal that perhaps the *waṣf* tradition evolved *from* the Song has yet to find provision within academia (as far as I can tell). It is a strong possibility.

As there are several translations and abridgments of the poem to be found online, the following selected highlights suffice to paint a familiar picture:[2]

★ Qays is called Majnun by those who witness his behaviour, i.e., it means mad, possessed (both the king in the Song and Nabonidus are depicted as being psychologically disturbed).

★ He has an obsessional love for a foreign woman, Layla[3] (Nabonidus is infatuated with Nitocris, the Egyptian, in the Song).

★ The name Layla means night/darkness (Nitocris, in the Song, is black/dark on multiple levels of meaning).

★ Layla has flickering eyes that "could have slain a whole world"; her hair/veil partially obscures her face; her lips and cheeks are red (Nitocris's eyes intoxicate the king from behind her veil; she has red lips and cheeks).

★ The two initially fall for each other under the influence of a heady drink ("wine") and a magical, mystical flower, the scent of which they inhale (the Elixir Rubeus and the lotus).

★ Because they are not from the same tribe, they cannot be together

---

[1] For example, Richard N. Soulen, "The Waṣfs of the Song of Songs and Hermeneutic," *Journal of Biblical Literature* 86.2 (1967): 183–90; J. Cheryl Exum, *Song of Songs* (Louisville: Westminster John Knox, 2005); Richard S. Hess, *Song of Songs* (Grand Rapids: Baker, 2005).

[2] The following references to the tale are thanks to R. Dikgunk, "The Story of Layla and Majnun," https://www.heliotricity.com/layla-and-majnun/; see also Wali Ahmadi, "The Story of Layla and Majnun: The Idealization of Love" (2016), https://ums.org/2016/09/23/the-story-of-layla-and-majnun-the-idealization-of-love/.

[3] The story attests that the two met as youngsters, which may well echo Solomon's youthful liaison with Naamah.

(extraneous biblical references to mixed marriage, and directly, that of Nabonidus and Nitocris).

★ Majnun retreats into the wilderness, where he becomes "king" of the beasts, writes love songs about his beloved, and falls deeper into madness, becoming dishevelled and unrecognizable (Daniel's 'prophecy' concerning the king's punishment and madness; Solomon's acclaimed writing of poetry/songs).

★ He claims to have fallen under her spell and to be the victim of the Evil Eye (Nabonidus becomes afraid of Nitocris's gaze and the symbolic power of the Eye amulet).

★ "Huntress, beautiful one, whose victim I am … I am the madman, I should be fettered (the king in the Song is depicted as the hunted gazelle, the queen the huntress; the idea of fetters is linked to her control over the king through the blood-rite).

★ "Bind me to you, wind again your tresses round my neck; … I remain your slave" (Nitocris mentions the binding 'seal'/fetter; the 'tresses' that make the king captive are mentioned by other characters in the Song).

★ Layla holds a glass of wine scented with musk (the Elixir is the highly scented "wine" of the Song).

★ An eager 'student' comes from Bagdad to learn at Majnun's feet; his name is Salem; this is etymologically linked to "Solomon" and Bagdad represents Babylonia. He finds the 'madman's' ways too daunting and fails in his quest to find wisdom from his master (Nabonidus worships at Nitocris's feet, coveting her esoteric insights but he fails to complete his training).

★ Layla is forced into a marriage she does not want and locks herself away from her husband, preserving her chastity (Nitocris does likewise, when all attempts to convert the king fail; there is evidence she did not go willingly to Tayma).

★ Layla's father claims he would rather see his daughter fed to the dogs than marry Majnun (Jezebel's fate is linked to the death of Nitocris).

★ Majnun's father takes him to Mecca to pray for help to get over Layla, but the mad poet chooses his love for her over his love for Allah (Nabonidus calls Nitocris the only "one," i.e., this indicates he raises her above Yahweh; of course, Solomon supposedly does likewise with his Egyptian wife).

★ It is Majnun who, after a lifetime self-analysing and teaching a youth the wisdom of his mistakes (cf. Eccl), desires an exalted type of love, *without sexual union,* i.e., truth, wisdom, and peace (the onus is shifted from Nitocris, whose role this is in the Song, to the king, in keeping with the male-dominant Arabic context of the medieval poem)

✷ When Layla dies, she says she wishes to be buried in a "blood-red garment" because she is a "blood witness" and "blood" is a constant motif in the poem (Nitocris's blood, of course, is central to the Song)

The text of "Layla and Majnun" is replete with *many* direct echoes of Song terminology and imagery, for instance: Woman as moon (and star/sun); blood; seal; stags and gazelles; wedding litter; fetters; huntress; tent curtains; blood as purple wine; "drinking" from the female to bring peace to the soul; shade/protection; lips dripping with honey; blossoms and buds; palm; garden; the power of words; magic; "closed door" as vulva; "fortress" as chastity; blood-covenant; evocation of the winds, etc. There is even mention of Venus (Ishtar), the plucking of the date from the palm by force (cf. Song 5:4 and 7:8), and the description of Majnun as being like an "exiled ruler" (as Nabonidus was). She is described as "a miraculous goblet whose mirror reflects the secret world." This is Nitocris, Nabonidus's mysterious, magical, priestly vessel for the Elixir Rubeus and thus the supposed fountain of the wisdom of the universe.

The most amazing connection comes from yet another Arabic legend that suggests Qays, the poet upon whom the epic is allegedly based, *lived in Tayma!*[4]

If the Song is composed by the woman I have suggested (see Part Two, Chapter 9), who is probably a native of Tayma, it is fully plausible that a very similar story to the Song should find its own roots in that area (rather than in Babylon). Nizami either knew the Song well and used it as the foundation for his poem, or the collection of legends that he was given to make sense of suggested much the same thing: The king went 'mad' because of a foreign woman who introduced him to a magical potion (i.e., the Elixir Rubeus), in a bid to find wisdom and some form of exalted love.

2. JOSEPH AND ASENATH

This story I *was* aware of, superficially, but when I later returned to read the tale in full, again, I was amazed. Recall that in the book (Part Two, Chapter 5), the honey and honeycomb 'consumed' by the king relates to (Egyptian) cultic rituals performed within the feminine sphere, and within the temple. In this context, it represents Nabonidus's initiation into Nitocris's secret world and the Elixir Rubeus.

---

[4] Fouzia Khan, "On the Trail of Star-Crossed Lovers," *Destination Jeddah* 39 (2012): 34–5, https://issuu.com/djmagzine/docs/binder40.

The story of Joseph and Asenath, via the exegetical processes of Midrash, develops from three short mentions in the HB (Gen 41:45, 50; 46:20) into a complex narrative that is now a Pseudepigraphal text.[5] Yet again, there are familiar themes and allusions that necessitate a consideration that it is based on, or at least profoundly inspired by the Song of Solomon— but only when read from a historical-cultic perspective, *including* the Elixir.

The name Asenath is traditionally translated as Belonging to Neith (which echoes our Nitocris). Abarim Publications, however, provides a more etymologically insightful rendition, suggesting a link to the Hebrew word *'ason*, meaning mischief, evil, or harm.[6] Thus, the anti-Egyptian, ant-Nitocris sentiment could well be maintained. Joseph's Egyptian name, Zaphenath-paneah ("The god spake, and he lives"), however, is said to embody "the tradition of creation by the divine voice. It is a well-known type of name, not ancient, used in the 26th Dynasty."[7] This provides a strong clue to the dating of the tale of Joseph and Aseneth.

The story is known: Joseph is given the daughter of a priest of On (Heliopolis), as wife. She becomes the mother to Manasseh and Ephraim. The Midrash version incorporates the following significant elements (and this is just a sampling!)[8]:

★ Asenath is the daughter of a priest of Re. As Pharaoh, Ahmose, Son of Neith, is *ipso facto* a priest of Re; some scholars do suggest Aseneth might be a princess but the tale accentuates the priestly context; Nitocris is First Prophet of Amun-Re.

★ She is isolated, protected by many soldiers, not seen or touched by any man, having a veritable hatred of them; she is surrounded by (seven) virgins. This comes across more in the final stages of the Song, where Nitocris is in Ur, in the temple, with the other women; it also echoes the tale of Neith and her female cult at Sais, whose 'veil', i.e., hymen, had never been breached by any man.

★ She lives this way, having been placed in a tower, out of harm's way

---

[5] For discussions, see e.g., Michael Fishbane, *Biblical Myth and Rabbinic Mythmaking* (Oxford: Oxford University Press, 2003); Geoffrey H. Hartman and Sanford Budick, eds., *Midrash and Literature* (New Haven: Yale University Press, 1986).

[6] "Asenath," https://www.abarim-publications.com/Meaning/Asenath.html.

[7] Alice Grenfell, "Egyptian Mythology and the Bible," *The Monist* 16.2 (1906): 169–200. http://www.jstor.org/stable/27899648.

[8] See David Cook, trans. "Joseph and Asenath." Online hyperlinked version by Mark Goodacre. The Aseneth Home Page. http://www.markgoodacre.org/aseneth/translat.htm.

(recall the legend concerning Solomon and his daughter, Kaziah). In the Song, Nabonidus's daughter is placed in the 'tower', i.e., the ziggurat at Ur, and the last chapter of the Song deals with her position as a sacred female in a world where she is protected but still expected to marry.

✶ She is described as being "tall and beautiful" (just like Nitetis), and about the age of eighteen; Nitocris was about nineteen or twenty at the time of the coalition/treaty.

✶ Her bed is covered with a purple coverlet; the seat of the king's palanquin in the Song is purple, i.e., suggesting female blood.

✶ She worships idols in the privacy of her own quarters. Nitocris creates her idol in privacy of her own chamber/cella.

✶ Her quarters are surrounded by ripening fruits and flowing waters; these are used to profound effect in the Song.

✶ She is identified as the "bride of God"; Nitocris comes from the realm of the God's Wife and in the Song, she appears to be God's Hand.

✶ Her marriage to Joseph is intended to 'save the nation', i.e., from the effects of famine; for Nitocris, the marriage is conciliatory, in a time of impending war.

✶ She initially refuses, vehemently, thinking Joseph to be a mere "shepherd's son." The wording of the Song does offer the possibility that Nitocris is taken from Egypt against her will, at first, though she soon determines to make the most of her situation; the courtship of Inanna and Dumuzi, e.g., her initial disdain for the "shepherd" should also be considered.

✶ When she is presented to her betrothed, she dresses in all her finery, including bracelets and necklaces bearing the inscriptions of the names of her deities. The symbolism of the necklace is strong in the Song and it is the inscription, or the image, of the Eye of Re that brings terror to the king.

✶ Joseph arrives in all his splendour upon an Egyptian chariot, with his purple robe and a hefty retinue. Nabonidus arrives for the *hieros gamos*, i.e., his official wedding.

✶ On seeing his grandeur, etc., Asenath regrets her harsh words and is embarrassed, desiring to run away and hide. References to hiding, clefts of the rocks, etc., are mostly in the early verses of the Song.

✶ Joseph has the effect of making all the Egyptian wives and daughters swoon over him; in the Song, Nabonidus is "loved" by all the daughters of Jerusalem.

★ When he learns that Asenath is a virgin, he calls her his "sister"; Nitocris is the sister-bride in the Song.

★ Joseph leaves for seven days, during which time Asenath experiences a form of 'descent', psychologically/spiritually. She removes all her finery and dresses in dark robes, covering herself in ashes. Nabonidus leaves Nitocris alone for several nights; she runs through the streets looking for him but is accosted by the guards, who remove her robes and submit her to humiliation; this is *her* symbolic descent.

★ Asenath calls upon a deity (the god of Joseph) to assist her in winning his love. Nitocris calls upon her deity, Amun-Re, to assist her in securing Nabonidus's mind, and thus his *dod*/love.

★ A golden, shining image of Joseph appears in response to Asenath's prayer; Nitocris symbolically creates a golden image of Nabonidus.

★ Asenath's spiritual ascension follows (Nitocris's 'spell' has the effect she hopes, and the king comes to her for initiation into her cult).

★ She is offered a drink from the "cup of immortality." The verses following the cultic image and the prayer to the gods, in the Song, depict the introduction of the Elixir Rubeus and the king's ingestion of the magical potion.

★ The divine image of Joseph requests honeycomb, which, itself, mysteriously appears within the inner sanctum of Asenath's quarters, and the two partake of the honeycomb in some quasi-eucharistic rite, echoing the occult, feminine aspect of the honeycomb in Egyptian cultic sources and thus the context of the ingestion/initiation in the Song.

★ Asenath asks where the honeycomb came from, suggesting it came from Joseph's mouth, "for it smells like myrrh" (in the Song, myrrh is symbolic of female blood but also death; to the Egyptian priestess, Asenath, the man's mouth smells of the blood of the Elixir, but we soon learn that to the Hebrew scribe, it is the smell of death, i.e., the death of Asenath's idolatry and perceived sinfulness).

★ To further accentuate the idea of blood, the golden image of Joseph touches the honeycomb and it, too, turns to blood where his finger falls.

★ White bees appear from the honeycomb and circle about Asenath, some landing on her lips. In the Song, bees are alluded to via the honey/honeycomb reference; bees are of paramount significance, especially with respect to Neith and the concept of hidden knowledge; in the Song, this further accentuates the priestly perspective and heritage of Nitocris.[9]

★ When Asenath prepares to meet Joseph again, she dresses in all her finery (just like Ishtar), and she is described as "shining" like the sun and the "morning star," i.e., Venus. In the Song, Nitocris is the avatar of Ishtar, the morning star, Venus, and of Hathor, the sun, or Shining One.

★ Asenath and Joseph "embrace" but this is a matter of contention for Nitocris in the Song.

★ Pharaoh puts the wedding crowns upon the couple but in the Song, it is the king's mother who is given the honour of crowning him.

★ The story moves rapidly from the wedding and the birth of Ephraim and Manasseh, to telling us that the period from the beginning of the famine to the establishment of the house of Joseph was "seven years." This is the timeframe for Nabonidus in Tayma (and he left during a famine).

★ Joseph is remembered for his fascination with celestial omina. Nabonidus, of course, runs his life according to such omens.

Although subsequent interpretations and retellings shifted to be more Christian-orientated, the early tale seems to be an attempt to take what was once the powerful, well-known, thus influential account of Nabonidus and Nitocris and mould it into pro-Hebrew-conversion propaganda. The story does open with the strong proviso: Asenath was "was quite unlike the daughters of the Egyptians, but in every respect like the daughters of the Hebrews." It also highlights the fact that as well as the north/south (i.e., Egyptian) alignment of her bedroom windows, there is also one facing east: she watches Joseph's arrival from the east, suggesting a messiah/saviour-like figure, which is then expanded upon in the ensuing narrative.[10]

---

[9] There is a fascinating interpretation of the bees, provided by Gideon Bohak in "Asenath's Honeycomb and Onias' Temple: The Key to 'Joseph and Asenath'," *Proceedings of the World Congress of Jewish Studies* (1993): 163–70, http://www.jstor.org/stable/23535762. Bohak argues that the description of the bees' colours parallels that of Jewish priestly vestments (167–8).

[10] R. T. Beckwith (The Solar Calendar of Joseph and Asenath," *Journal for the Study of Judaism* 90 [1984]: 90–111) makes the claim that Asenath's prayer toward the East, and the several indications of a solar calendar (in a symbolic sense Joseph arrives like a shining, rising sun), speak to an Egyptian Essene authorship for the tale. Interestingly, he also sees the consumption of the wine and honeycomb as some sort of "initiation" ritual (110–11).

3. WIFE OF PHARAOH

In Islam, there is the legend of Asiya bint Muzahim, purportedly the wife of Pharaoh who discovered Moses in the river. The story follows a similar vein to that in the Song, i.e., Asiya's marriage to the king is arranged; she does not love him. She harbours a faith that Pharaoh does not, and she becomes secretive about it. When she finds the child Moses, she hatches a plan to keep him because he may 'be of use' one day; she hires a wet-nurse, who turns out to be the natural mother; the child grows up in the palace. Eventually, Pharaoh and Asiya prove incompatible and the poor woman is tortured and killed (her *hands and feet* being nailed to a *palm* tree; see Part Two, Epilogue), becoming a martyr to her faith.

The name Asiya is not mentioned in the Bible or the Koran, however, and one scholar has conjectured that it...

> ...is a variant reading of the name of Asenath, the Egyptian wife of Joseph; especially as Joseph's wife in Arabic traditions is not given as Asenath but as Zulaikhah. In Arabic, written without the diacritic points, the names Asiya and Asenath would be alike.[11]

He then suggests a common rendering of the name is "Asiya Aikaterina," i.e., Asyia the Pure One (see the discussion on Nitocris as the "pure one" in Part Two, Chapter 7). Another scholar identifies Asiya with Bithiah of 1 Chronicles 4[12] (see the entry on Mered and Bithiah in Part One, Chapter 2).

***

What I suggest, therefore, is that the historical Nitocris and her life with the "mad" King Nabonidus, as recorded in the Song of Solomon, inspired many to appropriate specific details for their own cause, from the liturgy of the Egyptian Phibionites (see Part One, Chapter 3), to the Midrash of the rabbis, to the medieval poet Nizami (whose patron, clearly, had not read the Song of Solomon!), and the Islamic tradition. Their profound tale becomes a literary leitmotif, with the same details reorganised, embellished, and adapted to suit the needs of each successive retelling. There are researchers out there who have probably found strange links and odd insights in other texts, not knowing what to make of them, but with Nabonidus and

---

[11] John Walker, "Asiya, the Wife of Pharaoh," *The Muslim World* 18 (1928): 45–48.

[12] George Archer, "A Short History of a 'Perfect Woman': The Translations of the 'Wife of Pharaoh' Before, Through, and Beyond the Qur'ānic Milieu," Georgetown University (n.d.), https://pubs.lib.uiowa.edu/mathal/article/2738/galley/111540/view/.

Nitocris's story as a foundation, or framework, they may well learn that they have discovered a new rendition of the story to add to the growing list!

TIMELINE OF THE SONG OF SOLOMON

Verse(s)	Event in Song	Year BCE	Regnal Year	Historical Event
		554	2	13 Ulūlū (26 Sept) lunar eclipse
		553	3	Nabonidus leaves Babylon for Arabia (Iyar / April-May)
1:4–11	Bride brought from Egypt to palace of the king; king anticipates offspring	550/49 Year 1 in Tayma	6/7	King settles in Tayma; treaty with Ahmose; dream omen given to king (15 Tebet / 31 Oct); Nabonidus renovates first Ishtar temple
1:17–2:6	*Hieros gamos* 1; betrothal stage of marriage	548 Year 2 in Tayma	8	
3:6–11 4:12–16	*Hieros gamos* 2; Nitocris conceives; official marriage and mention of king's mother; queenship / deification; miscarriage	547 Year 3 in Tayma	9	Adad-guppi dies far from home (5 Nisannu / 6 April)
5:1 5:8	Nabonidus initiated into Nitocris's religion; feigned pregnancy	546 Year 4 in Tayma	10	
6:10–12	Child born; Nitocris celebrated as "mother"	545 Year 5 in Tayma	11	13 Ulūlū lunar eclipse (16 Sept); Nabonidus renovates second Ishtar temple

6:13–7:9	*Heiros gamos* 3; emissaries threaten to expose Nitocris's deceit	544 Year 6 in Tayma	12	Hathor's Festival of Drunkenness (20 Thoth / 30 Sept); Dedication of Ennigaldi-Nanna?
8:5	Family travels to temple site at Ur; Ennigaldi two years old	543 Year 7 in Tayma	13	Nabonidus completes his seven-year penance and returns to Babylonia (17 Tishritu / 28 Oct)
8:11–12	Nabonidus institutes Elixir 'prostitution' in temple in Babylon	Post-543		Herodotus tells of a peculiar form of prostitution in the temple at Babylon; Nabonidus boasts that he has received great wisdom, beyond the scope of the Babylonian sages and priests

SUGGESTED READING

The complete Works Acknowledged list is available on Academia.edu.

Ayad, Mariam F. *God's Wife, God's Servant: The God's Wife of Amun* (c.740–525 BC). Abingdon, UK: Routledge, 2009.

Beaulieu, Paul-Alain. *The Reign of Nabonidus King of Babylon 556–539 B.C.* New Haven: Yale University Press, 1989.

Bertrand, Seren and Azra Bertrand, *Womb Awakening: Initiatory Wisdom from the Creatrix of All Life*. Rochester: Inner Traditions/Bear, 2017.

Cohen, Shaye J.D. "Solomon and the Daughter of Pharaoh: Intermarriage, Conversion, and the Impurity of Women." *Journal of the Ancient Near Eastern Society of Columbia University* 16–17 (1984–5): 23–37.

De-Whyte, Janice Pearl Ewurama. *Wom(b)an: A Cultural-Narrative Reading of the Hebrew Bible Barrenness Narratives*. Biblical Interpretation Series, 162. Leiden: Brill, 2018.

Dick, Michael B., Ed. *Born in Heaven, Made on Earth: The Making of the Cult Image in the Ancient Near East*. Winona Lake: Eisenbrauns, 1999.

Dieleman, Jacco. *Priests, Tongues, and Rites: The London-Leiden Magical Manuscripts and Translation in Egyptian Ritual (100–300 CE)*. Leiden: Brill, 2005.

Dillery, John. "Darius and the Tomb of Nitocris (Hdt. 1.187)." *Classical Philology* 87.1 (1992): 30–38.

Dougherty, Raymond Philip. *Nabonidus and Belshazzar: A Study of the Closing Events of the Neo-Babylonian Empire*. Eugene: Wipf & Stock, 2008 (1929).

Foster, Benjamin R. *From Distant Days: Myths, Tales, and Poetry of Ancient Mesopotamia*. Bethesda: CDL Press, 1995.

Frankfurter, David, ed. *Guide to the Study of Ancient Magic.* Religions in the Graeco-Roman World 189. David Frankfurter, et al., eds. Leiden: Brill, 2019.

Graham, Lloyd D. "King's Daughter, God's Wife: The Princess as High Priestess in Mesopotamia (Ur, ca. 2300-1100 BCE) and Egypt (Thebes, ca. 1550-525 BCE)." https://www.academia.edu/34248896.

Haines, Alastair Ian. *Gender in Solomon's Song of Songs: Discourse Analytical Abduction to a Gynocentric Hypothesis.* Eugene: Wipf & Stock, 2016.

Hall, Nor. *The Moon and the Virgin: Reflections on the Archetypal Feminine.* New York: Harper & Row, 1980.

Hallo, William W., and J. J. A. Van Dijk. *The Exaltation of Inanna.* New Haven: Yale University Press, 1968.

Kaminka, Armand. "The Origin of the Ashmedai Legend in the Babylonian Talmud." *Jewish Quarterly Review,* New Series, 13.2 (1922): 221–24.

Koren, Sharon Faye. *Forsaken: The Menstruant in Medieval Jewish Mysticism.* Hanover: Brandeis University Press, 2011.

Kramer, Samuel Noah. "The Biblical 'Song of Songs' and the Sumerian Love Songs," *Expedition Magazine* 5.1, Penn Museum (1962), Online version, http://www.penn.museum/ sites/expedition/?p=488

Leick, Gwendolyn. *Sex and Eroticism in Mesopotamian Literature.* London: Routledge, 1994.

Lewy, Julius. "The Late Assyro-Babylonian Cult of the Moon and its Culmination at the Time of Nabonidus." *Hebrew Union College Annual* 19 (1945): 405–89.

Long, Asphodel P. "The Goddess in Judaism–An Historical Perspective." Pages 27–65 in *The Absent Mother: Restoring the Goddess to Judaism and Christianity,* ed. Alix Pirani. London: HarperCollins, 1991.

McDonald, J. Andrew. "Influences of Egyptian Lotus Symbolism and Ritualistic Practices on Sacral Tree Worship in the Fertile Crescent from 1500 BCE to 200 CE." *Religions* 2018, 9(9), 256.

Meacham, Tirzah. "An Abbreviated History of the Jewish Menstrual Laws." Pages 21–39 in *Women and Water: Menstruation in Jewish Life and Law.* Ed. Rahel R. Wasserfall. Hanover: Brandeis University Press, 1999.

Meador, Betty De Shong. *Inanna: Lady of Largest Heart: Poems of the Sumerian High Priestess Enheduanna.* Austin: University of Texas Press, 2000.

Meek, T. James. "Babylonian Parallels to the Song of Songs." *Journal of Biblical Literature* 43.3/4 (1924): 245–52.

_____. "Canticles and the Tammuz Cult." *American Journal of Semitic Languages & Literature* 39.1 (1922): 1–14.

Michalowski, Piotr. "The Doors of the Past." *Eretz-Israel: Archaeological, Historical and Geographical Studies* 27 (2003): 136–152.

Moore, Stephen D. "The Song of Songs in the History of Sexuality." *Church History* 69.2 (2000): 328–49.

Nissinen, Martti and Risto Uro, Eds. *Sacred Marriages: The Divine-Human Sexual Metaphor from Sumer to Early Christianity.* Winona Lake: Eisenbrauns, 2008.

Noegel, Scott B. "Scarlet and Harlots: Seeing Red in the Hebrew Bible." *Hebrew Union College Annual* 87 (2016): 1–47.

Pope, Marvin H. *Song of Songs: A New Translation with Introduction and Commentary.* New York: Doubleday, 1977.

Pryke, Louise M. *Ishtar.* Abingdon: Taylor & Francis, 2017.

Riddle, John M. *Goddesses, Elixirs, and Witches: Plants and Sexuality Throughout Human History.* New York: Palgrave Macmillan, 2010.

Ritner, Robert Kreich. *The Mechanics of Ancient Egyptian Magical Practice.* Thomas Holland, Ed. SAOC 54. Chicago: University of Chicago, 1993.

Roberts, Alison, *Hathor Rising: The Serpent Power of Ancient Egypt.* Rottingdean: Northgate, 1995.

Sandars, N. K. *The Epic of Gilgamesh.* Rev. ed. London: Penguin, 1972.

Sharlach, T. M. *An Ox of One's Own: Royal Wives and Religion at the Court of the Third Dynasty of Ur.* Berlin: De Gruyter, 2017.

Schulman, Alan R. "Diplomatic Marriage in the Egyptian New Kingdom." *Journal of Near Eastern Studies* 38.3 (1979): 177–93.

Silver, Morris. "Temple/Sacred Prostitution in Ancient Mesopotamia Revisited." *Ugarit Forschungen* 38 (2006): 631–63. https://www.academia.edu/2360254/.

Steinert, Ulrike. "Concepts of the Female Body in Mesopotamian Gynecological Texts," Pages 275–357 in *The Comparable Body: Analogy and Metaphor in Ancient Mesopotamian, Egyptian, and Greco-Roman Medicine*. Edited by John Z. Wee. Leiden: Brill, 2017.

Stol, Marten. *Birth in Babylonia and the Bible: Its Mediterranean Setting.* Cuneiform Monographs 14. Edited by T. Abusch, et al. Groningen: Styx Publications, 2000.

_____. *Women in the Ancient Near East.* Trans., Helen and Mervyn Richardson. Berlin: De Gruyter, 2016.

Suderman, W. Derek. "Modest or Magnificent? Lotus versus Lily in Canticles." *The Catholic Biblical Quarterly* 67.1 (2005): 42–58.

Szpakowska, Kasia. *Behind Closed Eyes: Dreams and Nightmares in Ancient Egypt.* Swansea: Classical Press of Wales, 2003.

Tanner, J. Paul. "The History of Interpretation of the Song of Songs." *Bibliotheca Sacra* 154.613 (1997): 23–46.

Van Buren, E. Douglas. "The Sacred Marriage in Early Times in Mesopotamia." *Orientalia*, NOVA Series, 13 (1944): 1–72.

Veenker, Ronald A. "Forbidden Fruit: Ancient Near Eastern Sexual Metaphors." *Hebrew Union College Annual* 70/71 (1999): 57–73.

Verde, Danilo. *Conquered Conquerors: Love and War in the Song of Songs.* Atalanta: SBL Press, 2020.

Wasserfall, Rahel R., Ed. *Women and Water: Menstruation in Jewish Life and Law.* Hanover: Brandeis University Press, 1999.

Weadock, Penelope N. "The Giparu at Ur." *Iraq*, 37.2 (1975): 101–128.

White, Gavin. *Queen of the Night: The Role of the Stars in the Creation of the Child.* London: Solaria Publications, 2014.

Wolkstein, Diane and Samuel Noah Kramer. *Inanna, Queen of Heaven: Her Stories and Hymns from Sumer.* New York: Harper and Row, 1983.

INDEX

THE TESTAMENT OF LAZARUS
The Pre-Christian Gospel of John

By Janet Tyson

Of interest to

★ HISTORICAL JESUS STUDIES

★ BIBLICAL STUDIES (EXEGESIS AND HERMENEUTICS)

★ MESSIANIC JUDAISM

★ SAMARITAN STUDIES

The Gospel of John is an eyewitness account of Jesus' mission to return Israel to its original status as the beloved Bride of God. He is depicted as the the Messiah ben Ephraim, and intends to return the locus of worship to Shiloh, Samaria. Lazarus is Jesus' chosen successor, not Peter; writing his testament is part of his duty as Jesus' deputy. Jesus' entire mission depends on Lazarus and Mary Magdalene.

ISBN Paperback 978-1-7393154-0-5
   Hardcover 978-1-7393154-2-9
   Digital 978-1-7393154-1-2

Milton Keynes UK
Ingram Content Group UK Ltd.
UKHW050624070923
428211UK00009B/34